THE NOVELS OF

HARVEY FERGUSSON

☀

BLOOD OF THE CONQUERORS

1921

CAPITOL HILL

1923

WOMEN AND WIVES

1924

HOT SATURDAY

1926

WOLF SONG

1927

IN THOSE DAYS

1929

FOOTLOOSE McGARNIGAL

1930

THESE ARE BORZOI BOOKS PUBLISHED BY
ALFRED A. KNOPF

RIO
GRANDE

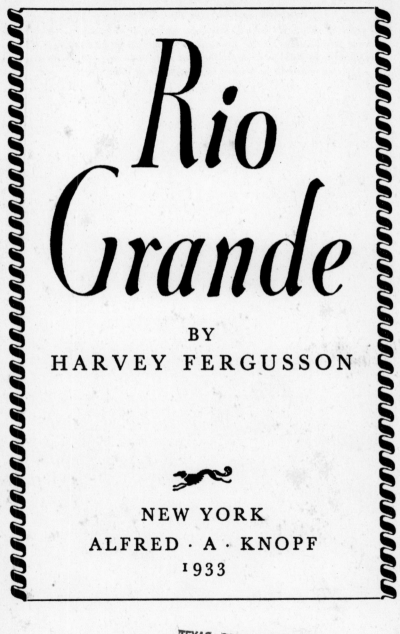

Rio Grande

BY
HARVEY FERGUSSON

NEW YORK
ALFRED · A · KNOPF
1933

CONTENTS

ILLUSTRATIONS

(THE ILLUSTRATIONS WILL BE FOUND AT THE
END OF THE BOOK.)

INTRODUCTION

THIS book is an attempt to portray a region, both as it is today and as it has been. It does not try to recreate the past for its own sake but to comprehend the present in terms of the forces that made it.

Its central scene is the Rio Grande basin in New Mexico. The narrative sometimes travels far from this, and even from coast to coast, but it always returns to the great valley which is the heart of the Southwest. For many generations this valley fed most of the region and it was always a main route of travel. It is a place where journeys and migrations began and ended, where battles were fought and destinies decided.

It is a tempting field for such a study as this because of its amazing ability to resist the effects of time and change. During the past two hundred years, and especially in the United States, the growth of populations and the invention of machines have changed the aspect of human life with a speed and completeness that men of an elder time could scarcely have imagined. Not only have the patterns of human destiny completely altered but whole races of men and species of animals have been wiped out and the face of the earth has been made over. The prairies are as completely obliterated as the wild herds they supported and there is hardly a vestige left of the giant forests that covered the eastern half of the continent. Most of the aboriginal tribes are extinct or nearly so, and the types of white men who killed them are figures in a legend. In most places the past survives only in tiny fragments that make it seem quaint, almost incredible. It is a refuge for the romantic imagination and a field in which pedants plough up dead facts but as a human actuality it is often hard to recover.

In the Southwest both the earth and the people are peculiarly resistant to this obliterating kind of change. A country of unwatered sand and lava and of mountains rising in rock-armored slopes from sterile desert to frozen summits, most of it gives sustenance only to wild things and to wandering bands of sheep. Over three hundred years of diligent search for gold and silver has for the most part merely pitted it with the scars of futile digging. Its arable valleys have been cultivated to some extent for thousands of years and in some places by the same families for centuries so that its agricultural life contains at least as much of survival as of progress. In a few large towns and along the railroads and highways the modern life of money and machines is fully established but elsewhere there are vestiges and even flourishing survivals of almost everything that went before. The Pueblo Indians are almost as many as ever they were and they preserve the essentials of their ancient life with a surprising tenacity. They are doomed, beyond a doubt, but they have survived three centuries of violence and injustice and present an implacable front to the far more insidious dangers of kindly patronage and impudent curiosity. The Navajos are even more successful in postponing their extinction for they are the one aboriginal people in the

United States that has multiplied its population since it was conquered.

Of the aristocratic Spanish life with its feudal character there is only a wistful remnant, but the common Mexican, wherever his tenacious grip on the soil has not been broken, is much the same man he has been for several hundred years.

By diligent research one can recover the outline of striking events and the material details of a vanished culture but the patterns of individual conduct are hard to imagine once they have ceased to exist. It is these patterns that persist in the Southwest and not only those of the aborigines but also those of their conquerors. The American pioneer, although his blood and something of his character survive in all Americans of the older stock, is in most places extinct as a type of man, but here one can still discover his distinguishing characteristics in the flesh. A few years ago I met a man under forty who had been born in an outlaw camp in the wild country near the Colorado River and raised by the Southern Utes who still roam that region about as they always did. His whole life had been spent in the strip of unsettled country which extends from northern Sonora through the intermountain region of the United States and into Alberta. He had trapped and hunted and chased wild horses for a living. He had fought Indians and bandits. In every essential respect his life had been that of the first men who crossed the wilderness from the Missouri River to the mountains. He was a perfect survival of the pioneer type with its courage and self-sufficiency, its incorrigible individualism, its restlessness and naïvely romantic outlook. To see him, as I did, trying to adapt himself to the life of a modern western city, gave me a vivid impression of American character in the making. In many ways, this man was the American prototype and it seemed to me that I could discern clearly just how much of him had gone into the common social heritage and how much belonged to the past.

Many such glimpses have gone into the making of this book. I have read much for detail and episode but a long association with the country and the people and the feeling of a personal relation to them are responsible both for the method of the work and the impulse to do it.

Just as any individual destiny, however peculiar, seems to have a universal quality when viewed with detachment and sympathy, so I am persuaded that this story has more than a local significance. It describes the aboriginal America which is typical of all primitive life. It recounts the last aggressive thrust of religious empire on this continent and the decay of a lost and isolated fragment of that world. It pictures the modern man in the sharp contrast of conflict with these older cultures, first as a fighting hunter, then as a trader and explorer and finally as the master and slave of his machines. These wider implications of the theme I have tried to suggest without expounding them and without distorting the material to give them emphasis.

RIO GRANDE

I
Country

RIO BRAVO DEL NORTE the Spaniards first called it, meaning the swift river of the North, but it finally came to be known simply as Rio Grande, the great river. This name testifies to its regional importance and its hold upon the imaginations of men for it is not a great river in anything except its length. Sometimes, worn thin by drought and bled by irrigation, it is not a river at all but only a wide strip of white sand baking and glaring in the sun. It becomes an impressive stream only in times of flood and then it runs in a red torrent often half a mile wide, lifting an angry crest of sand-waves, devouring its own low banks, earth, trees and all, as though in a furious effort to carry away the whole country and dump it into the sea.

It is a river not at all friendly to men, still a menace to what they build and plant in its valley. Except for a short distance from the sea it is not navigable. It is a hard river to bridge and a dangerous one to ford, even in low water. Its quicksands have swallowed horses, wagons, cattle, sheep and men. For hundreds of miles in all it growls along the bottoms of chasms where it can hardly

3

be reached, much less used for any human purpose. But in this respect it is better than other rivers of the arid region. Most of them, from the smallest mountain streams to the great Colorado, run in canyons that protect their waters from irrigation, but the Rio Grande for several hundred miles has a broad flat valley where crops have been grown for perhaps a thousand years. Sometimes it fails them in drought and sometimes it washes them away. Latterly it has filled up its own channel and made a marsh of much of its valley so that the roots of the corn rot in the ground. Yet this valley has produced much food for men and the Rio Grande, like the Nile, fertilizes the land in floods with its heavy burden of silt. For a long time this was the only considerable place where corn grew between the rich middle prairies and California. It was the chief granary of a region two thousand miles wide. It was also the natural route of travel north and south. These two facts made it a place where three civilizations met, traded, fought and interbred.

The river rises in the great mountain mass of southern Colorado. Entering New Mexico, it flows in the bottom of a deep gorge which is like a crack in the face of the country. For most of a hundred miles it is an inaccessible thing which cannot even be crossed except in a few places. Like the Colorado it turns all roads aside, it supports no farms or towns.

Where the Taos creek enters it from the west, this canyon widens enough to contain a road and as you travel south it becomes more and more a valley. Orchards and narrow fields are wedged between the walls of rock. At Espanola the cliffs fall away and an open valley lies between low hills. Once more the river plunges into the impassable White Rock Canyon for seventy miles or more and then emerges into the great valley which extends almost to El Paso without a break.

Seen from a distance, this valley is a long strip of green, stitched and spotted with bright waters, lying across a country that looks otherwise barren and dead. It is limited sharply on either side by low yellow sandhills. Beyond the sandhills are the mesas, flat and bare, and beyond the mesas always mountains that show as jagged blue silhouettes.

This is the typical New Mexican landscape as seen from the valley. The cultivated lands are like rich veins of green life in a great matrix of rock and sand and the mountains are so far away they often seem unreal. They float upon the horizon light and lovely as a cloud and almost as changeable in tint and shadow. Their waters are hidden in deep canyons and their forests, if visible at all, appear only as a dark crown. Yet they cover nearly half the country and are full of bright streams and tall trees. Snows lie upon the northern peaks all summer and melting snow is what feeds the river and keeps the country alive.

The Southwest has been so much described as a monotony of wide levels, tiring the eye and oppressing the spirit, that it seems necessary to say it has one of the most diverse landscapes in the world. Its elevations vary ten thousand feet or more and elevation changes the character of the earth. Starting at Taos last summer, on the edge of the sage-brush flats, I went up to the top of the Sangre de Cristo mountains, where Blue Lake, sacred

to the Pueblos of Taos, lies in a rockbound dimple at
the foot of Wheeler Peak. It was only a long day's journey,
yet it carried me through as many different zones of life
as though I had gone from North Carolina to Hudson
Bay. Just a little way up Taos Canyon the sage-brush disappeared and we climbed a ridge where stunted nut
pines grew and a few fine junipers. Over the top of a
low divide we passed into Canadian country where yellow
pine stood seventy-five feet high and blue spruce lifted
its perfect cones of shining foilage. Although it was
August the ground was bright with flowers. Wild oats
brushed our stirrup leathers and wild strawberries and
raspberries grew so thick that we could not resist the
temptation to dismount and eat them.

As we climbed the timber grew thicker and shorter.
It was all spruce and fir, a dense dark forest with only
mosses and lichens clinging to the damp ground where
the sun fell in scattered fragments — exactly the same
kind of forest that reaches farthest north toward the arctic
tundra.

It was late in the day when we came out of the forest on
a bare ridge above timberline and then we were in a truly
arctic country. All around us were bare peaks where the
timber had shrunk to a kind of crawling ground pine,
for nothing high can stand against the wind and snow of
those levels. Snow still stuck on the north slopes of the
peaks and a shower that came upon us suddenly turned
into hail and it was bitterly cold.

Next day I climbed Wheeler Peak, over thirteen thousand feet above sea level, and looked down upon the tops
of many other peaks and upon timbered ridges reaching

long crooked fingers north and south as far as I could see. From there the illusion was just the opposite of that one feels in the valley. The mountains that had been pale blue figures of distance now seemed to be the whole world and the intervals of valley and mesa were a vague emptiness, like the space between the stars.

To the west and the south the mountains are not so high. They seldom reach above the timberline. But they are all heavily timbered on their upper slopes and they all give birth to clear streams that run swiftly down to the mesas and are lost in the sands more often than they reach any river on the surface of the earth.

The mesas to the south grow more arid. In the north they are covered with sage and where they roll up into foothills they support a widely scattered growth of junipers and nut pines. But southward there are real deserts and especially east of the river where the Jornado del Muerto lies. Journey of death the Spaniards called it because it was eighty miles across without a sign of water except when rain has just fallen and many died there in the days when eighty miles was a long distance.

The valley itself is much the same from end to end and it is not a place of obvious attractions. Two or three miles wide, it is almost as flat as a floor, so that the river has run all over it at one time or another, scarring it with abandoned channels. These, except in very dry seasons, tend to fill with stagnant alkaline waters, breeding hosts of small but diligent mosquitoes, furnishing a refuge for wild fowl and for countless striped water snakes and green frogs.

Edging the river on either side is a strip of cottonwood forest. Then comes a narrow belt of marshy meadow where the coarse grass is grizzled with alkali and beyond that the land is a little higher and may be ploughed and irrigated. In the old days the grants of land were always divided in long narrow strips so that each man owned some arable land and some meadow and a strip of bosque where he might cut wood, such as it is.

Cottonwood is the only tree that is native to the valley and although it sometimes grows into a thing of beauty, it is a singularly useless one. Its wood has the quality of paper and burns almost as quickly. It cannot be sawn and never affords timbers long enough to be used in building a house. Its real function in the economy of the valley is to keep the river within bounds. It is quick of growth and its profuse seeds, winged with a soft white floss, fly over the flood plain. They alight upon every sandbar and if it lies exposed for a year or two they cover it with young trees. While the river is destroying the forest on one side a new one is growing on the other and but for this battle of the winged seeds floods would ravage the whole valley every year.

Most of the cottonwood forest never lives long enough to be more than a dense covert, twenty or thirty feet high, but wherever the trees escape the river for a period of years they grow into beautiful groves, and where they have been planted about the towns and houses they often reach a great size, lending the landscape its most charming touch. In the autumn their leaves turn a bright polished yellow and then, in good years, when all the houses are hung with scarlet strings of drying chile and the crops are ripe and the vineyards purple, the valley looks its opulent part of the great provider.

It is usual to say that this arid land supports little life and that the Pueblos became farmers because game was so scarce but this has always seemed to me a mistake. Both the Apaches and the Navajos lived here as hunting savages, and although the mesas are not rich in game, the mountains must once have supported a teeming life. In places they still do. Deer are as abundant today in some of the southern mountains as they are anywhere on the continent and wild turkeys still are seen in flocks that number half a hundred. Once there were great elk herds as well. The buffalo never came west of the mountains, but antelope lived on most of the plains in great numbers. The Rio Grande is a flyway for waterfowl. Early travelers tell of the myriads of wild ducks, geese and cranes that covered its sandbars and were so tame a man could ride within a stone's throw of them. In the foothills, quail, rabbits and turtle doves reach a swarming abundance in good years and all the mountain streams are full of trout. It is not a country where hunters would starve but it is one where rich and sheltered valleys invite them to stop and build.

The character of a country is the destiny of its people and that is peculiarly true of this one. It is a country where men can live only in certain places and these are surrounded by wide stretches of desert and by mountains that were often impassable — a country, therefore, of long isolations and long journeys. It has been a place of rebellions and mountains always nourish rebellion by affording a refuge and a stronghold for few against many. It has been prolific of legends, dreams and myths, and the fantastic shapes created by light and distance have certainly helped to sustain them. Above all, it is a land where water has always been scarce and therefore precious, a thing to be fought for, prayed for and cherished in beautiful vessels — a land where thunder is sacred and rain is a God.

~~~~~~~~~~~~~~~~~~~~~~~~~~~~~~~~~~~~~~~

II

The Dancing Builders

~~~~~~~~~~~~~~~~~~~~~~~~~~~~~~~~~~

1

ONE summer a vagrant impulse led me to launch a small folding boat in the Rio Grande near San Ildefonso and float down the reaches of White Rock Canyon, past the mouth of the Rito de Los Frijoles where the Pueblos lived a thousand years ago and on down the open valley to Bernalillo through the country which they still possess most completely today. Cochiti, Santo Domingo and San Felipe lay along the route within sight of the river and the Pueblos of the Jemez valley were a few miles to the west.

This was the heart of the Pueblo country when the Spaniards came and it still is. There may have been twenty-five thousand of them then and there are still about nine thousand. They once had seventy towns and they still have twenty-six. They still dance the same dances, sing the same songs and irrigate the same fields. They are the vestige of a civilization that was blighted by invasion, but a stubborn, resistant vestige which neither accepted the culture of its conquerors nor mingled its blood with theirs.

11

Secretiveness, cunning and a passive but implacable resistance, hiding under a surface of good-humored politeness — these are the qualities of the modern Pueblo. They make it hard for a white man to know him as anything but a quaint figure in the landscape. Even those who have lived among the Pueblos for long periods seem to have come away baffled. For my part I never achieved any conviction of insight into human personality by talking with Indians although I have seen something of them from time to time for twenty years. Neither have I learned much about Indians as human beings by joining the crowds that gather about their public dances, eager for a free show. But on this river trip, as on a few other occasions, I did obtain a slight but vivid impression of primitive men in a primitive country.

From the river nothing could be seen of roads or houses. White Rock Canyon is a wholly uninhabited place. No road enters it and not even a trail goes all the way through. It is a sharp jagged rent seven or eight hundred feet deep in a country of volcanic tufa, showing on either side of the river in sheer cliffs, brown red and white, crowning slopes too steep and too heavily armed with rock and cactus to be climbed. Here and there water seeps through the walls making bright green oases close to the river where grape vines tangle among junipers and box-elders. A few deep canyons break through from the west, bringing narrow tributaries to the river by way of cataracts and sheer falls of fifty or sixty feet.

For seventy miles or more we floated down long smooth stretches and bounced precariously through white-capped rapids that roared in their hollow bed so we could hear them half a mile away. It was easy to see why there never have been any boats in that country. It would be impossible to propel any kind of craft up the river and going down it was a damp and quixotic adventure rather than a practicable mode of travel.

Almost all the way through, the canyon looked like a place where no man had ever been, but when we landed to explore the walls and tributary gorges we repeatedly found the rocks marked with hieroglyphic designs and we knew that just three miles from the river, in the Frijoles Canyon, was the most perfect deserted cliff city of the whole region. This canyon is the center of a country where men have lived in permanent houses longer than anywhere else in the United States.

When we emerged from the mouth of the canyon the illusion that we were traveling into the primitive past was well sustained for the first sign of human life we saw was the Cochiti Indians and their village, standing a little way back from the river.

An Indian pueblo seen from a distance often looks less like a human habitation than like some queer natural upthrust of the country for it is built of the earth on which it stands and there are few marks of cultivation near it. The fields are usually a little way off, sometimes several miles, and in the natural levels and opens of the land. An Indian seldom cuts trees to plant a crop. He never changes the landscape as a white man does. He seems to be always a natural part of it, like a wild animal, and his structures are no more alien to it than bird nests or prairie dog towns.

Cochiti is now mostly a village of one-story adobe

houses. Taos still reaches five stories in height and
Acoma, perched on its narrow rock, has not changed
much in form, but the other pueblos have all become
lower and a little more scattered than they were in the
days when each of them was a fort.

Indians were busy everywhere about the pueblo, men
working in the fields and on the ditches and throwing one
of their wing dams across the river to turn its dwindling
waters toward their crops. Women were plastering walls
with the palms of their hands, washing clothes and carrying water jars on their heads. Everywhere there was chat-
ter for the pueblos are a civilized people and a garrulous
one. Talk begins with leisure and the pueblos achieved
leisure long ago. In the summer they work hard but in
the winter, with full granaries, they talk, dance, sing,
make love and work at their crafts. For hunting peoples
winter is generally a time of precarious struggle with cold
and hunger. For the pueblo it is the season when his
spirit expands.

Bandelier, who lived for years in Isleta and probably
came to know the Indians better than any other white
man, has described this winter life of the Pueblos and
it is plain that he felt in it something of the charm that
goes with all artful use of time for the purposes of pleasure. He says the men would often sit up all night telling
each other stories of the Gods and the olden times and
the young people would gather in groups to sing and
court. In winter are held all the most sacred dances, the
masked dances of initiation and phallic worship, full of
the grotesque humor of primitive eroticism. For the
Pueblo is a humorist and he does not miss the comedy of

sex. Every pueblo contains societies of clowns and these
have charge of the dances that are primarily erotic. Yet
sex is also a sacred thing because it is associated with
germination. In it the Indian sees a symbol of the sprout-
ing grain and the fructifying passion of the storm. The
corn dance, when the men and women meet and mingle
in a stately rhythm, seems to be a pantomime of the union
of earth and sky in the long caress of the rain. To the
Pueblo desire is at once a subject for laughter and for
prayer.

Down the river below Cochiti we saw none but Indians. On either side the banks were high and the cottonwoods, safe from flood and axe, formed fine groves with
short thick trunks and wide-spreading branches, often
heavily draped with mistletoe. Wherever the land was
clear Indians were working in their fields with the slow
intensive diligence which is the characteristic of the
Pueblo farmer. He will not cultivate much land but that
little he cultivates well. He has developed a kind of dwarf
corn with long roots, quick to mature, which will give
him a crop even in dry years. He is not a man to conquer
the wilderness and extend the areas of cultivation but
give him a basket of seed and he will make a crop and
raise a family where another man would starve.

At sunset we were passing the pueblo of Santo Domingo and the men and boys were just then coming home
from work. They came in groups of three or four or
sometimes a dozen, chattering, laughing, singing, and
when they reached the river all of them stripped and
bathed, so that the water was full of naked brown people.
Most of them were finely built, with flat hips and broad

shoulders, and their bodies were smooth and erect, never knotty with muscle and never stooped or twisted. Bathing naked in the river with the sun on their wet skins they were a more pleasing sight than in any other glimpse I ever had of them. They would splash and play but they seemed to care nothing for swimming or diving and they washed all over with much hard rubbing.

Many of them had probably never seen a boat before but ours did not seem to surprise them in the least. Some of them saluted us with loud good nature and some made jokes to each other but they evidently considered us merely comical.

We drifted half a mile past the pueblo, camped on a bare sandy spot beside the river and went to sleep almost as soon as we had eaten. I awoke just before sunrise at that hour when in summer every bird begins to sing. The valley rang with their voices — especially the soft throaty voices of blackbirds and the high clear bugle of the western meadow-lark who comes nearer than any other bird to the making of real music. Then, all at once, the Indians began to chant for they too salute the rising sun. Their voices carried half a mile with ease and at that distance had a rich resonant quality, making a deep accompaniment to the chorus of the birds. It was a charming performance and to me something of a revelation. I had seen the Indian so much as the pestered and evasive object of an impudent curiosity — a man who was hiding behind a surly or hypocritical manner — that it was refreshing to have an impression of him as one who could sing to the rising sun spontaneously as a bird.

2

This strip of the valley is where the Spaniards found most of the Pueblos when they came but they had not always lived there. The Rio Grande country was for them a refuge after long wanderings and after a long slow development toward some goal which now can only be imagined.

The aboriginal past for the most part is obscure but in this country where decay is slow, where roof beams and grains of corn and human bones last for a thousand years, the story of the Pueblo's struggle toward civilization has been worked out in clear and convincing detail.

It seems certain that these men came from the east several thousand years ago as nearly naked savages living in skin tepees, wandering over their range. They must have been driven back from the buffalo plains by stronger and better-armed enemies. As so often happens to peoples and to individuals their development sprang from an effort to compensate for their weaknesses.

The first signs of them are found in the valley of the Arkansas and of other eastward flowing rivers in the form of fallen walls built of loose rock. These they doubtless roofed with skins, converting their tepees into slightly more substantial and lasting structures.

Before they built their first stone walls they must have been savages of the most primitive kind. They did not even have bows and arrows but hunted with darts, clubs and throwing sticks, living on small game such as rabbits, prairie dogs, doves and quail and also on grass seeds, berries and locusts.

Their rise began when they got the first seeds of corn, probably by trade or capture. The wild ancestor of the corn is native to the plateaus of Mexico and Central America and doubtless they got the seed and learned to plant it from tribes of the south. At first the corn was planted on the open prairie and a precarious crop was raised without irrigation. At first too the grain was stored in caves.

But the man who has raised a crop that will feed him all winter has become a sedentary man and one who needs to defend his property. The first stone house was doubtless a granary and only later and by force of necessity a dwelling and a fort. The Indians still store their grain in the lower and inner rooms of the pueblo and live in the upper and outer ones. It became what it is by the building of rooms over and in front of a storehouse. As this structure developed its walls became thicker and the rough stones were laid in adobe mortar. Adobe was used exclusively when suitable rocks were not available but the characteristic construction of the great period began when walls were built of flat stones and these were carefully shaped and laid.

The Pueblo now became a householder and a man of wealth and his enemies pressed upon him. His stores of garnered grain were a rich prize for all the stronger more warlike Indians who hedged him about. His expansion to the North brought him in contact with the mountain tribes, such as the Utes, and to the South he encountered the even more deadly Apaches. He built his walls thicker and higher and entered his house through a hole in the roof by means of a ladder which he could draw up after him. He defied his enemies and sat safe in his castle.

Leisure begets both craft and art and at an early stage in his house-dwelling phase he learned to make baskets — or rather she did, for probably the women made the baskets to carry grain home from the fields. Probably too they made the first unglazed pots, frail and undecorated, of which the remains still are found.

The art of pottery may have been invented by the Pueblos but the probability is that an invasion from the South brought it to them along with cotton and the bow and arrow. They became better able to defend themselves, although they were never good fighters, and they learned to spin fiber and weave cloth.

As they moved westward into lands more and more arid they could no longer depend upon rainfall alone and they learned to irrigate their crops with the waters of rivers. Even so the rivers often failed them in time of drought. Cloud and thunder and storm became gods to them because they were so important. Prayer was even more necessary than work and the primitive prayer is a dance. Because they had leisure and a fixed abode and because their very lives depended upon the fickle gods of weather they developed an elaborate ritual of dancing prayer.

" Dancing and building are the two primary and essential arts," says Havelock Ellis. " Dancing stands at the source of all the arts that express themselves first in the human person, and building is the beginning of all the arts that lie outside it."

These men who had become great primitive builders

because they needed a shelter from enemies too strong
for them now became great dancers because they felt the
need and had the time for prayer. Their dances became
always more elaborate, more richly costumed and carefully disciplined. They became masters of measure and
rhythm, they became gifted mimics and clowns. They
learned to make masks for their faces and to personate the
Gods by walking on stilts.

They danced in the spring to encourage the sun and
thaw the ground, mimicking the motions and calls of
mating birds, decorating their bodies with wings and
feathers. They danced in the summer to bring the rains
and in the fall to celebrate the harvest and to make the
hunting good. They danced to make men and women
fruitful as well as the earth. Their dancing, like any art,
became a thing that existed for its own sake as well as
for religious purposes so that they had comic dances and
pleasure dances and even imitated and improved upon
the dances of their enemies.

Since water was such a sacred and precious thing they
devoted much of their long winter leisure to making vessels in which to carry and keep it. They had learned how
to make a crude pottery early in their history. Slowly they
perfected it by glazing and decoration until the rough
utensil of their first efforts had become a thing of beauty
and another art had been evolved.

3

These people must have enjoyed a period of rapid expansion. The ruins of their abandoned dwellings show

that they once had flourishing communities as far north
as southern Colorado and southern Utah, south to the
Gila valley in Arizona and west to the San Juan, while
the Rio Grande was their eastern border. This was the
period when the cliff dwellings of Mesa Verde were built
and also the great communal apartment houses of Chaco
Canyon and the Gila.

In the Mesa Verde country as at the Rito de Los Frijoles in New Mexico the Pueblos were occupying deep
canyons in a country of high and relatively well-watered
mesas. The canyons were cut in soft volcanic deposits
containing many natural caves. These are the cliff
dwellings which have been the subject of so much myth-
making by white men, who invented a race of dwarfs
solely because the doorways to the caves were low. It is
now known that the cliff-dwellers were simply the
Pueblos, who enlarged the caves, walled up their fronts
and finally added independent structures of the same
material standing on the floors of the canyons and also on
the mesas. In the Mesa Verde country they also built for-
tresses in the heads of the canyons. The remains of these
cliff cities give a vivid impression of how men might begin living in caves like wild animals and then enlarge them
and build them, reaching out and up with their walls,
creating larger and larger areas of warmth and security,
until what had been a refuge for a hunted creature became a home and a temple, a place of worship, leisure
and art.

On the San Juan and the Gila there were no caves and
they built houses in the open valleys. The Pueblo Bonito
of the San Juan country probably represents the highest

development of pueblo building. It was an apartment
house of about two hundred rooms built in a semicircle
four stories high with a sheer wall on the outside and a
terraced effect within. The front was closed by a straight
one-story structure. The whole was built of tabular stone
laid in adobe mortar, evenly arranged in courses that
varied in thickness, giving a beautiful surface as the remaining walls show. The roofs, doorways and corners all
show neat finish and accurate line. This building, which
must have housed between one and two thousand people,
was not a primitive structure in any proper sense of the
term but a work of architecture, soundly conceived and
executed by skilled masons.

The period when the life of this communal one-house
community was at its height was the great period of
pueblo culture and it must have presented a striking
spectacle, especially on the days when great public festivals were held such as the corn dance. Doubtless many
hundreds danced to a great chorus of drums and chanting
while others crowned the roofs with a throng dressed in
brightly decorated cottons of their own weaving. The
men, even in historic times, wore flowered pantaloons,
and the dresses and robes for great occasions were all
wrought in bright colors. Men and women wore about
their necks and arms ornaments of bone, wood and stone
inlaid with turquoise, jet and shell.

Just what happened to the communities of the Gila,
the San Juan and the Mesa Verde country can never be
surely known. It is certain only that all of these, the finest
cities the Pueblos ever built, were abandoned, probably
some time in the Middle Ages. Doubtless the pressure of

their enemies was one thing that drove the builders back into a smaller territory. As their stores of grain and their wealth in textiles and jewelry increased they must have become more and more a tempting prey to the roving fighters around them. They were essentially a civilization surrounded by barbarians. While their strong walls often kept them safe there must have been times when the great stone houses were besieged and sacked and yelling savages ravaged their granaries and their women.

There is much evidence, too, that throughout the period of their development the Pueblos fought a losing battle with a changing climate. It is a common belief among the native peoples to this day that the climate of the Southwest tends always to become drier and drier. Old men tell you that their fathers told them of springs where now there is not a drop of water and of streams that once ran always and now only when it rains. There is also evidence of a more reliable kind that the Southwest once had a greater rainfall than it has now. The country has been eroded by water where the present rainfall is not heavy enough to leave a scar and it is spotted with the beds of lakes that have dried up entirely and of others that have shrunk to marshes surrounded by fields of salt. It is also hard to imagine how some of the ancient pueblos supported their populations unless they had more water than is now found near their ruins.

Probably droughts and wars combined to drive the Pueblos back from their northern and southern strongholds, concentrating them thickly along the great valley which became their final home. This most likely happened by a slow process of infiltration. When a crop failed or a pueblo was overwhelmed by its enemies a group of hungry or wounded refugees would reach the river where water always ran and where they were as far as they could get from the savage tribes to the north, south and east. Here was little stone and they built adobe houses, not so good as those of their earlier cities but still rising sometimes to five stories, and here they had wide irrigable levels in which to plant their corn. Soon all of the pueblo people were concentrated in this valley except for a single extension westward across the desert country by way of Laguna and Acoma to the Hopi villages of Arizona.

The Pueblos of the Rio Grande valley were by no means a beaten people or a decadent one. They had met with a setback in their expansion and their culture had been concentrated and unified.

Unity was certainly what they had always lacked. Although they were all so much alike in essentials they spoke several different languages, which suggests that there was little contact among the different towns. Apparently they never made any attempt at forming a federation and acting together until after the Spaniards came and then they failed as might have been expected.

The pueblo settlements of the Rio Grande were an experiment in human living which was never to be completed, a burst of creative energy that was blighted and checked. These men had solved the problem of subsistence in a fixed abode. They had attained to leisure and art. Their social organization did not extend beyond a single town but the pueblo town was a perfect communism and a perfect democracy. They had gone much farther toward a complete civilization than most peoples

ever go without setting man against man in the competition of individuals and classes. In a pueblo town everyone has a right to food and although there are chiefs,
rulers and priests, none of these offices has created a permanent privileged class.

Along the Rio Grande these men who had learned
how to build and dance were holding their own against
drought and savage invasion but doom was closing in
upon them. From the south and from the east a race of
men such as they had never known was moving upon
their valley of last resort — men who fought with lightning and thunderbolts and rode on strange swift animals,
men who wore shining garments no arrow could pierce,
men whom no walls could withstand, preaching of a God
no dance could propitiate.

III
Explorers

1

IN the high dry country of the Southwest, illusion is not wholly a product of hungry imagination. Light and distance and the clear dry air work transformations so that fantasy is often a part of the very landscape.

This is a thing to be remembered when one comes to consider the fantastic myths that have flourished in that country, the gorgeous lies and romantic liars it has produced, the tremendous journeys that were made there in search of non-existent things. Men will travel far when they can see far and they will pursue a chimera more eagerly than they will a fact.

Even in this sophisticated and sceptical day these distances and horizons sometimes fool men and they still stimulate the imagination. The tall story is part of western tradition and the stranger is still regaled with circumstantial accounts of unbelievable things. The seven golden cities of Cibola are an almost forgotten legend and it has been proved that the Grand Quivira, with its emperor who slept under a tree hung with golden bells, was an invention by which a native beguiled a stranger. But only two years ago a native who took me for a stranger tried in all seriousness to lead me on a hunt for the mythical wampus cat. And the El Dorado myth is still alive in its essentials. Companies have been incorporated to go in search of lost mines where gold could be gathered in baskets.

The explorers who saw this country for the first time were men who believed in miracles, who accepted the universe as a mystery to be revered rather than as a problem to be solved. It is no wonder then that they went a little crazy, that they often died hunting for imaginary treasure and were always disappointed with what they found. Exploration there was always a far more dramatic and imaginative thing than it could possibly be in the regions farther east, where men crept up rivers, seeing only as far as the next bend, or made their way through dense forests that seemed endless, hoping for nothing more than a clearing where the sun would reach the earth and crops might grow. From the Atlantic coast to the middle valleys men paddled and gnawed their way like blind rodents, driven by an impulse they only half understood, fighting savagely against a solid wall of resistant wilderness. In the high dry country of the west their imaginations expanded and they followed visions that were fed by what they thought they could see.

Josiah Gregg, a thoroughly modern man, had much to say about these illusory effects of light and distance. He observed truly that in this country everything appears enlarged and elevated. Distance does not always perform its usual function of shrinking things. He records that ravens walking on the ground were often taken for Indians and also for buffalo, while more than one caravan was thrown into panic by bunches of weeds and sunflowers which looked like great hordes of savages. Buffalo grazing quietly were taken for groves of trees and rocks looked like houses. He considers at some length the supreme illusion of the mirage and debates learnedly whether it is due to reflection or refraction. I cannot settle this question but I have seen many mirages and what always amazed me was how faithfully they imitated wide blue water in the sun with low dense groves beside it, so that one would be almost sure he was seeing the Rio Grande, swollen by some great flood, where he knew there was not a drop of water.

It is not at all hard to understand how Friar Marcos, who was certainly an honest man, gave the impression that at Zuñi he had seen a town as great as Seville, and it is still easier to share the dream of the credulous negro Estevan, who must have believed that he was about to make up for a life of bondage by taking possession of an empire with great cities full of gold and jewels.

This Estevan deserves more attention than he has ever received, partly because of the dramatic nature of his story but also because he really explored more of the Southwest and perhaps learned more about its people than any other man of his day.

Estevan was an African negro slave and was owned by a Spaniard named Dorantes, a member of the Narvaez expedition that sailed from Spain to explore Florida in the early sixteenth century.

Spain then claimed all America as part of its empire. A new world had been discovered, an immense world.

No one knew how great or how wealthy it might be. Never had the imaginations of men had anything so rich to feed upon. It was a day of tremendous projects, of unlimited hopes. Moreover, it was a day of religious empire. There was a simple method for taking possession of this new world and a perfect philosophy to justify the act. Every man was to be made a Christian for his own good. If he resisted salvation he was likely to be killed and if he accepted it he had to obey his spiritual lords who were also in effect his temporal masters.

The interesting thing about Estevan is that in his simple way he seemed to embody the spirit of his time. This man, who did not even own his body, had nevertheless the idea of empire and not a little of the technique. He craved to dominate men and he knew well enough how to do it by posing as the agent of divine and supernatural powers.

A vessel of the Narvaez expedition was wrecked and one of its leaders, Cabeza de Baca, with a few companions, crawled out of the surf somewhere on the coast of Texas. Dorantes and his slave Estevan were among these survivors who wandered for eight years in a wilderness no European had ever seen before. It was one of the greatest adventures in the exploration of North America and that four of these men finally reached the northern settlements of Mexico alive seems almost miraculous. Part of the time they were the captives of wild tribes and more than once they saved their own lives by posing as priests and healers. They wandered all the way across the continent to the shores of the Pacific and then south to San Miguel de Culiacan where they finally came into con-

tact with civilization again. They had learned much
about the country and still more about the people but
most of the time they had not known where they were.
The route they followed is still a matter of learned
dispute.

Estevan was one of the survivors who reached Culiacan
and were taken to Mexico City. There they were entertained and queried by all the lords of New Spain. The
tales they had to tell quickened the lust for empire. De
Baca had explored a vast region filled with souls in need
of salvation and if he had not found gold he had nevertheless heard much about it.

There was then current in Mexico a legend of seven
great cities so rich that whole streets were given over to
the shops of workers in precious metals while the beams
of the houses were set with gems. How this legend came
into being and grew until it filled the imaginations of all
the Spaniards can never be determined. The growth of a
legend is always a mysterious process. Bandelier believes
the tale of the Seven Golden Cities originated in Europe
and was somehow transplanted to America where the
Spaniards avidly listened to everything that made it seem
a rumor of the truth. They questioned the natives and
the natives told them stories. It must be remembered
that the Indians knew no Spanish and most of the Spaniards had not learned the Indian tongues so that this wish-
dream of empire was fed largely upon information com-
municated by signs. Probably most of the Indians did
not even have a word for gold. Yet the Spaniards persuaded themselves that they had heard of gold in profusion. The Indians told them of great cities and doubtless

the Pueblos of the Rio Grande and west of it seemed great cities to the nomadic and hut-dwelling tribes of the south, especially as they saw them only from a distance, but the inflamed imaginations of the imperialists magnified these into great cities in the European sense. Don Antonio de Mendoza, the Viceroy of the Emperor in Mexico City, had already heard of the seven golden cities and De Baca's stories made him more than ever certain that they existed. He seems to have purchased the slave Estevan who had now a great value as a guide because he had seen so much of that fabled country to the north and knew so much about the people and how to get on with them. In fact, there is evidence that Estevan knew more about the Indians than any of his masters. Essentially a savage himself, he was perhaps better qualified to understand them than the Spaniards. He was made much of in Mexico City and doubtless praise and wine made the slave feel like a master.

Mendoza now determined to conquer these rich provinces to the north and to do it wholly by the cross rather than by the sword. This was a humanitarian idea and also perhaps a shrewd one. If he sent an army the leader of it might seize the golden cities, ravage them and found an empire of his own. The Spanish court was full of jealousy and suspicion and so was the viceregal court in Mexico City. So Mendoza decided to send a priest with the negro slave to guide him and serve him. Then if the cities were found the souls of the people could be claimed for Christ and the Viceroy could attend to the gold when he got around to it.

For the delicate task of converting a heathen wilderness

into a Christian Empire he chose a man known as Friar
Marcos of Niza, an ecclesiastic of great ability who had
served as commissioner-general to New Spain and had
been with Pizarro in Peru. He was accompanied by one
other priest, Friar Onorato, by Estevan and by a few Indians who had come to Mexico with Baca. They were
probably Pimas.

Friar Marcos, like most of the priests of his time, was
a genuinely consecrated man. He did not crave any gold
or any other earthly goods for himself. He wanted only to
win souls for Christ and extend the dominion of God on
Earth. He was probably willing to die in the attempt if
necessary and sure of his heavenly reward if he did. Friar
Onorato was probably an equally devout man but he was
not a strong one. Before they passed the outlying settlements of New Spain he fell sick and was left behind. So a
priest, a slave and a handful of savages set out to conquer
a wilderness and found an empire. It was a fitting task
for a man who was willing to die and for one who had no
choice of destiny.

Somewhere in northern Sonora Friar Marcos decided
to send Estevan ahead to reconnoiter. Just why he did
this is not made very clear by his report. There is a hint
that Estevan had a way with the Indian women which was
not altogether in accord with religious teachings and that
the Friar thought he could expound salvation better while
the negro was somewhere else. It is natural to suspect, also,
that the Friar was willing to let the slave take the first
brunt of contact with the savages. If they received Estevan maybe they would receive Christ. Anyway, he
instructed Estevan to go ahead and make diligent in-

quiry about the seven cities. If he heard no very promising reports he was to send back by an Indian messenger a small cross, about the size of a man's hand. If what he learned was more encouraging he was to send back a larger cross, the size of two hands, while if he got definite information about the seven cities he was to send a still larger cross. Should he reach the cities or learn where they were he was to wait for the priest before proceeding.

Estevan, it seems certain, stepped out with alacrity. He was his own man now, probably for the first time in his life, and as long as he stayed a day or two ahead of the priest he would remain so. Almost immediately he sent back by Indian messengers a cross as tall as a man which they could barely carry.

Evidently Estevan had heard much about the seven cities and his Indian messengers seem to have convinced the priest as well that Cibola was a splendid reality for his report mentions not only cities but provinces and kingdoms. Friar Marcos had persuaded himself that he was moving toward a great organized community — a heathen civilization which could be won for God.

It is evident too that Estevan was strongly in favor of going ahead. He considered the expedition a good thing from his own point of view and as he went along it became a better and better thing. It became nothing less than a slave's dream of empire come true.

The course of his journey ran almost due north across the plateau country of northern Mexico where giant yucca and branching cacti grow sparsely over arid levels and whirlwinds dance like tall yellow ghosts. The gulf of California was far off to his left and to his right the western Sierra Madre was a blue wall. He crossed and followed the narrow valleys of streams which poured down from the sierra and all of these valleys were inhabited by Indians of one great sedentary family, mostly Pimas and Opatas. These Indians were a somewhat degenerated people. The Pimas, according to their legends, had once built great adobe houses, like the Pueblos, but they had been harried and hunted by the Apaches until they had devolved into a semi-nomadic tribe, building dome-shaped huts covered with thatch and mud, raising small crops of corn and squash in the canyons, hunting deer and small game, even rats, mice and lizards. They had bows and arrows and carried clubs of mesquite wood and shields of rawhide. Most of them were half naked, the women often wearing nothing but a grass skirt. They were strong and well built but not warlike. A people much beaten in battle they sought to placate invaders.

Estevan, as the slave of Dorantes, had wandered for years among these same people or others like them and he knew something about their simple souls. While he was sending crosses back to Friar Marcos he sent ahead to each of the Pima villages a gourd decorated with two bells and two feathers, one red and one white. He had observed that important leaders and medicine men of these tribes all carried some such symbol of office. Along with this magical emblem he sent word that a great man was approaching who would heal the sick and that all who went in his company would be safe from every kind of harm.

This simple device worked wonderfully well. At each village the people gave the negro food and shelter and from each village some of them followed him to the next. He soon found that they would deny him nothing he wanted and for the glory of God he began gathering up everything that looked valuable to him — chiefly turquoise and other semi-precious stones. Then he began also gathering women. These Mexican Indians are all polygamous and have never been celebrated for chastity so that perhaps it was not hard for Estevan to acquire concubines. Soon he was choosing the best-looking girls in every village and adding them to his retinue while as a special favor he also allowed some of the men to follow him. His black skin, which had been a mark of bondage before, made him a strange and therefore a supernatural being to the Indians. He dressed himself in the finest skins and fabrics and decorated his arms and legs with primitive jewelry and the green feathers of parrots. With the symbol of his new-found power in his hand he marched at the head of a following which soon numbered three hundred men and women. Estevan, the slave, was an emperor with an army and a harem. To Friar Marcos he continued to send messages, telling of splendid things ahead, but to the priest's repeated demands that he stop and wait he paid no heed.

These desert Indians were, and still are, wonderful runners. The Tarahumares are said to cover as much as a hundred miles a day. So it was easy for Estevan to communicate with his chief while still keeping in the lead.

At the head of his savage army, surrounded by his court of love, Estevan was marching north to meet the spring. It was probably soon after Easter that he left the priest behind and it was early summer when he entered the mountainous country of southern Arizona. He probably crossed the Gila river, where he saw the last settlements of sedentary Indians and then entered a vast uninhabited tract of plateau country, six thousand feet above sea level, timbered with a scattering growth of the low, spreading nut pine, which gives those mesas the appearance of vast untended orchards. At that time of the year the spring rains would have covered the ground with grass and flowers and water was easy to find. There were no longer any villages to feed him but his followers hunted and brought deer, rabbits and quail into camp every night, and they built him shelters to sleep in, which were occupied in turn by the Friar, toiling along behind with a few Indians. This country was a hunting ground for Apaches and Navajos but Estevan apparently had no trouble with them. Either he failed to meet them or his following was strong enough to scare them off.

In fact, it was Estevan's dangerous fate to meet with no opposition of any kind. He had but to reach out his hand for whatever he wanted — food, women, beautiful baubles. And somewhere ahead were great cities with many-storied houses, cities filled with women, food and baubles — cities filled with gold. He was getting almost daily messages from the priest, commanding him in the name of the Lord to stop and wait. But there was no stopping Estevan now. He was making up for a lifetime of slavery in a splendid holiday of freedom, lust and power. The current of his destiny was running swift and full towards its inevitable end.

His followers had informed him that presently they would come to a wide valley in which lay the first of the cities they had told him about. It was not one of the greatest but it was a part of the Kingdom of Cibola.

The Kingdom of Cibola did not know that a new ruler, a man of supernatural power, was approaching to take possession of it, to heal the sick and bring permanent peace and security. But it was soon apprized. Estevan sent his messengers ahead as usual with his sacred gourd and his high promises.

In a few days they came back to the camp but when he called them before him they averted their faces. They at first refused to report. When Estevan insisted they told him with great reluctance that the chief men of the many-storied city had thrown his rattle on the ground, saying that it meant nothing to them, and had sent word that Estevan must turn back for they would not receive him.

But Estevan had no idea of turning back. He did not fear death, he did not believe in opposition to his will. All his life he had obeyed because he had been a slave. Now he had become a ruler and therefore all men obeyed him. He felt sure they always would. Those who have learned to obey are always the readiest to command and have the most absolute faith in authority. Every slave is a potential tyrant and Estevan had become an actual one. Doubtless in his own eyes he was now a ruler by divine right. With perfect confidence he marched upon the first of the cities of Cibola.

There is no longer any doubt that this city was a pueblo of the Zuñi Indians which has now been long deserted. Traces of it are still to be seen near the present Zuñi pueblo. The legend of the Zuñis, concerning Estevan's visit, is that long ago a " black Mexican " came to this pueblo and was at first received with kindness but that he made free with the girls and women and was killed.

The details of Estevan's end can never be known but they tempt the imagination. One pictures the swaggering negro at the head of his retinue, decked in his feathers and jewelry, with the symbol of rule and priesthood in his hand, entering this western outpost of the dancing builders. They were not like the beaten and degenerate peoples farther south who had followed him and submitted their wills and their women to him. They were a proud people, living safe and separate behind high walls. But he did not know that and when they admitted him to their city he felt sure that all was well. He made his usual declarations. By eloquent signs and grimaces he announced himself as one who healed the sick and warded off all harm from those who followed him. Then like a greedy child he went among the people, laying his fingers upon all that attracted him — upon comely girls and necklaces of brightly-colored stones. But these women shrank from his hand. There was a moment of frozen silence, a rising mutter of rage, a rush of savage warriors, a scream of terror. Clubs thudded on living flesh. Frightened Pimas ran for the hills, leaving Estevan to his fate. It is said that Zuñis cut his black body into many small pieces and distributed them among the principal men of the tribe that they might be sure he was dead. So perished a clown of empire who had enacted a tragic travesty upon the spirit of his time.

The Indians brought back to Friar Marcos word that Estevan was dead. What was Friar Marcos to do? He had

been called a coward, as also a liar, but it does not seem
probable that he was either. If he tried to enter Cibola
he too would very likely be killed and his first duty was
to report to the Viceroy the news that Cibola existed.
Friar Marcos compromised. He marched on to the top
of the mountain from which Estevan had first seen the
pueblo and saw it for himself. He then planted a cross
on the hilltop and with a prayer and a few gestures he
took possession of all this region for God and the King
of Spain. Then he went back rapidly to tell them in Mexico City what had happened and what he had seen.

In his report Friar Marcos said that this city of Cibola,
which he had viewed from a distance, was as large as the
city of Mexico. There were only about two thousand
people in Mexico City at that time and this pueblo of
the Zuñis may have contained half that number or a little
more so that the Friar had not exaggerated greatly.
Perhaps he did not consciously exaggerate at all.

What he looked at was a compact little adobe village
several stories high. But what he saw is another matter.
The pueblo, aglow in the sunlight, miles away, may have
looked to him as large as he wished to believe it. One can
never know how much of optical illusion and how much
of excited imagination went into the making of these
legends. Painters say they use much gold in rendering
the effect of sunlight on adobe. The whole association of
these cities with gold may have been originally a matter
of color, just as the myth of their size may have been due
to the effect of light. Here were cities of a golden hue,
magnified in a lens of crystalline air, and the men who
first heard of them from half-articulate savages and then

saw them from afar were men who hungered for great golden prizes and believed in their own dreams.

The one thing certain is that the Friar's report, amplified by what he said in conversation and embellished by gossip as it went the rounds, threw the Mexican capital into a fever of excited greed. It was the common report that these cities of Cibola were as large as Seville, that the roof beams of the houses were decorated with precious stones and the necks of the natives were heavy with golden trinkets.

Mexico City was then a little flat town of pale stone walls and narrow streets where soldiers and adventurers loafed and brawled. About half the population was made up of fighting men. Mexico was just then the principal frontier of Spanish Empire. Farther south most of the fighting was over.

A great many of these bellicose idlers in Mexico were young Spanish gentlemen of good family, out to find fortune and adventure in the Indies. They all had a certain claim on the viceroy by reason of their high connections and they were a burden and a nuisance to him. But now he saw a good use for them. He determined to organize them all into a great expedition which should go north and conquer the Kingdom of Cibola.

Everyone wanted to go on this jaunt. Everyone felt sure it was coming back loaded with gold. Many who could not go armed slaves or servants and sent them instead. An ambitious and imaginative young officer named Coronado was placed in command and no expense was spared on the preparations. Castaneda, who was a member of the expedition and wrote its history, describes it as the most brilliant company ever collected in the Indies to go in search of new lands. All the young gallants rode fine horses, many of them hung with trappings that brushed the ground. The men wore armor and helmets all burnished for the occasion — a terrible weight of metal which was scattered across the deserts and mountains as the hard realities of exploration proved its uselessness. Lances were lifted and swords were drawn as the expedition started amid the cheers of the people. Trumpets were blown and banners flew. There were three hundred armored soldiers and after them came the full-robed priests and a great troop of Pima warriors, painted and feathered.

This last great search for the mythical cities was an undertaking mediaeval in form and spirit. In Europe the mediaeval world was dying. Doubt had been born, faith was on the wane. Men were learning to look at the world with the sharp and sceptical scrutiny that became modern science and they were beginning that worship of themselves which became modern individualism. But this outpost of empire had not much felt the winds of change. These gallant followers of Coronado were like a troop of Quixotes, tilting against illusions hardly less preposterous than those of the comic knight. Coronado had even a Dulcinea to plague and inspire him for the historian of the trip attributes many of its misfortunes to the fact that the leader left behind a beautiful young wife who was always in his mind.

Coronado reached the Rio Grande, visited all of the principal pueblos and stormed and sacked several of them. He found the way to this valley of destination and he endowed its inhabitants with a lasting conviction that the Spaniards were a cruel, deadly and treacherous lot.

It was midwinter when he came to the river and it must have been an unusually hard winter for the Rio Grande was frozen solid. The mountains were white with snow, the cottonwoods were bare and stinging sand storms swept the flats. Coronado had to live off the country and when the Indians refused him food and clothing, he took them. His foraging soldiers got out of hand, stole whatever they could find and raped women. Open warfare broke out and the bringers of salvation brought death. At the pueblo of Tiguex, which has long been extinct but probably stood near the present city of Albuquerque, the Spaniards committed a bloody blunder that prejudiced their relations with the Indians for generations. They stormed the pueblo and two hundred warriors surrendered on the promise that they would not be harmed. The officer who had them in charge did not understand these terms. He could not feed prisoners. His own men were starving. And since these prisoners were obstinate heretics he thought the appropriate thing would be to burn them all at the stake. When the Indians saw what he was going to do they fought barehanded for their lives. The Spanish soldiers charged and scattered them and hunted them up and down the valley on horseback, spitting them on lances and splitting their skulls with swords.

In that winter of hunger and blood the beautiful legend of the golden cities perished. Coronado found no gold although he searched the hills for it as well as the houses. Moreover he could not fail to see that here was no ancient civilization of stored-up wealth, but only an arid country where a primitive people fought hard for bare survival. After Coronado no more is heard of the seven wonderful cities. He had performed the chief function of an explorer, he had pierced illusion and come to the hard unlovely truth. But that was not what he wanted. His King, his God, his Dulcinea, his own romantic credulous soul, fed on faith and miracle, all demanded fabulous wealth and brilliant conquest. And a man can always convince himself that what he wants is real. He can always find a witness to corroborate his dream.

Coronado found his prophet of glory in the person of an Indian whom he called the Turk because the man looked like one. This Turco was a gifted liar. He was probably a refugee or a prisoner from some of the prairie tribes. Talking mainly with his hands, he convinced Coronado that far to the east there were cities which would make the fabled ones of Cibola look insignificant. This Grand Quivira, as the Spaniards came to call it, was where the Emperor slept under a tree hung with little golden bells that played a tune in the wind. He told also of a great river and of galleons rowed each by forty oarsmen. Just how much he said and how much the Spaniards imagined is a question. Questionable also are his motives. It is probable that he was appointed by the Pueblos to lead the invaders away by telling them stories, and in this he succeeded, for Coronado started east in search of the Grand Quivira.

He was a deluded man but a brave one. His soldiers were ragged and starved and many of them were mutinous but nevertheless he crossed the mountains and entered the vast prairies. Nobody knows just where he went. Certainly he didn't know. He found himself in a world as flat and limitless as the sea. He saw buffalos and the great bellowing herds scared his horses and stampeded his cavalcade again and again. He wandered for weeks seeing nothing but prairie and sky. Probably he traveled in the circle of the lost for he seems to have ended up not far from where he started.

Suspicion early fixed upon the Turk. He was suspected of being in league with the devil and one of the soldiers set to guard him swore that he held conversations with the devil in a jug of water. Instead of leading the Spaniards to a Grand Quivira full of gold he brought them only to a camp of nomadic savages, probably Pawnees or Cheyennes, who attacked the troops and made them fight for their lives.

The Spaniards strangled the Turk in his sleep and began a long straggling march back toward Mexico City. Coronado's men had lost all confidence in him and the expedition fell to pieces as it went along. Many of the men deserted when they reached the outlying settlements and the rest dragged into the city a few at a time, bearded, ragged, dressed in skins of wild animals and bits of Indian clothing, devoid of all their chivalrous trappings — devoid, above all, of their illusions. Coronado was a disgraced man and Friar Marcos was denounced for a liar.

The effect of the Coronado expedition was to leave the Rio Grande to the Pueblos for almost forty years. During that period only a few Franciscan friars entered the northern country. Two of them accompanied Coro-

nado and stayed behind to try to convert the Indians and
later two lay brothers, named Rodriguez and Lopez,
went in with a small escort and founded a mission at one
of the pueblos called Puaray.

These Franciscans sought nothing but converts and
they were the only Spaniards whom the Indians did not
all fear and hate. Yet all of them, after a while, were
killed. Since they died alone among the Pueblos nothing
certain is known about their deaths but a letter one of
them wrote gives a probable clue to the fate of all. This
man, left behind by Coronado, sent a message to say that
he was winning the young people to Christ but that the
old men were all against him and he had no doubt he
soon would die. Doubtless these gentle priests, who
wanted neither women nor wealth, would gather the boys
and girls about them and gain a gradual ascendancy over
some, teaching them new crafts, offering them new images
to worship, telling them of another sacrifice of blood.
The religion they offered was after all not so strange in
its essentials. But to the elders of the tribe they were
simply rival medicine men, winning the young to new
Gods, threatening the ancient and necessary faith. In
the secret counsels of the khiva, where the Gods of the
earth were worshiped, their fate was decided. They
preached that death was a road to glory and they were
sent upon their chosen way.

The reports brought back by the escort that went with
Rodriguez and Lopez and by a volunteer named Espejo
who followed to see what had become of them gave the
pioneering impulse new life. It was recognized by this
time that all the dreams of Golden Cities and Grand

Quiviras were defeating the true business of empire. When the expeditions failed to find gold they lost both courage and purpose. The thing needed now was a colonizer and the Viceroy began a long and careful search for one whom he could trust. This search led eventually to the choice of Don Juan de Onate and to his conquest and settlement of the country but there was first an independent attempt by another man who is much less known and more interesting.

Gaspar Castano de Sosa was the Lieutenant Governor in charge of the province of Nuevo Leon and he lived at a little frontier mining settlement, digging silver out of the steep and barren mountains of north central Mexico. These diggings had been but recently opened and they were not panning out very well. Sosa was ambitious and it evidently occurred to him that while the politicians in Mexico City and Spain were fumbling about for a man to send into the unconquered north he could steal a march on them and make himself great. There was a law on the books which permitted the governor of a province to settle any lands already discovered and claimed for the Empire, provided he told the Viceroy of his intention and complied with all the requirements of imperial colonization. These were many and meticulous. The law instructed him exactly how to treat the Indians and how to build his towns, even to prescribing the width of the streets and where the church should stand. He was also required to write an elaborate report, recording almost every step he took, and Sosa wrote a very full and very good one. These Spaniards were not, like the Anglo-Saxon pioneers, bold individualists going their own way. They were men whose every move was governed by a double authority, that of God and that of Empire.

Sosa had first to persuade people to go with him for what he proposed was simply to move his whole settlement into the northern wilderness and there expand it into a great colony which he would control. He let it be known that some Indians from the north had brought him rich silver ores. He then had some rocks smelted and into the melting pot he threw a couple of large silver mugs so that the official assay showed an ore of unexampled value.

Here was a man who perhaps had no illusion himself that he was going to find great wealth in precious metals but who realized that he must provide his followers with some such belief. For his own part, he evidently dreamed not of wealth but of power. He sent word to the Viceroy, as the law required, that he was setting out upon this enterprise and he requested that messengers should follow him with the necessary permission. Evidently he expected that by the time the Viceroy's messengers overtook him his conquest would be accomplished and his superiors could not fail to endorse it.

Toward the end of July he set out with one hundred and seventy men, women and children. Their goods were loaded in wagons drawn by oxen and they drove a herd of cattle before them. These and some corn were their only provisions and only enough to last them a few weeks. Their very lives depended upon the conquest of an unknown country containing thousands of Indians by a handful of men, encumbered by women and children.

The reality of exploration is hard to imagine for those

who have never faced the hazards of a wild country. This caravan had not only no road to travel, it had not even a map. Sosa knew of the existence of the Pecos river. He conceived that the Pecos valley would be a short way into the Pueblo region and he boldly set out across country to find it.

Traveling over the bare plains of western Texas he soon came to the Pecos but only to find that it ran in the bottom of a gorge several hundred feet deep. He was not far from where the southern Pacific now crosses the stream on a trestle that spans one of the deepest and narrowest canyons in the country with a barren wilderness on either side. It seemed impossible to reach the river and already many of his followers wanted to turn back. From this time on Sosa kept his expedition going only by the force of his individual will in the face of constant objection and even of open mutiny and threats of murder. He was entirely willing to risk not only his own life but those of all of his followers.

They followed the gorge of the Pecos perhaps a couple of months for it seems to have been early fall before they found a way down to the river. Meantime they had killed most of their cattle for food and the clamor against the foolhardy expedition grew constantly louder. No gold or silver had been found. They were eating all they had and risking their lives for nothing.

When they finally found a way down to the river, probably somewhere in southern New Mexico, they were not much better off for the Pecos valley there is full of brackish marshes. They were always crossing the river to avoid bogging down in the mud. They saw little game and only a few Indians of a wandering prairie tribe. Early in November, half starved, they reached the vicinity of what is now Fort Sumner, New Mexico, and here they stopped to recruit their strength. The valley was full of the tall shrub known as mesquite and its sweet puffy seed pods were ripe. These furnished them with food of a sort and they also caught in the river a generous supply of coarse fish, mostly catfish and a kind of sucker known as buffalo fish.

Meanwhile Sosa had sent a few soldiers ahead to reconnoiter and they came back reporting that they had found a city with several thousand inhabitants who had jeered at them and chased them with rocks and arrows so that they had barely escaped with their lives.

This advance guard had reached the great pueblo of Pecos which stood at the foot of the mountains about forty miles east of Santa Fe. It was not abandoned until early in the nineteeth century and its ruins are still to be seen. They are pointed out to tourists from the windows of the Santa Fe Limited and archaeologists have been digging among them for years.

Sosa's followers had no wish to approach this community which outnumbered them ten to one and had shown plainly that it regarded Spaniards with aversion. But Sosa had now found what he was hunting. He divided among his people all the corn he had left except two fanegas which he kept for seed so that he could plant crops as soon as his new colony was well established. Then he went with nineteen soldiers and seventeen servants to claim the pueblo of Pecos for God and the King, leaving the rest of his expedition to wait for him.

One cannot refuse to admire the Spaniards for their courage — a courage based on faith. Sosa was bringing the word of God to these people. He must have believed absolutely that they would receive it and that God would protect him or he would not have dared to go ahead with such a puny force.

It was late in December when Sosa came to Pecos. He saw a narrow valley, bare and wind-bitten then, with a snow-covered mountain range behind it. On a low hill beside the river stood a massive adobe structure rising in tiers to a height of three or four stories. There were several units enclosing a large court and separate struc- tures were connected by wooden galleries high above the ground. As the Spaniards rode toward the pueblo the whole population swarmed out upon the roofs and stood staring at the invaders. The men wore brightly flowered cotton pantaloons and heavy robes of buffalo hide and they stood with bows and arrows and rocks in their hands. Women and children were gathered on the housetops, too, all dressed in cotton fabrics of their own weaving, many of the women wearing jewelry of turquoise and of shell obtained by a long process of transcontinental barter.

Sosa boldly rode into the pueblo and went about making signs of friendship. He was determined to carry out the letter of the law which forbade him to make war upon the people unless they attacked him first.

Had the Indians rushed upon the Spaniards in force they could surely have destroyed them, but this, for some reason, they never did. When Sosa tried to tell them in sign language that he had come as a friend and to save their souls, some of them jeered at him. Arrows were shot by warriors concealed in the crowd and stones were thrown. But the arrows failed to pierce the Spanish armor, the rocks bounced off iron helmets — and there was no concerted movement. The Indians huddled upon their housetops, helpless before these strange messengers of their destiny as though they had understood that any but a passive resistance was useless in the long run.

Sosa finally took his stand in the plaza and tried to make a speech in sign language but he was interrupted by a woman who emptied a pot of ashes on his head. His soldiers had wanted to attack the Indians all along and he had refused to permit it but he now considered that he had been sufficiently resisted to justify him in using force. He ordered his men to capture one of the housetops. There he planted his two small brass cannons and fired them off, laying down a sort of barrage, while his men scaled ladders and captured a few more roofs.

This move at least convinced the Pueblos that the Spaniards could not be driven away by jeers and indignities. They began to call out " Amigo," and to throw bits of food to the soldiers but they refused to come down from the roofs unless they were driven.

Sosa withdrew from the pueblo and camped near by, determined to complete the civilization of these people in the morning, but when he returned to the pueblo it was absolutely deserted. The Indians had all fled to the mountains during the night.

But Sosa was not to be discouraged. He went on to the vicinity of Santa Fe where he visited a small pueblo with only a few hundred inhabitants. These frightened people offered him no resistance. They looked on in silence while he erected a large cross in their plaza and explained its meaning to them. He then held up a crucifix and each of his men in turn knelt and kissed it, " at which the barbarians were seized with admiration," he reports, though he does not say how they showed their emotion. Sosa then appointed from among the Indians themselves an Alcalde and an Alguazil, which were the two essential officers of a Spanish village, and he explained their duties to these newly constituted dignitaries as well as he could. He had now, to his own satisfaction, converted a tribe of savage heretics into an organized Christian community.

In the face of freezing weather Sosa went on to the Rio Grande, visiting twenty pueblos in all, and in each of them he set up a cross, explained the Catholic theology in sign language and established a government. When he had done he returned to Pecos where he found all the Indians back in their homes and conferred the blessings of Christian civilization upon them also, finding them this time wholly submissive.

There is something at once absurd and heroic in the spectacle of this man, going about with his handful of soldiers who might have been destroyed at any moment, solemnly convinced that he was making Christians and and planting civilization in the wilderness. Nearly three hundred years later the descendants of those same Indians are still dancing in honor of their heathen Gods and still tolerating an alien faith just as they tolerated the crosses and speeches of Sosa. They still maintain, too, their ancient tribal government while keeping up the show of a civilized one to please their masters.

Yet Sosa's march down the Rio Grande was not in vain. All his predecessors had come to this country expecting to get rich and all had gone away in disgust when they found no gold. Sosa at least convinced the Pueblos that he had not come only to rob and kill. He opened the way for the settlement of the country. His sermons in sign language were laughed at and his crosses were tolerated only out of fear but from that time on the cross was supreme on the Rio Grande except for one brief interlude of revolt. The God of Heaven had triumphed over the earthborn Gods of the dancing builders.

Sosa had brought Christianity and civilization to the Rio Grande but it held a defeat for all his personal aspirations, just as it had for Friar Marcos and Estevan and Coronado. His followers had come for silver and gold and they were sick of their privations and took no interest in christianizing the Indians. They formed a plot to kill Sosa as the only way of bringing the expedition to an end. He discovered the plot and was about to kill the chief conspirators but at the last moment he changed his mind. He said that all who wished might go back but for his part he would go on alone and die alone if necessary. This shamed his men and they went on with him, down the Rio Grande to Isleta. There the starving troop was delighted to meet a force of fifty Spaniards from Mexico City. Sosa rode forward joyfully, feeling sure, so he says, that these were messengers of the Viceroy come to endorse his conquest. But instead of being congratulated he was arrested and accused of treason. Enemies at the court had convinced the Viceroy that he was trying to found an independent empire. He was taken to Mexico in chains, tried, convicted and sent into exile in China. Later his case was reconsidered and it was decided finally that he had acted within the law and done a great work for his King. He was appointed governor of the new province and messengers were sent to bring him back from exile. Meanwhile he had started on a Chinese junk for the Moluccas, the crew had mutinied and Sosa had been killed fighting the mutineers.

He was the last of the Spanish explorers who reached the Rio Grande. All of them had started with visions of gold or of power, temporal or spiritual. All of them had found death or disgrace or both. But they had also found the way.

IV
Conquerors

1

IN every Pueblo village one building stands apart and is different from all the others. Often oblong or circular, it is usually half buried in the earth and sometimes, set in a hillside, it is almost wholly so. It has neither doors nor windows. A broad adobe stairway gives access to its roof and the long tapering ends of a pueblo house-ladder jut from a hatchway which is its only entrance.

This isolate and secretive structure is called a khiva and it is a temple where many gods are worshiped. Somewhere in its earthen floor there is always a hole, symbolizing the entrance to Shipapu, the place in the bowels of the earth from which the gods emerged. For all the gods of the pueblos are earthborn gods serving the earthly needs of men. They are gods of fertility, love and rain, gods of hunting and battle. Everything man lives by is a gift of these gods and the Pueblo cannot conceive of life without prayer to them. That is why the khivas still stand and still shelter a primitive religion after three hundred years of proselyting and persecution by civilized men of two races and three governments.

55

Churches of other kinds have been built beside the khivas and their rituals are duly enacted. The Indians are perfectly willing to assume another religion if they can thereby achieve peace but they are not willing to abandon their own. When the corn festivals are held in late summer a bower is always built to shelter the patron saint of the pueblo, offerings of melons and bread are laid at his feet, muskets are fired in his honor. But always down the broad steps of the khiva comes the bright throng of half-naked dancers with painted faces, the drums rumble and the voices of men and women blend in a deep chant of supplication to the god of rain while they dance in his honor from noon till sunset.

All the ancient dances still are held, many of them in secret, and inside the Khivas are enacted ceremonies no alien eye has ever seen.

Each year the dances become smaller as the pueblos dwindle and more and more of the young people go away to schools and jobs. Each year the alien crowds of curious spectators grow. Thousands now see the snake dance of the Hopis and visitors stay up all night to claim a bit of standing room. When the Zuñis bring out their masks and stilts and costumes to bless their new walls and their new brides in the Shalako dance, the Indians are almost crowded out of their own houses by staring throngs. To the rest of the world the religion of the dancing builders has become a show and it has even been put upon the stage like vaudeville but to the Indians themselves these dances still are necessary prayers for rain and corn and babies.

It is only a matter of time until the pueblos will be

crushed out of existence by the sheer weight of civilization pressing upon them in a hundred ways but their religion will probably last as long as there is any organized pueblo society.

When the last dance is over and the drums are still it will be the death of a culture that began thousands of years ago when wandering savages first built walls to hold their grain and in a rhythmic pantomime begged sky and earth to let them live.

A few years ago government officials announced that the dances of the Pueblo Indians were to be stopped. They said the Indians wasted their time and energy in dancing when they should be hoeing corn and also that many of these dances were obscene and offensive to the morals of civilization. They may have been right but they were not original for in the seventeenth century the Spanish rulers and prelates denounced the same dances in almost the same terms and with exactly the same unwavering conviction of their own righteousness. To read the words of Governor Otermin, who faced the fury of the one great Pueblo rebellion, is to know how constant a thing the spirit of intolerance may be. It is one of those forces that unify human experience and enable us to comprehend the past through the present. The inquisition is dead but its soul goes marching on.

2

All of the explorers tried more or less to christianize the Pueblos but the effort did not become systematic and continuous until after Don Juan de Onate had conquered

New Mexico at the end of the sixteenth century, built the city of Santa Fe and begun the settlement of the lower Rio Grande valley. The colony grew slowly. After almost a century only about twenty-five hundred Spaniards were scattered along the valley from Taos to a point somewhere near the present Socorro. About a thousand of these lived in and near Santa Fe which stood just where it does today. It was grouped loosely about the present plaza, a sprawling adobe village with corn fields and orchards between the houses. The old Palace, which still stands, was the capitol building, the headquarters of the governor. Behind it was a square enclosed by high walls with little watch towers at the corners. About a hundred Spanish soldiers, clad in armor, carrying lances, swords and the crude firearms known as arquebuses, represented the military power of the Spanish Empire in this remote and isolated colony. By way of artillery they had a couple of small brass cannon.

The Pueblos in their seventy towns outnumbered the Spaniards about ten to one. Most of them had nominally accepted Christianity, churches had been built in most of the pueblos and about fifty priests administered the Catholic rites. They were nearly all devout and zealous men in those days. They herded Indians into church, told the story of Christ, pointed to his image. They threatened hell and promised heaven. They baptized Indian babies with good Spanish names and married Indian couples for a Christian eternity. They heard confessions and granted absolutions. The Indians, or at least some of them, went through it all with unrevealing faces and the good friars felt sure they were winning souls for the one true God.

And so they were, a few. But still the khivas stood —
those rival temples — the great drums rumbled and the
padres saw their charges dancing naked in the sun, chanting their prayers to a pagan pantheon.

This was not only impiety, often it was crime, and the
civil authorities took a hand. They arrested revered old
men of the pueblos, charging them with sorcery, witchcraft, idolatry and obscene practices. Khivas were torn
down and burned. Pagan masks and images were thrown
on the flames. Governor Trevino had three Indians tried
for witchcraft. They were found guilty and hanged.

A rumble of rage ran through the pueblos, but the
Spaniards, secure in the approval of God, were undaunted. A mere handful of fighting men surrounded by
thousands of Indians they proceeded industriously with
the business of killing the men and burning the structures
which were to the Pueblos symbols of universal power
controlling the very sources of life. In a bold drive against
heresy forty-seven pueblo medicine men were arrested
and taken to Santa Fe for trial. A few days later seventy
warriors surrounded the governor's palace and demanded
the release of the prisoners. The governor, smelling dangerous rebellion and having no adequate forces at hand,
released the prisoners.

Among these pueblo shamans who had been imprisoned was a San Juan Indian named Popé, and he is
one of the few Pueblos who are remembered by name,
who stand out as individuals and leaders.

It must be understood that in the American Indian,
as in all primitives, individual personality does not exist
as it does in civilized men. The Indian is not the free being

of romantic legend. On the contrary, almost everything he does and everything he believes is dictated by tradition. He is surrounded by social taboos and compulsions and more completely controlled by them than is even the most conventional of civilized men. The individual part of him is small and weak, the communal and traditional part massive and rigid. The Indians produce few great leaders in any line because greatness is individual. Indian leaders for the most part are figureheads who merely repeat traditional words and acts. The training of a shaman or medicine man is largely a matter of learning rituals from the lips of old men. Indian art is traditional and the gifted individual dares add but little to the accepted patterns. Only in war does individual leadership have any scope at all and even there it is narrowly limited.

The tragedy of the Indians, facing a civilized invasion, lay in the fact that they could not combine against their enemies for great human organizations are the creations of great individuals. Leadership was what they needed and they had not quite reached the point, in man's long ascent toward consciousness, at which great leaders are produced. Now and again as the irresistible machine of militant civilization rolled across the continent, Indians arose who had something of the gift and inspiration of leadership, who saw the need and tried to serve it. Almost all of the few Indians whose names are remembered — King Philip, Tecumseh, Osceola, Sitting Bull — were such primitive geniuses groping toward organized power. Invariably they failed. The organizations they created were destroyed by treachery, by jealousy, by the dead hand of tradition holding the Indians apart in little groups, making it impossible for them to grasp the ideas of solidarity and co-operation.

Popé was another of the same kind. The rest of the pueblo shamans who had been imprisoned probably went back to their people, glad to be free, asking only to be let alone. Popé went back to San Juan an impassioned and inspired man. The rest of his life was a conspiracy and a struggle.

Of Popé as individual little is known. It is said he had wandered widely and had lived among the Apaches and Navajos and this suggests the restlessness and originality of impulse which is associated with unusual men. He tried even to draw the Apaches, the deadliest enemies of his people, into a league against the Spaniards. It seems probable that he had a vision of complete Indian solidarity — of an aboriginal world organized against a civilized one.

Popé worked upon his conspiracy five years before he struck. His native pueblo of San Juan was not congenial to it. The Spanish Maestro there suspected him of dangerous tendencies and persecuted him. Some of the Indians were against him too. So he went to Taos, one of the strongest and most recalcitrant of the pueblos, where an abortive conspiracy had been started once before.

The dark, half-buried chamber of the Taos khiva now became a womb of rebellion. Popé, like Joan of Arc and many another deliverer, had direct communications from God. Three spirits came to him in his retreat to prophesy the destruction of the Spaniards. It is said that he rubbed his body with some phosphorescent substance so that it glowed in the dark and his hands and feet appeared to

burst into flames. News of his plan was spread by runners. Chiefs and shamans from all the rebellious pueblos
came to Taos and heard the fiery words of a prophet who
appeared as a shape of flame. Only important men were
admitted to the conspiracy. They were to rouse their
people when the time came. All were given to understand
that treason meant death.

Even so it was inevitable that rumors of the plot should
leak out. Not all of the pueblos could be enlisted. Isleta,
always the most friendly to the Spaniards, refused to fight,
and individual Indians in many pueblos were faithful to
the conquerors. Popé came to suspect his own son-in-law,
Nicholas Bua, of treason, and went to the man's house
and killed him. Probably he had others killed too. He was
at once ruthless and patient.

Intimations of danger reached the Spanish priests but
they could make little impression on the governor. Moreover, not much could be done. Some word of impending
trouble seems to have gone south and a few more soldiers
were sent to Santa Fe but the colony was remote and its
pleas were little heeded in Mexico City.

Popé finally decided upon August 11, 1680, as the
day for his revolution and he sent runners to all the
pueblos bearing knotted cords to fix the date. But on
the ninth it became known that some Indians had betrayed the plot to a priest and on the morning of the
tenth the revolt began.

Despite betrayals, the Spaniards were surprised in some
places and had short warning in others. Santa Fe first
learned of trouble when a priest went to Tesuque to hold
services. His Indian parishioners, instead of kneeling at

his feet, rushed upon him with clubs and beat him to death while a soldier who had accompanied him galloped back to the capital to give the alarm.

Popé had planned his rebellion well. He was going to take Santa Fe in a surprise attack by all the northern Pueblos while the capital was to be cut off from the lower valley by holding the roads between. But his plot had been betrayed. His revolt began in a ragged fashion, some of the Pueblos starting before others had gotten word. His plan only half succeeded, for neither Santa Fe nor the lower valley was wholly surprised, but he did let loose a terrible storm of primitive wrath and vengeance.

3

The Pueblos had never been a warlike people. They had fought off the Apaches and Navajos, mostly by standing siege in their citadels. They had fought small wars among themselves. But now, perhaps for the first time in their history, almost the whole race of them rose up with weapons in their hands against a common enemy. They rose up to avenge their insulted Gods. This was a holy war on both sides.

In every pueblo the chiefs called out the people and told them that God, the Father of the Spaniards, and Mary, their Mother, were dead, and that the old Gods were supreme again. They told them that all the Spaniards were to be killed or driven from the country. They promised the warriors a woman each for every Spaniard killed — not Spanish women, for none were to live, but women of their own kind.

The Indians tore the rosaries and crosses from their necks and burned them on bonfires. They set the churches afire, looted the altars and galloped yelling through the streets of the pueblos dressed in the vestments of sacred office.

The priests, who had been their best friends among the Spaniards, were the first to feel their wrath for these men were the symbols of the alien faith. In Santo Domingo they killed three priests and piled their bodies on the altar. In Zia they routed the priest out of bed, mounted him naked on a hog and whipped him through the streets until he died. Only a few priests escaped alive and almost all of the Spaniards who lived near the pueblos were killed. Seventy died in the Taos valley, where the revolt began, with three thousand Indians of Taos and Picuris on the warpath.

Meanwhile all the Spaniards in the north were running for Santa Fe and those in the south got word to gather at the friendly pueblo of Isleta. About four hundred were killed but the rest assembled in these two strongholds and prepared to fight for their lives.

In Santa Fe a thousand men, women and children, with many horses and cattle, were crowded into the little square behind the Palace. All the royal arquebuses, blunderbusses, swords, lances and daggers were gathered there and the two brass cannon were mounted on the walls. Soldiers manned the roofs and dug trenches outside the walls.

A few Indians from near-by pueblos were caught and these were questioned about the conspiracy. When all possible information had been got out of them they were absolved by the priests and then hanged. One Indian refused to tell anything or to receive unction. He said he would rather die and go to hell than confess so they killed him unpenitent.

Presently the watchers on the roofs saw the northern Pueblos coming across the flat mesa that lies south of Santa Fe. There were about five hundred of them, led by a Taos Indian named Juan, and they came on leisurely, stopping to loot and burn every outlying house. As they drew nearer Juan rode out in front of his troops. He wore a broad sash of red taffeta, recognized as part of the hangings of a convent. He was mounted on a fine Spanish horse and armed with an arquebus, a sword and a dagger, all taken from fallen Spaniards. He offered Governor Otermin his choice of two crosses, a red one and a white one. The red meant fight, the white meant go. The governor chose the red cross of battle.

Then began the five day siege of Santa Fe. The Indians never tried to take the place by storm. They lacked artillery and organization. They simply waited for the Spaniards to starve and all the while their numbers were growing, as recruits from other pueblos arrived, until there were several thousand of them outside the walls, showering the defenders with arrows and with unskillful volleys from stolen guns.

Only five Spaniards were killed but inside the crowded palace conditions were becoming unendurable and they became hopeless when the Indians succeeded in cutting off the water supply. The ground soon was littered with animals, dead of thirst, bloating and rotting in the sun. Provisions were low and it was only a matter of time till the last of the water would be gone and men and women would die too.

Outside the Indians were already celebrating a victory, dancing war dances, shouting again that God the Father and Mary the Mother were dead and that their own Gods had never died as the priests had claimed.

They celebrated too soon. The Spaniards gathered all their armed men together and made a sudden deadly charge upon the unprepared Indians, fighting with the fury of desperation, invoking the name of the Virgin Mary with every blow. They scattered the Indians and chased them, killing hundreds and driving them back from the walls. Then the whole troop of refugees marched out and started south.

The Indians from the hilltops watched them go. They did not attack again. They were satisfied to see these deadly men depart. Otermin and his followers reached Isleta unmolested and were there joined by fifteen hundred refugees from the lower valley. The whole troop made a slow and painful march to El Paso.

The Pueblos had lost hundreds but they were victorious. For the first time in nearly a hundred years not a Spaniard was in the country and for the first time in all their history they had acted together.

For days Santa Fe was the scene of a pagan celebration. The church was burned and in the plaza the Indians built little stone squares oriented with the four cardinal points which to them were sacred. Around these improvised altars they danced for days and nights and made offerings to their Gods. All of those who had been baptized by the priests went to the mountain stream that runs through Santa Fe and scrubbed themselves with amole root to take off the taint of the Christian touch. They dropped their baptismal names and they were forbidden by their chiefs to speak a word of Spanish. They put off the wives they had married in church and held a great orgy of new matings.

Popé had not appeared in the fighting. He was not a warrior but a man of words and visions. The fighting had been led by his chosen captains and especially by one Catiti. But now that victory was won Popé came forward in glory. Mounted on a black mule, dressed in the finest fabrics and furs, with a bull's horn fastened to his forehead he toured all the pueblos as the Spanish governor had been wont to do and everywhere he made the people turn out in his honor just as they had been made to do for the governor. Evidently when it came to ruling his kingdom, Popé could do no better than to imitate the conquerors for there was nothing in his own traditions to guide him.

The pomp and privilege of the governor he mimicked perfectly. He went everywhere accompanied by a retinue, he exacted large contributions of corn for the support of his government and he took all the prettiest girls as consorts for himself and his captains. But when it came to organizing his federation he would seem to have had no plan. He was not an executive, he was a prophet and he went on prophesying. Now that the Spaniards were driven out, he proclaimed, and the ancient Gods appeased, rain would fall and crops would grow, game would abound and peace would be everywhere. He made overtures to the Apaches again and he even proposed intermarriage as a way of sealing an intertribal pact.

Popé had talent but no luck. The very first summer after the rebellion was one of almost unprecedented drought. Crops failed and game was scarce as it always is in dry years. The Apaches proved treacherous and attacked the Pueblos, sacking and destroying several villages, while others were forced by famine to move and build new towns. Factional wars broke out among the Pueblos themselves. The ancient Gods were angry still.

4

Meanwhile the Spaniards were getting ready to return. They had made a starving march down the Rio Grande to where El Paso and Juraez now stand with only the river between them and there they had begun a settlement. They were aided by the Franciscan friars and especially by Father Ayeta who held the office of procurador-general and was thereby the official representative of the Viceroy at El Paso. Speaking for the government he demanded that Otermin go back and reconquer the lost province.

Neither Otermin nor his followers had any stomach for this attempt. They were a band of half-starved refugees, many of them sick or wounded, living miserably in mud huts, mourning their four hundred dead. They had found saving heretical souls a grievous business and they wanted no more of it. But the word of the Viceroy was the word of God. Otermin mustered a hundred and forty-six soldiers, something over a hundred friendly Indians, a few armed servants and a cavalcade of nearly a thousand horses and mules to carry the men and their provisions. Padre Ayeta provisioned the expedition and armed it as well as he could. Most of the Spanish armor was worn out but shields and jackets were made of rawhide to protect the soldiers against the Indian arrows and all the arms in the settlement were gathered together. Padre Ayeta himself accompanied the expedition and since he knew all the churches had been destroyed he took along a portable altar mounted on an ox cart so that he could be prepared to do the service of God.

The Spaniards marched up the valley first to the pueblo of Isleta which had never revolted. All along the way they saw black columns of smoke signals rising above the sandhills so that they knew the Indians were watching and word of their advance was traveling north by primitive telegraph.

Otermin entered Isleta with seventy men, with trumpets blowing and banner aloft, " extolling the holy sacrament." Although this pueblo had supposedly remained faithful to the church, Padre Ayeta was shocked to find that all the crosses had disappeared and he immediately set the soldiers to work making a profusion of new crosses — big ones to put on the houses and little ones to hang on Indian necks.

The Indians watched all these proceedings in surly silence. They submitted to having all the new babies baptized and all the couples remarried. They did not even dare to protest when the khiva was sacked and feathers, idols and masks were burned in the plaza.

Otermin then went into camp a few miles up the valley and sent forward one of his captains, named Mendoza, with a substantial troop. He was to enter each of the pueblos, by force if necessary, and to burn all khivas, "refuges of the devil, and houses of idolatry, ravishment and obscenity," while granting absolution to all repentant Indians.

Mendoza went to Alameda, Puaray, Jemez, San Felipe, Santo Domingo and Sandia. He met with no resistance anywhere for the Indians had deserted their towns and fled to the mountains. They were as sick of battle as the Spaniards were but still determined to escape salvation at any cost. Mendoza could destroy khivas and burn masks and images to his heart's content but souls to save were few. In Sandia they found the body of a cripple who had hanged himself because he was unable to flee and a very old blind man. This one declared that he had been misled by the devil and begged to be absolved. He was duly restored to good Christian standing and given food. Mendoza wrote a special letter about him to Padre Ayeta, asking that the father come and work on the old man "so that his soul might not be lost."

All the rest of the souls from these pueblos were somewhere in the high mountains and there they stayed despite the fact that it was the dead of winter and the mountains were deep in snow which also covered the valley a large part of the time. Mendoza thought one reason the Indians did not attack was that the snow had softened their bowstrings. It is a fact that Pueblos do not like snow. Whatever its effect on bowstrings it softens their moccasins and impedes their movements. They do not like to hunt in snow. The weather may well have saved Spanish lives.

Mendoza saw none but a few cripples and aged until he

came to Cochiti. Outside that town he was confronted by a band of three hundred Indians who demanded to know what he wanted. He called out that he had come in search of them that their souls might not be lost. At this the Indians laughed and hooted and called the Spaniards cabrones which is still in New Mexico the chief fighting insult.

This parley led to nothing. The Indians withdrew to the hills and the Spaniards entered the pueblo of Cochiti, which they found as empty as the others, and spent the night there. The next morning they went out to meet the Indians again and found the hilltops west of the pueblo covered with them. There were many hundreds of warriors and the Spaniards could see that this was a force recruited from all the northern pueblos. They greeted the Spaniards with war whoops and the situation seemed hopeless for the little band. But Mendoza went bravely forward and called for Catiti, the leader. This Catiti, according to Otermin's report, was part Spanish, but he had nevertheless become the chief military leader of the Pueblos. Mendoza told him the Spaniards had returned because the souls of the Indians would otherwise be lost, that they could fight if they wished, but in that case they would pay " with their women, their children and their souls."

This oration had apparently all desired effect on Catiti. He broke into loud sobs and said that he feared his soul was lost in any case because his sins had been so great. Mendoza reminded him that the mercy of God is infinite. Padre Guerra, who was the priest with Mendoza, came forward bathed in tears and begged Catiti to repent. Both

Spaniards and Indians wept and a true revival spirit was
apparently rising but it was marred by some of the Taos
Indians in the background who began to yell in loud
derision. Catiti left his spiritual comforters and held a
conference with these irreverent brothers, after which
they kept quiet.

He then assured Mendoza that everything was arranged. He said that he would have the Indians all back
in their pueblos in two days and that triumphal arches
would be erected in honor of Padre Ayeta and Governor
Otermin. The Spaniards went back to Cochiti for the
night feeling that the business of the Lord prospered.

But soon they began to be a little nervous. They were
surrounded by many times their number of Indians and
treachery was always possible. Certainly some of the Indians had seemed honest enough in their repentance.
They had wept loudly and shed real tears. They had
fraternized with the Spanish soldiers. But one Luis
Tupatu, governor of Picuris pueblo, had been heard to
threaten to kill his own brother, Lorenzo, for embracing
a Spaniard. Lorenzo had cried out that God would protect him, whereupon Luis shouted in a great rage: " Don't
speak of that man God in my presence! "

Aside from evidence that some of the Indians were
not truly penitent it was noticed that they all wanted to
trade with the Spanish soldiers for powder and lead.
Some of them also borrowed horses and these never
came back.

The nervousness of the Spaniards became a panic when
some Indian boys came to the pueblo and said they
wanted to repent their sins, be absolved and make a con-

fession. The first of these only hinted at treachery, but the other two, Juan and Joseph, after having been granted the mercy of God, told the Spaniards of an elaborate plan for their destruction. They said all the penitence had been but a blind to conceal it. That night a group of the prettiest Pueblo girls was to come to the Spanish camp, cook a meal for the men and seduce them. When all the Spaniards were in the arms of love one group of warriors was to rush into the pueblo and kill them with clubs while another made off with their horses.

This was too much for Mendoza's nerve. He abandoned Cochiti and went back down the river to rejoin Otermin, taking with him the two boys, Juan and Joseph, and a few other Indians who had confessed and received absolution. He told Otermin that in his opinion it was a hopeless task to make the Indians conform to Christian ways of living, that all of them were traitors and idolaters at heart.

Otermin was of the same opinion. His supplies were exhausted and so were his horses and men. He composed a sad report for the Viceroy in which he said: " We found them very content in their accursed witchcraft and idolatry and very stubborn after having burned churches, images and even bells."

It was incredible but it was true. The Pueblos preferred freedom and their own Gods, even with drought, starvation and Apache raids, to comparative security under Spanish rule.

The only souls Otermin could surely save were those of the Isleta Indians. He went back to that pueblo and found that its population was steadily diminishing. He had left five hundred Indians there and he found only three hundred and eighty-five when he returned, the rest having fled to join the rebels in the mountains. In order to secure those remaining for God he resolved to burn the pueblo and take the Indians back to El Paso with him.

Then began a long ignominious march back down the Rio Grande. Otermin records that he had a severe headache and sore eyes as a result of his diligence in burning masks and feathers with his own hands. Padre Ayeta's portable altar, which had brought so few souls to grace, was always getting stuck in the mud and once they spent half a day pulling it out again.

When they were far down the valley, the two boys, Juan and Joseph, disappeared from camp one night and were seen no more. It then struck the humiliated conquerors that perhaps the whole confession of a plot to slaughter them in the arms of Indian maidens had been only a story to scare them out of the country.

They had been beaten and expelled again and this time wholly by a cunning which was not without a certain salt of humor. But it was the last triumph of the Pueblos and a futile one. For eight more years they owned their country and their souls. Popé once more rode abroad on his black mule and prophesied a future of peace and plenty. The northern Pueblos grew tired of his words and his taxes and deposed him in favor of Luis Tupatu. That chieftain did no better and Popé regained his power in 1688, only to die the next year. Some said that he was poisoned by jealous rivals and some that the devil carried him away in a cloud of smoke.

Whatever the mode of his going he went at the right time. Within a year De Vargas came marching to reconquer New Mexico in a war that left the Pueblos little more numerous than they are today. The reign of Popé was the apogee and the end of the Pueblo culture. What might have become a civilization and a state was thereafter only a relic — a quaint survival of the childhood of the race when all men danced before their Gods and built with their own hands.

V

The Right People

1

THE SOUTHWEST is a land of fallen walls, littered with ruins of all ages and in all stages of decay. Tribes, cultures, classes have lived and died here, leaving their shells to crumble slowly in the dry preservative air. From the first rude buildings of the pre-pueblo people, lasting for centuries, to the ghostly mining camps of the seventies and eighties where two or three old men live in towns built for thousands and spiders spin their webs over bars and pool tables in ornate deserted saloons, the whole procession of human life down the Rio Grande has left its record in adobe, stone and wood. Usually it has left some human vestige too, for the descendants of the men who built the first walls still are building new ones and almost every deserted gold town shelters some oldtimer who remembers the booms and battles of fifty years ago.

Of all the walls men built in this valley none has more nearly disappeared than those of the great adobe houses that belonged to the aristocracy in the years of Spanish empire. Adobe houses are many and there are still a few

large ones built around courtyards but usually the spot
where one of the famous families lived is marked, if at all,
by a pile of sand.

Gente de razon these people called themselves, and
the phrase, ringing with pride, means literally " the right
people." They were called also ricos or rich ones and
gente fina, the fine people. Their descendants still live
here and many of them are valued citizens but these are
triumphs of adaptation to a way of life wholly alien to
their traditions. As a class the right people are gone.

In old Mexico the same aristocracy is now falling to
pieces under a proletarian revolution, just as it fell after
the invasion of the gringos in New Mexico three generations ago. To visit Mexico City now and meet the wistful
remnant of the people who ruled under Diaz is to go back
into the past. There one may still encounter the pride,
the perfect courtesy and the absolute self-assurance which
are born of the conviction that the right people should
rule because they are the right people — that human life is
a hierarchy based upon land and blood and privilege. And
there one feels the same fragrance of charm that one dis-
covers in the records of old days on the Rio Grande. These
men were proud and lazy and often they were cruel but
the society they created had charm because it was imbued
with respect for the past. Charm in human society is a
cumulative thing and it does not survive rapid change.
It depends upon the faithful observance of customs and
traditions, slowly perfected. It requires that men shall live
for generations in the same houses, tilling the same lands,
having the same relations of class to class and man to man.
Perhaps this aristocratic ideal was never more completely

realized, on a small scale and in a rude way, than it was along the Rio Grande when the wars with the pueblos were over and the great valley was settled.

For a while after the conquest of De Vargas many settlers came to this new colony of the North. Soon fifteen thousand Spaniards lived along the river. New towns were built, campaigns were launched against the Navajos and Apaches, new missions were established to convert the Pueblos. Armed expeditions set out to conquer new lands. Daring priests mounted their mules and departed to risk their lives preaching Christ to the Moquis. The barren New Mexico hills were searched for gold and silver.

This burst of colonizing energy soon subsided. Neither gold nor silver was found in paying quantities. Even precious metals to make ornaments for the churches had to be imported. The Spaniards were always treasure-hunters and when it was learned that New Mexico contained little gold interest in it waned. It was found too that the country was a lean one and its arable lands soon were all taken up. But there was another reason why this colony became an isolated and neglected place. The Spanish Empire was dying. Power had passed to England. The splendid discipline that had conquered South America and Mexico was falling to pieces. This colony was the last expansive thrust of religious empire in America. Faith in God and King had been its spiritual nourishment and both were on the wane. The rest of its story is a study in decay — the inevitable decay of pride and privilege sitting in isolation.

The lands of the Rio Grande region were granted in great tracts by the King of Spain, some of them to com-

munities but most of them to individuals, so that a few
aristocrats literally owned the earth. This land-owning
class was probably never more than one-fiftieth of the
whole population. The pueblo Indians were granted the
lands about their villages and they maintained a precarious economic independence, tilling their own fields. The
priests still tried to make good Christians of them but the
effort became more and more perfunctory as its futility
became apparent. The Pueblos tolerated the churches
and went to mass on Sunday while still keeping their own
heretical faith intact. In the early eighteenth century a
junta was held to discuss whether they should be allowed
to paint their faces. They are still painting their faces.

Some small landowners took up homesteads, mostly in
the less desirable sections north of Santa Fe where the
valley is narrow and rugged. But in the South, where it is
wide and fertile, nearly all of it was owned by a few rich
men who claimed to be of pure Spanish blood. This
southern region came to be known as Rio Abajo or lower
river, the northern region as Rio Arriba or upper river,
and the geographical division became more and more a
social one. It was in the rugged upper valley that the fra-
ternity of the Penitent Brothers, wholly a plebeian organization, had its headquarters and its greatest strength.
There, too, the Pueblos were strongest and most independent.

In this northern region the Pueblos still are strong and
the Penitent Brothers still lash their bare backs every
holy week. The Matachines still is danced, witches fly,
serapes are woven on handlooms and magical cures are
worked at the shrine in Chimayo. The life of the humble

still goes on much as it did a hundred years ago but their
first lords and masters have disappeared. Here once more
the mighty have fallen and if the meek have not inherited
the earth they have at least clung to some of it with an
astonishing tenacity. And here the collapse of pride and
power has the beauty of completeness because this little
aristocracy was so long cut off from the rest of the civilized
world to work out its destiny alone.

It was about eight hundred miles from the Rio Grande
to the nearest American settlement on the Missouri and
more than a hundred years elapsed after the conquest
before men found their way across that thirsty plain.
Chihuahua was almost as far to the south. North and
west lay wilderness, unexplored and impassible. But on
the Rio Grande life became safe and easy for the right
people. Apaches and Navajos raided outlying settlements
and stole cattle and sheep but they seldom if ever struck
the great houses of the rich.

These houses had been built as forts. With walls three
or four feet thick they enclosed each a courtyard, called
a placita, and behind this was always another square enclosed by a high adobe wall with quarters for slaves and
peons built inside it. Here the carts and wagons were
kept and the horses could be driven in when danger
threatened. Windows were barred and a trusted servant
asked every comer his name and business before doors
were opened. Storerooms were filled with grain and dried
buffalo meat and a well in the courtyard supplied water.
Life here was secure. It was shut in and well nourished.
Each great house reproduced the isolation which beset
the colony as a whole.

The men who owned these houses lived pleasant lazy lives. In the valley they raised grain, vegetables and grapes and on the mesas they pastured great herds of scrubby sheep, yielding little wool but abundant meat. All the work was done by peons who in effect were serfs. They were paid in goods and were never out of debt. Sons inherited the debts of their fathers and generations lived in bondage.

Law held the peon but not the patron. It provided that officers in the army and priests of the church could be tried only by their own peers. The army in New Mexico was at best a few hundred ragged peons but it provided berths and immunities for young men of the right people as did also the church, and the powerful landowner was just as immune as these by reason of his property. Always less than a thousand soldiers priests and gentlemen ruled the country.

2

This lower valley in the early eighteenth century, then, although surrounded by unmapped wilderness, was itself a well-settled and well-cultivated place where men had lived for generations. From Bernalillo to Socorro the great houses were only a few miles apart — long low recumbent structures with porches, supported by round wooden pillars, extending the full length of their gleaming whitewashed fronts. They looked as solid as the mountains but they existed only by the incessant toil of slaves who plastered the earthen walls and mended the flat dirt roofs after every heavy rain. They were all sheltered by old cottonwood trees with their generous spread of thick whispering foliage which seem designed to create havens of shade in a land of burning sun. Sometimes the houses were surrounded by adobe walls and often in the old days the bushy vineyards and the fields of grain were enclosed by lower ones for labor was cheap and there were no other fences.

Along the roads passed many riders. Rich men rode fine horses with heavy silver-mounted saddles housed in bearskin. Poor men bestrode burros, sitting well back on a humble rump, dispensing both guidance and encouragement with a club which is all the equipment necessary for burro-riding. Women rode rarely, sometimes in chair-like side-saddles, sometimes on postillions. The peon commonly held his woman before him on his steed as he did a sack of corn for the mill. The only common vehicles were one-horse carts, made without iron, the huge wooden wheels sawn from the trunks of cottonwoods. The terrific screech of their ungreased wooden axles was a familiar voice of the valley. Quite early a few great coaches were imported by the richest men, and these, rolling on important social errands, were impressive symbols of an unquestionable power.

Within, the homes of the rich were Moorish. An oriental influence had been brought from Spain and it was strengthened by the scarcity of furniture. Bedsteads there were none but only mattresses, folded against the walls in daytime and covered with Navajo blankets, black red and white. The wealth of a man showed in the quality of these coverings rather than in the amount or kind of his furniture for it was all home-made and included only a dining table, a few wooden chairs with rawhide seats and heavy carven chests for clothes and jewels. Most preferred to sit on the floors which were earthen but often covered with woolen carpets of native weave in black and white checker patterns. The walls were washed bone-white with gypsum and covered with colored cloths to a height of four or five feet so that the whitewash would not rub off. Pictures were few but mirrors in gold frames were much esteemed and these multiplied after the wagons began to come from Missouri until some of the salas offered the guest his own image from every angle. Nearly all the houses had sacred images in little corner shrines.

The principal room of every house was a long reception hall. Scant daylight shone in through translucent windows, wooden-barred. Cool dim and quiet were these great rooms — carefully guarded sanctuaries of faith, power and family life, where idle, soft-voiced women chatted away their long days, waiting for men who were truly both lords and masters.

For this society belonged to the vanished world in which man was supreme and woman only his pleasure and possession. Here the father was an absolute ruler by divine right and treated as a sacred being. His children, no matter how old, uncovered when he approached and they dared not smoke in his presence. He could chastise a grown son or give his daughter in marriage as easily as he could sell a horse or kill a slave. His power sprang from his loins and multiplied with his family. One man had thirty-six legitimate children by three wives and almost all had large families of a darker shade by Indian concubines.

When men rule and women are subject the differen-
tiating qualities of the sexes are always exaggerated, just
as they are minimized when men and women meet on
equal terms. So these men were belligerently, aggressively
masculine. They were arrogant, lazy, truculent, cruel and
brave. They ruled, fought, wandered, and made love.
Cock fights and gambling were their sports. Commerce,
except in slaves, horses and the products of their own
lands, was beneath them, as were the professions. In 1831
the province contained only one doctor and no lawyers.
There were almost no books except bibles.

Feuds were many and generally sprang from love
affairs, for this was a time and place of romantic passion,
furious and blind. There were few formal duels but many
fights, especially at dances. A beauty promised the same
dance to two young men of the proudest blood. The lie
was passed and they met at dawn in the plaza. Their pistols cracked and both fell dead. They were men of honor,
as were all of these ricos, and in a country where every
man carried pistols on his saddle and a Spanish dagger at
his belt, honor cost blood.

Life was not dull for these men. There were three long
and adventurous journeys to be made every year. In
August or September a fair was held at Taos where tribes
of the plains and mountains came to trade with the Mexicans, offering captives as slaves and also furs and skins for
knives and beads. Horses were sold and swapped and
much property changed hands over races, cock pits and
monte games. There were dances and fights and a great
flow of red wine.

Those must have been strange and dangerous gatherings. Navajos, Apaches, Comanches, Arapahoes, perhaps a few Cheyennes all came to Taos and they were not peaceful Indians but warriors fresh from their raids with scalps at their belts and captive girls to sell, observing a precarious truce. The Taos Pueblos held a fiesta with ceremonial dances and footraces. Mexicans came, of every degree from ricos looking for bargains in human flesh to the poorest peon that could get there on a burro. Early in the eighteen hundreds tall blonde mountain men began to appear with their long rifles and packs of beaver — deadly men, forerunners of change and destruction.

Later in the fall the New Mexicans went east by way of Pecos across the mountains to the buffalo ranges in organized communal hunts. The buffalo furnished the province with most of its beef for there were never many cattle on the Rio Grande. In the late eighteenth century these hunters from the valley killed as many as twelve thousand buffalo a year and rich and poor had meat. Almost every family had one horse that was kept for buffalo-hunting and nothing else — a swift horse trained to stick to his prey like a dog. The rider carried a lance with a twelve-inch blade, sharp as a razor, and he drove it through the crook of his left arm into the buffalo's heart and out again. If his weapon stuck between the ribs he was in for a fall.

Rich young men hunted luxuriously with peons coming behind to skin and butcher the kill and hang the meat in strips a yard long to dry in the sun. Dried buffalo meat cooked with chile and beans was the staple of the poor and a dish to be found on every table.

Sometimes they hunted wild mustangs on these expeditions, wearing them down by a relentless relay pursuit
or driving them into some corner of the country where a
trap-corral had been built. Often the wild horse, when
he had been roped and thrown, was tied neck and neck
to a burro half his size and the burro would always master him and bring him to camp.

In January there was another trip, called a conducta,
to the southern fair at Chihuahua — a perilous journey
of six hundred miles with danger from Apaches and from
death by thirst in the desert. This, like the Taos fair, took
a large part of the male population away. It was apparently led and organized by the ricos while many poor men
went along to trade their woolen weaves for chocolate,
silver and silks. The conducta that Lieutenant Pike saw
drove also a herd of fifteen thousand sheep and was
guarded by a small detachment of Mexican troops. It was
the custom among the gente de razon for an affianced
youth to make one of these expeditions for his prospective
father-in-law and he was expected to bring back an Indian slave girl as a present for his beloved. This trip to
Chihuahua was the only contact the New Mexicans had
with the outside world. There they saw men and goods
that had come across the sea and got some faint inkling
of what lay beyond the Rio Grande.

In all this life of adventure and movement the women
had no part. Their lives, before marriage, were a guarded
and cloistered virginity and afterward one long series of
pregnancies. It was necessary that many babies be born
because so many died. The death of an infant was accepted as a matter of course. " One angel more " was the

usual spoken obituary, and the first gringos who came to New Mexico were shocked to see children's funerals moving through the streets at a brisk trot and to cheerful music with the tiny corpse often uncoffined.

These women tended, by reaction, to be everything the men were not. As the men were cruel the women were notably tender and compassionate. Kendall records how they saved the lives of the Texan captives, bringing food to them, secretly if need be, and he broadly hints that they brought love as well. For these women, after marriage, were not celebrated for fidelity to their proud masters. All early observers testify to this. Gregg remarks that "marriage changes the legal status of the parties but it scarcely affects their moral obligations," and Abert said that "nowhere is chastity less valued or expected."

This last is not exact. The male expected chastity of his bride and considered himself cheated if he did not get it. He would resent any invasion of his family with knife and gun. Yet infidelity was all but universal for this was almost the only possible form of feminine revolt against a complete and brutal masculine domination. To the blond invaders the women gave themselves especially, as though there had been some instinct in the blood to breed to the coming conqueror. Both of the Taos conspiracies against the American occupation were betrayed to the Americans by Mexican women. When Doniphan evacuated Chihuahua his army was followed by a crowd of Mexican girls in men's clothing who trailed his soldiers and camped with them in the desert until he drove them all back home.

These women in all essentials were slaves and they had
the deep duplicity and the spirit of revolt, unresting even
when only half conscious, which tyranny always breeds.
From this same source doubtless sprang their quick warm
sympathy for everything helpless and oppressed — for
children, captives and motherless lambs. " Pobrecito! "
(poor little thing) was an exclamation often on their
lips. It comforted the ears of the Texan captives all
through their march. The word is still often heard all
through Mexico, old and new, and almost always from
a woman. It articulates a feminine protest against the
cruelty of man, which perhaps never achieved a more
complete and bloody expression than it did in the Empire
and colonies of Spain.

In their Moorish houses these women lived like in-
mates of a harem. Slaves did all the work — ground the
corn on metates, baked the bread in hive-like outdoor
ovens, tended the cauldrons that hung before the wide
cooking-hearths, beat thick chocolate to a froth in wooden
bowls. There were five meals a day and three of them were
heavy ones. It is no wonder these women, married at
fourteen and fifteen, were fat and middle-aged before
they were thirty.

All smoked corn-husk cigarettes and all drank native
wine, copiously, with meals and between them. Grape
brandy was made but used sparingly and chiefly as a medicine. One old man, who had been a youth of the aristocracy in its decline, assured me that American whisky
had done much to ruin the ricos. Accustomed only to
wine they could not stand the deadly corn juice of the
invaders.

For marriage the girls could only wait and take what their masters willed. Some were promised before they could walk. Usually a suitor called with his parents on the parents of the chosen girl, and if they agreed she might be called in, as a special indulgence. If no refusal was sent in eight days the man was accepted. Betrothals were often long as they still are in Mexico City where the girl dare not even dance with any but her affianced though he keep her waiting for years while he has the run of the town. One wealthy New Mexican, becoming engaged to a girl of thirteen and humanely judging her too young for marriage, sent her to a convent for four years to keep her safe and she became celebrated as the best-educated woman of her time. A few of the girls went to Durango to school but many never learned to read. Small private schools were kept in New Mexico but only for boys.

There was much visiting among the houses of the rich, especially late in the afternoon when chocolate was served, and then this society exhibited all its graces. It moved with grace, as Spanish society always does, and it had an eye for appearances. You must picture the men of that early day dressed in buckskin dyed black, well cut by native tailors and ornamented with silver buttons. Their hair was long and hung in queues on their necks. They wore full beards and moustaches and wide flat black hats imported from Mexico. Each had over his shoulder a blanket called a serape, of bright colors and striking pattern, and it might be worth as much as two hundred dollars. The women wore short skirts, often of red wool, and low cut bodices, and each always carried

a shawl. The quality of this reboso marked her wealth
and station as did the serape that of the man.

Manners were elaborate, ceremonial and truly charming, as they still are wherever Spanish influence lingers.
Bows were profound and a man took off his hat even to
offer a light for a cigarette. Salutation was an art, with
room for originality. " May you live to be a thousand,
sir! " " And may you, sir, live to see the last of my years! "
Where men go armed they speak with exaggerated
deference.

These people were not afraid to touch each other.
When old friends and relatives met, all embraced and
kissed — a custom still sometimes to be seen. Girls publicly embraced and kissed male friends whom they would
never see alone unless in marriage or by stealth. Men embraced each other, kissed on the cheek and expressed the
degree of their affection by the heartiness with which they
hammered each other on the back.

All sat usually on the floor and drank their chocolate
from hammered silver mugs. All service was silver —
even the bowls and ewers used for washing.

These people were without a formal art but not without a culture. Where there is no written literature poetry
escapes the danger of becoming the possession of a class.
Here almost everyone was a poet of a sort. Almost every
youth could strum some kind of stringed instrument,
serenade his lady and sing verses of his own making.
They varied in kind from the innumerable couplets and
quatrains that embodied the folk wisdom to long narrative poems celebrating important events. The latter were
sometimes written down but they seem never to have

been associated with the names of authors. All poems and
stories were common property as were also the dramas
and charades they enacted. Some of these came from
Spain but there was a great deal of indigenous work,
most of it now forever lost. It was the kind of rich
compost of folk tale and folk fancy, of rhythm and tradition from which a literature may spring but here it was
doomed never to bear its fruit.

There were many dances and everyone danced, rich
and poor, layman and priest. Formal dances were held in
all the houses of the rich and these were called bailes or
balls while the dances of the common people were called
fandangos. At the bailes they performed all the old
square dances with intricate figures, requiring both
knowledge and command on the part of the leader. The
musicians were commonly peons and often blind. They
played fiddles and a stringed instrument like a guitar
which was often home-made. Sometimes a woman with a
special gift for verse sat on the platform beside the players and as each couple passed she improvised a rhyme
about them, to the hilarious merriment of all. They
danced also waltzes both fast and slow and their most
distinctive dance was called Cuna or cradle waltz. The
whirling dancers embraced each other loosely about the
shoulders, making a cradle, " which was never bottomless " as one shocked observer from Missouri remarked.

About Christmas time all New Mexico danced. There
were dances of every kind, both sacred and profane, for
in winter the Pueblos held their most elaborate dances
and in the holidays there was dancing in every great house
and blind men rode fiddling through every village to

gather the slaves and peons for fandangos. To violins from across the sea and to savage drums, to courtly minuets and to the rolling chant of the Katchinas, all up and down the valley feet went dancing.

3

Such was the life within walls of the right people — a life of feasting, dancing, fighting and amorous intrigue. Outwardly it was a struggle with savage tribes. The vital and determining factor in the fate of these people for over a hundred years was their relation to the Indians — an intimate and subtle relation of blood shed and blood mingled. For the whole of the eighteenth century, while the rest of the world was making over its ideas and institutions, the written annals of New Mexico are little more than a list of Spanish governors with long resounding names. Forms and customs did not change but change was working under the skin.

With the Pueblos there was peace since they had nominally accepted the cross. They were a part of the community but a separate and self-sufficient part. They traded with the Mexicans, raising most of the fruit for the valley, but there was little social intercourse. Mexicans were not welcome in Pueblo villages and some of the Pueblos still will not let a Mexican stay within their walls at night.

So these sedentary Indians ceased to be a problem but on all sides the settlement was beset by savage nomads — Navajos to the west, Apaches to the south, Comanches and other prairie tribes to the east, Utes and Arapahoes in the northern mountains. These tribes surrounded the

little civilization on the Rio Grande much as the barbarians surrounded Rome. With all of them the New
Mexicans were sometimes at war and with all they traded,
but the Navajos were their most persistent and intimate enemies. Fighting is always an intimate relation,
and when captives are carried into slavery on both sides,
then the most implacable enemies are struggling to
become one.

The northern Indians seldom invaded New Mexico
and the Apaches generally preferred to prey on the richer
provinces to the south. For a while in the early eighteenth
century the Comanches were a scourge. They had killed
and robbed and taken Mexican children captive. Don
Sebastian Martinez of San Juan, who had lost relatives
to the savages, called for volunteers and five hundred
young men came forward, each well mounted and leading
a pack mule. Some of them had blunderbusses and muskets and there were horse pistols and a few swords but
many had only the bows and lances of their foes. They
traveled east by way of Pecos across the mountains to
where they knew the Comanches were camped. The
Spaniards then all threw away their hats, let down their
long hair, painted their faces and rode forward chanting
and yelling like Indians. They knew the Comanches had
war parties out and they were taken for one returning.
Suddenly they charged upon the unprepared warriors
and slaughtered most of them. Seven hundred Indians
were taken prisoner and there was a long discussion of
what to do with them. It was finally and appropriately decided to present them to the Spanish crown and it is a
matter of record that several hundred Comanches were

taken to Vera Cruz and shipped to Spain. The miserable and bewildered savages touched the heart of Queen Isabella who had them baptized and allotted them lands in Cuba. There speedily they all died of the climate in the odor of sanctity.

The New Mexicans composed a long narrative poem commemorating this campaign and for generations it was recited and enacted as a drama at Christmas time.

The Comanches never became a serious danger again. When the young warriors wanted to raid the settlements, the old ones would lead them to the spot where the massacre had happened and point to the whitening bones and skulls that littered the ground for many years.

No such easy triumph could be won over the Navajos who were numerous, proud and powerful and never far away.

Navajo is a Spanish word. These Indians call themselves Tinneh, meaning simply " The People," with the accent on the first word. They still consider themselves superior to all other men and they condescend when they speak to any stranger. They also long believed they were the most numerous and powerful people on earth. When he heard that the United States army was to be sent against his tribe, a Navajo scornfully picked up a little sand to represent the army. He waved his hand at the prairie and said the Navajos were as many as the blades of grass on the earth. These warriors were entirely willing to take on the United States with the Utes and Piutes thrown in to make it interesting. It took fifteen years for the Americans to subdue them. Three proud generals marched into Navajo-land and were glad to march out again. Almost every campaign against them ended in the deep red sandstone gorge of the Canyon de Chelly. The Navajos had the rocky walls fortified and they could be neither surrounded nor dislodged. Kit Carson finally starved them out in a hard winter and put them on a reservation. There were estimated to be six thousand of them then and now they number over thirty thousand. They are the only American aborigines who have increased since they were conquered. Sheep-herding and silver-smithing they learned from Spaniards and weaving from the Pueblos. They were proud but not too proud to learn. Neither were they too proud to accept into the tribe any man who proved his metal. All sorts of renegade Indians joined the Navajos. Their blood was not pure but it was rigorously selected. And they were always at war. While the Mexicans were getting fat and lazy in the valley, the Navajos were keeping themselves fit by incessant fighting and weeding out weaklings and cowards on the battlefield.

It was an arrogant and deadly tribe of barbarians that the ricos of the Rio Grande fought for over a century and it was from these people that they took most of their slaves. Indians of many tribes were both captured and bought but the Navajos made the best slaves. They were tall, well built and intelligent. The Navajo women were especially prized because they were lighter in color than most Indians, had better figures and were reputed to be especially voluptuous. A Navajo girl would generally fetch a higher price than one of any other tribe.

The valued captives were boys and girls under fourteen and provided they were weaned from the breast the younger the better. An adult Indian was nearly always untamable. Even a girl of sixteen would often steal a horse from her captors and run away at the risk of her life. But young children were baptized and given Christian names and they became good Catholics and good Mexicans. They would have nothing to do with their own people. Moreover, the same was true of many Mexican children taken into slavery by the Navajos. When they had grown up among the Indians they generally refused all offers to purchase them and return them to civilization. So many a good Mexican was a Navajo and many a good Navajo was a Mexican.

Literally, the right people took their enemies to their bosoms. It was the peons for the most part who worked the land and herded the sheep while Navajo slaves became house servants and also and inevitably the concubines of the men. The children of these unions were of course born slaves and in time many slaves must have had more Spanish than Navajo blood and many were close relations of their masters. This doubtless happens in all slave-holding societies, as it certainly did in our own South, but there the slave blood could never invade the ruling class because color would betray it at once. No such bar existed in New Mexico. Some of the right people were Catalans and Basques and there were some blonds and red-heads among them, but many, of the Moorish strain, were nearly as dark as Indians. How a mixture of Navajo blood got into the veins of the right people must be left to the imagination. Doubtless there were likely boys among the slaves as well as likely girls. It is certain that some of the proudest families came to show the high cheek bones and the coarse hair of the Indians though none of them ever acknowledged a drop of Indian blood and to call a man an Indian was an insult. Their pride of race never abated but the right people grew steadily swarthier as though a dark flood were seeping up from the earth to engulf their pretensions.

Perhaps there was never a better example of a contact long continued between a civilized people and a primitive one that remained unconquered. Anglo-Saxon pioneers, ruthless and puritanical, have generally exterminated primitive peoples when they could not rule them and kept their blood comparatively pure. Their racial instinct may have been sound. Certainly the contact between the Mexicans and the Navajos seems to have worked always to the benefit of the Indians. Mexican blood probably improved the Navajo stock but Indian blood was a doubtful asset to the right people. Moreover, in a desperate effort to keep their lineage pure, the members of this small and isolated group were always interbreeding. Marriages between cousins, even first cousins, were common, and in time almost all of the best families were interrelated.

In war also the Navajos had all the advantage. They had little to lose and everything to gain. The Mexicans were the producers and the Navajos came to occupy the status of a powerful race of bandits who levied tribute. They made peace only to be given presents. They roved in small bands over a vast wilderness of high mesas and low mountains cut with deep impassable gorges. In summer they lived in brush shelters and in winter they built brush huts wattled with mud, called hogans. They had no permanent settlements to be attacked and when they fled they were as hard to find as a scattered covey of quail. When they needed meat they swooped down on a herd of sheep, shot the peons in charge and made off with what they wanted. They sacked lonely ranches and sometimes villages but I can find little evidence that they ever struck the ricos in their homes. The great houses were nearly impregnable and all their retainers as well as their walls stood between the ricos and their enemies. It was the peons and the small independent ranchers who suffered and they knew almost nothing of security. They had few guns but fought with bows and knives and their horses were seldom as good as those of the Indians.

The Apaches said they always sent a few of their number to be captured by the Mexicans in Chihuahua and baptized so that they could report to the tribesmen. It is probable that the Navajos did the same in New Mexico and that some of the slaves were spies. Certainly the Navajos seemed to know always when to strike and where.

This guerrilla warfare was cruel and treacherous on both sides. The Indians tortured and killed without mercy all they did not want for captives. The Mexicans once lured a band of Navajos to Jemez, under the pretense of talking peace, got them all drunk and murdered them with clubs. It is said that a foetus was torn from the body of a Navajo woman and baptized in the church.

4

Despite these wars on all their borders throughout the eighteenth century the right people were gaining in wealth, in power, in arrogance. Their slaves increased and they held more and more of the common people in peonage as the Indians robbed them and drove them to the rich for protection. They were always acquiring more of the land because poor men were not strong enough to hold it and much of it lay uncultivated. Nearly all the sheep were theirs and some of them owned more sheep than they could count and land they had never seen.

They were rich and they held power in their hands but both as a stock and as individuals they were weakening. Not only had slavery and intermarriage weakened their blood but their young men became idle and dissipated in the comparative security of their wealth. Moreover, although they were despots they increasingly neglected their obligations as leaders. They were hated and feared by their retainers whom they left at the mercy of savages.

Yet as long as the Spanish Empire lasted this aristocracy could stand. It was wholly feudal in form and spirit — in all essentials a fragment of the mediaeval world, surviving long after the rest of that world was dead. Men cannot live without a faith and a discipline and these men had both as long as they were part of an empire. They believed in God and King and their discipline was obedience. Every man owed allegiance to God and King and every man was both a God and a King in his own house-

hold. This was a lazy and voluptuous people but everyone knew whom he had to obey, from the humblest peon
up to the Governor and Captain-general who was the
representative of the King who derived his power from
God. Obedience here was beautiful and as nearly perfect
as anything human can be. The peon without question
accepted the debts of his father and resumed his status.
A daughter bowed her head and married the man her
father chose. If one obeyed his masters it mattered little
what else he did. The individual was nothing, the order
of society everything.

The Spanish Empire had long since lost its vitality but
it remained as a symbol and its visible representative in
New Mexico was the Governor and Captain-general.
These governors were sometimes titled men and often
they were men of ability. Coming direct from the Spanish court the Governor kept alive in the New Mexicans
the consciousness that they were part of a great empire,
that they lived in a great tradition. Ceremoniously the
Governor ruled from the ancient Palace in Santa Fe, creating there in replica the dignity and authority of the
court. Each of them, too, brought a fresh access of administrative energy which would doubtless have died
had anyone of them long remained. José Chacon Medina
Salazar y Villasenor, Marquis of Penalosa, who ruled in
New Mexico from 1708 to 1712, was a true servant of
God and King. He had the church at Santa Fe rebuilt and
all of the principal churches in the province were improved in his time. The priesthood was already degenerate but at least he could refurbish the temples of God.
He made three campaigns against the Navajos and

while he could not conquer them he could give them something to do besides stealing sheep and girls.

As late as 1810 the New Mexicans sent a delegate to the Spanish Cortes. He was Don Pedro Bautista Pino of Santa Fe, a fat, good-humored gentleman of great wealth and of the very best blood. His fellow ricos raised nine thousand dollars to help defray his expenses and he went to Vera Cruz and crossed the sea — an envoy from a dying colony to a dying empire. He told the gentlemen of the Cortes, among other impressive things, that there was great danger of an alliance between the United States government and the wild tribes of the plains, which would overwhelm New Mexico, and he asked for troops to protect the province. The Cortes listened, probably it yawned, certainly it did nothing. Don Pedro Pino, having talked, had done all his duty as a statesman. He stayed three years abroad, spending all the money they had given him and much of his own besides. In state he visited London and Paris and then returned to Santa Fe, expensively bringing with him a magnificent landau, probably the only vehicle of its kind that had ever been seen in New Mexico. A few years ago very old men could remember that equipage and its owner and how irreverent souls of inferior birth used to shout after him in the streets a couplet which summarized his achievements: " Don Pedro Pino went, Don Pedro Pino came."

For a few years more, representatives of God's empire would futilely come and go but that was all. In 1822 Mexico declared its freedom from the Spanish Empire and the New Mexicans awoke one morning to learn that they were the citizens of a republic. Then they belonged to an Empire again — an American empire — and almost before they had gotten used to the idea, it was once more a republic.

What of it? Nothing visibly had changed here in New Mexico which was so far away from all capitals. And yet, subtly, everything had changed. This last bit of the feudal world had been cut off from the sources of its spiritual life. No more Spanish governors came, bringing the divine authority of empire. Life was no longer supported by a changeless hierarchy. Obedience no longer was enough. Democracy had reached New Mexico, and individualism. These ideas had affectively reached a people who could never have conceived them, who could not understand them.

In Mexico there were twelve presidents in eight years. The New Mexicans duly celebrated each change of government. Speeches were made by important persons, oaths of allegiance were sworn and always there were balls that lasted until early in the morning. If the world was falling to pieces, at least one still could dance. It took so long to get reliable word from Mexico City and changes of administration were so rapid that the New Mexicans were always in danger of celebrating a conqueror after he had fallen.

Important men of the right people were appointed governors and some of these tried hard to exercise a real authority — to hold back the Navajos and keep order within the province. But their tenure of office was too uncertain. Many of them held office for less than a year. And they got little or no support from the government in Mexico City, corrupt as it was and torn by endless revolution. In 1827 the unspeakable Armijo got himself appointed governor. He did not hold the place long but his administration meant that Democracy had fully arrived for he was a man of lowly birth who had stolen sheep for a living. Yet he had curried favor with the politicians in Mexico City, and what could anyone do?

Who now were the right people? Not those born to power but those who could seize it. Ability and money were what counted now. Gertrudes Barello had been a common prostitute in Taos, so Gregg assures us. She became one of the most skillful monte-dealers in the province and she moved to Santa Fe where everyone gambled and opened a gambling hall. She was a born administrator, that woman, and knew how to hold onto money. Her gambling hall was a show place with magnificent chandeliers and it ran all the way through a block. She had been called Tules in her days of ill fame when she had had a figure that aroused the lust of men. Now she was a mountain of fat and was called Doña Gertrudes. She had money and she knew where to lend it, where to give it. This woman, a whore and gambler, became a person of political importance and even of social consideration. Gregg says that some persons of the best families entertained her in their houses. Truly, on the Rio Grande one more world was coming to an end.

The Navajos more and more had their own way. Who was to fight them? There was neither leadership, troops, nor money for arms. One Colonel Vizcarra of the Mexican army made the last effective campaign against them about 1830. From then on they robbed and murdered as they would. They called the Mexicans their shepherds and said the only reason they did not take all the sheep was that they preferred to leave a few for seed. Even so the herds declined eighty percent and even some of the ricos began to feel poor. The Navajos would kill herders and run off with sheep a few miles from the capital. The Apaches came to Santa Fe to make a treaty, received presents and killed a few people on the way out of town. Every spring the Navajos would solemnly make peace so the Mexicans might shear their sheep and plant their crops and in the fall they would make war so they could steal the fat wethers and the ripe grain. Small land holders in outlying sections ran to Santa Fe for safety. The government decreed that all who abandoned their holdings must lose them and so the number of the dispossessed was always growing. The gap between rich and poor was widening. Drought struck the country and there was famine although thousands of good acres, owned by rich men, lay untilled. As though God himself were angry a scourge of small pox came to kill nearly ten percent of the people.

It seems probable that if the civilization of the right people had been left to its destiny it would have been overrun and destroyed by the Navajos. The union of bloods and cultures, begun in war and slavery, would have been complete.

This was not to be. A deadlier race than the Navajos was on its way to the Rio Grande. Even before the revolution there had begun to appear in Taos a few tall Yankees with long rifles who bribed the Alcalde to let them trap in Mexican streams. The men feared and hated them, the women adored. Then one day came more men of the same breed, driving a pack train laden with goods, cheaper and better than those the conductas brought up from Chihuahua. The pack train was followed by wagons and the common people turned out in crowds to greet them, all the women decked in their best. A road was forming across the prairie — across the thousand miles of wilderness which had been for two centuries an impassable barrier. The wilderness had been a wall between the right people and all the rest of the civilized world. The wall was broken, the infidels were pouring in and slaves and women were shouting them a welcome.

VI

The Men of the Soil

1

THE HIGHWAY between Taos and Santa Fe runs along the Rio Grande but a shorter road, almost impassable for a car, cuts across the mountains that dwindle down from the snow-flecked peaks to the river. It follows closely the contour of elevation at which the pine and spruce give way to the bushy fragrant growth of piñon and cedar, the ridges flatten out into narrow mesas, the canyons become little valleys that may be plowed and irrigated.

In each of these valleys is a village, sheltering a few hundred people. Chimayo, Cordova, Truchas, Trampas, Chamisal, Penasco — each town with a singing name sits beside its singing water. These are cold clear streams full of trout, running straight from the snow. Each of them waters just enough land to keep a village alive. Between the valleys the wilderness is unbroken.

Few Americans have ever gained a foothold in this region and it is probable that none of the ricos ever lived here for this is the heart of the up-river country where the small ranchers of mixed blood always owned most of the land. And it is here that the New Mexico of a hundred years ago is still almost unchanged.

Mountains shelter the past. In their arable crannies human life catches and clings like ore in the rock. Mountains check both expansion and invasion, the two great agents of change. In the lower valley the great houses of the rich have disappeared but here on the heights the houses of the humble are much as they always were except that they have windows of glass and here and there a tin or shingle roof. Most of the villages still are compact clusters of earthen houses, gathered together originally for protection, with their fields spread about them, the wooded mountains rolling up toward the peaks on one side, falling away to the river on the other. Almost every house has still its conical adobe oven outside the door and in the fall the walls are hung, as always, with scarlet strings of drying chile. The wide-hatted men and the black-shawled women are figures little changed. And here is an atmosphere, too, that belongs unmistakably to another age, before hurry began or machinery was invented. It is profoundly quiet but with a quiet that never seems dead. One gets from the faces and movements of the people and from their voices an impression of indolent vitality — of life that is never driven or frantic as it is wherever machines set the pace and the hope of progress an ever-receding goal.

These owners of tiny farms were sometimes called paisanos — men of the country, men of the soil. And true peasants they are, perhaps the only ones that ever existed within our borders. For the peasant is a lover of the earth who asks nothing better than to live his whole

life on one patch of soil, scratching it for a living, laying
his bones in it at last. And there has never been much of
this resigned sedentary spirit in the American farmer
of the Anglo-Saxon breed. He was originally a wanderer
and always an exploiter. He settles down only when there
is no place else to go. He does not cherish the earth, he
longs to conquer it. Always he tends to exhaust the soil
and move on, whether in a few years or a few generations,
as did the tobacco planters in Virgina, the cotton planters
farther south. His interest is always in a " money crop."
He believes in progress and longs for change.

No wonder he has always despised these men in whom
the blood of an ancient European peasantry mingles with
that of sedentary Indians. They ask of the earth only
a living and imitate the past because it has seemed good.
For men who accept life as it is progress must be a meaningless word and it has never meant anything to the
paisano, at least as long as he could cling to his patch
of land.

From the earth he draws his strength, even his identity,
for when he loses his hold upon it he becomes another
man. But his instinct is to cling to it and he has done so
with a time-defying tenacity. All his masters have tried
more or less to rob him of the land but in the upper valley he still owns nearly all of it and even in the lower
valley Mexicans still hold most of it except around a few
large towns.

For centuries he persisted quietly in raising crops and
children while his lords raised revolutions and pretensions. They are gone, he is the survival, here as in Old
Mexico. The new order there, just beginning to emerge,

is his creation as is the new art. Apparently the future
of all Latin-America belongs to this man of mixed blood
who lives by faith and farming and endures the scourges
of government, like those of drought and storm, as the
disciplines of a just God.

2

When New Mexico was conquered, along with the
proud families who were granted most of the lands came
a following of humble folk, some of the southern Indian
stocks, Tlascan and Aztec, some of mixed blood and some
that were soldiers, workmen and artisans of Spanish
peasant class. Doubtless some of these common men took
wives from the Navajos and other nomadic tribes. The
lineage of the paisano is mixed beyond all hope of exact
analysis but time has produced a homogeneous people.

These common men came as the servants and workmen of the ricos and many of them remained bound in
peonage to the lands of their masters. But in addition to
the individual grants of land there were community
grants where the poor could take small homesteads along
the arable valleys and hold the grazing lands in common
so that from the first there were independent small landowners as well as peons. Between the plebeian and the
aristocrat was an impassable gap that widened with time
but there was probably never any sharp line between
the independent ranchers and the peons. A peon who
paid his debts might take up land of his own, and a poor
ranchero, falling upon hard times, would relapse into
peonage. In course of time the ricos held more and more

of the land, until in the early nineteenth century the poor were often threatend with famine.

In fact there was probably never a more oppressed and harried people than the paisanos of that period when the right people were in their glory. If the poor man was not in debt as a peon to his master he was in debt to the traders who brought up from Chihuahua everything he needed that he could not produce himself. The government took a heavy tax and the trader a heavy profit. The Navajos constantly threatened not only his crops and his sheep and goats but even his wife and children. And if he saved anything from his masters and his enemies it was promptly gobbled up by the church. Weddings, baptisms and funerals were the great events of his life and for the proper celebration of each of these the padres charged exactly what the poor man had. Marriage was often a luxury the poor could not afford. They lived loyally enough in open concubinage, their children often went unbaptized and the dead were sometimes buried in the desert with the rites of the Penitent Brothers. In that dark period after the pioneering Franciscan friars had left and before the reforms of Bishop Lamy, the priesthood in New Mexico was profoundly corrupt. The priests drank, gambled and danced and many of them kept veritable harems. Their offspring were known and even acknowledged and often a woman would proudly tell that one of her flock was a child of the padre. Perhaps he at least was sure of baptism.

It was the exactions of the Church more than anything else that brought on revolution in Old Mexico but in New Mexico the poor man bore the padres' greed with

incredible patience and with unshaken faith. Frank M.
Edwards, who was one of General Kearney's Missouri
volunteers, tells of a poor couple who wanted to marry
and went to the church to arrange for their wedding. The
priest, a great fat man, tonsured and robed, demanded
so large a marriage fee that the groom had to sell his three
cows to pay it. The priest took what he brought but said
more would be necessary before the ceremony could be
performed. The groom's father then sold his few head of
stock and raised about a hundred dollars more which
the priest took but still refused to proceed. Drained of all
their wealth, both families went to the Alcalde who inter-
ceded with the priest in vain. They went to the store-
keeper, an American, who had come to be a power in the
community as the storekeepers did everywhere after
the Americans began to come in. He, too, plead with the
priest but the man of God stood firm. He must have
another hundred dollars. Thereupon both families went
home and held a council. Finally they decided with much
laughter and many blushes on the part of the bride to
have a grand ball instead of a wedding. It would be more
fun and cost less money. The ball was given and afterwards the young couple went to bed in a state of blissful
sin, considering themselves united for life without benefit
of clergy.

In such a state of society a man must live as he can.
"The poor will pilfer anything," Edwards wrote, and
he and others also found that both thievery and banditry
enjoyed a sort of social tolerance. "I couldn't think of
exposing the poor fellow," said a rico who had seen a man
stealing a sheep.

The ricos, the traders, the church all robbed the poor but all felt that the poor man must be somehow kept alive. The placer mines in the Sandia mountains were set aside by government edict as a sort of charitable foundation for those who could find no other way of getting bread. That opulent dream of seven golden cities, of emperors lulled to sleep by golden bells, here found at last its meager fulfillment in a streak of sun-baked sand where a man with a pan and bucket could wash out a few grains of gold in a day. What was to have been the source of wealth for kings and nobles became the last resort of the very poor. Men who had neither land nor stock went and camped upon these sands, often carrying the water they used for miles. It was the law that anyone could open a pit provided it was ten feet from the next nearest and it was his as long as he worked it. So any poor man could own a gold mine and make perhaps seventy-five cents a day. Abert found at the mines the raggedest wretches he saw anywhere, sleeping between dirty sheep skins, living on tortillas, goat cheese and brown sugar. There was one old man named Candelario who had once found a nugget worth over seven hundred dollars. "As soon as my luck was known, I became Don Candelario," he told, "and within a week I was Don Juan de Candelario and then Don Juan de Candelario, Caballero. My name kept on growing for three weeks, until the money was all gone and then I became Old Candelario again."

A young man came to Abert at the mines and said that he knew of a rich vein of ore far up in the mountains and offered to lead the young Lieutenant to it. Abert asked him why he didn't develop the mine for himself.

"You know the ricos take everything in this country," he said. "If I came in with gold they would soon have my mine but with your protection I would be safe."

Edwards also encountered a rico who had been put in jail for killing one of his peons but it was explained that he had been the victim of political enemies and would soon be free again.

The effect of all these oppressions was to throw the poor man back upon his own resources, both material and spiritual. Cheated by traders and ricos he tried to produce everything he needed on his own few acres when he had any. Overtaxed by the padres he dispensed with their services when he could not afford them, keeping still intact his own faith, which was always a graft of Catholic dogma and ritual upon a primitive idolatry and drew its strength more from earth than from heaven. Denied protection and even arms he learned to fight the Indian with his own weapons. He was often called a coward but Gregg testifies that he was a good fighter when given anything like an even chance. After the American occupation, when the governor called for volunteers to fight the Navajos, more came forward than could be used and they made a splendid holiday of beating their ancient foes with good guns and under able leaders.

The domestic economy of the common man at best was simple and meager. Often the whole family lived in a single room, sleeping on mattresses of sheep skin, sharing their shelter with dogs, lambs and the family game cock. Chile, beans and buffalo meat or mutton were cooked together over the fire in the corner hearth.

Tortillas were baked on a hot stone and each served himself by rolling one of these thin corn cakes into a cornucopia and dipping it into the stew.

Life was simple but never rude. Manners were just as perfect among the poor as among the rich and hospitality just as generous. Here too was the same rigorous precedence, the father supreme and the mother bearing a reflected glory. Nor was any man ever too poor to observe the ceremonies and celebrate the joys of life. All Latin-Americans love ceremony and ritual and among them the established forms of human conduct seem never to go dead as they do among us where formality is almost a synonym for dullness and spontaneous joy in generally a violent smashing of traditional restraints. Weddings and baptisms were always celebrated among these people with all the ceremony they could afford and every such event ended in feasting and dancing. Even the funerals, with professional mourners wailing till the coyotes answered from the hills, were occasions for much feasting and drinking of red wine. All saints' days were celebrated not only with feasts and dancing but with games. The favorite of these, still to be seen in the more isolated villages, is called Gallo. A luckless rooster is buried alive to the neck in loose sand and the horsemen of opposing teams ride by in turn, stooping from the saddle and trying to snatch the bird out of the earth. When one succeeds he runs away at full speed and if he reaches a goal uncaught he may present the bloody trophy to his chosen girl. Here is a game that has in it something of the mediaeval tourney and something of a savage sacrifice of blood.

They played also a game like shinney, whole villages against each other, fighting over a wooden block all up and down a course a mile long. They had horse-races and everyone gambled. Santa Fe, with its many monte tables was the gambling center for rich and poor alike but games of chance were played everywhere and cock-fighting for stakes was universal. It was a poor man indeed who did not own a rooster he was willing to bet on. One traveler tells of spending a night in a humble house where he lay down on the floor with the whole family and all the dogs while a magnificent red game cock occupied a perch that hung from the roof and annoyed him all night with its crowing. Each time the bird threw back his head and uttered his ringing challenge, the father of the family would awake and proudly exclaim, " How sweetly sings my bird! "

Original sin was one article of Christian dogma the paisano never grasped. Perhaps he was too near to nature to pay such a tribute to any God. At any rate he regarded love as a free boon or a commodity rather than as a spiritual discipline. The invading Americans found it easy to rent or purchase mistresses among the poor and there was not felt to be anything wrong about such unions which had their own governing terms and their own dignity. One describes a mother chastising a twenty-year-old daughter for speaking impudently to the gentleman who had paid good money for the privilege of her society.

It is an apparent contradiction in the character of the common Mexican that he may be the most proudly independent of men or the most servile. It seems to depend less upon the individual than upon the relation to him in which you stand. If you go as a guest to his house, however humble it may be, he is a grand gentleman who tells you that all he owns is yours. Unless he has been too much corrupted by contact with the Americanos he will often refuse payment for his hospitality though nothing averse to accepting suitable gifts. But if you hire a Mexican to work for you he is likely to regard you as a potential source of all things needed and to become a somewhat importunate solicitor of favors. Give him half a chance and he will get himself into your debt and stay there. In a word, he will relapse into peonage. Doubtless the tradition of his experience accounts for both of these attitudes. When he had land, a hard-bitten self-sufficiency became his necessary virtue and when he could not feed himself then he became the abject dependent of some rico. Both political and economic life in New Mexico still suffer from his instinctive love of a feudal relationship to some leader. Shrewd politicians have built up some of the most perfectly working and perfectly corrupt political machines that ever existed by taking proper care of their henchmen. Of one of them it was said that when an election was in doubt he could always win it by voting the sheep.

3

In almost every Mexican village there is still to be seen a strange building that stands apart from the others, apparently deserted. This is the Morada, headquarters of the Penitent Brothers. Like the khiva in an Indian

pueblo it is usually distinguished from all other buildings by the fact that it has no windows or only a tiny
one too high for peeping. Sometimes, like the khiva, it
is partly buried in the earth nor does the resemblance
end with these physical similarities. For the Morada, like
the khiva, is the secret and unpenetrated stronghold of
a primitive faith. Here, too, rites are still enacted that no
alien eye has seen and that despite the official frown of
the Church and the endless prying of the laity. The
Morada is the heart of primitive New Mexico.

Sometimes a great wooden cross, ten feet high, stands
before the structure or leans against its wall. More often
the cross is on some distant hilltop and you catch a surprised glimpse of its outline against the sky. The cross
is never lacking for by origin and profession the Penitent
Brothers are members of a Christian sect, deriving from
the Middle Ages, who gash and whip their flesh for the
glory of their souls and enact at every Eastertide a primitive passion play. It is known that formerly they nailed
a man to the cross. Some aliens have witnessed cruci-
fixions with ropes, drawn tight enough to stop the circulation of the blood. There are many rumors of Penitentes
who have died on the cross as of other tortures. Nowadays
one may see only the whipping of bare and lacerated
backs and the crucifixion of an image but what goes on
in the night and in the secret chamber of the Morada
none but the Penitent Brothers know.

The flagellant sect from which this one takes its name
and origin came to New Mexico with the conquest and
with the Third Order of Saint Francis. Oñate records
that he and his men performed its rites. But in Old

Mexico this sect had already absorbed an aboriginal one which practiced self-punishment. The society was from an early date as much Indian as Spanish, as much pagan as Christian. It is of a piece with the faith of all Mexicans of the mixed blood. Everywhere they have substituted Christian images for those of their native idolatry and made over Jesus into a symbol of their own sacrifices of blood. That is why Mexico can fight the Church and expel its ministers and still remain a devoutly religious country. And that is why the New Mexicans remained devout while the priests robbed them of the rites of marriage, of baptism and even of burial from the Church.

It was into the society of the Penitent Brothers that the common Mexican fled from spiritual persecution as the land was his refuge from his temporal masters. Whatever its social standing may have been at first it speedily became an organization of the common man against his masters — a brotherhood with temporal benefits and a fierce solidarity and a secretiveness so relentless that it punished betrayal of its laws and business with burial alive. And as a religion, although its rules and its songs came straight from the mediaeval church and were never changed, it became more and more a primitive penance and a primitive worship of death. The church formally pronounced against it in the eighties and it must have suffered the opposition of many of the padres long before that for its tendency was to free the common man from their exactions. It was the flower of a spiritual integrity which had its roots, lower and deeper than those of any church, in an ancient sacrifice of blood, in the ecstatic acceptance of pain and death.

Like everything about the paisano it has an astonishing vitality. There are still many Moradas, perhaps nearly as many as ever. An educated Mexican who has known the Penitentes all his life told me that the society still numbers thirty-five thousand. It extends into southern Colorado and perhaps into Old Mexico and Texas but its headquarters are in the New Mexican town of Mora and most of its membership is within the state.

In most of the Mexican villages the Church stands in the center of the town and the Morada is apart and alone but in the isolated towns of Rio Arriba the Morada may be the most prominent building in the place. In Truchas the Morada is almost as large as the Church and it is the only one I ever saw that has a bell tower. In Las Trampas there is no Morada, for the secret chambers of the order are built onto the rear of the old church itself, the cart of death stands in a room of the main building, bloody whips hang in the gallery and the walls are spattered with the blood of many Good Fridays. Here, it is plain, the Penitent Brothers were so strong that they simply absorbed the church and hold it still. There is no resident padre but only a circuit-riding priest who comes once or twice a month.

It is said that the Penitent Brothers have secret rites on many saints' days and they have an elaborate and hidden system of meetings and benefits like any other secret order. It is only in the Lenten season that they come before the public as penitents. The curious, if they rise early and ride far, may then see the processions of the flagellants and even the crucifixion of an image and if they stay the night they may hear the weird screech of the flute which is the only music of the nocturnal processions and the terrific uproar of the tinieblas when rattles, bullroarers, chains and tin cans filled with rocks simulate the din of universal catastrophe.

I saw the Penitentes first in 1903 when I was thirteen years old. Pop-eyed with excitement I went home and wrote a description which I paraphrase here because it is more complete and exact than memory. In fact, what I remember best is the all-night ride in the bitter March weather with freezing hands and feet. The wind had piled tumble weeds along the road and every few miles we would touch a match to a pile of these and warm ourselves at a brief flare that lit the mountains, still patched with snow, and made a dance of shadows among cedar brush and boulders. I remember dawn-light shining on an adobe town and a breakfast of crackers and cheese in a little store and then excited Mexicans coming to tell that the Penitentes were marching to the graveyard.

A dozen men, naked to the waist, their heads enveloped in black caps as for a hanging, marched slowly, chanting in perfect time. Their backs, gashed with sharp flints, were wholly covered with blood and their white drawers were bloody to the heels. Each swung a great whip of braided yucca fiber in time to the chanting and at every sixth step brought it down upon his own bare back. The whips were saturated with blood so that each blow resounded like a slap with a wet towel. Slowly the procession whipped its way to the barren little graveyard, fenced in barbed wire, with its scant wreaths withering on graves with wooden markers. The Penitentes knelt briefly before the large wooden cross in the middle of the yard, then whipped and chanted a slow course back to the Morada on the hill.

After some minutes of excited hesitation all of us — four or five eager, awestruck boys — climbed the hill and with bared heads bowed filed into the chapel room among a crowd of Mexicans. A smoky lantern hung from the middle of the roof and two candles lit an altar at the far end. It was draped and curtained in black and a human skull occupied its very center. Not the cross, but the skull and cross bones were embroidered or painted in white on the black altar cloth. Plainly this was a shrine of death.

The light was so dim that some minutes passed before we saw the Penitentes lined up along the walls on either side, bowed and veiled. Presently they all filed into the back room where none but members are ever admitted and they passed so close to us that we might have touched the bloody flesh of their bared backs. As soon as they were gone a crowd of men and women pushed through the door, singing in shrill doleful Spanish, and all knelt, the crowd movement bringing us to our knees in a meaningless genuflexion. Then for the first time we saw that a small dark figure knelt before the altar. It rose and became a man, certainly less than five feet tall, in a black robe with a horsehair rope about his middle. He spoke fervently in Spanish for several minutes and when he had done all went silently out again.

Before the door the Penitentes stood in terrible marching order. Now the ascent of Calvary began. First came a man whom four others held by short ropes and as he walked they jerked him savagely this way and that. Two following whipped alternately themselves and another who walked before them. Then came a man with his arms bound tightly to a pole behind his back. Two others bore small crosses and the rest came behind, whipping themselves with long swinging strokes over their own shoulders.

The cross was only a little way off behind the building. It was about ten feet high and swathed in white sheeting. All of the Penitentes knelt on one side of it and a funereal huddle of black-shawled women on the other while the crowd gathered loosely about. A man stepped forward and jerked the sheets from the cross, uncovering a wooden image of the Saviour, absurdly small, grotesquely crude. From somewhere the tiny gnomelike figure in the black robe appeared and spoke again in a wild rapid patter that seemed to communicate an excitement to the whole crowd. Women wailed, men groaned and clapped their hands. One whirled a wooden rattle, another blew shrill discords on a flute and a man in the background seized a crowbar and pounded on it with a shovel. So Christ died amid pandemonium and lamentation. Then he was taken down in reverent silence, the great cross was uprooted and laid upon the shoulders of a giant penitente and in slow procession all whipped themselves back toward the Morada. Just before they reached it the man of the four ropes cried out and fell and his brothers picked him up and carried him into the house. The two who whipped another laid on with a sudden burst of energy and he too fell upon his face and was carried through the door. One man fell senseless under his own efforts. The giant bearer of the cross leaned it against the wall, fell out from under it and crept into the Morada on all fours. The public penance was over.

Riding home we met another group of penitente-hunters who had seen a man hurl himself naked into a cactus patch and heard a rumor that a real crucifixion with nails was to take place in secret that night.

The Penitentes were only a delightful horror then. It is the diversities of life that strike us first. Time reveals the unities, bringing a sort of comprehension for anything men may do. Those whips laid on bloody backs now seem only a brutal and forthright form of the discipline which every man must lay upon himself — symbols of the guilt and fear which are the penalties of human consciousness. And even more than it is a discipline, the rite of the penitent brother is a worship of death. It is a manifestation of that intimate concern with death which seems to be the vital religion of all Mexico. Formerly every penitente procession included a " cart of death " in which rode a skeleton draped in black, with a drawn bow and arrow in its hand, and it is said that once the arrow flew and killed a man.

The Mexican embraces death because he loves life, because death is a part of life and until death has been accepted life is but a subterfuge. On the Day of the Dead in Mexico City the people picnic in the graveyards, spreading their lunches on the tombs. Children crunch candy skulls between their teeth and bakeries sell dead man's bread. At funerals Mexicans feast and drink and even make a little love while watching beside a bier. In the rite of the penitent brother this worship of death, like his discipline, is simple, naked and realistic. It is not death as an abstraction that he accepts, after the fashion of philosophers, nor any poetic sublimation of it, but the stark and awful physical reality. He does not need to declare death beautiful or make it lyric. He waters the earth with his blood and kneels before a skull in reverent acknowledgment of the day when he shall be a bit of dust and bone.

4

In the rites of the Penitent Brothers and in the mountain towns where they have their greatest strength is seen the most enduring part of what Spain left in this country. This native peasant stock is what took root in the soil and survived all changes. And it is by no means a perishing or a decadent stock today. All through the Rio Arriba country, where one can ride many miles without meeting any but Mexicans, the people are prosperous in their own crude and self-sufficient way. Their houses are well-plastered and their horses are large and fat. Valleys are green with well-tilled crops and sheep fatten on the communal range lands.

As you go down toward the river and southward the character of the civilization changes gradually as does that of the vegetation. Even in the upper valley, men from Missouri and Oklahoma have bought in, often cultivating lands the Mexicans had neglected. There are tow-headed children and tin roofs. Little Methodist chapels of an uncompromising ugliness are as many as the old adobe cathedrals, the nasal wail of the Protestant hymnology rivals the chant of the Penitent Brothers and the subtle scourges invented by John Calvin replace the bloody whip. As you near one of the larger towns, such as Albuquerque, the proportion of Mexicans who own and cultivate land steadily decreases and those you see are obviously products of adaptation. They ride in Fords and if you speak to them in Spanish they reply in excellent idiomatic English, including the latest slang. When he comes in contact with the Americans the native of the younger generation shows an adaptability in manner and language as surprising as the earth-rooted resistant conservatism of his fellows back in the hills. When it comes to learning the current values of time and money he is not so quick. He has a tendency to buy whatever takes his eye, on the installment plan, and keep it until they take it away from him again. He seldom becomes a rich man or a thorough-going puritan. The virtues of thrift and repression elude him. He remains always a man of pleasure and of leisure. Doubtless he is in process of being absorbed but he seems likely to leave his mark upon the society that absorbs him.

From the Rio Grande south, clear to the frozen lands of the Argentine, this same man of mixed blood, more Indian than Spanish, is the prevalent, the surviving type. He varies widely in build and complexion according to the aboriginal stocks that went into his making but later immigration has changed him little and everywhere that I have seen him — in Mexico, in Central America and in the islands — he is much the same man. Unmistakably he is an emergent type — a man half primitive just beginning to grasp the tools of industrial civilization and the mysteries of democratic government. His period of incessant revolution is drawing toward an end. He is just beginning to find himself in the arts. His fertility, both spiritual and physical, seems to be unimpaired.

For a hundred years all immigration across the border was southward. Men from the old Southwest, of the Bowie and Crockett type, had pre-empted a large part of Texas before the guns of the Alamo began a revolution. The wagon merchants from Missouri had taken New Mexico away from the ricos and were supporting the government ten years before Kearney hoisted a new flag at Santa Fe. Lately the spontaneous movement of population has in a measure reversed itself and the fact seems to me not without significance. The Americans who go south now are salesmen rather than settlers while thousands of Mexicans have been crossing the border every year, looking for easy American dollars, alarming Nordic congressmen. These humble track-workers and fruit-pickers are pioneers just as much as the early Texans were and so are the Mexican painters and cartoonists who invade the literary teas in Manhattan. Indo-Spanish America is coming toward us, bringing both its gifts and its needs. The Rio Grande is now, as it has been for a hundred years, the frontier between two races and two cultures and the outcome of that contact is a thing that still remains to be seen.

VII
The Mountain Men

1

WHEN civilization penetrates a new country mountains are always the last barriers to be crossed and the last areas to be settled and tamed. Mountains are never wholly subdued as valleys and prairies are. Even when cities sit at their feet they still keep in their hearts some unconquerable wilderness where roads cannot go and the earth will yield nothing to human labor.

Few mountains ranges have more of this resistant quality than the Rockies. Only a tiny fraction of their surface is arable and all of their upper levels are buried under deep snow more than half the time. In the North their summer is only a few weeks of feverish warmth and color and then they are ravished by torrents and by slides of earth and snow like a world in the travail of creation. The arctic zone of their summits reaches south as far as Santa Fe and recurs again on the giant peaks that stand over Mexico.

It was at the mountain barriers that the Spanish pioneering stopped. The wave of civilizing energy that surged northward from Mexico City just sufficed to reach and settle the Rio Grande valley and conquer the valley tribes before it spent itself. For two centuries after the conquest the mountains remained unmapped, seldom crossed, and the Indians that lived in the mountains and beyond them were a scourge that descended from the heights and went back to their impenetrable security.

Both the Spanish and the Mexican governments were evidently aware that their pioneering had failed in this respect. The Spanish government had various plans for crossing the mountains and exploring the prairies to the east and north and a few attempts were made. But there was no sustained effort to explore the mountains or to map them. No settlements were established in or beyond them. None of the mountain tribes was ever subdued. When the Spanish Empire collapsed the Rockies still belonged to Indians and wild animals.

When Mexico became a republic the Mexican government made grants of land in the mountains and east of them to members of the aristocracy. These ricos were supposed to settle the wild lands, building a line of communities and great haciendas between the valley and its foes to the east. They were to stop both the prairie Indians and the greedy infidels from beyond the Missouri. But these grants of land, some of them as large as European kingdoms, were for the most part never even seen by their owners. The ricos had lost all capacity for pioneering.

If the West as a whole was ever to be a part of civilization — and few believed it ever would — men must be found who were not afraid of the mountains, who would learn all the mountain trails and fight the mountain tribes and finally open roads and settle valleys. It was a task in primary pioneering of the most heroic kind like Boone's crossing of the Alleghenies and De Soto's march to the Mississippi. It called for the kind of man who can leave everything behind except a weapon, who can go for years without woman or bread or the support of organized society.

No ordinary comfort-loving man can do this — the task calls for one who is possessed of a demon. He must have a tension that will not let him rest. He may call himself an agent of God, as both Boone and De Soto did, or he may profess to be seeking his fortune or he may be too simple a man ever to need a conscious motive, but the sign of his curse is that he cannot stop. He turns away from the very thing he seeks and squanders wealth when he wins it. He turns instinctively away from woman for she is the enemy of his urge who can both bind him down and take the tension out of his body. He avoids organized society as he would a trap. He lives by his needs and not by his satisfactions.

The Spanish Empire produced such men for a while and then no more. The sons of the conquerors were content with love and farming. But when they dropped the task men came from the east to take it up — men different in almost everything except the possession of this same urge. Mysteriously an impulse died in one race and was reborn in another.

The Spanish pioneers were men of a religious discipline for whom gold was the material talisman. The mountain men were for the most part Godless indi-

vidualists and fur to make hats was their excuse for court-
ing death and hunting the unknown.

Beaver hats became the rage in London. It is said Beau
Brummel started the fashion. If so, the disguise of trivial
chance that often hides the moving forces of human destiny never had a more striking manifestation than this
of a dandy strutting down a London street in a great
shining tile and thereby sending a thousand hardy men
to explore a wilderness. For beaver fur became as good
as gold and almost worth its weight in silver and the
Rocky Mountains contained an untouched store of it.

For generations after the great trapping period beaver
were almost extinct in the Rockies but lately they have
come back to their old range under rigorous protection.
It is easy to imagine what myriads of them must have
existed a hundred years ago and how perfectly they were
distributed to lead men into every part of the mountains,
through every pass, up every river to its source and down
it almost to the sea. Their only needs are running water
and deciduous trees with an edible bark. Almost all the
creatures of the mountain region are distributed in zones
of elevation but the beaver live at every level from just
below timberline in the mountains where the streams
are born to the lower reaches of the Rio Grande and the
Gila where muddy rivers make timber grow in the desert.
They are still trapped in the gorges of the Colorado and
in the Rio Grande where it marks the Mexican border.
They can build houses and survive seven months of ice
and snow and they can dig holes in the bank and live
where the water never freezes. In the high country they
cut aspen and down on the flats cottonwood and willow

are their staples. They are prolific and relatively helpless. Men with traps can gather them almost as boys
gather melons in a field.

It was in this period of the beaver hat that the great
fur companies were formed and men of money sent
highly organized expeditions into the mountains. They
recruited almost any kind of men and led them like
soldiers. But in addition to the organized companies
there were many free trappers and traders and these were
the true mountain men. Jim Bridger, Kit Carson, Joseph
Meek, Lucien Maxwell, and almost every other remembered pioneer of that period served his apprenticeship
and learned the trails and the Indians as a free trapper.
These were the men who afterward led the official " explorers " and the troops that conquered the savages,
pointed the way for wagons and railroads, built houses
and planted corn where none had ever dared to live
before. And hundreds who died unknown did their share
of the work.

The mountain men ranged and trapped from Canada
south to Chihuahua and from the headwaters of the
Missouri drainage to the Pacific coast but like nearly all
other westering men they were bound to the Rio Grande
region by peculiar ties. The chief of these was Don Fer-
nando de Taos, a settlement which has had a hundred
and fifty years of vivid life and is still officially only a
wide place in the road, without any kind of government.
Situated just south of what is now Colorado, Taos was
then the most northern of the Mexican settlements. It
lay in the heart of one of the best beaver regions and it
occupied also a cherished place in the hearts of moun-

tain men. It was the one place in all their range where they could expect to meet civilized women and buy bread, coffee and sugar. From the time they left the old Rocky Mountain House in St. Louis until they struck Taos they lived at best like savages, at worst like wild animals. It was in Taos that they briefly and violently renewed their contact with society, gorged themselves on its fleshpots, and then turned again to the wilderness, except for an occasional renegade who could not tear himself away from the arms of some Mexican girl.

It was in Taos that the two American civilizations first made contact. Pike had reached Santa Fe before the mountain men were many and so had a few traders but the gangs of trappers riding into the little mountain village were the first regular visitors from the East.

Certainly there was never a ruder invasion outside of war. These men were all poachers and interlopers for it was against the Mexican law to trap in the Mexican streams. The Mexicans knew well enough the value of beaver and intended to keep their own beaver streams as preserves for their own people. But none of the Mexicans would trap or could. The aristocracy was too lazy. The paisano had neither arms nor traps nor any tradition or experience to fit him for such a task. Among the regular trappers was only one Mexican and he completely repudiated his own people. " Me no Mexican. Me mountain man — waugh! " so Ruxton quotes him.

As poachers the mountain men ranged all over Mexican territory and even sold their furs in Taos, bribing the alcalde to close his eyes. Later Governor Narbonna agreed to issue licenses to American trappers provided each party would take along a certain number of Mexicans to learn the trade. It is not of record that any Mexican ever went but this ruling opened the way for more bribery. Milton Sublette and Ewing Young, both famous mountain men, got a license from Narbonna and came back to Taos with many bales of beaver. Meantime Armijo had succeeded to the governorship and he revoked the license and seized the furs. Finding them wet he spread them in the sun to dry before the garrison in Santa Fe. Sublette came single-handed and took his furs and hid them in a house across the street. Armijo blew trumpets, shouted orders and turned out his entire military force to hunt for the trapper and the furs but neither could be found, even under the governor's nose, because nobody had the courage to lay a hand on either. Sublette and Young departed in the night for St. Louis.

It has been said that the mountain men held their rendezvous at Taos but I am inclined to believe that the great annual gathering which brought together thousands of Indians, trappers and traders, including representatives of the Northwest Company and the American Fur Company, was always farther north. Certainly the favorite place was at Brown's Hole, in the Green River valley, which was near the center of the whole vast fur country. There, when beaver trapping was at its height, whole tribes of mountain Indians came to trade, stringing their white tepees along the river for miles, turning out in their finest buckskin trimmed with beads and porcupine quills, filling the night with the rumble of their drums, dancing themselves into a frenzy. Traders came, driving pack trains loaded with whisky, powder and lead, sugar and coffee, knives, beads and cloth. The free trappers drifted in singly and in groups, each with three or four horses and mules packed with baled beaver fur. Lanky blond men from Kentucky and Virginia, French Canadians, half-breeds, a few Swedes and always a few men from New England — especially from Connecticut for a Connecticut yankee or two would be found in any western gathering. Trading was fast and lubricated by a steady flow of corn liquor. Indians and mountain men alike were cheated by the traders. Mountain men traded quickly, getting what they needed of powder and lead, traps and knives, then letting all the rest go in liquor and gambling. The air was filled with the dust of incessant horse-races and blankets were spread on the ground for games of coon-can. Everybody would bet on anything. Indian girls rode up and down on their ponies with tinkling bells in their hair and about their necks. They were bought and sold like horses and men fought for the prettiest. There were innumerable fights in the traditional rough-and-tumble style of pioneer America with kicking, gouging and biting of noses and ears. Sometimes there were duels to the death with rifles and Kit Carson fought a boastful French giant on horseback with pistols and brought his adversary down. Some trappers dropped as much as three thousand dollars in a week. As the liquor ebbed in the kegs the gathering became a primitive orgy where every lust and hunger, denied for months, had its undisciplined innings. For this was the rhythm of the mountain man's existence — first a long time of privation and hardship, sometimes of absolute solitude, often of semi-starvation, and then a week or two of splendid drunken release. There were a few shrewd and careful men among them who made money but typically they spent everything at every rendezvous and even had to ask credit for the powder and lead that would keep them alive till the next year. They divested themselves of goods and money as of a superfluity that weighed them down, hampering the act and spirit of their essential destiny.

Taos probably saw no such great gatherings as Green River did for Taos was a place where a man could trade, drink, dance and make love any time he could get there. Small groups of mountain men were in and out of the town at all seasons but especially in the spring and fall. When a gang of them arrived they would first hire a hall and give a dance and almost always the dance would end in a fight between the Mexicans and the mountain men with the girls for a cause of war. The mountain men, fighting one to five or six, would generally rout the natives and pay the Alcalde damages for broken heads and knife wounds.

These rude and truculent gatherings were the first and for a long time the only social contact between two civilizations. Here the Mexican men learned to hate and fear the gringos and the Mexican women learned to love them, somewhat precariously.

All observers testify to the fascination that Taos had for the mountain men and it seems certain that the women of Taos, more than any other one element in their lives, represented civilization to them. In Taos they tasted charm and comfort and here if anywhere they formed bonds that held.

All of them knew Indian women and a few married squaws but for the most part these did not civilize them or tie them down any more than their horses did. A squaw was something to be taken along or left behind, to be bought or sold or traded. They gave a doglike devotion which was seldom requited. They were beaten with lodge poles and made to work like slaves. It is said that deserted squaws were known to kill both their masters and their rivals but doubtless the rage of a woman was a minor hazard in the mountain life.

The American women of their own breed the mountain men almost all held in contempt and this is perhaps the measure of their alienation from the society that produced them. White women were too fond of " fofarraw " (fanfaron) , meaning finery. Their cooking made no appeal to a mountain palate and they knew nothing about the indispensable business of tanning hides and making moccasins which was one of the chief uses of woman. They had little capacity for hardship and they were then as now accustomed to rule the family. The American woman demanded children and an establishment. She was an anchor and no mountain man wanted one. But the Mexican girls knew that complete submission to the male will which was a part both of their Indian heritage and of their European tradition and they shared something of the primitive aptitudes and hardihood of Indian women. Many mountain men married Mexican girls, leaving them here and there while they went on expeditions, ultimately settling down to raise crops and babies when the price of beaver dropped and the streams were depleted.

The Mexican men, poorly armed and weakened by generations of indolent living, were all but helpless before the trappers, who were tense and truculent, hardened by every privation, equipped with the best of rifles, pistols and knives, expert in the use of every weapon. But the women fared better. They found the vulnerable spot in the invader's armor. They could sometimes tie him down and tame him and so play a part in the making of a new order.

There was another place, a few days journey north of Taos, that bound the trappers to the region. This was Bent's Fort on the Arkansas, near where Pueblo, Colorado, now stands. The Bent brothers themselves were mountain men, probably the first of them to build in the wilderness where Mexicans would not have dared to go. It is significant that they did not think of farming or of founding a town. What they built was a fort, a permanent armed camp, to serve as a trading post and an outfitting point for mountain men. It was an enclosure of adobe walls topped with growing cactus, impregnable to any savage attack. Over its iron-bound gate was a watch tower where a guard sat all the time and swept the prairie with a telescope. The American flag flew above the walls and a bald eagle was the fort's pet and mascot. In the center of the square was a fur press and all around the inside rooms were built. Table was set for all comers by a celebrated negro cook. Here mountain men could always get supplies and credit and here they often left their Mexican wives for safe keeping. Here all the wild tribes came to trade and often battles among them were watched from the walls of the fort which never was assailed.

At Bent's Fort and at Taos the mountain man knew something of comfort and safety. When he left these havens, often for most of a year and sometimes for longer, he lived off the country like a wolf and trusted himself for everything. In him self-sufficiency reached its highest development. His necessary outfit included a long rifle, a pistol, a knife with a fourteen-inch blade and half a dozen traps. His bed was a buffalo robe to lie upon and a heavy Navajo blanket to cover him and shed the rain. He was dressed in buckskin, clean and fringed when new, but after a few months in the wilderness it was both blackened and waterproofed by much wiping of greasy and bloody knives and all the fringes had been used for strings. His hair was long and so were his whiskers though he shaved when he came near women. If he was prosperous he might have three or four pack horses and several squaws but both horses and Indian women were subject to loss by war. He carried no food except a little sugar and coffee and these were apt to be exhausted long before he returned to a trading post. Tobacco he must have but he mixed it with the inner bark of red willow to make it last and he smoked it like an Indian, sparingly and only at night. Often he went alone, sometimes in a party of three or four, rarely in larger groups, and these were held together by no bond except expediency.

That he loved his lean and dangerous career there can be no doubt. "A sort of homesickness seizes him when he retires from his mountain life to civilization" wrote Wislizenius, the German botanist who rode with the mountain men and saw their rendezvous at Brown's hole. Ruxton, a wealthy young Englishman who spent years among them, not only observed this fascination of the mountain life but fell a victim to it himself. He went back and tried to live in London but gave it up and returned to the mountains where he finally lost his life.

For months at a stretch these men ate nothing but meat and when powder and lead were gone or game failed they ate literally anything alive. More than one man kept himself from starving in the desert by eating rattlesnakes and some came to esteem them a luxury as the Comanches did. They were also fond of the flesh of the mountain lion and they did not scorn the stewed puppies of the Indian camps. Some even descended to cannibalism. Ruxton tells a story of a gang of trappers lost in the desert near Salt Lake who captured three Digger squaws. They could find no game and were near starvation. All went on a last desperate hunt but one Forey who stayed to guard the camp and the captives. When the others came back he had meat hung on a tree and roasting on the flames and they all fell upon it ravenously — until they realized that one of the squaws was missing. These Diggers were the lowest of all American savages and the trappers also found cooked flesh of a white man in a captured Digger camp.

These men who went alone into the wilderness make it starkly clear what a precarious and artificial thing civilization is. Some of the stronger and more intelligent never lost their social consciousness but the simpler ones shed it as a useless baggage. Many of them became wholly Indian in feeling and spirit. Ruxton describes one,

known only as old Rube, who prayed at a sacred spring
for luck, blowing smoke from his Indian pipe to the four
quarters and to the sky. Many worshiped the moon and
the stars and consulted medicine men for auguries.

The strangest of all these renegades was old Bill
Williams. No one knew where he came from or when
but it was always said that he had been in the mountains
longer than any other white man. It was also known that
he had been in his youth a circuit-riding Baptist preacher
but he had long since lost all trace of Christianity and
had apparently become an adept of Indian faiths in an
unusually elaborate way. He spoke many Indian languages and he probably had a vast knowledge of primitive ceremonial and belief.

In his old age he became almost completely solitary.
It was woman that bound the mountain man to human
society and brought him back to it for rare visits and
woman had probably ceased to interest old Bill. He
would appear briefly at the rendezvous for necessary supplies and then plunge into the wilderness alone, riding
a crop-eared, sore-backed Indian pony, as evil-tempered
as he was and as wise in the ways of the wild. He is described as a very tall gaunt man with long hair and beard,
his blackened buckskin hanging upon his frame in loose
folds like the hide of some prehistoric being. When he
mounted his runty steed his feet in great wooden stirrups
were not far from the ground and he always rode with
huge iron spurs. If he met with a party of trappers he
might consent to travel with them for a while and they
were always glad of his company because of his almost
supernatural faculty for finding his way about and for

detecting the presence of Indians. His pony could smell Indians a long way off and it seemed almost as though Bill could too. Whenever real trouble threatened he would desert his companions and "cash" (cache) himself so successfully that neither foe nor friend could find him.

" Do ee hyar now boys? There's sign about. This hoss feel's like cashing."

He would saddle his pony, talking to it volubly and exclusively and disappear into the wilderness, perhaps not to be seen again for months.

As he aged Bill Williams became increasingly obsessed with the doctrine, found in various forms among the Indians, that the souls of the dead pass into the bodies of animals. He at last became completely convinced that his spirit after death would inhabit the body of a bull elk. He repeatedly described to his companions the exact appearance of himself in that future avatar and he besought them all not to shoot him. Here was a man who had been once a preacher of Christianity, had then become wholly a savage and finally in spirit and imagination a wild animal. He had all but renounced the human race and there is evidence that he had little left of human feeling. When a half-breed was killed who had been a loyal member of his party he remarked merely that the man had been " no account nohow."

Doubtless it would be a mistake to regard Bill Williams as typical. In fact none of these men could fairly be regarded as typical. They were a distinctive group, speaking even a language of their own, hard for others to understand, having a lore and fable of their own making,

but they were individualists of the extremest kind and
they were exceedingly diverse by origin as well as by
adaptation. Frontiers lure men of many kinds who have
nothing in common but their restlessness. The worst of
the mountain men might have become criminals in a
civilized society but some were men of high courage and
imagination who could not endure the dull and limited
life of pioneer farming communities. Nearly all the best
of them were men from Kentucky, Virginia and Tennessee, of the Scotch-Irish breed, and many of these were
the sons of men who had crossed the Alleghenies when
those were the unconquered mountains. Kit Carson was
a relative of Daniel Boone.

The notion that the pioneer was merely a vagabond and
a renegade from social restraints surely does not account
for such a man as Carson. He was for many years a trapper
and shared the life of the mountain men to the full. He
lived by his rifle and took a willing part in brawls and
battles. Perhaps there was never a man who shed more
blood with his own hand for all of these men literally
lived by killing. He married at least one Indian woman,
conveniently lost her, and took to wife a Taos girl who
made him a home that he visited once in a while. Yet
when his trapping days were over he became the one
most useful man in the Southwest. It was Frémont's explorations that advertised the West and opened it to civilization and it was Carson who led the dreamy Path-
finder and at least once saved his life. He guided Kearney
into New Mexico for his bloodless occupation. It was
Carson who conquered the Navajos after three governments had tried and failed. Moreover, when they had

been put on a reservation in a hot country that threatened to kill them all it was Carson who insisted that they be restored to their native range. Patience and a dogged will were his winning qualities in action. He was excessively modest and wholly without greed. In his later years he showed the fine sense of justice and the selfless devotion to social purposes which are certainly elements of greatness. When he came to die he asked for a dish of his favorite food, called an old friend to his bedside and swapped yarns about his trapper days until his breath failed him.

Carson was the supreme product of his period. He was the instrument selected and formed in that conflict between men and mountains to do necessary work. He was the man of opportunity and he became the hero of a legend so that his posthumous fame has overshadowed that of other men who did important work.

Uncle Dick Wootton has been almost forgotten and the excellent memoir he dictated in his old age, absolutely convincing in its naïve directness, is seldom read. He was a man of almost exactly the same type as Carson and even looked much like him, to judge by their pictures. He had the same long firm slit of a mouth, downcurving at the corners with an upthrust lower lip, and the same stocky powerful body. Like Carson he came of the best American stock. He was born in Mecklenburg county, Virginia, in 1816, the son of a tobacco planter, and christened Richens Lacey Wootton — a name which suggests a family proud of its descent. He went west when he was only nineteen. Like nearly all of his kind he went to make his fortune and was always meaning to return. Repeatedly he wrote his mother that he would be back next year but his parents died without ever seeing him again. " It was about the same with all the old trappers," he wrote. " When they once got into the mountains they seemed, some way or other, to get chained to the country, and a great many of them became lost entirely to their early friends and associates and even to their families."

His capacity for leadership was recognized at once. During his first year in the West he led a trading expedition into the Sioux country with thirteen men and ten wagon-loads of beads, knives, powder, lead and other trade goods. The Sioux were not hostile then and never killed a man who came into their camps voluntarily. They would post a guard over the traders' goods and give them a lodge to live in and Wootton was astonished at the roomy comfort of these tepees, even in the dead of winter.

This was a strictly business venture and a very profitable one. A beaver hide worth fifteen dollars was bought for about thirty cents in trade.

Wootton afterward spent a winter and spring at Bent's Fort and in 1837 went on his first trapping trip with a party of seventeen. They trapped the Rio Grande, among other streams, and after nine months of work young Wootton went back to Missouri and cashed his peltries for four thousand dollars. He meant to go home with this stake but started instead on another expedition, which lasted two years and was typical of the tremendous journeys these men made — journeys that were for the most part never recorded, any one of which would have made the reputation of an explorer and furnished him with material for a couple of volumes.

This expedition enlisted nineteen men of whom six were Indians and fifteen of the party got back alive. Their route, as nearly as Uncle Dick could trace it on a modern map, was up the Arkansas to its source in Colorado, north to the Green River in Utah, up that stream to Wyoming, west to Idaho where they trapped the Snake and Salmon rivers, and across the divide to the Columbia. Here they turned south and saw the Pacific again at San Luis Obispo, California. They trapped up the Colorado River to the Gila, up the Gila into Arizona, and finally reached New Mexico by way of Utah. They found the fur poor in California and Arizona and counted their time wasted. "But we got to see some new country," Uncle Dick remarks. They estimated that they had traveled five thousand miles, all of it in an unmapped country inhabited by Indians that were often hostile and they carried no supplies except powder, lead and traps.

This party had many encounters with the Indians, mostly Snakes and Blackfeet, and Wootton gives us an admirably specific account of what Indian warfare was in those early days before the Indians had acquired guns or organized against the whites. Indians were always trying to steal their horses but many were not openly hostile. Now and then a group of warriors would make an attack. It was nearly always made in the morning, never after dark. A volley of arrows opened the battle and then the wild men charged, yelling terrifically, trying to stampede the enemy. When fired on they invariably retreated. They might charge repeatedly but it was a long battle that lasted three or four hours. Indians were always killed and trappers seldom. Only two of this party were killed in open battle.

It is significant that the trappers fought without leadership, each for himself. Parties of free trappers seldom had a leader. They had only one inviolable rule in battle and it was that never should all of them fire at once for to do so would leave them open to a charge.

It was not pitched battle with the Indians that the mountain men dreaded but a shot from the brush when one of them was alone on his trap line. One member of the party, Le Bonte, was ambushed and killed by the Payutes and his companions had reason to believe that he was eaten. Another was shot with a poisoned arrow and died after twenty-four hours of agony. The oldest man in the party, August Claymore, was caught alone by a band of Snakes and beaten over the head with clubs. The Indians left him for dead and his companions took him for dead. Wootton says that " his skull had been crushed, his brain lacerated and a portion of it destroyed." One of the trappers contributed a clean suit of clothes in which to bury the old man and the simple obsequies were under way when Claymore sat up and demanded water. He got well and boasted for the rest of his life that he had worn out his burial suit.

A French Canadian named Charlefors, who had probably lived among the peaceful Indians in Canada, annoyed his fellows and especially Wootton by telling them that the Indians were not a bad lot. This was before the trappers had encountered any hostile ones. Presently a band of Blackfeet got after the Frenchman and chased him to the brink of a narrow fissure. He tried to make his horse jump it, fell in and broke both his legs. The Indians left him there. His companions found him and carried him for two months on a litter until he got well. From his convalescent couch he denounced the aborigines daily and profanely and all the rest of his life he was a confirmed Indian hater as were most of the mountain men. When an old man he sat on a jury at Taos that was trying an Indian for murder and he slept soundly throughout the trial. He was awakened and asked his opinion. " Hang him, of course," he pronounced. " If he ain't guilty, he would be."

The accident to Charlefors was a double catastrophe because he was time-keeper for the party. He recorded the days by cutting notches on a stick and in this fracas the stick was lost. After that they knew only the seasons and in the California climate they lost track even of these. Often they did not know where they were, either in time or in space.

When the beaver boom was over Wootton, like Carson, became a pioneer man of all work — an instrument of expansion and conquest. He held the same job that Carson had for a while as professional hunter for Bent's Fort, killing as many as thirty buffalo a day, hunting with a pack train and a retinue of butchers. Lost on the prairie one night he sat by a fire and held off the wolves by tossing them heads and entrails of his kill. He tamed two buffalo calves and made them draw a plow. He went back to Indian-trading and made money buying stolen Mexican mules from the Apaches. He explains that it would have been intolerably bad manners for him to inquire where the mules came from. When the gold rush was on in California he drove a great herd of sheep across the desert from New Mexico, miraculously escaping the Apaches, and got back with fourteen thousand dollars in gold and thirty thousand in drafts. Always he was out to make his fortune but repeatedly he was drafted by the government. He went with Doniphan on his celebrated march to Chihuahua and his most important job was to find water for eight hundred men in the Mexican desert. He believed that he had a special gift for finding water. He found it every night and Doniphan would never have occupied Chihuahua if he had failed. Doniphan then chose him to carry dispatches back to New Mexico and he rode from Chihuahua to Albuquerque in nine days through a desert occupied by hostile Indians, traveling only at night.

Like Carson he was chosen to fight the Navajos but unlike Carson he was not given the command. He had to defer to West Point officers and he quit in disgust because they would not do as he said.

He, too, married and settled at Taos where, like most of the mountain men, he became intensely bored with peace and domesticity. To break the monotony he went hunting the mythical lost mines of the Sandia Mountains. One Indian who had promised to lead him to a mine was found murdered. He crawled into many caves and crannies and found bobcats, owls and bats but no gold. He finally settled in Colorado where he was one of the first to raise cattle and corn. He made money out of a toll road and helped to hold the right-of-way for the Santa Fe in the great railroad war. In Colorado he lived, a widely known and greatly respected old man, until about 1898.

Wootton had the incurable restlessness of the true pioneer but he remained always a good business man. He lived wholly in action and had no need of God. He never traveled too fast to gather gear. His bargains were all good ones and he handled much money for a man of his time and place. Like the ideal rotarian he had both feet on the ground and he was as hard as it. In him one sees emerging the victorious unreflective materialism of the great national expansion for which he opened the way. He made buffaloes work and Indians pay all the traffic would bear. He was the original go-getter.

James Ohio Pattie swung toward the opposite pole. He rode through the West like a knight on a quest that was never defined and never abandoned. He renounced both love and wealth, deliberately, for movement and danger. A pious man he was one of the few who remained a professing Christian in the wilderness and called on God when other expedients failed. He was evidently a puritan and certainly a man of courage. His story is excessively romantic but it has been carefully checked by Reuben Gold Thwaites and found to be accurate wherever it is subject to corroboration.

Like Carson and Wootton he came of the old American blood-stream that flowed irresistibly westward for four generations. His grandfather followed Boone and Logan into Kentucky and his father, Sylvester Pattie, who shared many of his adventures, pushed on to Missouri, built a sawmill on the Gasconade and made a good thing of selling lumber. As long as his wife lived he stuck to business but when she died of tuberculosis in 1824 he farmed out all his younger children among relatives and neighbors, took his eldest son, James, and struck out for the Rocky Mountains. It was a characteristic gesture of the time. Any catastrophe meant a move westward and neither family nor property weighed against the urge to go. The Patties planned to trap beaver and they joined a caravan of over a hundred men for the trip to Santa Fe. Sylvester Pattie, a veteran of the war of 1812, was elected leader.

The prairies had been crossed by white men for the first time only a few years before and the Patties saw them as a trackless wilderness. On the upper Arkansas the flats and valleys were black with buffalo, there were great herds of elk and wild horses. Grizzly bears, which then came down from the mountains to hunt, were so abundant they were a menace. Pattie records seeing twenty-seven " white bears " in a day. They killed several and one of their party was so badly mutilated by a wounded grizzly that he died.

At Taos they saw Mexicans for the first time and were evidently disgusted with their laziness and dirt. The men, armed only with bows and arrows and knives, stared at them with hostile eyes. A woman invited them into a house and offered them chile con carne but they could not swallow the burning food nor could they exchange a word with their hostess. On they went to Santa Fe where they applied to the governor for a permit to trap in Mexican streams, offering to pay for it five percent of all they made. The governor took the proposition under advisement and the Patties sat down to wait. They spoke no Spanish and they were not diplomatic men. They might have fared badly but for a romantic chance which not only won them a trapping license but affords an illuminating glimpse of an early contact between Mexicans and American pioneers.

While the Patties were camped in Santa Fe a band of raiding Comanches struck the outskirts of the town, killed several Mexicans and made away with a large number of sheep and with three women captives. Like all Indian raids, the thing was swiftly done, and the Patties learned of it only when they heard the yells of excited Mexicans and the bustle of a badly organized pursuit. They immediately offered to help trail and fight the Indians in the hope that they would get in return what they wanted of the government. The hope was well-grounded for one of the women captured was the young and good-looking daughter of a rico who had once been governor of the province. He lived somewhere near Albuquerque and the girl had been merely visiting in Santa Fe.

Pattie, like all men of action, is sparing of detail. He does not give us the name of the rico but only that of the girl who was called Jacova. His story of the pursuit is also vague. He tells only that they sighted the Indians at last in the distance, going through a low pass in the mountains and evidently not expecting any pursuit at all. The elder Pattie now proposed that he and his followers make a laborious detour through the mountains and get in front of the Indians while the Mexicans were to attack them from behind. The Patties carried out their part of the plan and took up a position directly across the trail the Comanches were following.

What they saw first was the herd of stolen sheep and these were being driven by the three women captives who had been stripped naked, although there was snow on the ground. The Indians came on behind and the mountain men waited until the women were quite near them and the Indians well within range. When they fired the women ran toward their lines. The Indians were completely surprised but sent a volley of arrows after their captives, killing one of them. Young Pattie ran forward to meet the other two and the beautiful and distraught Jacova hurled her lovely nakedness into his arms. He gallantly took off his hunting shirt and put it around her.

The Comanches rallied and charged and the mountain men, with the two surviving women, reached some thick timber just in time to save their lives. The Mexicans, who were to have attacked the Indians from the rear, apparently ran in the other direction. For a while the mountain men were in a tight place as the Indians wheeled and charged again and again. The mountain men broke each charge with a volley from their rifles and the Comanches finally gave it up and rode away, leaving a good many dead and wounded on the field. The Mexicans now came back and joined in the pursuit. When the Comanches had disappeared into the mountains, they returned to the battlefield and rode their horses up and down over dead and wounded Indians in a yelling orgy of hatred until the Patties put a stop to their cruelty. The Mexican leader then formally demanded of Sylvester Pattie the custody of the two women, saying he considered them no safer with the mountain men who were not Christians than they had been with the Indians. Syl-

vester with dignity replied that if cowardice was the mark
of a Christian the Mexicans were Christians indeed and
he said the women themselves should choose who would
escort them back to Santa Fe. They both elected to stay
with the mountain men and the beautiful Jacova now
came forward to thank young Pattie for saving her
life.

"I cannot describe the gratitude and loveliness that
appeared in her countenance as she looked on me,"
James wrote. "I did not know how to meet her acknowl-
edgments."

What is worse he never learned. She insisted that he
come to call upon her that evening. When he appeared
both she and her sister came forward and embraced him
which was well within the rules of Mexican etiquette but
wholly confusing to James. He sat down for a few minutes
but being unable to say a word he presently rose and
tried to go. "But Jacova, showing me a bed prepared for
me, placed herself between me and the door. I showed her
that my clothes were not clean. She immediately brought
me others belonging to her brother-in-law. I wished to
be excused from using them but she seemed so much hurt
that I finally took them and reseated myself. She then
brought me my leather hunting shirt, which I had taken
off to aid in protecting her from the cold, and begged the
interpreter, who was now present, to tell me that she
meant to keep it as long as she lived. She then put it on
to prove to me that she was not ashamed of it."

If James made any response to all these blandishments
he does not admit it. If he was tempted to linger in
Jacova's arms, he put the temptation sternly aside. He

might presumably have married not only beauty but wealth for Jacova's father was one of the rich men of the province but James did not even tarry any longer than he had to. There was never a man more hopelessly possessed by the urge to wander and James's wanderings had just begun.

Coming to Santa Fe as strangers the Patties had found the Mexicans hostile and suspicious, cruel and intolerant. Now that they were friends and heroes they saw the other side of that primitive-feudal character. They were given a license to trap and taken as guests to the house of Jacova's father in the lower valley. His house was theirs for as long as they cared to stay and they stayed three days. James says the place was " large and even magnificent " but he gives not a single detail of its magnificence.

Their host tried to load them with gifts but they refused everything except a horse apiece and the luxury of a little flour. The two Patties, with a small party recruited from the caravan, then followed the Rio Grande south to Socorro and cut across country to the Gila. It was afterwards famous as a beaver stream but they were probably the first trappers to see it. Beaver abounded but when they had gathered bales of fur so many of their horses had been stolen and killed by Indians that they could not carry their wealth. They buried the furs and struck back for the Rio Grande, arriving starved and dirty, with matted hair and beards. Once more James called upon his Jacova and this time he was the one in distress. He records that she burst into tears at the sight of him. She clothed him and fed him and she must have hoped that this time he would stay. But no. Supplied with horses and flour again by her father he went back to get his buried furs, only to find that the Indians had stolen them.

The Patties started back once more and got as far as the Santa Rita copper mines — those ancient diggings which had already been worked for perhaps a hundred years when the Patties saw them and are still yielding copper today. The Apaches had long before beaten off the Mexican owners. They now attacked the Patties who beat them so badly that they made a formal treaty of peace. Here once more the mountain men took up work the Mexicans could no longer do. Sylvester leased the mines from the Mexican owners and began to work them very profitably.

Once more James had his chance at security and rest and once more he rejected it. He was bored with life at the mines and the Gila, which had defeated him twice, was a challenge he could not refuse. Against the protests of his father he organized a party and started out again. This time he followed the Gila all the way to the Colorado, turned north as far as the Yellowstone and then south again to Santa Fe. For the first time he had brought his furs out of the mountains but he was again cheated of his profit. The governor ruled that his license had expired and confiscated his furs. He went south to Santa Rita to visit his father and stayed three days which seems to have been his idea of a long visit anywhere. Then he was off again on a trapping trip into Chihuahua, returning to the mines in the fall.

This time he found his father in distress. A Mexican whom Sylvester trusted had absconded with a large part of his capital. Father and son once more joined forces to make their fortunes and once more, with a small party, they set out for the Gila on what proved to be the most adventurous and disastrous of all their journeys. They built canoes and went down the river to the Colorado. From the natives they got the mistaken idea that a Spanish settlement had been built at the mouth of the river. In their crude boats they navigated the lower gorges of the great river all the way to the Pacific, only to find themselves on a desert and uninhabited seacoast. Across salt marshes and waterless wastes they made their way north to the first Spanish mission where they were arrested and sent as prisoners to San Diego. There the elder Pattie died in his cell. He was refused even the comfort of a last visit from his son and James was filled with a great bitterness against all things Spanish which even the memory of the gentle Jacova did not mitigate. He finally gained his liberty by reason of his usefulness as an interpreter, went north to the Russian settlements, played a part in the Solis revolution, went to Mexico City to seek redress for his grievances, got no satisfaction and finally reached New Orleans by boat. His narrative ends with his return to the ancestral home in Kentucky, and his final fate is unknown, but there is evidence that he was again in California and it is more than probable that he died somewhere in the West.

Most of the mountain men did. At every rendezvous many who were expected failed to appear. Men asked for old friends and got often the same vernacular answer — " rubbed out." Not much time was given to mourning. These typically were men who kept going until they were killed. They were like wild animals in that for them a violent death was the natural one.

The whole period in which the mountain men flourished was not more than a quarter of a century. By 1840 the price of beaver had dropped and the streams were depleted. The great annual rendezvous dwindled and finally died. Taos saw no more of those wild bands, laden with bales of fur, who had formerly bought the town and thrown money into the streets to watch the urchins scramble for it.

It is said that when Kit Carson saw the trapping days were over he organized a last expedition which had no other purpose than to live for a last time the kind of a life he loved. He summoned all of his surviving cronies and they rode away into the mountains with their long rifles across their saddle bows, traps jingling in their ruck sacks, to light last fires beside the beaver streams, to sing their songs and tell their stories — and go their separate ways.

The day of the mountain men was over. As a class they had done their work. They had found the Rocky Mountains an unexplored wilderness and a barrier before which civilization had stopped. They had camped on every stream, followed every trail, located every pass and beaten every tribe of mountain Indians in pitched battle. Enough of them survived to point the way for everything that followed — explorers, soldiers, wagon-trains, even railroads. Jim Bridger told the surveyors where the Northern Pacific could cross the mountains and Uncle Dick Wootton's toll road preceded the Santa Fe. These men did more than any others to open the way from sea to sea.

VIII
The Prairie Man

~~~~~~~~~~~~~~~~~~~~~~~~~~~~~~~~~~~~~

1

T HE PRAIRIE land between the Mississippi and
the mountains is now the vital and social center
of our country. It grows the grain and pork and
fattens the beef that feed us and it contains the society
that grew most purely out of our pioneer beginnings, far
from seaports, complacent and self-contained. Europe has
captured the Atlantic coast north of the Potomac. California is an Asiatic frontier and a place where good
farmers go to die. American civilization lives and works
in the midlands.

Nowhere has the earth been more completely subdued
and transformed. Almost every acre is fenced and plowed.
The traveler's eye tires of corn and wheat reaching clear
to the level skyline and it escapes them only in glimpses
of little wooden towns grouped in shabby reverence about
their grain elevators and in the sudden roar and smoke
of great inland cities.

It strains the imagination to comprehend that little
more than a long human lifetime has elapsed since this
was no man's land, that settlements stood on either side

of this region for five generations before white men found
their way across it and that for two generations more it
was only a wilderness to be braved in the hope of
profit. Far-sighted men thought it would never be settled.
Daniel Webster was in favor of leaving it to the Indians
and Josiah Gregg believed settlement would never reach
beyond the headwaters of the Missouri.

What made them all think of the prairie as uninhab-
itable was the lack of navigable rivers. Civilization then
traveled by water and lived in valleys. Men had gone
up rivers from the Atlantic and crossed the Alleghenies
to go down rivers on the other side. It was not to plant
settlements that they invaded the prairies but to trade
with people on the other side. Merchants bent on selling
cotton cloth to Mexicans at three times what it cost were
the ones who found the way across and finally made a
road. Here again the Rio Grande was the destination.
The trail ended in Santa Fe and the road still bears its
name.

The crossing of the prairies is epitomized with rare
completeness in the life of a single man. Josiah Gregg
grew up on the edge of the prairies, spent years in the
wagon trade and wrote a book about it that is still an
authority. His book, his letters, and the facts about him
recorded by others make a picture of an epoch and of
the kind of man the epoch produced. In Gregg more than
in any other man I know of, the American pioneer became articulate. Many of them recorded their adventures,
Gregg also reflected upon his. He tried to understand the
world he lived in, he tried to understand himself and
he tried to find a faith to live by. He was a gifted man.

In rudimentary ways he was both an artist and a scientist. He was an explorer and a historian. He was unusual, yet he was typical. Traits suggested by the lives of many pioneers are in him exaggerated and by him explained.

Josiah Gregg was born in Independence, Missouri in 1806. His forebears were Pennsylvania Quakers of Scotch-Irish descent and like those of so many other Americans of his time they had been pioneers for two generations. His grandfather had crossed the Alleghenies, his father had pushed on to Missouri and Josiah finally and appropriately left his bones on the Pacific coast.

Independence, now a suburb of Kansas City, was then a small pioneer settlement and one of the newest and farthest west in the United States. It was a straggling group of log houses on the Missouri River, surrounded by farms that scattered out to the edge of the prairie. It lived by farming and trade, its sports were hunting and drink, its cultural life consisted of politics and the narrowest kind of sectarian Christianity. In all essentials it was like a thousand other American pioneer communities. Like them, it was an excellent place for a simple man of action to live and work. He had boundless outlets for his energy and an unlimited hope of reward. Land and timber were his for the taking and the country swarmed with game. But for a reflective and imaginative man, a pioneer settlement was a barren place. It contained few books and fewer thoughtful persons. It needed no writers or thinkers. It regarded originality with suspicion and art with contempt.

Josiah Gregg was a man of thought and imagination born into such a community. He was a sickly boy and doubtless for that reason read and thought more than his fellows. Somehow he taught himself French and Spanish, he learned the rudiments of several natural sciences and he read both in the classics and in eighteenth century literature. Independence had been settled mostly by men from Tennessee and Kentucky and perhaps some of them brought books along. At any rate, Josiah evidently found books to read and the rest of his time he spent hunting and roaming alone in the beautiful country that surrounded the settlement. From the first he felt a profound aversion to society and he never got over it. In that respect he was like many other sensitive Americans of his time.

Independence became the starting point for all who crossed the prairies to the Rio Grande. Josiah grew up in an atmosphere of adventurous departures. While he was a child McKnight led a pack train to Santa Fe, was imprisoned by the Mexicans and held for years. James Pursely, a wandering carpenter, reached the settlements on the Rio Grande, pushed north into Colorado, found the gold in the Platte River which afterwards started the Pike's Peak rush and threw it away because he had lost all interest in what it would buy. Baptiste La Lande was sent to Taos as a trader and stayed to found a family without even accounting to his employer for the goods he had sold. A few years later Lieutenant Pike set out on his celebrated expedition, discovered Pike's Peak, estimated it to be much higher than it was, raised the American flag by mistake on Mexican soil, was politely taken prisoner, entertained by the Spanish governor and returned to make himself and the West famous. Soon after Pike's expedition pack trains were setting out regularly from the Missouri for Santa Fe. They were harassed by Indians and some traders were killed but the business grew because it paid. Soon the traders found they could cross the prairies in wagons. In 1829 all of them for the first time were gathered into one great caravan and escorted by troops. From then on the caravan was a regular annual event. Beginning in 1831 it started every year from Independence in the month of May.

At this time Josiah Gregg was twenty-five years old. He had apparently found no place or occupation in Independence and he certainly longed to escape it. He was considered by himself and by others a chronic invalid. He tells us that he suffered from a "complication of chronic diseases" but the only one he mentions by name is dyspepsia. It is evident at least that life in Independence had given him an acute pain in the stomach. He persuaded himself and his relatives that his health would be improved by a trip with a wagon train to Santa Fe. This involved sleeping on the ground, standing guard in the rain and living on wild meat, camp-fire bread and strong coffee. It involved a complete separation from comforts and from medical attention. It was a peculiar prescription for dyspepsia but it was good for what ailed Josiah Gregg. He tells us that the trip "restored my health at once and begot a passion for prairie life which I never hope to survive." He never did.

Josiah Gregg was both a man of action and a man of thought. He was at once a pioneer and an intellectual. It is hard to discover another pioneer who thought and read and wrote as much as Gregg did but it is easy to see that in his time the pioneer and the intellectual had a similar origin and often shared some of the same qualities. Both were men who rebelled against the narrow restraints of a primitive community life. The pioneer set out to discover a new world in reality, the intellectual idealist to create an imaginary one, but often the two impulses mingled in a single man and they are never quite distinct in any case. Writers such as Thoreau and Melville felt the pioneer's need of physical escape. Thoreau fled to his hut on Walden pond and Melville to the South Seas. Bronson Alcott, the dreamiest of the Transcendentalists, tried to found an ideal community, just as did Brigham Young, one of the greatest of the pioneers. Young built a city that still stands and Alcott committed an absurdity that is still remembered and written about. Many of the pioneers had something of the artist about them and wrote crude narratives of their adventures, filled with a somewhat sentimental idealism.

In Gregg, these two impulses, toward the real and the ideal, were about equally strong. He fled into the wilderness and he wrote books. He tried to escape society and he tried to resolve his conflict with it by thinking and by presenting it with the fruits of his intellectual labors. But he never quite succeeded in either. He was always destroying the wilderness he loved, fleeing the civilization he helped to create. He achieved no adjustment, found no rest. His life is a tragedy of subtle but inexorable causes.

2

Independence in the month of May was a transitory pioneer metropolis, briefly crowded with many kinds of men — teamsters, soldiers, merchants, buckskinned hunters and trappers bound for the mountains, rich Mexicans on their way back to Santa Fe, and a few exotics such as health-seekers from the states, British younger sons in search of adventure, men of science and men of mystery, going west for reasons they kept to themselves. The saloons were full and the nights were bright with camp fires. All day long hammers rattled on wagon tires and horse shoes and men shouted and cursed and laughed as they went about their preparations. For the atmosphere of the expedition, Gregg makes it clear, was that of a splendid lark.

One by one the wagons with their white covers, drawn each by six or eight horses, mules or oxen, stretched their traces, cracked their whips and pulled out for Council Grove. It was the last of the woods and there all stopped to cut timber for spare axles, tongues and singletrees. There too the caravan was formally organized and always a captain was elected after much and passionate electioneering. Many candidates were put forward, eloquent speeches were made, men went about with jugs of corn liquor soliciting votes for their favorites. But once chosen the captain was practically forgotten. He had no real authority and these men were wholly unaccustomed to obedience. He usually picked the camping place but even his choice of that was likely to be disputed, while in case of emergency the expedition developed almost as many plans of action as it had members.

Once it was organized the caravan got under way as a unit for the first time. It moved to shouts that went from mouth to mouth. "Catch up!" was the signal to harness. "All's set!" went around when this was done. "Stretch out!" meant that every whip cracked and every team strained at its traces. "Fall in!" And the wagons formed a line crawling across the trackless green.

From the seat of a carriage, Josiah Gregg, the invalid, the social refugee, looked out upon a world unmarred by men. Grass grew belly high to a horse. Silver-rippled by the wind it covered the gently rolling land from sky to sky. Wild roses, phlox and cluster lilies sprinkled the green with blossom. "The soil is black as your hat," a traveler wrote. "The earth is so fat it looks as though it would laugh if you tickled it." Prairie chickens skimmed the grass and the antelope fled and turned to stare, flashing their white rump-patches in the sun.

Crossing the prairies at this time, and for a generation after, was not a very dangerous business. Gregg says there were not a dozen deaths on the road in twenty years. Many of the Indian tribes had not yet become hostile, as they did when the buffalo began to disappear, and they seldom struck a caravan. They were just menacing enough to lend the expeditions a pleasant air of excitement. Nearly every trip had its Indian scare. A band of wild riders would be seen on the horizon. Every man would grab his gun and begin shouting orders, wagons would be formed in a circle, the captain would try in vain to assert his authority — and then it would be found that the Indians only wanted to trade or beg or that they had no idea of coming within gunshot and everyone would be half relieved and half disappointed.

Indians would seldom fight but they would steal horses at night if given the slightest chance and this made it necessary always to mount a guard. None were exempt from guard duty except women and the sick. Every caravan carried a contingent of loafers who went along just for the ride and for free board. The hospitable traders would refuse no man a plate by the camp fire but these parasites partly paid for their keep by doing their share of guard duty.

There were difficulties enough. Herds of buffalo sometimes ran over the camp, stampeding the animals so that it took days to gather them again. Hail storms killed mules and horses, winds blew wagons over and they bogged down in flooding creeks and mudholes. But it was the rule that everyone helped everyone else and a wagon stuck in the mud was sure of all the mule power it needed to pull it out.

The first sight of buffalo was always one of the great excitements of the expedition. All turned out, on foot or on horseback, armed with rifles, pistols, shot guns, even lances and bows and arrows, and there was a tremendous and often wasteful slaughter. Gregg was a sensitive man and when he sat down to write he deplored the senseless killing of animals left to rot on the ground. At the same time he admits that he was often carried away by the excitement and bloodlust of these great hunts which evidently had somewhat the character of mob movements, submerging individual consciousness in a burst of primitive excitement. After the killing there would be great feasts and men would gorge themselves like savages.

This wagon business, like so many other phases of American pioneering, was almost wholly a man's world. Generally there were no women and if two or three went along they were the objects of awed admiration and of elaborate gallantry. In the early West men learned how to get along without women much better than they learned how to get along with them.

All the way across the prairie these men of many kinds worked and hunted and fraternized around their fires in high good-fellowship and loyalty, marred by occasional arguments and fights. They lived in a moving world of their own with few and simple obligations and they liked it but as they drew near to Santa Fe an intense anticipatory excitement ran through their ranks. Two hundred miles from town messengers were sent out on horseback to dicker with the Mexican customs officials and bring back supplies. On the morning of the last day every man washed himself and put on a clean shirt and every teamster tied a new cracker to his whip. When they topped the hills east of the town and saw its flat roofs huddled at the foot of the mountains a great shout went up from all of them. Whips were cracked and guns were fired. " I doubt whether the first sight of the walls of Jerusalem was beheld by the crusaders with more soul-enrapturing joy," says Gregg.

As the wagons rolled into Santa Fe most of the town turned out to greet them. The ricos held aloof for to them these men were invaders who threatened the established order and infidels who defied the will of God. But the common people welcomed the traders from the first. They felt no loyalty to the order that had crushed them for centuries. The wagons brought them cheap and needed goods and flooded the town with money and with gayety.

Santa Fe was a ragamuffin capital — a bare adobe town with narrow crooked streets full of dogs, pigs and naked children — but it knew how to celebrate. The night the wagon train arrived there were dances in every available hall, the monte tables were banked with players, the saloons were full. No man lacked a girl or a drink or a chance to spend his money. Everyone studied Spanish with a sleeping dictionary. To these men out of hardshell Protestant pioneer settlements Santa Fe was Sodom and Gomorrah and they plunged into its dissipations with the violence and unrestraint of impulse long denied.

Nothing was denied them here for they brought life to a perishing society. In the course of a few years they not only dominated the town but almost owned the government for it lived on the heavy tariffs they paid and it was always insolvent. Soon everyone, from the governor down, was in debt to the traders. Some of the more enterprising ricos went into the trade themselves and they proved unexpectedly successful at it for the Mexican has a genius for any kind of transportation. But these men were apostates. Most of the ricos to the last met the traders with secret implacable hostility and the politicians who lived on their bounty seemed to hate them most of all.

It is evident that to Josiah Gregg the wagon trade

brought the greatest happiness he ever knew. He cared
little for the dissipations at the end of the trail but he
loved the peace and freedom of the prairies. There for
the first time he found health and serenity. The trouble
was that the longer he lived in the wilderness the less
could he tolerate the society of his time and this troubled
him sorely. For he could not become a contented vagabond like so many of his fellow traders. He had high
abilities to use and he had a social conscience. He knew
instinctively that he was wasting himself as a wanderer.
But when he tried to live at home he became sick both
in mind and in body. He fled again to the prairies but
he fled with the guilt of a conscious renegade. Again and
again he tried to justify and explain his flight. He never
saw the United States as a crude and undeveloped society
nor did he think of seeking a better one. He clung to
the notion that his country was the greatest and most
enlightened on earth and he believed the wilderness had
a fatal fascination that no society could rival.

"In the first place" he writes, "the wild, unsettled
and independent life of the prairie trader makes freedom
from every kind of social dependence an absolute necessity of his being. . . . No court or jury is called to ad-
judicate upon his disputes or his abuses; and no powers
are invoked to redress them, save those with which the
God of Nature has endowed him. He knows no government — no laws save those of his own creation and adoption. He lives in no society which he must look up
to or propitiate. The exchange of this sovereign independence . . . for a life in civilization where both his
physical and his moral freedom are invaded at every

turn . . . is certainly likely to commend itself to but few."

It certainly did not commend itself to him and he evidently had no conception of a society in which both his physical and his moral freedom would not be invaded at every turn. He knew only the American society of his time and he repudiated it. He bought goods and wagons and became a trader on a large scale and a very successful one.

Evidently he did not lack an aptitude for business. One of his transactions is recorded in detail. He got a contract to install a clock in the tower of the church at Santa Fe for a price of one thousand dollars. He had a gift for all kinds of machinery and he built a clock of ingenious device. At every hour a wooden figure of a little negro emerged from a door and bowed in unison with the chime. All of the people were delighted but the Vicario, who hated gringos anyway, decided that he had been overcharged. He refused to pay Gregg more than seven hundred dollars. Not long afterward the little negro ceased to appear and the clock stood silent. The pious people of Santa Fe became greatly worried. They were sure this was a judgment of God upon the Vicario for not keeping his bargain and they were afraid the divine wrath would be inflicted upon the whole parish. The Vicario was finally compelled by public opinion to give Gregg the rest of his money, whereupon the clock was repaired and the little figure appeared once more, to the great relief of the whole town.

Gregg made eight trips across the prairies as a merchant and he speaks of himself as having lived nine

years in Mexico although he evidently included in this
estimate the time spent on the road. Undoubtedly he was
much in Santa Fe but there is no evidence that the sensu-
ous decaying society of the New Mexican capital meant
any more to him than that of his native Missouri. The
one nourished his restless and hungry spirit no more than
the other. He observed the Mexicans with complete detachment as he observed the prairie dogs and the buffalo.
Apparently he wanted a Mexican mistress no more than
he wanted a yankee wife for one can discover no hint of
a love affair. If he had one it must have been a minor
incident in his life. Neither does he seem to have known
intimate friends and his family he seldom saw. His
brother accompanied him on a few of his trips and then
abandoned the prairie life to return to his wife and children. Gregg mentions him only to say that a prairie trader
has no business being married.

Isolation is despair and socially Gregg was one of the
most isolate of men. He knew no warm gregariousness.
He knew the terrible loneliness of those who never find
their peers and cannot tolerate their inferiors. The
United States as a society he could not endure but the
United States as a nation he literally worshiped. He
despised it as a society and doubtless for that very reason
he loved it as a great expanding, conquering power to
which he belonged. For he had to feel that he belonged
to something.

His book is full of naïve and eloquent expressions of
his patriotism. He always celebrated the Fourth of July,
no matter where he was. He kept track of his position
on the prairie with compass and sextant, like a mariner,

and ascertained the exact moment when he first set foot upon American soil.

"Those who have never been beyond the purlieus of the land of their nativity" he writes, "can form but a poor conception of the joy which the wanderer in distant climes experiences upon treading once more his own native soil. Although we were yet far from the abodes of civilization, nevertheless the heart within us thrilled with exhilarating sensations, for we were again in our own territory, breathed our own pure atmosphere."

Yet in the same book he tells us that in American society there is neither physical nor moral freedom, a little later he is calling the rulers of his native land nincumpoops, and he ends by saying that he prefers the society of wild animals and Indians to that of his fellow citizens.

This contradiction between his love of the United States as an abstraction and his contempt for it as a social reality seems absurd enough in retrospect but to him it was a tragic dilemma. For the country he loved and longed to serve was killing the wilderness he loved and lived in.

He was never content merely to seek his fortune. Always he was consciously the servant of society, both as a man of action and as an intellectual. He explored new routes across the prairie and on one of these adventures he fought a desperate battle with the Comanches. From the first day of his first trip he took elaborate notes about everything. His curiosity ranged from the most immediate and practical questions to the most purely scientific.

He wanted to know why the great salt deposits of the West could not be used and he speculated about the origin of the Indians, the nature of mirages and the formation of the great western river gorges. With him the modern spirit went into the wilderness, undaunted and uncorrupted, perhaps for the first time. The Spaniards had been mediaeval men, living in a supernatural world. The mountain men were spiritually subdued by the wilderness even while they conquered it. Literally or figuratively they knelt to savage gods. But Gregg was a perfect embodiment of the scientific spirit — detached, skeptical, enquiring, realistic, wholly without superstition. He considered that his mission was to see and understand.

At the end of nine years he had a mass of valuable information and he determined to present it to his beloved country, at whatever cost to himself. He had written nothing for publication except a few newspaper articles. Captain Marryat, then a best-selling novelist, had paid him the compliment of incorporating some of these, almost verbatim, in one of his stories, but Gregg nevertheless felt the need of expert assistance in preparing his work for publication. Someone gave him a letter to John Bigelow, a prominent journalist in New York City. Gregg abandoned his business and with his work in his hands journeyed to the metropolis of his country, as do all gifted men seeking reward and recognition.

With what hopes and expectations he made that pilgrimage we do not know, but we do know something of how he fared, for some of Bigelow's letters about him and some of his letters to Bigelow have been preserved.

Bigelow describes him as the shyest man he ever knew. Gregg stayed in New York nearly three months and he achieved almost no living contact with the place. Bigelow says that he did not make three acquaintances, that he remained shut up in a single room most of the time and that his health suffered incessantly. New York gave him even a worse stomach-ache than Missouri had done. Ill and lonely and bewildered he nevertheless completed, with Bigelow's assistance, a two-volume work. Bigelow testifies that his notes were very well written and needed little revision. One suspects that Bigelow tried to make the book more sensational and popular than the material warranted and that Gregg resisted him firmly for he says that Gregg was intolerant of literary frills and had a passion for exactitude. He told Bigelow that if he put in any fancy writing his old companions of the plains would make fun of it as borrowed plumage. Evidently nine years on the trail was not without value as a literary discipline.

As soon as the book was done Gregg gave it to the first publisher who offered and fled New York. The publisher went bankrupt and Gregg got nothing out of his contract but the book he wrote is still reprinted and still quoted. He called it " The Commerce of the Prairies " but it is far more than an account of the wagon trade. It is also a history of New Mexico, based upon documents in the Palace at Santa Fe some of which have since been lost. It includes an account of the prairies — their plants and animals and their geography — and a description of the Indian tribes. By intention at least, his book is a work of history, of science and of art, and incidentally it is a work of self-revelation. It must have been in his lonely room in New York that he wrote its closing pages.

" Since that time," he says, referring to his return from his last trip across the prairies, " I have striven in vain to reconcile myself to the even tenor of civilized life in the United States, and have sought in its amusements and its society a substitute for those high excitements which have attached me so strongly to prairie life. Yet I am *almost ashamed to confess* that scarcely a day passes without my experiencing a pang of regret that I am not now roving at large upon those western plains."

He is ashamed that he cannot endure society but he is about done trying. He predicts that his passion for prairie life will be very likely to lead him back to the great plains " to spread my bed with the mustang and the buffalo under the broad canopy of heaven — there to seek to *maintain my confidence in men* by fraternizing with the little prairie dogs and the wild colts and the still wilder Indians — the unconquered Sabaeans of the Great American Desert."

Surely there was never a more complete revelation of that impulse of social avoidance which drove men into the wilderness to subdue it. What Gregg expresses again and again is suggested by the story of every pioneer, and in him, too, one sees an early example of the typical American individualism, which combines an intolerance of restraint with a craven fear of public opinion and the social discipline, making us at once the most lawless and the most conforming and herd-ruled people on earth.

John Bigelow was apparently a commonplace man but he was perhaps the closest approximation to an intellectual peer and companion that Gregg had ever found for he wrote Bigelow many long letters, recounting his adventures and expounding his irreconcilable conflict with society. Leaving New York he returned to the West and immediately joined a party who went upon the prairies to hunt and gather wild honey and he reports that "the little jaunt contributed very much to strengthen the tone of my stomach." But as soon as he returned to town his stomach got worse and he caught cold. He has "contracted a perfect disgust for anything that savors of town life" and he concludes that "my organ of inhabitiveness is entirely annihilated."

Nevertheless he went to Shreveport, Louisiana, to visit relatives and in that community he took a look at local politics. They gave him something like a nausea. "The most ignorant and ill-fated nincumpoops are continually being elected to fill posts of honor, trust and profit," he reports to Bigelow with naïve indignation. Once more the "pure atmosphere" of his native land was too much for him and in 1846 he is again starting from Independence with a wagon train.

He had presented society with a book for which society gave him nothing. He had tried life in three communities and found it intolerable and he had also tried to join the expeditionary forces of the United States which were marching upon Mexico City and Chihuahua in a war of ruthless aggression. In Gregg's eyes, whatever his country did was right. "I am willing to undergo any privation and labor which my physical powers can endure when there is even a remote chance of serving my country," he wrote to Bigelow and he proved that he meant it.

His offer of services had apparently been ignored but when he was a hundred miles from Independence on his way to Santa Fe, messengers overtook him to say that he had been assigned to the division of General Wool which was marching to join Doniphan's expedition at Chihuahua. Gregg at once abandoned his business, turned back and rode twelve hundred miles alone on horseback through a wild country to join Wool at San Antonio.

It is hard to discover what purpose he served in the war. His status was purely civilian and he probably acted as an interpreter and an adviser about the country and the people. Doniphan had already taken Chihuahua when Wool got there, so that the whole expedition was largely futile, but Gregg had the satisfaction of serving his beloved country to the best of his ability. Connelly gives us a single revealing glimpse of him in this patriotic capacity. As the returning army marched across the burning desert of northern Mexico Gregg suffered intensely from the heat. He procured a huge red umbrella and rode along holding it above his head. When the soldiers began to laugh at him he was so incensed that he rode the whole length of the army with his sunshade defiantly aloft and lodged a complaint with the commanding general.

Probably Gregg enjoyed the jaunt despite its gibes and discomforts. He saw a new country and witnessed battles with Mexican guerrillas and with Apache Indians who had gotten so rich preying on the Mexicans that they wore golden ornaments and blankets worth hundreds of dollars. He met Dr. Wislizenius, the scientist who accom-

panied Doniphan and who took the skull of a slaughtered
Apache chief back to the Smithsonian Institution.

3

For the next few years after his return from Chihuahua
Gregg's life is obscure but it was still a restless quest.
Apparently since his first departure he had never stopped
anywhere for as much as six months. He writes Bigelow
again from Saltillo where he followed the army of occupation as a newspaper correspondent. He went once more
to New York to see about his book but he did not tarry
long. In 1848 he was again in Missouri and again apparently at loose ends. Then came the California gold
rush and inevitably it carried him on to the Pacific.

For years neither friends nor relatives heard anything
about him but the last act of his life is fully recounted in
an old book by A. J. Bledsoe on the early explorations of
California. From this we learn that in 1849 Gregg was
living in a mining camp on the upper Trinity River,
known as Rich Bar. It was badly named for the sands
yielded little gold and everyone was discouraged. Indians
told the miners of a rich country by the sea eight days'
travel to the west. Their descriptions suggested a great
valley beside a harbor — an ideal location for a settlement. Gregg proposed to his companions that they organize an expedition to discover this new land and
twenty-four of them agreed to follow him.

Gregg's motive in this expedition is mysterious. It had
every appearance of being a wild goose chase. He was
not looking for gold. Did he really think he could found

a settlement in the wilderness with his few followers, without tools or equipment? Or was he merely driven by the impulse of flight that had hunted him all his life — an impulse grown desperate and perhaps a little mad?

We cannot know how Gregg felt about this last departure but it is of record that when the day of starting came most of his followers pronounced it a folly and refused to go. Gregg called for volunteers and seven of the twenty-four agreed to follow him. These men were all young and strong. Gregg was their leader by common consent but he had no authority except that which his personality created. He was forty-three years old — a man of slight build and uncertain health. Each man had horses and a gun and they carried provisions for only ten days. It was November of 1849.

The narrow ridges of the coast range they crossed after five days of bitter struggle. The lower slopes were slippery with mud and the crests were covered with soft snow. On the sixth day they reached the lower Trinity River and came upon a village of Indians who had never seen white men. The Indians fled, leaving their huts deserted. Gregg and his party, wet and hungry, occupied the deserted village and made a meal of dried salmon they found there. At night eighty painted warriors came and surrounded them. They seized their guns but found all of them too wet to shoot. While parleying precariously with the Indians they dried enough powder to fire a single shot. This frightened and impressed the warriors who then agreed to let them stay the night and advised them to leave the river and travel straight west across the mountains.

After eight more days of travel across unexplored mountains their provisions were exhausted. They held a council and took a vote as to whether they should go on or return. Those who wanted to go ahead were in the majority with Gregg their leader. They stopped for a few days to hunt, killed deer, smoked venison and pushed on.

Day after day they crossed the endless ridges and to all of them except Gregg the ocean began to seem a myth. The sixteenth day of travel found them out of meat again. Moreover grass was scarce, horses weakened and two of them died. They pushed on for ten days more, crossing ridge after ridge through forests that became daily more dense and impassable, living mostly on wild nuts. They were nearly spent when they came to another open valley where grass grew and deer, elk and grizzly bears abounded. Here they spent five days making meat and resting and then went on. The morale of the expedition was collapsing but they had gone too far now for turning back.

As they traveled westward the ridges became lower but the forest rose as the mountains fell. They were in the region of the great trees. Giant conifers towered hundreds of feet above them, and the ground was littered with fallen trunks six or seven feet thick, piled and crisscrossed one above the other. Often they had to build platforms up one side of a log and down the other to get the horses across. It rained incessantly and there was no game. They all began to hate each other and especially the others all hated Gregg, for he was the one who had led them into this hopeless plight, and he was the only one for whom the trip still seemed to have a meaning. He was still undaunted and he still made his scientific observations. The rest of them were desperate animals fighting for their lives.

After five days of struggle through the forest two of them went ahead on foot, reached the sea and returned. It was only a few miles away but it took them three days to get to it with their horses and two more of these died on the way. They came to the Pacific near a point which they called Gregg's Point and which is now known as Point Trinidad.

Here a wrangle took place as to which way they should go. The great rich valley and the harbor which they were to discover were forgotten. The only object of the expedition now was to get out of the wilderness alive. Finally they agreed to strike south along the coast in the hope of reaching San Francisco. As often happens when men are desperate group spirit had almost disappeared. It was each for himself. Gregg fell behind, his horse mired and he yelled for help but none paid any attention. He finally got out of the mud unaided.

After days of travel along the coast they came to another village of Indians who seemed friendly. One of the men, Wood, wanted to desert the expedition and stay with the savages. Anything human looked better to him than this wilderness of mountain and forest but he was finally persuaded to go on.

A wide river blocked their progress but they found an old Indian canoe and were starting across when Gregg insisted on stopping to take the latitude so that he would know the location of the river he had discovered. His devotion to science at such a time threw his companions into a frenzy. They cursed him and started to paddle off without him. He called them back. Some of them wanted to throw him and his instruments into the river. He finally waded out to the boat and climbed in. When their blood had cooled they named the stream Mad River and it is still so called.

That night they camped in the hills back of the river and one of the men, Buck, went in search of water. Gregg tasted what he brought and found it salt. He demanded to know where it had come from for he knew they were far from the surf and must be on some great bay. In the morning they found it and called it Trinity Bay. It was later known as Humboldt Bay.

They were now in the region which they had come to discover and settle and they could only sit and wonder what mad impulse had started them on such a journey —all, perhaps, except Gregg. He had spent his life in such journeyings and he must have known that for him there was neither rest nor destination.

On December 21 they found it impossible to follow the coast any farther south and they turned inland for some miles. On Christmas day they roasted the head of an elk and ate its brains for Christmas dinner. Again they had a discussion, which rapidly became a quarrel, as to which way they should go. This time their differences could not be reconciled. Four of them, led by Gregg, continued south, paralleling the cost. The other four, led by Wood, turned inland. Wood was nearly killed by three grizzlies which he attacked when no other game could be found. He was carried for days in a litter but he and his companions all reached the settlements alive. So did the other party — all except one.

Gregg remained their leader although physically he was by far the weakest. They ran out of ammunition and their march became simply a race against starvation. One morning Gregg mounted his horse as usual and led the way. Suddenly he wavered in his saddle and fell. When his companions reached him he was dead. Hunger and fatigue had killed him.

They buried him in a shallow hole they dug with sticks and covered him over with rocks, not to mark his grave but to keep the wolves from eating his remains.

He had completed the migration of his family across the continent. He had conquered the prairie and reached the other sea. He had found the only resting place there was for him.

IX
The Revolutionist

1

EVER since the Spanish Empire fell to pieces government south of the Rio Grande has been a bloody farce of revolution. Some countries fare worse than others but in nearly all of them " liberators " periodically arise, put on gaudy uniforms, issue bombastic proclamations, lead ragged armies in desperate conquests, seize offices, greedily gobble their revenues and are in turn shot or driven into exile by other hungry patriots.

From the north the antics of these political clowns are watched with contemptuous and uncomprehending eyes. It seems to be never sufficiently recognized that in all of the Latin-American countries a feudal discipline was destroyed almost in a day and that all of them embraced the forms and pretensions of Democracy without having the social and industrial organization necessary to support them. As in New Mexico, so all over Latin-America, Spain left a small feudal aristocracy and an illiterate, half-savage proletariat. There was no middle class and Democracy is certainly a product of the middle class. It derives all its strength from those who have a little property and a hope of social advancement. Such a class has just recently begun to appear in Mexico and some of the other countries to the south, bringing with it a measure of stability. As long as there are only hungry demagogues and an ignorant and expropriated peasantry for them to lead, revolution is the inevitable mode of government.

General Manuel Armijo of Albuquerque, who had the honor of presenting New Mexico to the United States, was one of the earliest and one of the most perfect specimens of this Spanish-American demagoguery. His significance is not reduced by the fact that he performed in a small theater and his career has the advantage that it can be examined in detail and in a long restrospect. Although he shed much blood he was essentially and even consciously comic for he was a professing rogue who elevated cowardice to the dignity of a philosophy and practiced treachery as an art. It is almost as though he had set himself to enact a bloody satire on Democracy, war, diplomacy and all the other creaking machineries of government.

Manuel Armijo was born in Albuquerque near the beginning of the nineteenth century. The name belonged to some persons of excellent birth and position and it was also taken by their henchmen. We are assured by Kendall and others that the parents of Manuel were both poor and disreputable. Undoubtedly he came of slave or peon stock and of mixed blood. He was in effect a cross between a mediaeval Spaniard and an American Indian. In person he was large, robust and handsome, endowed with great strength and energy, enormous appetites and a resounding voice. Like most successful politicians he was a gifted actor. He knew how to stage himself and this was perhaps his most important talent but it was not his only one. He had in a high degree that intuitive grasp of the lower human motives which is known as cunning. His gift was to discover and use the weakness in every man and in every class. He looked for a traitor in every group and for a greed or a fear in every individual and he seldom failed to find what he needed. He was an executive of ability and had a gift for words. Wholly uneducated in childhood he taught himself to read and write after he was grown. For political purposes he had an unfailing flow of bombast in the best Spanish tradition and to his cronies he revealed a private philosophy couched in aphorisms, a few of which have been preserved. " God in Heaven and Armijo on earth " was his announced motto, and he laid it down as the rule of his career, from which he never departed, that " it is better to appear brave than to be so."

What he lacked completely was a social conscience. It is impossible to discover that he felt any attachment to any interest but his own. Undoubtedly he was a sincere and thorough-going rebel. Born under the sneer and lash of a decadent and tyrannical aristocracy he repudiated its discipline even as a boy. He aspired, simply and boldly, to take for himself its goods and prerogatives, to live in its houses and possess its women. Doubtless something of this motive is to be found in all rebels but most of those who rise to political power identify themselves with their fellow proletarians. They cannot stand alone and so they make their cause that of a class and even persuade themselves that they are bringing salvation to the entire race. Armijo needed no such delusions and self-justifications. His motives had a magnificent and illuminating simplicity. He was greed and hatred and a sense of inferiority moving toward their compensations and pretending to no other goal. He murdered, stole and lied with good humor and enjoyment. He made no apologies and engaged in no heroisms. When he was scared he ran just as he ate when he was hungry.

To the superstitious ricos he must have seemed a scourge of God. Certainly he brought upon them a sort of poetic retribution for he was exactly what they had made him — an ignorant savage who hated his masters because they had robbed and beaten him. To that extent he was a typical peon but he was one who could see the weakness of the mighty and strike at the right time. With amazing adroitness he took their power away from them and used it for a spoon to feed himself. But that was all he could do except to deliver them into the hands of their enemies and depart with a whole skin and a full belly.

The ruling rico in the neighborhood of Albuquerque, during our hero's boyhood, was Don Francisco Chaves. He was one of the largest sheep-owners in that period when New Mexico contained the greatest sheep herds that ever existed in America. Over hundreds of wilderness miles the sheep of Don Francisco wandered in little rippling, scattering herds, following the spring grass into the mountains, drifting before the autumn snows back to the barren flats, tended by ragged, half-wild men who carried slingshots and packed their homes on burros. Don Francisco probably never counted his sheep but they numbered tens of thousands and most of the poor in his neighborhood were his shepherds. If a poor man possessed a few sheep of his own Don Francisco would buy them for what he chose to pay and drive them to Chihuahua where he made large sales every fall. As no poor man could reach a market unaided Don Francisco in effect owned all the sheep in that part of the country.

Young Armijo, a mere boy, proceeded to remedy this injustice, so far as he was concerned, by devoting himself to stealing Don Francisco's sheep. When the Don went out to buy, Manuel always had sheep to sell and they were always the Don's sheep. After he became governor Armijo boasted that he had sold one old ewe to Don Francisco fourteen times and had stolen her from him in the first place. "So lucrative did young Armijo find the business that in his own neighborhood he gave it an air of respectability," says Kendall.

It is evident that Armijo was doing more than stealing sheep. He was conducting a personal revolution and also building up a political machine. He often bribed the Don's herders and it is safe to guess that soon many of them were working for him more than they were working for the Don. This handsome, boisterous young man would ride into a sheep camp, feast on mutton, pass out pesos and ride away again with what he chose to take.

His rise was rapid. He soon owned both land and a store. He paid for everything in his own goods at an enormous profit and gathered an army of debtors. He must have been one of the first men of lowly birth in New Mexico to achieve the economic status of an aristocrat and it is to be said for his methods that they were probably the only ones possible in the circumstances.

Like all men of destiny he had been born at the right time. The revolution of 1822, which destroyed the Spanish power, must have coincided nearly with his majority. Mexico became a republic and a career was open to any man of brains and energy with no premium on scruples.

How Armijo rose from sheep-stealing to his first political preferments is not a matter of record but it was a logical progression and not hard to imagine. He had many men in his debt and so could command a following. He could make himself useful to the men of transient power who ruled in Mexico City. He had energy and ambition at a time when the ricos of New Mexico were declining in both. He was a realist and they were doctrinaires of a dead idealism. They believed in the dominion of God on earth and he believed only in that of Armijo. With the collapse of the Spanish power the only kind of order they understood had been destroyed. All the records indicate that an apathy, almost a despair, had fallen upon them. They withdrew into their great houses, hoping for a restoration of the old order, wholly unable to cope with the new, just as the survivors of the Diaz regime have done in Mexico since the revolution.

Their catastrophe was Armijo's opportunity. It is said that he consciously modeled his career and character upon those of General Santa Ana. Probably he went to Mexico City and curried favor with that ruthless opportunist of the wooden leg. At any rate he gained minor political appointments and in 1828 he was appointed governor of New Mexico. It was the initial triumph of Democracy in New Mexico, as was the election of Andrew Jackson to the presidency in the United States. But as governor Armijo did not last long. Probably his administration was too corrupt even for the revolutionary government in Mexico. He was in power less than a year and was then permitted to retire to his estates for a long rest.

2

About the year 1835 opportunity came along again. Reaction prevailed in Mexico City and it promulgated a new system of government by which the country was divided into departments instead of provinces, chiefly for purposes of taxation. New Mexico now belonged to the Department of the North and a Mexican gentleman by the name of Albino Perez was sent from Mexico City to govern in Santa Fe. Perez was the first outsider who had been made governor in New Mexico since the revolution and he was resented. Moreover, it was his hard duty to enforce a new system of direct taxation. Heretofore, the New Mexicans had paid only import duties on their goods. This tariff had always been a robbery but they had been used to it for generations. The prospect of direct taxation stirred the whole country to discontent. For the first time since the rebellion of the Pueblos New Mexico was in a revolutionary mood. It was intensified by the fact that Perez maintained an expensive court in Santa Fe with a great retinue while drought and small pox ravished the country and the Navajos locked men into their own houses, set them on fire and rode away with sheep and women.

Armijo was always on the side of the strong as long as they paid him. He was given the post of revenue collector under Perez but presently he lost it. Doubtless again his shameless stealing was too much for his superiors. He retired to Albuquerque a disgruntled and dangerous man.

Some of the ricos were disgruntled too. They hated Perez but they didn't know what to do about it. Armijo did. It is said he made a bargain with three men of the gentry by which he was paid to go about fomenting revolution. Everything was done in such deep secrecy that nothing certain is known about it. Probably the aristocrats planned only to use Armijo's cunning and his influence with the peasantry for their own ends, not knowing what a dangerous man they had to deal with. At any rate, Armijo was presently deep in a plan to promote rebellion, working through agents and keeping his own hand concealed.

Now his great gift of demagoguery was seen at its best. He knew the credulity of his public and he had a talent for dramatic invention. He spread the word that the new system of taxation would invade the privacy of every life. Every time that a chicken laid an egg, he let it be known, a duty would have to be paid upon it. Every time that a man embraced his wife he would have to report the fact and pay a luxury tax and there would be spies and agents to see that the law was enforced.

The mood of revolution grew. It spread from the paisanos to the Pueblo Indians. Ever since the conquest there had been a belief among them that they would some day smash the Spanish power and that a fighting race would come from the east to help them. This belief now crystallized in a plan of rebellion with a hope that the Texans would come to their aid. The plot had its greatest strength in the north where the Penitent Brothers put their heads together in the windowless secrecy of their Moradas and the Taos khiva once more sheltered plotting war chiefs and medicine men prophesying bloodshed, as it had in the days of Popé.

A trifle started the revolt. A poor man had been arrested for debt and the local Alcalde had released him. One Ramon Abreu, an officer of the government under Perez, who had come with him from Mexico City, had the Alcalde arrested. A roaring mob of Pueblos and Mexicans descended on the gaol and released the prisoner. A Taos Pueblo by the name of Gonzales, a buffalo hunter by trade, was chosen leader. He proclaimed a revolution and called a meeting of all the Alcaldes he could reach. They endorsed everything he had done for there were no forces to resist him. He was the de facto government of New Mexico.

In this revolt Armijo had not shown his hand at all. Yet secretly he had fomented it and from behind the scenes he had directed it. Subsequent confessions and certain documents show that both he and Padre Martinez of Taos were present at a meeting of the revolutionaries and that he served as a member of a committee to draft the grievances of the people. Immediately after the meeting he returned to Albuquerque and was living quietly at home when the trouble began. It seems certain that he deliberately planned and started a revolution without openly committing himself to it and with the purpose of joining whichever side would profit him most.

Evidently he decided at once that the cause of the people was no longer his. It is said that Gonzales talked openly of sending to the Texans for help. If so this probably alienated both Armijo and the Padre for both of them hated the Texans. Besides, Armijo must have seen that Gonzales and his rabble could not stand against any force that might be sent from Mexico City. Before his carefully planned revolution had fired its first gun he had seen clearly that his own fortune was to be made by putting it down.

Gonzales established his headquarters at La Canada de Santa Cruz, an admirably defensible position a few miles from Santa Fe. Governor Perez called for volunteers to march against the rebels but got almost no response. The Santa Fe militia had been disbanded for lack of pay. The Captain of the troop called upon all loyal citizens to meet in Bernalillo, organize their forces and choose a leader.

Meanwhile Perez had recruited a small force from Santo Domingo and other Pueblos to the south. Gonzales had all of the Taos Pueblos and those of many other northern villages in his own ranks. The Pueblo Indians were expected to do the fighting for both sides, chiefly because they were the only forces available. They were organized after a fashion, had some arms and were willing to fight, while the Mexicans were deficient in all three respects.

At the head of his Indians Perez marched against the rebels. Near Pojoaque he was ambushed and at the first

fire all of his forces except about twenty-five men went
over to the enemy. The Pueblos declined to fight each
other. Gonzales was victorious without a battle. Perez
got back to Santa Fe but gave up all hope of holding the
capital and started south for help. He was intercepted
and killed by the Gonzales forces, now a yelling, pillaging
mob. They cut off his head and carried it to camp where
they played football with it while Gonzales took the governor's property as his own. About a dozen other officers
of the government were killed. Don Santiago Abreu,
brother of Ramon, was captured by the Santo Domingo
Indians. They put him in the stocks, cut off his hands and
feet one by one, shaking them in his face, pulled out his
tongue, gouged out his eyes and capered around him till
he died. The ancient hatred born of the conquest once
more tasted blood. Armijo had released a savage fury.

The whole of the lower river country was in a panic.
It was fully expected that Gonzales and his mob would
descend upon this stronghold of the ricos and kill and
pillage, perhaps with a force of Texans to back them up.
There were no troops to resist them. Apparently there
was no one to lead. But someone sent out a call for all the
men of the best families to meet at the village of Tomé.

Tomé had long been the most important town in the
lower valley — a place where great fiestas were held and
all the fine people came to trade. Even then it was decadent. The Navajos had sacked it and killed many people.
Small pox had taken more. The town still stands today —
a few crumbling adobe houses and an ancient church
grouped about a soggy plaza where stagnant seepage
water gathers in the streets.

Here came all the ricos in desperation — Pereas, Chaveses, Romeros, Bacas — descendants of the conquerors, bewildered, frightened and unorganized. And here came also General Manuel Armijo, not so well born but a man of property and power. In an interview given when he was an old man one of the Pereas described the meeting as it had been described to him by his father. It appears that for a time no one knew what to do or say. Then Don Mariano Chaves arose and proposed that General Armijo be appointed to organize a force and defend them all against the rebels. It is probable that at this meeting were all the ricos who had backed Armijo in the plot against Perez and that they dared not desert him now because he knew too much. The rest were apathetic. Armijo's nomination was neither opposed nor applauded. No other name was suggested. No one else wanted the job. Armijo, the sheep-thief, the upstart of peon blood, was chosen by the ricos without a dissenting voice to their defender.

He at least knew what to do. As soon as he was empowered he went about the valley, invaded every house and seized all the guns he could find, at the same time impressing into his service all able-bodied men of the peasant class. With all the man-power and all the arms in his hands he departed for Santa Fe, taking over the forces gathered at Bernalillo on the way. Don Perea testifies that many of the best families, his own included, packed up all their valuables and followed, for the General had left them absolutely defenseless. They were dependent upon him now for their very lives.

Arrived at Santa Fe Armijo issued a proclamation in

which he formally accepted the responsibilities of governor and commanding general, "an assignment which I could not refuse without failing in the duty of a citizen highly interested in the happiness of his country." He concluded this and all of his other pronunciamentos with the words " God and Liberty."

A small detachment of dragoons had come from Mexico City to assist him and also a representative of the civil government who gave him some sort of endorsement. Approved and re-enforced he marched against the Gonzales troops and found them, an unorganized, half-armed rabble, entrenched in the canyon at Santa Cruz.

It is said that Armijo took one look at his enemies and pronounced their position invulnerable. He was afraid to attack. The Captain of the Mexican dragoons was disgusted. He said that with the General's permission he would undertake to rout the rebels with his own troops alone. Armijo graciously gave him leave, the dragoons charged and the rebel army scattered in the mountains, except for a few who were killed and captured.

Among those taken was Gonzales, the rebel leader, who had sat with Armijo in council as a fellow conspirator a few weeks before. He came forward with extended hand, confident of mercy. " How do you do, Companero? " he greeted the general. "How do you do, Companero," Armijo answered with great cordiality. " Confess yourself, Companero," he added. And then, turning toward his aides: "Now shoot my Companero! " It was immediately done. Gonzales knew too much.

Armijo was always uneasy on the field of battle but as a dictator he was at home. He at once organized a court martial, found four more leaders of the revolution guilty and had them shot in Santa Fe. It is said that he had many others secretly assassinated. Probably all that knew of the double part he had played were planted deep.

3

The sheep-thief now was ruler of New Mexico and no more absolute despot ever sat in the chair of power. In Mexico City he was regarded as a patriot who had put down a dangerous rebellion and saved a province for the republic. He was confirmed as governor and with one brief interruption he held the place for eight years. Moreover, his glory was still to grow for he was to save his province for the government once more and this time from the feared and hated Texans.

Texas then was a republic and one of the most aggressive and optimistic young nations that ever lived. It claimed the Rio Grande as its western border and if this claim had been allowed most of New Mexico, including Santa Fe, would have been a part of Texas. President Lamar decided to take formal possession of this disputed part of his domain. A troop of three hundred men was organized and sent across the plains. It was armed by the government of Texas, it carried goods for trade and it was accompanied by three commissioners who bore proclamations in two languages designed to explain to the inhabitants of New Mexico the great advantages of accepting the Texan administration. The avowed plan was not to make war. The Texans believed that as soon as the proclamations were read all the New Mexicans would become loyal citizens of Texas and the lone star would be hoisted in Santa Fe. If the New Mexicans objected the Texans were to sell their goods and return peacably home.

It was a bold plan but it failed to take account of several facts. Mexico had never conceded the Texan claim to New Mexico, the Texans had every appearance of an army of invasion, and Armijo, who was milking the government in Santa Fe, had everything to lose by their success.

No one ever caught the General asleep. He knew of the Texan expedition long before it reached New Mexico and immediately he made two moves. He sent an officer by the name of Damasio Salazar with about one hundred men to patrol his eastern border and he sent out his agents among the people to tell them all about the invaders. He gave the natives to understand that the Texans were a terrible and ruthless race of infidels who murdered men and raped women on sight and would pillage the whole country.

The Texans were unlucky from the start. Their story was told in detail by a young New Orleans newspaperman named Kendall who went with them. They did not know the way across the prairies and soon were lost and out of provisions. Moreover they could not find game. They became completely demoralized and drifted across the plains like a flock of starving crows, greedily seizing everything that would serve as food. Snakes and terrapins and wild berries helped to keep them alive before they reached the Pecos River.

Three men — Howland, Baker and Rosenbury — had

been sent ahead to negotiate with Armijo. It was a foolish move. Armijo promptly took them prisoners and pumped them for information. He had known Howland before and he tried to bribe the man to betray his companions. Howland refused to tell anything and the three tried to escape. Baker was killed and the other two retaken after Howland had been slashed with a saber so that one whole side of his face was almost cut off.

Meanwhile another group of five men, including Kendall and a Texan named Lewis, had been sent ahead to reconnoiter. Salazar came upon these, surrounded them and took them prisoner with the most accomplished treachery. He told them that if they would give up their arms they would be permitted to trade and return to Texas. As soon as they were helpless he lined them up before a firing squad and was about to shoot them all when a neighboring rico by the name of Vigil came to their rescue and persuaded Salazar to let them live. They were then imprisoned in the town of San Miguel on the Pecos River.

Kendall says that at first the common Mexicans trembled and turned pale at sight of them for Armijo had made his subjects believe that all Texans were agents of the devil. But when they discovered that the captives were merely a few hungry and bewildered young men the paisanos were all compassion. The women and girls especially came to the house where they were kept, bringing eggs and tortillas and milk, staying to talk and flirt. The prisoners, who had nearly starved for weeks, now were fairly stuffed. If they did not eat everything offered their gentle visitors were insulted. Even their guards were kind and while Salazar was away they held shooting matches with the bows and arrows of his soldiers. At night they built a huge fire, told stories, sang songs and entertained the girls. They had no notion what Armijo would do with them but they enjoyed their precarious existence while it lasted.

After a few days the great General arrived and granted them an audience. Kendall says that Armijo was a truly splendid figure, over six feet tall, powerful and portly. His mount was a huge dun mule, caparisoned like the charger of a mediaeval knight. He wore a blue military coat of the finest broad cloth, a cocked hat with a plume and a blue serape embroidered in gold and silver. He informed the Texans that he was a great warrior, that he had thousands of men under arms and that he was prepared to resist invasion to the last man. His visible army consisted of a few hundred ragged peons and several ancient cannon drawn by oxen who lay down in the road and chewed their cuds when the army paused. He proceeded to recruit his force by impressing into his service the entire male population of San Miguel. Most of his troops were armed like Indians with bows and lances.

He brought with him the two captives, Howland and Rosenbury, and having failed to seduce either of them by bribery he proceeded to have them executed before the eyes of their companions. Kendall caught a brief glimpse of Howland. One whole side of his head was a mass of blood but he had not lost his nerve. As he passed them on his way to death he turned and smiled with the other side of his face. " Good-bye, boys," he said " I've got to suffer." He was then made to kneel outside the window of their prison and shot in the back. Rosenbury was also executed and the bodies were dragged out upon the prairie to be eaten by coyotes or perhaps buried by some pious peon. The rest of the Texans were bound and marched to Santa Fe. One of the Mexican girls who had befriended them went into hysterics when her gringo lover was led away.

Meanwhile Armijo had asked for one of the men to act as interpreter. Lewis, who knew Spanish well, volunteered. After a brief consultation with him Armijo had him unbound and mounted upon a horse. He had found what he was looking for — a traitor.

The main body of the Texans reached the Pecos in two detachments a few days apart, having heard nothing from any of their advance agents. The first of these, like the advance guard, was met by Salazar and his forces, accompanied by Lewis. Salazar assured the leader, Captain Cooke, that the Texans would be well treated if they gave up their arms. Lewis advised his compatriots to surrender, telling them that the whole country was up in arms and that they were helpless in any case. Cooke made him swear on his honor as a Mason that he was telling the truth. The Texans then gave up their arms. Immediately they were searched and bound with ropes and they then listened to a long discussion among their captors as to whether they should be executed on the spot or taken to Mexico City as captives. The latter plan won by a single vote. Cursing Lewis, they were marched away. The second detachment of Texans was taken by a similar ruse. The whole troop was marched to Mexico City with the exception of a few who were killed on the way by Salazar

and his men just for fun. All of the survivors were finally
released by the Mexican government.

This episode gained Armijo great credit with his superiors in Mexico City. Without firing a shot, except for
purposes of execution, he had taken prisoner a force
of three hundred armed men who had every appearance
of being an army of invasion. He was now at the height of
his power but he was not yet done with the Texans. They
made one desperate effort to get revenge. A troop was
fitted out under a Colonel Warfield and marched upon
New Mexico. The plan this time was to waylay a wagon
train that belonged to Armijo. The Texans had reason
to believe that he would be with it and they proposed to
make off with both his goods and his person. Warfield was
supplied with arms by the Texas government and he
seems to have had somewhat the status of an Elizabethan
privateer.

Armijo again knew all about his enemies' intentions
long before they made a move and again luck was all on
his side. He sent an advance guard of a hundred men,
mostly Taos Pueblos, to meet the invaders. The Texans
gave them five minutes to decide whether to fight or surrender. Their leaders chose to fight although some of the
mercenaries had to be tied onto their horses to keep them
from running. The terrible invaders then charged and
almost wiped them out in fifteen minutes of brutal hand-
to-hand fighting. General Armijo was camped with a
much larger force forty miles to the rear but when he
heard of the battle he beat a frantic retreat, leaving the
road littered with hats, quirts and other impedimenta.
He imagined the Texans were hard on his trail. So they

would have been if a troop of United States cavalry, escorting a wagon train, had not come along and arrested the Warfield command for being on American soil. As a matter of fact they were still in Texas but they were compelled to give up their arms until they disbanded. Armijo reached home safely in a dead run and again was able to report a great military triumph to Mexico City.

4

In Santa Fe he had established himself by this time as an absolute monarch. He was not only the governor but also the commanding general, the legislature, the customs service, the judiciary and the treasury. His administrative genius was chiefly devoted to getting the largest possible amount of money out of the customs. Finding that an ad valorem duty did not pay enough to suit him, he levied a tax of five hundred dollars on each wagon that entered the territory. The wily traders loaded one wagon with the goods from three at the frontier, burned the other two wagons and thumbed their noses at the general. He then went back to the old system.

Sporadically he made war upon the Apaches and whenever one was killed he cut off the Indian's ears. For a time the Mexican government paid a bounty on dead Apaches. To impress all with his prowess as an Indian fighter the General festooned his office with long strings of drying Apache ears. At the same time he was accused of selling guns to the Apaches in Chihuahua.

His court was maintained with the utmost dignity. A soldier with a musket paced back and forth before the door of his office in the old palace. When Armijo came out this man would shout: " The governor and commanding general appears! " The cry would be taken up by guards stationed at intervals about the plaza so that the General moved to an incessant clamor and all were required to get out of his way. Often he stopped to beat with his cane someone whose conduct did not seem sufficiently respectful.

His wife was an enormously fat woman who kept a retinue of lovers and at the same time acted as her husband's chief pimp. When she walked abroad the feminine equivalent of the general's official titles had to be shouted by all the guards and all had to stand aside while " La gobernadora," a blowsey squaw, marched down the street with her nose in the air.

The testimony is unanimous that this pair were hated by rich and poor alike. Once a prominent rico waited for hours outside the General's door with the avowed purpose of putting an arrow in his heart but Armijo was the more patient of the two. That he escaped assassination is surely a proof of his cunning. Only the complete demoralization of the aristocracy can explain the fact that he did not face a rebellion.

Only once did the ricos threaten to organize against him and it was not his corrupt administration but his lecherous career among their women that provoked the attempt. The General devoted most of his leisure to his amours and especially to the rape and seduction of women of gentle birth. Not only his wife but many of his military and civil subordinates were his panders. More than one husband who stood in his way disappeared suddenly and forever while others achieved promotions and emoluments.

Soledad Abreu, daughter of that Santiago who had died in the stocks at Santo Domingo, was the girl who gave him trouble. She was fifteen years old when the General's eye first fell upon her and Mexican girls of fifteen are women ripe for love. Soledad spurned the General and did it in a loud voice so that everyone knew he had been thwarted. But he was both patient and resourceful. He found that Soledad was in love with a young officer named Esquipula Caballero. He encouraged the match and himself attended the wedding and drank the bride's health. Then he opened to Esquipula large possibilities of advancement and wealth with Soledad as the only consideration. It was a method that had worked often before but this time it didn't work at all. Esquipula behaved like the perfect hero of romance. He told the governor to go to hell and defied him to do his worst.

Armijo acted without delay. He first degraded Caballero to the ranks and then had him jailed and put in irons on the charge that he had tried to foment a mutiny. Finding Soledad still invulnerable he moved against her uncle, a young officer named Ramon Baca who was Caballero's best friend. On some trumped up charge he ordered this man into exile.

To Baca belongs the distinction of making the only attempt to overthrow the General. A day had been appointed for him to leave the country and meantime he was at liberty. He announced that he would not go, that he would kill Armijo or die trying. With his sword buckled on he walked the plaza in Santa Fe soliciting recruits for a rebellion. Even under Armijo's window he button-holed brother officers and begged for their support. Most of them, in true Mexican fashion, agreed to all he proposed. They would be ready with men and arms on the day set for Baca to go into exile. Victory looked easy. Everyone hated the General. At the first shot most of his supporters would desert. But when the day came Baca found himself an army of one. The stuff of rebellion simply was not in the ricos. Baca might have done better if he had gone to the Indians and the common pelados. The weary aristocrats no longer cared for desperate chances or believed in better governments. Baca finally assembled a few of his brother officers, made them a sarcastic speech of farewell and rode alone into exile. Armijo was told of the aborted plot, sent after Baca, had him arrested and threw him into jail with Caballero. He then sent both of them to Mexico City to be tried for treason. But these were young men of important families. In Chihuahua they were released through the influence of powerful friends. They went on to Mexico City as free men and preferred charges against Armijo, determined to 'show the government just what sort of man he was. Luck saved him. It was just then that the Texans marched against New Mexico and Armijo persuaded the central government that but for him the whole province would be lost.

For a few more years the General sat secure, rewarding himself with the public revenues, pursuing his lecheries unmolested, growing enormously fat in person and overbearing in manner. Then in 1846 came war between the

United States and Mexico. General Stephen W. Kearney marched upon Santa Fe with something over fifteen hundred men, mostly volunteers gathered in Missouri. He camped near Bent's Fort on the Arkansas and sent to Santa Fe as his emissary a Captain Cooke, who was unofficially but importantly accompanied by a wealthy Irishman, long resident in New Mexico, by the name of James Magoffin.

The exact facts about the bloodless conquest of New Mexico and the last public acts of General Armijo are still obscured by doubt and secrecy. It is certain that the great majority of the people — the Indians and the paisanos — felt no allegiance to the Mexican government. The wagon trade had taught them to know and like the Americanos. Some of them welcomed the change, some were indifferent and probably many of them did not understand what was happening. Most of the ricos were loyal to Mexico but they were a hopeless people, ridden by tyranny, unable to resist. Only Armijo and the rest of the politicians, who fed like buzzards on the dying provincial government, really had anything to lose by Conquest.

When he heard of Kearney's approach Armijo, on August 8, issued a magnificent proclamation, calling for volunteers. " At last the moment has arrived when our country requires of her children a decision without limit, a sacrifice without reserve, under circumstances which demand everything for our salvation."

Such was his first paragraph and the rest of the composition sustains its tone of lofty eloquence. Quickly he gathered a force of several thousand men and a few cannon and prepared to make his stand in Apache canyon, fifteen miles from Santa Fe. This position was chosen with judgment and fortified with skill. It was almost impregnable by nature and he strengthened it with breastworks and with an abbatis of tree trunks set in the earth, their sharpened ends toward the enemy. His cannon were planted in the pass and troops were stationed on the mountainside above its narrow walls. Military experts testify that a hundred men might have held the position against thousands. Everything was set for a glorious defense.

On August 12 Captain Cooke entered Santa Fe under a flag of truce, accompanied by the aforesaid Magoffin —a large smiling Irishman, celebrated for his wit and his hospitality. During many years of residence in the country he had become almost one of the ricos and was the friend of most of them. He had been doing missionary work among them, preparing their minds for a change of government, trying to convince them that it was inevitable. It is hinted that he had handled certain funds which were never accounted for, either as to source or as to disposition, but which helped greatly to keep the government in Santa Fe friendly to the wagon traders from Missouri. It is also said that on this occasion he carried a large sum of money which had its source in Washington and has never been the subject of any public accounting.

Cooke and Magoffin conferred at length with General Armijo and returned to the troops. These marched on to Las Vegas and then, with some trepidation, approached the position of General Armijo at Apache Pass. Advance guards reconnoitered. They found all of the fortifications ready, just as had been reported, but the army was missing. Word came to them presently that the General had dismissed his forces, spiked his cannon and departed for the City of Mexico. There was not a man to meet the invasion.

Kearney marched into Santa Fe unresisted, was entertained by Lieutenant-governor Vigil, read a proclamation and hoisted the stars and stripes. Vigil gave the allegiance of the entire province to the United States of America. "Do not find it strange if there has been no manifestation of joy and enthusiasm in seeing this city occupied by your military forces," he said. "To us the power of the Mexican republic is dead."

The power of the Mexican republic had departed rapidly southward in the person of a fat middle-aged general named Armijo. Whether he ran because he was scared or because he was bribed will never be certainly known. Whatever his motives his departure was perfectly consistent with his whole career and it had a sort of shameless wisdom about it. He ran to save his skin and maybe to bulge his pocket but he also saved many lives besides his own. He expedited the inevitable when a brave and honorable man would only have delayed it a little while by pouring blood across its path.

Ruxton, the wandering Englishman, gives us our parting glimpse of General Armijo. The year after his masterly retreat from Apache Pass, Ruxton met him near Durango in Mexico. Armijo, he says, had become a mountain of fat. He was traveling toward Durango with seven American wagons loaded with merchandise and his first question was about the prices of cotton cloth at his destination. He and Ruxton chatted for a long time about this and that. Just before they parted Armijo asked casually what was being said in New Mexico about him and his departure. Ruxton replied it was the unanimous opinion that Armijo and all of his followers were a pack of arrant cowards.

" For the love of God! Don't they know that I had but seventy-five men with which to face three thousand? "

With this final lie, with a shrug and a wave of the hand, the General heaved his bulk upon a wagon seat and went his way.

He died in 1853, when the legislature of the territory of New Mexico was in session. One of the members, Dr. Henry Connelly, had been a friend of Armijo. There is reason to believe that he had a sense of humor. At any rate he offered a resolution " that this council has heard with profound regret of the death of our distinguished citizen, General Armijo . . . that in respect to the memory and distinguished services of General Armijo this council now adjourn until ten o'clock tomorrow."

The resolution was unanimously passed and it remains inscribed upon the records of the State as an immortal tribute to a man who never compromised his principles.

X

The Man of God

∿∿∿∿∿∿∿∿∿∿∿∿∿∿∿∿∿∿∿

1

MANY Gods now live at peace along the Rio Grande. All the Gods of the Pueblos still are potent and send rain and babies when their people dance. Gods still live in the bottomless sacred Lake near Taos and the Indians of Taos wait for a day when the antelope and the buffalo shall come back by that blue door from Shipapu. The Hopi priests still dance with sacred rattlesnakes in their mouths and the Navajos worship fire in a dance of burning brands about a flame. The Penitent Brothers still bow their bloody backs before a skull. The Church of Rome is still the faith of most of the native people and almost every Protestant sect has both its churches and its missions. Now there are Methodist Mexicans and Baptist Pueblos. Worship is undeniably free, whether or not it is fervent.

All the Gods are still alive but they have grown a little weary. They sit peaceably side by side and compromise with one another. The Church frowns upon the idolatries of the Indians but it closes its eyes when they dance so long as they are married in the church and come to

Mass. The Christian government of the United States officially asks visitors to the Indian dances "not to encourage these ceremonies" but the ceremonies still go on. Even the Ku Klux Klan could not stir up much feeling here.

Certainly the great days of the gods are over — the days when priests died for Christ in the wilderness, Spanish soldiers slaughtered infidels and Indians tore down churches, murdered friars and scrubbed the taint of Christian baptism off their heads with the root of wild amole.

The gods are still alive but they are no longer terrible and being a man of God is not the splendid adventure that once it was.

Perhaps the gods have weakened because they no longer drink blood. In the old days they were well nourished. Most of the blood poured out upon this country was for some god or other. Nearly every war and rebellion had some religious motive. Every other man who died a violent death was an infidel to the man who killed him.

Padre Martinez of Taos was a man of God who lived the transition from the old ways to the new. He was born at the wrong time. By temperament and conviction he belonged to that great age when religion was a power that transcended all human restraint, when priestcraft was the greatest art, when faith was a thing that justified whatever was done in its name. For a little while he created a miniature of that mediaeval world and ruled it. The Taos massacre, in which he played such an obscure but important part, was among other things the last avowed effort to exterminate infidels here. And he

uniquely proved both the quality of his faith and that of
his egotism when he accepted excommunication rather
than submit to men, founded a church of his own and
served God in defiance of the Pope until he died.

Padre Martinez is a rare and significant character im-
perfectly revealed by his record. A supremely secretive
man he covered his tracks with care. He must remain
enigmatic but a few of his characteristics stand out
clearly. Beyond a doubt he loved power above all other
things. He probably thought of God chiefly as a source
of power. He was an uncompromising individualist. He
would serve none but God and he would serve God only
in his own way. There is little doubt that he was the most
intelligent man of his time and place. All of his recorded
words are full of wisdom. He denounced the granting of
land to wealthy men in huge tracts when the poor were
landless and in so doing he was denouncing the privileges
of the class that produced him. He denounced the heavy
tithes by which the Church was pauperizing the people
and he refused to collect them in his own parish. It is
said that he even spoke openly for freedom of worship.
He believed in education and founded schools when
many men of wealth could not write their names. He
saw the great possibilities of journalism, owned the first
printing press that was brought to New Mexico and
printed the first newspaper. He was an idealist and potentially a reformer but above all he was an egotist. He believed in change but he wanted to bring it about himself and in his own way. All through his active life change
was marching steadily upon New Mexico. First it came
in wagons and then with an army and finally with a gov-

ernment and a population. The Americans promised many things that he professed — religious liberty and education and a free press — but their coming meant the end of his power. Therefore he hated them. He preached against them. Finally he plotted against them. He dreamed of a sea of blood. He planned so craftily that although every record of the Taos massacre credits him with its leadership his enemies could never get any evidence against him. By craft and stubborn courage he survived all changes. By sheer personal force he created his own environment and sustained it until he died. His immense vitality alone entitles him to be remembered.

By birth he belonged to the aristocracy. His father bore the title of a General and came to New Mexico from Chihuahua in the early eighteenth century. The Padre was born in Abique, west of the Rio Grande, in 1793, and christened Antonio José Martinez. He married early and begot a daughter. Both wife and child died in a few years and young Antonio entered a Seminary in Durango where he spent six years studying for the priesthood. Having lost his loved ones he dedicated himself to sorrow and to God — perhaps. It seems more probable that a little of domesticity and farming had been more than enough for young Martinez with his eager mind and his longing to dominate. Ambitious men then always entered either the church or the army and if they had intellect it was the church they chose.

Antonio, like all Mexicans, was deeply rooted in his native soil. He came back to New Mexico, served briefly as presbyter in various parishes and in 1830 became the curate of Taos with several churches and an assistant.

He donned the robe when the priesthood in New Mexico was at its worst. In Taos he succeeded the Franciscan brothers who were leaving the province after centuries of heroic service. Most of the priests who followed the conquerors and explorers were Franciscans. They were the ones who stayed in the wilderness to preach of Christ until the Indians killed them. They had built most of the missions. They had made whatever sincere converts there were among the Pueblos and many of them the Indians had come to love. But when the conquest was over the life of a priest in New Mexico became an easy and an empty thing. He preached to Indians who listened politely and then went back to their dances and their idols and planted a prayer plume more often than they knelt to God. He preached to paisanos whose real church was a Penitente Morada with its skull and cross bones. He preached of Christ and the Virgin of Guadalupe was the true goddess of all Mexico. She was a purely native deity born of a native legend. Her image was to be seen in every church and in almost every saloon. Christ was only one God among many to the primitive New Mexicans. They carried his image into the fields when they wanted rain and they planted a cross to protect the crops from storm. They adopted Christ and God Almighty into their native pantheon and asked them to be useful along with the other gods. All of the poor and many of the rich believed in witches. As late as 1853 an Alcalde bound a man over to answer to the district court on a charge of witchcraft and the judge was hard put to explain that no such crime existed.

For an ambitious and intelligent priest New Mexico

was barren ground, and doubtless it tended to get the worst of the Church, but it would have required an almost superhuman power to triumph against the primitive inertia of the country. The wilderness conquers its conquerors. The primitive spirit works on a man as opium does, transforming him subtly. Just as the ricos absorbed the blood and color of their Navajo slaves and enemies, just as the mountain men learned to kneel at sacred springs and scalp the fallen foe, so padres in lonely missions became like those they were supposed to teach. With one eye on the clouds they prayed for rain, competing with medicine men, pitting Christ against the Gods of thunder and lightning. What the people loved about the church was its gaudy ceremonials. Their parishes were poor at best so the priests took what they could by pocketing heavy fees for weddings, christenings and funerals. The Christian ideals of chastity and monogamy meant nothing to their flocks and finally meant no more to them. They had not merely mistresses but harems. " It is not unusual for one to have three or four wives," wrote Frank M. Edwards, one of Kearney's volunteers. Their women served them like slaves, kissed their hands and the hems of their robes, knelt when they passed in the streets, boasted of the children they bore them. It was no unusual thing to see a priest, robed and tonsured, shaking a sandaled foot at a baile or bucking a monte game. The worst of them sank deep in primitive sloth, living dirty and barefoot among their women and brats, drinking huge quantities of red wine. The more sensitive were often epicures who chose both women and wine with care. That credulous young romantic, Lieutenant

Zebulon Pike of the United States Army, was entertained
in Albuquerque by the curate, Father Ambrosio Guerra.
The gallant Lieutenant was surprised by the cool adobe
comfort of the Padre's house and by the excellence of
his wine and meat and he was still more surprised to find
him surrounded by pretty young girls whom the Padre
introduced as his adopted nieces. Father Guerra was a
veritable connoisseur of nieces. He had Mexican girls,
girls of several Indian tribes, French girls and two who
appeared to be English. All of them were shapely and
handsomely dressed. The Padre hospitably bade the two
whitest girls embrace the delighted Lieutenant and he
and his guest were then served by three of the nieces,
" who, like Hebe at the feast of the Gods, converted our
wine into nectar and with their ambrosial breath, shed
incense on our cups." Anyway, the Lieutenant had a
good time.

Of their ecclesiastical superiors outside the province
these padres knew almost nothing. When Bishop Zubiria
visited Santa Fe in 1833 it was the first time in seventy-
one years that a prelate of his rank had been in New
Mexico. He is described as a devout man who was at
once appalled by the condition of the clergy and touched
by the piety of the people. Christ on his second coming
could hardly have created more of a stir. Bridges were
decorated, arches were built, the very roads he traveled
were swept. Every householder hung from his windows
the finest fabrics he had — Navajo and Chimayo blankets, embroidered serapes, silken shawls. As the Bishop,
robed and mitered, walked the streets, all the people fell
upon their knees and remained with downcast eyes until

he had blessed them or passed on. Even those of highest rank knelt and kissed his ring before they spoke. The church had lost nothing of its power.

2

It was doubtless this power that Padre Antonio José Martinez loved. Nor did he fear the primitive character of the country and the people. Presumably he might have gone to Mexico City or even to Spain, but instead he asked to be sent to Taos, the heart of primitive New Mexico, the place where the Penitent Brothers were strongest, where Popé had nursed his plot and where his dream of Indian empire had never been forgotten.

Every man with a yearning for power must perceive, more or less clearly, a choice of destinies. He may go to the centers of civilization to struggle with his peers and perhaps feel the strength of better men or he may fatten his self-esteem with easy victories on smaller fields. The Padre, whether consciously or not, had chosen the easy way.

Taos was long a walled town and doubtless the wall still stood when Padre Martinez first went there. In all essentials it was like the walled towns of mediaeval Europe — a self-contained social unit ruled by church and aristocracy. Taos is still the same cluster of adobe houses about a plaza on a hill with a lovely green valley spread about it and mountains lifting to rocky peaks six thousand feet above. It still has the look of a place apart from the world but its wall has long since fallen. It was built for defense against the Indians but Indians became

steadily less of a menace and no wall would stop the new
invaders. It never stopped the mountain men nor the
traders from Missouri. Little by little the wall crumbled
and disappeared and its decay was a symbol, but when
Padre Martinez went there, a lean young priest hungry
for power, the wall still stood. Kit Carson had come just
a few years before, a ragged young bullwhacker without
a penny or even a good gun. Lucien Maxwell, who was
to rule two thousand square miles just across the mountain, was another like him and Charles Bent, who was to
become governor of the province and die in the massacre,
was a poor Indian trader.

Padre Martinez knew these men and he covertly hated
them. From first to last he was uncompromisingly against
the Americanos and it must have been his foresight that
made him so. He knew they would break down the wall.
He did everything he could to turn his simple parishioners against them. He corresponded with ricos all over the
province, seeking to hold them together in an alliance
against the gringos. For within the walls of Taos the
Padre's power steadily grew. He was the religious head
of this principality, he was a little pope in a little Rome.
He preached not only in Taos but in several neighboring churches and not only in churches but in Penitente
Moradas.

What the Padre wanted was power and in that country
he had to stoop for it. The Penitentes were only nominally Catholics. They were a primitive sect of death-
worshipers. They were also, in a measure, a league of
the common people against their masters but they were
potentially a great political machine. They were highly

organized and completely obedient to their leaders. A man who could command the allegiance of the Hermano Mayor, the ruling brother, could command the whole chapter. Through a few score men he could rule thousands.

Padre Martinez was probably the first man of rank and influence to use the Penitentes as a source of personal power but he was not the last. The Republican machine in New Mexico long drew much of its strength from the Penitente vote and it still cultivates the bloody brothers. Ambitious Yankee politicians have walked barefoot in Penitente processions for the sake of votes and these may be said to have walked in the Padre's footsteps. But not too literally. It is doubtful whether he ever had to walk in any processions but he must have seen many a man bound to the cross. Every holy week he heard the shrill scream of the petate and the uproar of the tinieblas. In many a dark Morada he stood before the primitive altar with its human skull and its cart of death and preached to men half-naked and soaked in their own blood. He was a genuinely learned man who believed in education and justice. But he was also one who wanted to rule and a man who wants power must take it where he can find it.

In Taos he was not only a religious despot and a political boss but also a man of property. He owned wide lands which he farmed on shares so that many of his parishioners were also his renters and debtors. He had a large house near the plaza, built about a courtyard, and there he established a school to train young men for the priesthood. At one time he had forty pupils. There is abundant evidence that he was a magnetic man. These youths were attached to him personally, they were sharers of his convictions. Doubtless he looked forward to a time when every pulpit in New Mexico would be filled with his disciples — if only his power was not destroyed by change.

In addition to his boys' school the Padre had a class for girls. This must have been one of his most startling innovations for girls even of the best families often never learned to read.

Women were necessary to care for the Padre's great establishment. How many of them were his mistresses it is impossible to say but like other priests of his day he had a harem. One woman, named Theodora, seems to have achieved a sort of social recognition as his consort. She lived with him many years and bore him several children. Most of his descendants have been proud to acknowledge his paternity. One of his sons became a Presbyterian minister and one of his grandsons is a man of means and political power. All of his children were well educated and well cared for. He was a good padre in the flesh as well as in the spirit.

Taos is still full of stories about the Padre and it is hard to separate the true from the apocryphal but his friends and foes are agreed that he ruled the town with autocratic and absolute power. He was unwilling that anything be done without his approval — and his disapproval was a dangerous thing. It is said that he would go into the courts, sit down beside the judge and dictate decisions. It is also told that one Alcalde on such an occasion took him gently by the hand, led him to the door and told him that the church was his province and not the court. But such rebellions were rare. For the most part the Padre was the state as well as the church.

Like Armijo he was a man drunk with power but unlike Armijo he was always an intellectual and an idealist. It is said that his schools produced a generation who were not only better educated than any previous one but also better educated than several subsequent ones under the enlightened government of the United States. When Antonio Barreiro, who represented New Mexico in Mexico City, brought the first printing press to the province he apparently did not know what to do with it. Padre Martinez bought it and founded a newspaper, called El Crepusculo (the Twilight) — an oddly appropriate name, still carried a few years ago by a local publication. The Padre issued only four numbers of his journal but he continued to publish books and pamphlets.

In 1832 he went as deputy to the provincial legislature which was no more than a polite and ridiculous pretext at local self-government. Some of its members could not write their names and it is impossible to discover that it ever did anything. The Padre shocked all his colleagues by rising in his place to ask what powers the deputation had, if any, and on what they were based. It was then discovered, to the embarrassment of all, that the Republic of Mexico had neglected to provide in its constitution for any provincial legislature and that a law of the defunct Spanish Empire was its only excuse for existence. The Padre then offered the deputation a resolution to the effect that it had no powers and might as well adjourn. He also presented the gathering with a resolution in which he denounced the church for the heavy fees and

tithes it laid upon the people, saying that the poor buried
their dead in the desert, left their children unbaptized
and lived in concubinage because they could not pay for
the services of the church.

Surely it was a man of rare courage who would thus
denounce both his spiritual and his temporal superiors
and it was a man of power who could do it with impunity.
The Padre was probably more secure in his power than
any other man in the province. In the first place his
strength was personal, based upon magnetism and intelligence, and in the second place it embraced both high
and low. He was the acknowledged head of the large and
aristocratic Martinez family and through them he had
influence with many of the ricos while at the same time
to thousands of paisanos and Indians he was the lord,
both temporal and spiritual.

Evidently the Padre had in him the makings of an enlightened and benevolent despot. Left to himself, he
would have taught the people to read, or at least some
of them, and he would have lifted the crushing burden
of church taxation. He would have given them a press
and an educated and liberal clergy. But he was not to
be left to himself and it was interference from without
that he could not tolerate. In his influence over the
ignorant poor he had a terrible weapon. Any threat to his
power could change the Padre from an idealist preaching of enlightenment to the hidden leader of a savage
mob.

Evidently he saw such a threat in the coming of Albino
Perez from Mexico City to establish the new depart-
mental system of government. Perhaps he thought he

also saw an opportunity. Twitchell says he plotted with
Armijo against the Perez government and helped the
rebels draft a revolutionary program. But his part in the
conspiracy was not known until long afterward and its
failure left him as strong as ever. Armijo ruled in Santa Fe
and the Padre still ruled in Taos.

He was too intelligent a man not to see that he belonged to a waning power and that a new language and a
new government were to dominate the Southwest. When
Kearney had hoisted his flag and read his proclamation
in Santa Fe the feudal epoch in New Mexico was over
and Padre Martinez, in his own way, acknowledged the
fact. The same month that the government changed
hands he made an address to the pupils of his school
which has been remembered and written down.

" Boys," he said, " you came to this school for the
purpose of studying for the priesthood and I have done
what I could that you might attain the desired end. But
with the present change of government a change of ideas
may be necessary. The genius of the American government is in entire harmony with freedom of worship and
with the complete separation of the church and the state.
From this you will gather that for the clergy the foot
of the knife has been broken."

One of his pupils asked what kind of a government the
American was. The Padre replied that it was republican
and he added that a republic was " a burro on which the
lawyers jog along much better than priests."

Surely there were depths in this man, both of insight
and of cynicism. Frankly he had been educating his
young disciples for the priesthood because it had been

the great repository of power and clearly he saw that its power was gone. Succinct and ironical was his definition of change. The old world had been a jackass ridden by a priest, the new one was a jackass ridden by a lawyer. He was not one to keep up an empty pretense or to deceive the young. From that day on his school studied theology and canon law no longer. Instead he taught civil law and the English language.

He was not one to keep up a pretense or shut his eyes to facts, yet where his power was concerned he was capable of hoping against hope. All the citizens of New Mexico had been given their choice of taking an oath of allegiance to the American government or of moving out. A great many of the poor people had welcomed the change. In Santa Fe the Americans had quartered troops and were building a fort. The town was flooded with American money. Many girls had soldier lovers and many men had government jobs. The saloons and the gambling halls were full. For the poor in Santa Fe the bloodless conquest had been a boon.

Many of the rich had welcomed the change too. Some of them had entertained Kearney in their great houses and some had sent their sons to St. Louis and even to New York to learn the laws and language of the new government. Some irreconcilables had moved out. But there were those who neither accepted the change nor left the country and they included ricos, politicians, and priests.

The head of the church in New Mexico was Juan Felipe Ortiz, the Vicar General of the Diocese. Like Padre Martinez he belonged to a large and aristocratic New

Mexican family. He was a fat, pompous, red-headed man, immensely proud of his power — the same who had refused to pay Gregg his full price for the clock in the parish church. At a certain hour every day he used to walk in the plaza in Santa Fe that the people might kneel and kiss his hand while he gave them his blessing. One of his brothers was Tomas Ortiz who had been an officer in the Mexican army. This General Ortiz became the nominal leader of those who secretly repudiated the new government and plotted against it.

It is said that twenty Dons, including some of the most honored names in New Mexico, took part in the conspiracy. Whatever they may have lacked these men had a gift for intrigue. They plotted so carefully that the names of most of the conspirators became known only years afterwards through the confessions of other participants. Nearly all of these confessions seem to have agreed that two churchmen were leaders of the conspiracy — the Vicario Ortiz and Padre Martinez of Taos. The government of the United States tried in vain to get evidence against both of them. To this day their participation is a matter of hearsay but all authorities are agreed that the two priests sat in the councils of the conspirators and that Padre Martinez must have been its ruling mind. For one thing he was by far the most intelligent man among them and besides he never played second fiddle to anyone. Certainly he dominated the vicar, a stupid man, and his great influence with the Taos Indians and the Penitent Brothers was the chief asset of the rebellion.

This conspiracy was many things to many men. It was

to be a slaughter of infidels for the glory of God and the Vicar General may have thought of it as such and gone about his bloody preparations in a spirit of pious exaltation. It was to be a great patriotic enterprise that would restore the lost province to the fatherland and Ortiz and Archuleta, his chief aid, must have figured in their own minds as conquering patriots. To the Indians and peasants who followed these leaders it was one more revolt of the primitive against civilization. What they were promised no one knows, but for the Pueblos at least it held some obscure hope of deliverance from all the forces that were destroying their world. It revived the ancient prophecies that Popé had shouted as a battle cry.

What it meant to Padre Martinez is not so clear. His followers believed that the few troops the United States had sent to New Mexico represented all of its power but he knew better. He did not share their ignorance nor their credulity. What he shared was their savage hatred of the usurpers and one can only conclude that it blinded him to the weakness of their cause and the brutal futility of their plan. He seems almost a dual figure as one pictures him, telling his pupils that the days of priestcraft were over, teaching them law and English, and at night squatting on housetops with his fellow conspirators, plotting a massacre of all the gringos and all their sympathizers. Of course it can never be known just what he sanctioned or how much of the thing that happened was what he had planned. It is known only that he advised with the rebels and that he worked with a hidden hand.

3

The first attempt of the conspirators was a comical fiasco, the second a tragic one. Their first plan was to make Santa Fe the center of their operations. At a preliminary meeting Tomas Ortiz was elected governor of the state they proposed to found and Don Diego Archuleta was to be commanding general. Twitchell publishes a list of all the men engaged in this first conspiracy, including Padre Martinez, and he says they were all related either by blood or by marriage. In a word, this was a cabal of the ricos, belonging to the oldest families in the state.

Christmas eve was chosen by the conspirators as the date for their attack. All of the people then would be in their houses, many of the American soldiers would be drunk. Don Tomas Ortiz and his followers would gather in the church and toll the bell as a tocsin of revolt. Then they would rush to the palace, seize the officers of the American force, plant artillery in the streets and hold the town. Meanwhile Archuleta would rouse the rebellious populace and descend upon the city. The gringos and their government would be exterminated and so would the Mexicans who had given their allegiance to the invaders.

The plot was betrayed. Some say the wife of one of the conspirators went to Colonel Stirling Price, in command of the American forces, and told him all about it. Others say that Doña Tulles Barcello, the celebrated woman gambler, was the one who gave the American officer the names of the leaders. At any rate the United States troops set out to arrest Ortiz and Archuleta. The latter was warned in time and departed for old Mexico. Ortiz took refuge in the house of a friend. There he was disguised as a woman and carried out in the arms of a peon, who pretended that he was taking a sick wife to the doctor. Ortiz then walked out of town with a water jar on his head. The American soldiers who were searching for him stopped him and asked if he had seen Don Tomas Ortiz and he told them where he lived and then went his way. It is said that a Mexican woman recognized him and shrieked after the soldiers in Spanish, " There goes Tomas Ortiz, you fools! " But they could not understand her and the would-be ruler escaped in his petticoats to Chihuahua.

It was generally believed by the Americans that the flight of these two had made an end of the conspiracy but as a matter of fact its real leaders were untouched. Its greatest strength was not in Santa Fe but in Taos. A new uprising was planned, to begin in the walled stronghold of Padre Martinez on the 19th of January. Here all the rebellious Mexicans and Pueblos of the North were to gather, kill the gringos and march to meet the American forces. Charles Bent, who had been appointed governor of the territory, lived in Taos and had gone there to get his family and take it to Santa Fe. He was the one who, with his brother William, had built Bent's Fort on the Arkansas. Later he had founded a store in Santa Fe together with Colonel Ceran St. Vrain. It is said the conspiracy was again betrayed and the governor warned but he was so sure of his influence with the Mexicans and Indians that he refused to believe.

On the night of the 18th everyone in Taos knew

that rebellion was afoot. The rebels had gotten out of hand, the rule of secrecy was broken. All of the Taos Pueblos poured into the town and hundreds of Mexicans came from the surrounding country. One Pablo Montoya was the appointed leader of the Mexicans and a Pueblo named Tomasito Romero led the Indians. These two harangued the mob in crowded saloons. Whisky and eloquence worked them into a frenzy. Most of these men knew nothing of politics. They were illiterate savages. What flared into life that night, briefly and for the last time, was the ancient hatred of a savage world for its conquerors, the ancient hope that invading civilization might be destroyed and the old Gods, the earth-born Gods, restored to power.

The killing began about midnight. The mob went first to the house of Governor Bent. His daughter, who still lived in Taos when I first went there in 1917, told many times the story of that night. She remembered that they were all awakened by a crowd thundering at the door. Her father went and opened it and talked to the people, telling them to be quiet and disperse. There were three women in the house including the wife of Kit Carson. Carson himself was away with General Kearney. The women, using a poker and an iron spoon for tools, dug a hole through the wall of the house into the one adjoining. Meanwhile the Indians had cut short the Governor's speech by shooting him in the face with arrows. It is said that he stood his ground, plucking several arrows from his head, until he fell. They then scalped him alive and left him and he followed the women through the hole in the wall, covering his lacerated head with his hand, but Indians broke into the second house and shot the Governor to death. They debated whether to take the women prisoners but finally left them cowering beside the dead man. Narcisso Baubien, a boy of eighteen, hid under a pile of straw in a barn and they found him there and thrust him through and through with lances. They killed also the sheriff, the prefect, the district judge and a few others connected with the government. They looted and wrecked the houses of their victims and then marched to Arroyo Hondo, twelve miles away, where an American named Turley had a distillery. Eight Americans were in the house and seven of them died after a long siege in which many of the rebels were killed by the fighting gringos.

The conspirators had hoped that the people would rise everywhere as they had at Taos, kill the gringos and seize the government. It was a plan of revolution by massacre, exactly like that of Popé except that it did not include the killing of women. At Mora a few wagon traders were captured and shot by a mob of Mexicans but elsewhere the uprising simply didn't rise. It was only in the Padre's own little domain that it had purpose and effect.

While the mob went about its bloody business he sat safe in his great house. One longs to know what that inscrutable man thought and felt as he listened to the voice of the monster he had set afoot. For whatever his part in the conspiracy may have been that mob was more his creation than anyone else's. For twenty years he had preached hatred of the invaders. He had formed of this primitive mass a rude organism responsive to his will. It was the source of all his power. It embodied one part of his spirit as surely as his schools and his printing press embodied another.

However he may have justified his adventure in violence he must early have had a sickening conviction of failure. His revolution had proved to be nothing but murder, his army only a mob. His first care was to disown them both.

A little girl, daughter of a leading Spanish family in Taos which was friendly to the Americans, remembered that night and her story has been handed down in her family. She remembers that with a crowd of women and children she sought safety at the house of her grandfather, which was across the street from that of the Padre. The house was not large enough to hold them all and the Padre hospitably took some of them as his guests. After the killing while the troops were on their way from Santa Fe Pablo Montoya, the active leader of the rebels, came to the Padre's house. There can be little doubt that this man had sat with the Padre in the councils of the rebels or that he came to the house at the Padre's command. Before all his guests the Padre denounced Montoya, long and eloquently, as a murderer. It is remembered that Montoya stood covering his face with his handkerchief and afterwards went away without saying a word. He was a doomed man and already knew it. He took thus publicly all the blame upon himself and gave the Padre an opportunity to pose before witnesses as one who deplored all violence and bloodshed. Montoya later was hanged in the plaza and the little girl, peeping through a forbidden door, saw him die. She remembered the priest who uttered the prayer for

the dead and then ran away and she remembered that
when the trap was sprung Montoya's neck seemed to
stretch as though it had been made of rubber so that
she had to turn away her eyes for fear of seeing it pop
off in a spurt of blood.

After the massacre there was a lull in Taos. Word of
it had been carried to Santa Fe. The American troops
were on their way, toiling through two feet of snow, and
the rebels, led by Montoya and the Indian Tomasito,
went hopelessly to meet them. Montoya had about fifteen
hundred men, many of them armed only with bows, arrows and lances. They took their stand at Santa Cruz,
about half way between Taos and Santa Fe, and there
awaited the forces of the United States of America. These
consisted of several troops under the command of Colonel
Price and a band of mounted volunteers led by Ceran
St. Vrain, the partner of the murdered governor. Nearly
all of the men in this troop were Bent's friends. Uncle
Dick Wootton was among them and so were many other
famous pioneers and Indian fighters. Volunteers and
regulars together numbered only a few hundred but
they were equal to half a dozen armies like Montoya's
and the whole strength of the United States was behind
them if needed. There were two skirmishes, with the
scattered mob shooting like Apaches from behind rocks
and bushes, running before the well-directed charges
of the troops. Had Padre Martinez or anyone else
believed this mob could win a victory and found a
government?

The worst enemy the troops had to face was the
weather. It was bitterly cold and two feet of soft snow

had just fallen. They did not reach Taos until the third of February and they dragged into the town sick and weary, many of them frost-bitten. There they learned that most of the rebels had fled to the pueblo and forti- fied themselves in the old mission church with walls four feet thick. The church was surrounded, batteries of howitzers were planted and the mounted volunteers took their stand between the pueblo and the mountains so that none should escape.

This was the last battle on the Rio Grande between the old order and the new. A few hundred Indians and Mexicans, frightened and bewildered now, prepared to make their last stand. The Church had led them to be- lieve they were fighting a holy war and into the church they had fled for safety. This was traditional sanctuary and for a time it promised to be a real one. It is said that Colonel Price, himself a devout Catholic, at first refused to train his guns upon the ancient mission but he was overruled by the volunteers and by all the people of Taos whose friends and relatives had been murdered. For the first and only time the United States troops assaulted an Indian pueblo and a Catholic church.

The heavy earthen walls were hard to breech. All of one day the howitzers buried their futile balls in thick adobe while the beleaguered rebels shot from windows and roofs. All rested for one night, the Indians merely waiting for death. On the second day the troops charged the walls, got under them, chopped holes with axes and tossed hand grenades among the huddled Indians. Some of them broke out and tried to reach the mountains and the mounted volunteers, hungry for revenge, hunted these like driven game, killing fifty-one of them without the loss of a man.

For a while after this slaughter a few bands of the rebels were hunted by the troops in the northern mountains. It was a year before any of the surviving Indians of Taos came to the Mexican village, which is only three miles away, and they have never forgotten or forgiven that bloody day. But it was not long before life in Taos was outwardly what it had been before. Padre Martinez still preached and taught and ruled. There were whispers against him and the Americans tried to find evidence of the part he had played but none would testify. Apparently he sat secure as ever but in fact his day was over. His feudal world had perished in that deadly struggle about the ancient church.

It was never rebuilt but the Catholic church in New Mexico was about to be reconstructed, not as a feudal power, but as a respectable mode of worship. In 1851 a young French priest, the Reverend John B. Lamy, was appointed Vicar Apostolic of New Mexico for the express purpose of reform. He succeeded the Vicar Juan Felipe Ortiz, the friend of Padre Martinez. He was sent to do the work that Padre Martinez had dreamed of doing. He was young and of good repute and filled with an almost fanatic zeal. Padre Martinez was old and stained with dark suspicions and full of the bitter wisdom of living.

Lamy, beyond a doubt, was a devout and moral man and one of courage and energy. In New Mexico he has become a figure of legend — a sort of uncanonized saint — and it is hard to see the real man through the fog of reverent tradition. But it seems clear that Father Lamy

was above all a puritan. He exhibited a zeal for improving the morals of others and a faith in the perfecti-
bility of human nature which are not typically Catholic
at all but much more like the philosophy of American
Protestantism. It was not only the abuses of priestly power
that he proposed to correct but the moral delinquencies
of the whole community. " The Bishop has directed that
the confessional and communion be denied to all females
who are known to lead immoral lives," says Davis, who
is almost always reliable and was a great admirer of Lamy.
This is a strange pronouncement to be made in the name
of Him who defended the woman taken in adultery and
a naïve one in any case. It makes one doubt whether
Father Lamy knew anything of life in New Mexico or
much of life anywhere but there is no doubt at all of his
purpose and energy. He and his assistant went up and
down the territory, enduring great hardships, ousting
licentious priests, marrying couples who had been living
together and raising children for years, lifting the bur-
dens of church taxation so that the poor might enjoy its
services once more. He was generally revered and honored for his integrity but some of the more powerful
priests had loyal followers who regarded the young reformer as an impudent upstart. There were threats of
rebellion when he ousted Padre Gallegos at Albuquerque but he finally triumphed.

Padre Martinez of Taos was his most formidable an-
tagonist. He had ousted priest after priest for immorality
and the Padre's immoral life was a matter of common
knowledge. His offspring were numerous and acknowledged. But his power in Taos made him hard to attack.

His relations by blood and marriage alone were an army which he commanded and the poor still followed him faithfully. In 1856 he was still the vicar of Taos and in addition to this power as a churchman he had become a politician of wide influence. He had sat in both of the two legislative councils which had been called since the American occupation and he seemed likely in his old age to wield an even wider influence than he had before.

The Padre's political activities gave Lamy the opening he needed. He let it be known that he disapproved of all political activity on the part of priests. The Padre was sixty-three years old and weary of strife. He promptly resigned the Parish of Taos and Lamy appointed to the vacancy one Padre Damaso Talarid, a Spanish priest whom he had met in Rome.

It was a tactless choice. Father Talarid was a Castilian and his attitude toward the New Mexicans was condescending. Padre Martinez continued to say Mass in the church from time to time and doubtless he remained for most of the people their true pastor. A clash now was inevitable and it came over the question of who should perform a certain marriage ceremony between two relatives of Padre Martinez. At once the town was divided into two camps. Talarid had his followers among those who hated the Padre and these included such powerful persons as Kit Carson and Ceran St. Vrain whose friends and relatives had died in the massacre.

The Padre had resigned his parish, doubtless fully intending to keep his power. Now he was to be told what he could do and what he couldn't. Old and weary he was, but still indomitable. He promptly built a church of his own and went on serving as a pastor for all who chose to follow him — and his family alone could fill a church.

Now the issue was clear and a clear issue was just what Lamy wanted. Twice he went to Taos to reason with the Padre and in vain. He then suspended him from the exercise of all priestly functions. Padre Martinez went on saying Mass and preaching in his own church. He was followed into schism by one of his disciples whom he had educated in his own school, Padre Lucero of Arroyo Hondo. It was an unheard of situation and it admitted of but one course. Both of the erring priests were solemnly excommunicated.

The dread sentence of an eternity in hell was read in a church crowded with the Padre's loyal followers and also with his enemies. It was received in a dead silence and there was no disorder, then or afterward, but old-timers remember that as a moment big with war. It is said the adherents of the Padre were gathered on one side of the plaza and his enemies on the other and both parties were armed and ready. What prevented bloodshed is not certainly known. Perhaps the presence of Kit Carson did more to keep the peace than any other one thing. Relatives of his wife had been killed in the Taos massacre and she had been in the house when Governor Bent was murdered. Carson let it be known that he was ready to fight and he was the mightiest warrior in the Southwest. The story is also told that someone sent an alarm to the United States troops who were still quartered near Taos, that they rode into the plaza just as fighting was about to start and that when the bugle was heard the adherents of Padre Martinez went over the back fence. They had had enough of the United States army the other time.

At any rate, Padre Martinez was officially denied communion with God through the Church of Rome and he went right on to the end of his life communicating with God through the church of Padre Martinez. Nothing but death could break this man's spirit, nor his personal power, and he apparently feared neither the Pope nor the devil. He died in 1867 at the age of seventy-four and at his own request he was buried from his own chapel by his faithful fellow schismatic, Padre Lucero. It is said that in his will he made provisions of lard and bacon and flour for all the poor people who would come from distant ranchos to pay him a final homage. And they came and accepted his bounty and knelt at his bier — the swarthy men with whip-scarred backs who worshiped death in the image of a skull and power in the image of their indomitable Padre.

XI
Longhorns and Six Shooters

1

CATTLE have generally thriven best where once the buffalo ran. The pastoral epoch began in the West when the buffalo were slaughtered and the scrubby longhorns of the Mexican plateau were driven north to take their place.

With the buffalo went the Indian and with the cattle came the cowboy. Created by that northward sweep of the longhorned herds he was briefly the dominant figure in the whole Southwest as the mountain man had been before him and the Mexican rico before that. He was a figure as distinctive as either of these but the period of his importance was hardly more than a generation. It came to an end when money and fences laid hold of the grasslands. But he survives in the imaginations of men — he is an immortal stereotype. First the old-fashioned dime novel seized upon him as its hero. Along in the nineties he was promoted to the popular novel, bound in boards and higher in price but ruled by the same conventions of childish romance. The popular magazine took him up and more forests fell to spread his legend and spread it

thin. Finally the movies found in him their perfect mario-
nette and he galloped through a million reels, performing
incredible feats of arms and horsemanship, sustaining in
all his amours a flawless chivalry derived from Sir Walter
Scott. He is now a possession of all the civilized world, as
widely known as Falstaff or Don Quixote, as dear to little
boys as Santa Claus. In the flesh he survives chiefly as a
mountebank, not only before the camera but in the rodeo.
He has his annual innings at Madison Square Garden
along with six-day bicycle races and the heavy-weight
champion. His final apotheosis is seen in the astonishing
figure of Will Rogers who began his career as a cowboy-
clown and came to rule in Hollywood, to twirl his rope
in New York and London and bandy wise cracks with
presidents.

2

The Rio Grande country in New Mexico was never
buffalo range and it never held many cattle. It has belonged to the sheep for two centuries and sheep and
cattle never mix. Yet the story of this region in terms of
human type cannot be told without a chapter on the
cowboy for the great cattle range was just over the mountains from the river. All the Rio Grande towns heard
the bark of the six shooter and the shrill yells men learned
on the range. Las Vegas was briefly a cow town and Socorro lived under six-shooter law. Even Albuquerque had
its bad men in the early railroad days. And New Mexico
produced Billy the Kid, the most perfect example of the
cowboy-badman myth.

For the cowboy is now a figure almost wholly en-

veloped in myth and little effort has been made to dispel
it. No first rate artist has ever used him for material
and it is only art that can make the past humanly real.
The cowboy is a mechanical toy worn shiny and char-
acterless by much vulgar handling. To make him live
again is difficult and in a short space impossible. But it
is possible to describe his origins in the Southwest, his
incidence upon a region, and perhaps to catch a few
glimpses of him in revealing attitudes.

The final slaughter of the buffalo and the northward
movement of the longhorns both took place mainly after
the Civil War when the first transcontinental railroads
were reaching out into the prairie, linking the wilderness to the civilization east of the Mississippi. It was then
that the hide-hunters set out from Dodge City, armed
with their terrible fifty-caliber Sharp's rifles that would
kill at half a mile. The hide-hunters were the forerunners
of the cattlemen and many of them turned cowboy or
rustler when the wild herds were gone. Dodge, the toughest town of the old West, was first a headquarters for
hide-hunters and then a terminus of the long cattle trail
from Texas.

These hide-hunters were by all accounts the hardest
men that ever looked over gun sights. The cowboy was
a herdsman. His occupation had an element of hus-
bandry. But the hide-hunters were engaged wholly in
slaughter and in battle with the Indians. They were
agents of destruction and they were nothing else. Each
of them carried a long rifle, two six shooters and a knife.
Many of them were men who had gone to the buffalo
ranges because they were badly wanted back home. They

were quarrelsome and deadly, they were lousy and dirty. Jim McIntire was a famous one. " I have killed Comanche and Kiowa Indians by the score," he boasted, "and once I killed and skinned a squaw and made a purse of her breast which I carried for nine years." The hide-hunters were hard to love and never found a place in romance but they were immensely efficient in their necessary task which was to clear the range of buffalo and Indians. Frank Carver killed 5500 buffalo in a year. Sam Case was a lone worker and he could kill fifty buffalo a day and skin them and pack the hides to camp. That Herculean butchery makes one reflect men must have lost in energy as well as in their taste for blood. One firm in Dodge shipped a quarter of a million robes the first year it did business. Some meat was shipped but most of the carcasses were left to rot and the country was swept by a charnal stench that carried for miles. The prairie was one huge slaughter pen. As though there had been some mysterious imperative about it, all comers took a hand in this carnival of blood. When the first transcontinental trains plowed their way through the black masses of the herds, sometimes stalled by them for half a day at a time, passengers poured a murderous fire from the windows, shooting down buffalo just to see them fall. Railroads ran buffalo hunting excursions at reduced rates.

In 1879 the southern herd suddenly vanished. In 1882 the northern herd still numbered many thousands and hunters came home with robes. In 1883 they outfitted as usual and went to the range but the buffalo were gone except for a few old bulls wandering lonely and lost. For

years thereafter gathering buffalo bones was a trade of
the poor and whole freight trains went East loaded with
this last vestige of the herds. Comanche and Kiowa, starving and degraded, lived by gathering buffalo bones on
their ravished hunting ground.

The killing of the buffalo was doubtless the greatest
act of destruction in man's conquest of the wild but the
suddenness and completeness of the buffalo's disappear-
ance has never been adequately explained. It was almost
as though the doomed creatures had gone down into
the bowels of the earth, where Indian legend says they
still abound, in a land called Shipapu, guarded by jealous
Gods.

At the end of the Civil War, when this slaughter began,
there were few cattle north of Texas and the prairie
country was not regarded as potential cattle range. But
from the Big Bend of the Rio Grande south, all over
the Mexican plateau, cattle had ranged for generations.
The technique of raising cattle on a wild and unfenced
range was invented and perfected by the Mexicans a
hundred years before ever a gringo swung a rope. There
were no cowboys then but only vaqueros and the first
Texan cattlemen of Anglo-Saxon breed called themselves vaqueros too. These first American herdsmen
were adventurers from the old South — from Tennessee,
Louisiana, Kentucky and Virginia — who poured into
Texas when it still was Mexican soil. Texas then was
the region that lured adventurous men. Those were the
days when Aaron Burr dreamed of a southwestern empire
with himself upon a throne, when Sam Houston looked
to Texas as a place to repair his scandal-damaged for-

tunes, when James Bowie, inventor of the famous knife, began crossing the Mexican border in search of gold, when Davy Crockett set out to find his grave at the Alamo. These men were the famous ones among thousands. By the time the Alamo fell Texas contained an army of these immigrants — hardbitten, land-hungry, fighting men. They made Texas free and they made it a state of the union. They grabbed land and they grabbed cattle. They learned the arts of the vaquero and they stole his stock. For generations a bitter guerrilla warfare, mostly unrecorded and forgotten, was waged all up and down the lower Rio Grande. Texans stole Mexican cattle and ran them across the border. Mexicans stole Texan cattle and ran them back. How many men were killed nobody knows. But by the time the Civil War broke out the brush country of Texas was full of scrubby longhorned Mexican cattle wearing the brands of Texan ranchers. During the war these cattle ran wild. Afterwards their unbranded increase belonged to the man who claimed it. Anyone with a rope and a branding iron could found a herd but he would then be rich in nothing but beef. There was no market for cattle and meat was as free as land. If one wanted beef he shot down the first yearling that took his eye. Cowboys seldom carried provisions and it was common practice to butcher a calf for breakfast, cooking a few steaks over the coals and leaving the rest for the coyotes.

Men felt poor in a country where everything could be had for the taking except cash. All sorts of expedients were tried for making money out of cattle. Along the Texas coast tallow-making plants were built and thousands of cattle were slaughtered for their fat and hides. There was again a tremendous waste of meat, as there had been on the buffalo ranges, and the tallow plants perfumed the prairie air as the shambles of the hide-hunters had done.

So the cattle business began in a region of unfenced lands and ownerless herds and the fact is important. In the seventies branding mavericks was a legitimate and respected way of getting a start in life and in the eighties it was a crime for which men were hung. For cattle speedily became valuable property. War sprang up between those who had and those who hadn't and many a man never knew exactly why he was on one side or the other. It was in this way that the cowboy achieved his dual role of outlaw and herdsman. Billy the Kid was at times a cowboy, at times a cattle thief and at times a hired gunman on one side or the other in a struggle where ethics and issues were alike confused. And there were many less conspicuous destinies similar to his.

What made cattle suddenly valuable was the building of the transcontinental railroads. Each of the successive railhead towns became a shipping point. In the early seventies there were already refrigerator cars and packing plants. Chicago had begun its career as butcher to the world. Then gold was found in Colorado and the mining towns provided another beef-hungry market. The beaten redskins were planted on reservations to be fed by government dole and men made fortunes out of contracts, often corruptly lucrative, to supply the reservations with beef. Immense herds wended northward along the foot of the mountains and the most spectacular phase of

cattle history had begun. When the trail-driving epoch
was at its height an almost continuous procession of longhorned herds followed these vague meandering routes,
some of them a thousand miles long. Each herd had its
quota of cowboys, its huge remuda of saddle horses, its
chuck wagon and its trail boss — a commander of infinite
dangers and tribulations. Indians, rustlers and Mexican
bandits preyed on the herds. Thousands of cattle and
many men drowned in the great rivers that had to be
crossed. Stampedes scattered the herds over the prairie.
Horses were run to death in the effort to stop these panic
flights and men were pounded to pieces under the hooves
of the herds.

The period of the great trail drives was hardly more
than ten years long but it provided the authentic basis
for almost all the heroism and melodrama of the cowboy
legend. Beyond a doubt there was heroism in these trail
drives and there was melodrama in the track-end towns
when the cowboys struck them. Towns were shot up by
each successive outfit as a matter of course. Horses were
ridden into saloons, dance halls and theaters. A man
would "run" a town for a day or a week until someone
quicker on the draw came to take his place. It was at
this time that the Colt revolver, commonly called a six
shooter, produced its greatest practitioners.

3

The six shooter now is chiefly a symbol of melodrama
or a tool of crime but in the whole of the trans-Mississippi
West, for a generation following the Civil War, it pro-

foundly affected the character of society. The ethics of that time and region were built around it. It was an instrument of change. It produced both a type of man and a pattern of society. With it individual destinies and social conflicts were settled in a swift and deadly fashion.

What the rapier was to seventeenth century Europe the six shooter was to the West of the pastoral and mining period. Like the rapier it gave rise to a kind of impromptu duello with a code of its own and like the rapier it endowed men of exceptional skill and nerve with a great prestige and power over their fellows. But the six shooter was by far the more deadly and effective weapon. More men were wounded in fencing duels than were killed while the forty-five Colt filled cemeteries. The most gifted fencer could fight only one man at a time but a six-shooter expert could paralyze a roomful of opponents and often beat five or six in pitched battle. Billy the Kid briefly ruled a region as large as France because he was faster on the draw than any other man in it and Ben Thompson long dominated the city of Houston with a power of life and death based solely on personal prowess.

The sword was never important in America. Its place was taken in early pioneer society by the knife and to some extent by the old-fashioned muzzle-loading pistol. These were the side-arms of the mountain men and they were as turbulent a crew as ever lived but as far as one can learn they seldom killed each other. Personal quarrels among them were often settled in rough and tumble fights and a celebrated bully was one who could make another man admit he had enough. With the perfection of the revolver and the metallic cartridge all this changed. Hand-to-hand fighting almost ceased. A trifling insult meant sudden death for somebody. Armed conflict, whether between individuals or groups, became sudden, deadly and decisive. When every man packed a gun every man became the arbiter of his own destiny and the law was what he made it. Neil B. Field of Albuquerque practiced law in Socorro when that was the toughest town in New Mexico and averaged about one homicide a week. He defended many killers and he told me that to secure an acquittal it was only necessary to prove that the dead man had had a fair chance for his life. If he had been shot in the back or had been unarmed a true bill might be found against his assailant but otherwise his death was regarded as the judgment of a just God. The effect of this code was to produce not so much a period of chivalrous combat as one of easy and unpunished murder but it had its heroes as well as its villains and it made for a quick and final settlement of many issues.

Joe Fowler of Socorro was a perfect specimen of the licensed killer at his worst. He was a cattleman from Texas, a man of means, and when drunk a homicidal maniac. He was commonly credited with the killing of thirteen men and he killed most of them with little risk to himself. It is said that he killed two cowboys with a shotgun while they sat by a fire, that he killed men who worked for him to save their wages and that as a deputy sheriff he shot unarmed prisoners. He liked to use a knife as well as a gun and always carried a sawed-off shotgun across his saddle.

Fowler was feared and hated and yet Fowler throve for

years. Like every successful bully he had a following and he had money. Whenever he came to trial he had the best of legal talent on his side and witnesses to swear he had killed in self-defense.

Finally Fowler sold his ranch and came to Socorro with twenty-five thousand dollars in his pocket for a celebration before his departure. He lined men up at the bar and made them drink at the point of a gun. He shot at the toes of their boots and made them dance. He let everyone know that he owned the town and ruled it.

A barkeeper by the name of Monroe disputed his sway. He had two of his assistants grab Fowler across the bar, pinioning his arms, while Monroe took his guns away from him. Fowler pretended to take it as a joke. Then he sidled up to Monroe, drew a knife and disemboweled the man.

He was rushed to jail by his own friends who were afraid this last little exploit might be resented. It was — so much so that Fowler for the first time was convicted. While he was in jail awaiting sentence a rumor spread that a gang of his fellow Texans were coming to deliver him.

The rumor was not well received in Socorro. Men began gathering in the yard about the jail. Fowler saw them and tasted terror. He sent for his attorney, he demanded to be gotten out of jail, he demanded to be given a gun. All his demands were refused. His fate was in the hands of the mob.

At a certain moment its mind was made up. Its mumbling and whispering became a roar of rage. It rushed the jail, smashed the door and dragged out the man who had ruled the town by murder. He begged and wept, he screamed and bellowed with fear. He fouled himself like a frightened child. They stood him in a wagon, tied a rope around his neck and drove the wagon out from under. As his body danced grotesquely in the air it was riddled with bullets and then it was left hanging for a long time with its face twisted into a grimace of terror.

The six-shooter epoch produced many like Fowler — tolerated killers who ran a course of blood and died by a bullet or at the end of a rope. Killing, it would seem, has a strange fascination and men learn to like the taste of blood. Many who began by killing in their own defense ended by killing for fun. One who was half a second quicker on the draw held a power of life and death over his fellows and it is not remarkable that the power was often abused. But there were genuine heroes of the six shooter. The cowboy Galahad of popular legend had some existence in fact. Elfego Baca's battle with the mob at Frisco was certainly an heroic one and Elfego then and afterwards was truly the champion of an oppressed people. He was one Mexican who was not afraid of the Texans or of anything or anybody else.

4

Elfego's celebrated battle, with its social setting and all its antecedents, makes the best picture of six-shooter society on the Rio Grande that I can find. Many of the terrific exploits of celebrated gunmen dwindle sadly under critical examination but Elfego's defense stands the test of research. There are three written accounts of it, each from the viewpoint of a participant, including the hero himself, and although they differ in detail they all agree that Elfego staged a truly great display of courage, skill and endurance.

Elfego Baca still lives in Albuquerque and is still a leader of his people. His authorized biography was recently written by Kyle Crichton and published in Santa Fe and this narrative leans heavily upon it. But not exclusively. The Honorable William French, a young Irish gentleman recently out from the old country, was present at the Frisco battle and wrote an account of the affair. He exchanged shots with Elfego during the siege and took him to dinner after it was over. J. H. Cook, a celebrated scout and Indian fighter, figured as chief peacemaker and he too put the story into a book. This is to be regarded as a critical and imaginative synthesis of all three narratives.

Elfego Baca, like Fowler, was a product of Socorro and much more completely so for he was born there and his story must begin with some account of the town.

Socorro is the one town on the Rio Grande north of El Paso which felt the full shock of gun-rule. Its story is almost an epitome of southwestern history for it was by turns a Mexican village, a mining town, a railroad town and a cow town. Santa Fe and Taos were never wild after the American occupation. Seated far back from the railroad they went peacefully to sleep. Albuquerque had a few wild years when the railroad was building but it was always a well-governed place and bad men found it a hard one. Several of them briefly decorated its ancient cottonwoods with their suspended persons. But Socorro lay right in the path of trouble.

The trouble began after the war with Mexico. Before that Socorro had been a peaceful Mexican town, ruled by its ricos and its priest, fed by its sheep herds and fields and vineyards, served by peons and Indian slaves. After the war with Mexico Texas claimed the Rio Grande as its eastern boundary. Socorro was just over the river, safely on New Mexican soil, but it was a focal point for west-ward-drifting Texans. These early Texans were hard men, fighting men, and they hated Mexicans. A few brave words about the Alamo and Davy Crockett would work any Texan into a Mexican-killing mood. The Tex-ans came armed with " head rights " which were bits of paper issued by the government of Texas to veterans of its wars and other settlers, entitling the holder to any quarter section of Texas land not already occupied. Head rights were bought and sold and were practically currency.

The Texans came also armed with six shooters and rifles. Literally every Texan was a gunman. A Texan of that period was no more dressed without his Colt than he was without his pants. Texas was then perhaps the most heavily armed community in the United States and very likely it still is. The habit of bearing and using arms dies slowly and it also grows slowly.

The Mexicans as a whole had never learned much about the use of firearms. The vast majority of them were peasants, too poor to buy guns, who had fought always with the primitive weapons of their savage enemies. They had a certain skill with knives but they were helpless be-fore these men with six shooters on their hips. It was a part of the Texan tradition that all Mexicans were cowards but in fact the westering Texans were an armed invasion of an unarmed community. It was one of those gradual and unrecorded movements that work more change than formal wars and often spill more blood.

The Texans were not empowered to take occupied lands but Mexicans did not count with them as occupants. They took lands that had been supporting families in undisputed possession for a century. Murder and bluff were their methods and the short and deadly six shooter was their only attorney. The Texans were all cattlemen. They came driving their herds of longhorns before them. The Mexicans were shepherds and sheep were driven off the range wherever the cattle went. Whole herds were stampeded over cliffs and killed. Sheep-herders were terrorized or killed. It was a favorite device to surround a sheep camp at night and shoot into its cooking fire as a gentle intimation to move on.

Many Mexicans gave up their homes and migrated. The town of Doña Ana was spotted with Texas head rights and filled with belligerent Texans. Sixty of the inhabitants packed up their goods and led by Don Rafael Ruelas, their ruling rico, departed to find new homes in Old Mexico.

The gold rush of forty-nine meant more trouble for Socorro. It was on the route of the transcontinental emigrant trains. The passing wagons brought the town an influx of floating desperadoes who were even worse than the Texan cattlemen. Bartlett records that when the United States boundary commission got there the town was in danger of being depopulated. The emigrant gun-

men had all but taken it over. They quartered themselves on Mexican families, taking possession of houses
and women. They lined the plaza with gambling dens and
bawdy houses. Mexicans were moving out steadily and
those who stayed locked themselves in their houses at
night.

While the boundary commission was there a fandango
was given. Like all Mexican dances it was open to all
who chose to come. The ruling gang shot out the lights
and started a free for all battle in the dark. A member
of the commission was stabbed four times and died. Forthwith the commission constituted itself a posse vigilante,
rounded up about ten of the offenders, held a court in
which the judge used a six shooter for a gavel and hung
four men from the limbs of cottonwood trees. Socorro
was pacified for a while but the boundary commission
soon passed on and the Texans kept coming. Then silver
was found in the hills behind Socorro and the hard-
pressed town was deluged in sudden money. Three million dollars were dug out of the mountains, much of it
to be spent in saloons and dance halls, and the fierce race
of underground miners poured into its plaza every night.

The mining boom subsided too and Socorro quieted
down but the invasion of the Texans continued for a
generation. In the early eighties there was a new movement of Texas cattleherds across the Rio Grande to take
possession of the rich pastures in western New Mexico
and eastern Arizona. The plains of St. Augustine became
a cattle range and they remain one to this day. Magda-
lena, New Mexico is one of the best surviving cow towns
in the Southwest. Its annual rodeo brings out a splendid

show of horses and riders, just for the amusement of the home folks, and almost everybody calls everybody else by his first name. If some mysterious stranger tops a bronk and wins a prize, he is most likely "that fellow from Texas." For the migration has never wholly ceased though it is no longer an armed invasion.

5

Elfego Baca, then, was a native son of this town of trouble and he belonged to the race of the bullied and dispossessed who knew so little of the handle of a six shooter and so much of its business end. But he had a unique upbringing. His father moved to Kansas when Elfego was a baby and the boy was educated there among the gringos. When he came back to Socorro at the age of fifteen he spoke English perfectly and Spanish with difficulty. Gringos were no mystery to him. He had been fighting them with his fists for years and arguing with them in their own language. He had probably already learned that most men, of whatever race, are not as brave as they sound.

Just when his education in the fine art of the six shooter began is not of record but he was packing a gun at sixteen and he must have known even then that he had genius for its use. At this time his father was arrested by political enemies and jailed in Los Lunas. Elfego got him out but did not have to use his gun. He foiled his pursuers by hiding in a patch of weeds right across the street from the jail while the posse searched for him in remote places. At seventeen he made the acquaintance of

Billy the Kid, then a happy but deadly boy of about his own age. The two of them went on a little spree together in Albuquerque and Billy terrorized the place by firing a six shooter which he concealed under his hat with such swift skill that his little prank was never discovered. Elfego's association with the Kid was brief but momentous. Billy was the most gifted gunman of his day and doubtless Elfego both learned from him and gained confidence in his own comparative skill.

In the early eighties, when the last wave of Texan cattlemen were crossing the Rio Grande and locating their herds west of it, Elfego was a youth under twenty and by ambition and inclination a man of politics. He was admirably equipped for such a career. He had great facility in the three languages of his time and place — Spanish, English and the short decisive utterance of the gun. Moreover he had both courage and intelligence above the ordinary.

Every election in Socorro county was then a struggle between the races. The lucrative and powerful office of sheriff was the chief prize and always the Texas Democrats were solidly for one man and the Mexican Republicans for another. The choice of the native vote this year was the incumbent, a gentleman ambiguously known as Don Pedro Simpson. Whether Don Pedro was Spanish on one side or whether a Pete had become a Pedro for political purposes I cannot ascertain but Don Pedro had the native sons behind him and was opposed by the Texans. They charged that sixty thousand dollars of county funds collected by the sheriff could nowhere be found.

While this campaign was at its hottest young Elfego

Baca mounted a good horse and went electioneering for his friend Don Pedro. It is a matter of record that he wore, among other things, a Prince Albert coat, two six shooters and the badge of a deputy sheriff. This latter, by his own account, represented no official preferment. He had bought it and he wore it merely as a personal adornment that might have a moral value in emergencies.

Far west of Socorro on the San Francisco River stands a town then known as Frisco and now called Reserve. This change in name is perhaps the greatest one that has ever come to it for it is ninety miles from a railroad and off the main auto routes. At that time it was a small adobe Mexican village grouped loosely about three plazas. It was also in the center of the cattle country which had been pre-empted by migrant Texans and this made it a social center for the cowboys of several large ranches.

These were cowboys of the most perfect traditional pattern — Texas cowboys who packed their guns always and everywhere, wore twenty-dollar Stetsons and high-heeled boots and spurs as big as prairie sunflowers. Gun-men and horsemen and cowmen they were and very little else. They had almost forgotten how to walk and would mount a horse to cross a street. They were chivalrous fellows — that is, they lived in awe of women because they seldom saw one. Theirs was a world of men, horses and beef, with strong liquor and sudden battle for its necessary relief. Their chief tradition was derived from the short and heroic history of their native state. They all regarded Texas as the perfect blossom of human wisdom and courage and they all professed hatred and contempt

for Mexicans as a class and as a nation, whatever excep-
tions they might make of individuals.

Into this center of belligerent and primitive Texanism
rode young Elfego Baca — a Mexican by derivation, a
Spanish-American for political purposes, a greaser in the
language of Texas, a knight-errant from the romantic
point of view if ever the six-shooter West produced one.
With his long black coat and his bogus badge and his
two guns he went to the heart of the enemy country to
speak for the candidate of his people. If he was not looking for trouble he must nevertheless have known that he
was likely to find it. And he must have known he would
have to face it alone for he had no more illusions about
his own people than he had about gringos.

In Frisco stood a combined saloon and hotel known
as Milligan's and all cow-punchers went straight to it
when they struck town. On the day of Elfego's arrival a
young cowman of the Slaughter outfit, named McCarthy,
was taking a day off in town. Having eased his inhibitions
with several jolts of Milligan's best squirrel whisky he
was riding up and down the main street of Frisco shooting his gun in the air and at various inanimate objects
in the manner which has since been made familiar by
the fine arts. It was a usual sport of cattlemen in Frisco
and by them regarded as an innocent one. McCarthy
was not trying to kill anyone and nobody was in any danger provided he had the good sense to go into his house,
shut the door and lie down on the floor. Most of the
natives had done something of the kind. It was customary
and also expedient. But in Frisco that day was a young
idealist who put principle above expediency, and who

had great faith in his gunmanship, a yearning to distinguish himself and a desire to champion his people against the usurpers.

Elfego went to the native Justice of the Peace, often still called the Alcalde, and demanded the arrest of McCarthy. The Alcalde refused on the ground that if anything was done to or with McCarthy large numbers of Texans would ride into town bent on revenge. Elfego delivered the Alcalde a lecture which was probably hot and long but the substance of it was that if the Mexicans let the Texans think all Mexicans were afraid of them then the country was no longer habitable for its native sons. He, Baca, would demonstrate that one Mexican at least was not afraid of Texans. He would arrest McCarthy.

He did this with ease. McCarthy was not a bad man and doubtless Elfego took him by surprise. He also took him before the Alcalde who again refused to function in his official capacity. Elfego announced that he would hold his prisoner and take him to Socorro for trial.

About this time the predictions of the Alcalde began to come true. Several more cowboys of the Slaughter outfit, led by their foreman named Perham, rode into Frisco and heard that McCarthy had been arrested and by a Mexican. In the name of the Alamo and the Lone Star, what the hell? They rode to where Baca was and demanded the person of McCarthy. Baca emerged from the house where he had confined his prisoner and confronted the horsemen. It was dark and the Texans could barely see Elfego, but Perham rode a white horse, which made a shining mark. Elfego said he would count three and if the gathering had not dispersed at the third syllable he would consider that the occasion called for the use of arms. Again Elfego must have had the element of surprise strongly on his side. Probably the Texans did not take him seriously. But he counted, in all seriousness, and at the word of three he opened fire. The horse of the foreman, Perham, did some kind of a backward somersault and killed its rider. A cowboy named Allen was shot in the knee. The rest of the party disappeared suddenly. Elfego retained his prisoner, his dignity and his arms.

Now there was excitement on the San Francisco River. Word of what had happened was carried to all the neighboring ranches — word of what had happened and of much more. Battles grow in the telling. Reveres inspired by Milligan's whisky galloped from ranch to ranch, spreading the news and also their own imaginations. What they reported was nothing less than a Mexican uprising. Not only then but long afterward the incident was spoken of as the Mexican War and Elfego was thereby reckoned an army for he did all the fighting on the Mexican side.

It was a Mexican uprising that was reported at the S–U ranch where young William French, lately out from Ireland, was acting as greenhorn manager. He and his cowboys immediately started for Frisco, first sending a messenger to the town of Alma for a deputy sheriff named Dan Bechtol and elsewhere for a justice of the peace whose Nordic extraction would guarantee justice from the Texan point of view. Everything was going to be perfectly legal. This was customary throughout the six-shooter period of American history. Whenever a pitched battle was fought each side had its sheriff or its deputy and its warrants for the arrest of the other side.

French and his friends rode into Frisco late that day and found themselves part of a growing crowd. It is said no less than eighty cowboys came, all of them armed with six shooters and many with rifles besides. In groups and pairs and singles they rode clattering into town. Before Milligan's hotel hard-ridden cowponies came to a squatting stop in a cloud of dust and were left heaving at the hitch rack while their riders lined the bar inside, filled the room with talk and smoke and the jingle of spurs and the smell of whisky. Everybody was excited. Everybody was delighted. Whatever else he had accomplished Elfego had certainly started a fine party.

Where was the war? They started out to look for it rather late at night. All the inhabitants of Frisco had gone to bed. Some were routed out and enquiries were made. It was then definitely ascertained that the uprising consisted of but a single man and that he had gone to bed too. There was general disappointment. Nobody, apparently, wanted to wake up Elfego Baca. Perhaps they felt that if the uprising had a good night's rest it would work better in the morning. Anyway, they all went back to Milligan's and to their cups.

Until late in the evening there was excited talk about what they would do in the morning. Dan Bechtol, the deputy sheriff, was the drunkest and the loudest talker. He gave them all to understand that in the morning he would take Baca firmly in hand. But in the morning it was found impossible to get Dan out of bed. His expressed intentions were as belligerent as ever but neither his mind nor his legs would function effectively.

Deprived of a leader the mob gathered again at Milligan's and held council. With the chief fire-eater asleep surprisingly moderate views prevailed. It was decided to send word to Baca that he must produce his prisoner for trial. Baca responded at once. He came with his prisoner, a Mexican Justice of the Peace and several followers. After a conference with Dan Bechtol, now on his feet again, the party went into a house for the purpose of holding the trial. This was done in a small room with most of the mob waiting outside. The trial evidently was held before the American Justice of the Peace. McCarthy was fined five dollars for disturbing the peace. He was congratulated by all his fellow Texans and the proceedings adjourned. Apparently the trouble was over but in fact it had just started.

The subsequent events make an interesting study in the operations of that mob spirit which was the real ruling power in pioneer times and still in many disguises plays so great a part among us. What this mob craved was blood and excitement but it was ostensibly a gathering of civilized men and its lusts had to be suitably disguised as a love of justice. If someone suggested a trial everyone else agreed and if someone started shooting everyone else drew a gun. The mob was a highly suggestible monster and what made it dangerous was that every man in it was armed.

Now the crowd began dispersing. Some men mounted their horses and started for home. Others hung around in little groups, talking.

Elfego Baca evidently knew well that the trouble was not yet over. It is said that after the trial he walked rapidly from the court-room with his hat pulled down over his eyes. He went a short distance down the street and entered a small house of the type known in that country as a " jacal." A jacal is made by planting posts upright in the ground, chinking the cracks with mud and topping the whole with an earthen roof. This jacal was occupied by an old Mexican woman and a boy and it contained also a wooden image of Mi Senora Santa Ana — one of the many saints revered by Mexicans in the spirit of their ancient idolatry. Elfego told the old woman and the boy to get out quick but he kept the saint with him. His fort was a fragile structure but it had one great advantage. Its floor was about a foot below the level of the ground. Here Elfego sat down alone to await developments and he seems to have been in no doubt that there were going to be some.

Young William French was among those who considered the incident closed and had started for home. He was overtaken by a party of several Texans who told him they had a warrant for Baca and proposed to arrest him and try him for the death of Perham. French thought this reasonable and four of them rode back to town and approached the cabin where Baca awaited his destiny. A cowboy named Hern knocked on the door and demanded admittance. When this was refused he began kicking the door, presumably to break it down. This got him a prompt answer. Elfego shot twice through the door, hitting Hern in the abdomen. The friend of justice collapsed with a great oath into the arms of French and was dragged to a near-by house. There he died slowly, begging for revenge.

A man named Moore then rode up to the door of the cabin but before he had made his intentions known a bullet took off his hat and he retired. French had left his hat on the ground when he assisted Hern off the field of battle. He ran back, picked it up and ran away again while fire spurted from one of Elfego's loop holes. When he reached cover French found three holes in his hat. There is reason to believe that Elfego did some neat hat-shooting when he might have shot men.

After this unsuccessful attempt at arrest the survivors went once more to their leader, Dan Bechtol. It was found that he had again retired. He agreed with them that the thing to do was to take Baca out and lynch him but he declined to take an active part in the enterprise on the ground that he was sleepy.

By this time most of the crowd had returned and the siege of Elfego Baca was begun in earnest. Perhaps it would be more correct to say that it was begun in a spirit of play for to most of the participants this was purely a sporting event — a community hunt with a man for the quarry. Several of the besiegers — young William French among them — concealed themselves behind an adobe house across the street from Baca's fort. One of them, in a true sporting spirit, would stick out his head to draw Baca's fire and the others would return it. Baca was then addressed from the shelter of a wall and invited to come out and surrender. He replied with several shots. The entire assemblage then surrounded his hut and poured a fire into and through it for twenty minutes. It was then agreed by all that Baca must be dead. One man approached the jacal to reconnoiter. Baca testified to his survival by driving the bold one to cover under a hail of bullets.

Repeatedly during the day the besiegers renewed their volleys. It was great sport for everyone except Baca. He had long since given himself up for dead and was determined simply to die fighting. Surely his feat deserves to be remembered as one of the most heroic single-handed battles in all six-shooter history and one of the most miraculous survivals. Those on the ground estimated that at least four thousand shots were fired through the walls of the jacal. The door alone showed over three hundred bullet holes. The handle of a broom standing in a corner was hit nine times. Everything in the tiny room was riddled — everything except the person of Elfego Baca. Many of the primitive Texans carried away the conviction that he bore a charmed life. At his subsequent trial for murder a cowboy expressed on the witness stand his conviction that Elfego was bullet proof and that if he were stood up and shot at in the court-room he would remain unscathed. The Mexicans attributed his survival to the presence of the saintly image. Baca afterward tried to buy this from its owners by way of a souvenir but his own explanation of his escape was more realistic. He attributed it simply to the fact that the floor of the hut was a foot below the ground level. Whenever the firing became hot he lay down flat and when it ceased he sat up and popped at his assailants through chinks in the wall.

They discussed an assault in force but leaders and vol-

unteers for the enterprise were lacking. They tried to set
his house on fire and they tried to dynamite it but both
attempts were frustrated by Baca's prompt and accurate
shooting. Sunset came and darkness. Most of the besiegers retired for needed rest. Sentries were posted and most
of these went to sleep too. It was the general opinion that
Baca must be either dead or so nearly dead that he was
not worth worrying about.

In the morning William French, who seems to have
entered fully into the sporting spirit of the occasion, volunteered to put the matter to the test. He ran across the
street directly in front of Baca's stronghold. Several shots
tearing up the earth close to his heels proved to all that
Baca was still alive and shooting. He was now treated to
another volley by the entire gathering and the siege was
formally renewed for its second day.

During the afternoon a large crowd of mounted Mexicans was seen in the distance and word went around that
they were coming to the rescue of Baca. The uprising at
last was about to occur. Thereupon a considerable number of the assailants mounted their horses and departed
rapidly for home and their neglected chores. Others fired
on the Mexicans at long range without doing any damage.
It was presently ascertained that these compatriots of Baca
had no idea of coming to his rescue with arms but were
bound for Socorro to solicit the aid of yet another officer
of the law. Not one Mexican dared to fire a shot for Baca
although all of them were in sympathy with him and they
must have greatly outnumbered the Texans. The fact
testifies to the complete domination which the Texan
and his six shooter had achieved. Kyle Crichton, the

leading authority on Elfego Baca, states that the entire
Mexican population of Frisco was that day afflicted with
yellow jaundice.

Toward the end of the second day the native emis-
saries who had gone to Socorro for help returned with
yet another deputy sheriff named Rose and several others
who proposed to act as peacemakers. Among those present at the siege was J. H. Cook, a famous pioneer who
wrote a book entitled " Fifty Years on the old Frontier." Therein he gives himself almost complete credit
for getting Elfego Baca out of his riddled fortress
although other eyewitnesses do not mention him at
all.

The ascertainable facts about the ending of the famous
battle are as follows. Many of the cowboys had evidently
tired of the siege. Some of them had gone home. Others
had gone to hold a funeral over the remains of Hern, the
man killed by Baca on the first day. Cook or Rose or both
of them addressed the crowd and urged that an attempt
be made to get Baca out alive and place him in custody.
It was argued that if he were killed, whether by gunfire
or lynching, his death would bring on an inter-racial
conflict that would seriously interfere with business and
cause loss and trouble all around. On the other hand if
he were tried for murder he would certainly be executed
in an orderly manner. The suggestible crowd apparently
accepted this view of the situation. Baca was now addressed by a Mexican who was a close friend of his and
whose voice he recognized. He was advised to surrender
and assured that Rose and his party would protect him.
Baca now spoke for the first time since he had entered

the jacal. He replied that he would come out provided Rose and his friends would stand in the open and in full view, that everyone else should withdraw and that he should be allowed to keep his arms. These terms were accepted. French, who witnessed the recrudescence of Baca, testifies that he emerged not through the door but through a small window. He was clad only in his underwear, his hair stood on end, his eyes were wild and he grasped a six shooter in either hand. He looked more like a wild animal than a man.

For nearly thirty-six hours he had sustained almost incessant bombardment and for that same period he had contemplated what seemed to be certain death. Yet neither his nerve nor his judgment had deserted him. As he crawled out of his window the Mexican spectators on the hilltops behind the town shouted to him to run toward them. Baca knew that if he ran he was a dead man. He walked quietly up to Rose and placed himself in a state of armed surrender.

Once he was out of his fort and in the hands of the law the crowd seems to have lost all interest in him. He was no longer fair game. Most of the cowboys went home. French tells that he personally escorted Baca to Milligan's hotel, procured him a bath and a meal and had a long talk with him about the battle. These two young men, one a native of the Rio Grande valley and the other an Irish baronet, had been shooting at each other most of the time for two days. Now they sat down in a spirit of perfect amity and mutual respect to discuss their mutual efforts at homicide. That conversation somehow seems to embody all that was best in the spirit of the time and of the occasion. It would seem, French remarks, that the honors belonged to Baca.

Elfego the next day rode to Socorro in a buckboard, a prisoner of the law but with his guns still on him. In due course he was tried for murder and acquitted. Not only was he acquitted but he was famous. The battle at Frisco was his start in life. He came in a few years himself to occupy the coveted position of sheriff in Socorro county. Upon taking up the duties of his office he wrote a pleasant personal letter to each felon and murderer, proved and presumptive, inviting him to come in and surrender and explaining that if he refused it would be the painful duty of the sheriff to shoot him on sight. And they came, one and all, and laid down their guns with a smile.

" Who the hell are you? " asked a man whom he approached with the authority of his badge.

"I am Elfego Baca," he replied. And it was enough. The man handed over his gun. Elfego had become one of the great men of the six shooter like Billy the Kid and Bat Masterson and Wild Bill Hayward and all the rest of them, whose words were law, whose names were terror, who packed sudden death in a trigger finger.

How quaint their fame seems now! They belong to another of those brief and vivid epochs that make up the American story, each producing its type of man, its type of society and vanishing suddenly and finally in our swift pageant of change. The time has gone forever when a man can face life single-handed with a weapon and hope to win. The modern gunman is a gangster and often part of an organization almost as large as a major industry.

That was a wild and brutal time when the six shooter

ruled. It offers a spectacle of society in liquidation, reverting to modes and forces that belong to the childhood of the race. But it had its values and the best of these was an embattled individualism which threw a man squarely upon his own resources of skill and courage. It was a sad day for stuffed shirts. William French has a sentence of commendation which he applies to several of the men he admired in the old West. " He was a whole man." It would make a fitting epitaph for any of the best of them — those men who looked at life along the barrel of a gun.

1

OLD TOWN and New are one at last, in fact if not in law. I can remember when they were nearly a mile apart and you might start a jack rabbit along the dusty road between them. That was because the railroad wouldn't go out of its way to touch the old town. It was willing to do so if it could have what it wanted but someone asked too much for his land. The invader passed the Old Town by and built a New Town of its own.

It was a proud and independent invader. Santa Fe, capital for three centuries under three governments, was left sitting twenty miles off the main line at the end of a spur. Taos, visited by every conqueror from Coronado to Carson, for two hundred years a center of trade and battle, was on the wrong side of the mountains and has never heard the whistle of a train.

The Rio Grande valley had suffered many powerful invaders but this one with the belly that ate coal and wood, the eye that bored a hole in the dark, the voice that shouted across the miles, made all the others seem puny.

272

All previous invaders the country had absorbed. They were made of flesh and blood. Some of them could be married and some of them could be killed. They sank into the earth, they fell into the arms of women. They were human. But this machine seemed to have an independent and inhuman being of its own. It was made by men and they thought they owned it but they found that it owned them. The others had taken the world as they found it. This one created a world of its own — a world of iron, work and money.

Men had always worked, of course, whether as slaves or as masters. Work had been a part of life — but only a part. In the harvest season they worked while the light lasted, swinging their scythes in hearty competition, quenching their thirst from jars of red wine waiting in the shade. In shearing time they worked day and night and a man was known for the number of fleeces he could lift in a day. They worked in the spring planting the crops and cleaning the acequias for the muddy fecund waters that ran from the melting snow. The men of the Old Town knew how to work and how to make a game of it, but work to them was only one thing and largely a seasonal thing. There were long winter times when little work was done and summer days too hot for work and a great many days sacred to saints and Gods when all men danced and prayed and played games. Except when emergencies pressed the favorite time for work was tomorrow and all work ended in some kind of fiesta. One man might own another, might beat him or even kill him but he could not hope to make him work on a fiesta day.

The men who built the railroad and the men it brought

along knew neither seasons of idleness nor seasons of feast. They had but one day of rest in a week and they didn't always honor that. All the way across the prairie they worked like madmen, driven by the machine behind them. They built towns almost in a day and then went off and left them dead. They were men who lived to work and worked for money.

The men of the Old Town knew nothing about that kind of work. But they were soon to learn. In the New Town the railroad company built a machine shop to repair cars and locomotives and it had to have labor. The roadway needed labor too. New Town now took notice of Old. A mule-car line was built between the old and the new to carry men to work. Many Mexicans refused to work for the railroad but it got what it needed. It paid more cash for labor than that country had ever seen. For big round dollars men left their ranches and their patrons and went to work for the railroad.

To these men the great shop-whistle must have seemed, more than anything else, to be the voice and symbol of the new regime. All their lives they had been taking orders, they had been listening to voices of authority. But here was a voice that would take no answer and make no compromise — an inhuman voice that measured time in a world where time was money. You could hear it for miles and it murdered sleep. It blew at six and men jumped out of bed and reached for their shoes. At quarter of seven it tooted a brief note of warning. At seven it filled the air with its final summons and every man who hoped to eat must be at work that minute. It made men as much a part of the machine as any wheel or drum.

New Town was built around the railroad and the shops. It was called a railroad town and rightly so. Nearly all of its inhabitants owed their lives to the railroad directly or indirectly. It began with the railroad station and reached a single wide street toward the Old Town. Another street paralleled the tracks so that the Town had roughly the form of a cross.

This New Town deserved its name for it was new in kind as well as in being. It bore no relation or resemblance to anything that had gone before. It was built of wood, for one thing, and although most of it was only one story high many of its buildings had two-story fronts. It was pretentious and it was ambitious. It projected its own future in empty streets and vacant lots and its creators spoke of it modestly as a metropolis in the making. Meanwhile it was a town of shacks, stores, boarding houses and saloons and most saloons were also gambling houses and houses of prostitution.

Wherever industry strikes virgin soil this same kind of town grows up. It runs as true to type as a white rabbit. Not only every railroad town but every mining town reproduces the pattern and the new oil towns still take the same form. It is amazing how much Hobbs and Borger look like pictures of Dodge and Deadwood in their days of boom. Cars replace buckboards and ponies but there are the same streets lined with shacks and shanties, honky-tonks and baudy houses, speakeasies or saloons. There is the same scene of crowded struggle and desperate revelry, the same mob of restless men and shrill money-hungry women — above all, the same impression of a great outburst of driven energy, harsh and terrible,

only half human, wholly self-sufficient, without the power
or the need to adapt itself to anything.

The town itself was a machine and the saloons and
roulette wheels and baudy houses were a necessary part
of its mechanism. If you are going to give men money
on Saturday night you must take it away from them
again so they will come back to work for more on
Monday morning. Gradually you may teach them how to
save but first you must teach them how to spend for that
is more easily learned. So every Saturday night Railroad
Avenue blazed with light and jangled with the music of
honky-tonk pianos. Men crowded the high board side-
walks, poured into every saloon, surrounded gambling
tables like puppies around a plate of milk, lined the bars
in solid ranks, followed beckoning women into cribs and
dives. Money that went out of railroad pay windows Saturday afternoon was thrown down on bars and tables
Saturday night, raked up like a ripe crop, returned to its
rightful possessors — the men who knew how to hold it
and how to use it.

They had come with the railroad, these money masters.

The older West had been romantic, childishly so perhaps. Men had always come west to make their fortunes
but they often threw money away as fast as they made it.
They often threw their lives away too. They were childishly fond of heroic gestures — of challenges to men and
destiny, of high-sounding slogans. " Pike's Peak or bust! "
" Fifty-four forty or fight! " That sort of thing was going
out of fashion now. A new slogan was to replace all
others. " Six per cent and safety." Only it was more likely
to be eight or ten per cent in those days.

Money makes men careful. Men who don't throw away money don't throw their lives away either. Money is subtly allied with respectability, just as it is the enemy of heroism and romance. Men who hope to gather money must look safe and staid. They go in for stiff collars, wives and sober faces.

They were of many kinds and races — these money masters — but they all had one thing in common. They put money first. One of them was an Italian with an organ and a monkey. It is said they threw rocks at him when he first struck town and that a woman of the cribs was the only friend he could find. But he saved dimes and nickels and made them grow. In just a little while he was running the biggest saloon in town. He was a master of girls and gaming tables. And people who wanted to build found that he owned the earth.

He was a little fellow like that other Italian who conquered the world. Nobody ever saw a gun on him. He packed a bank roll instead. He was very quiet, reticent and soft spoken. He never needed to raise his voice. Money talks.

Another man of destiny was a Jew. He opened a store in a small Mexican town and did a good business for a while. He was getting rich. Like everyone who makes money he also made enemies. They gave him to understand that they were going to get him. Did he assemble his friends and defy his enemies? He did not. His line was dry goods, not heroism. He loaded his stock on one hundred burros and with the help of fifty Mexicans moved it across a mountain range to a larger and safer town, and from there inevitably he moved to New Town, which already was established as the home of money, morality and safe returns.

Money men gravitated to New Town by that unfailing process which brings each to his own. There was a refined young lawyer from a southern state who had a little political influence. It got him an appointment as postmaster in a tough town far from the railroad. He was told by certain men with guns on their hips that they didn't like the way he sorted the mail. He knew they could shoot better than he could. He was not a man of battle but a man of law. He was an exact and severe logician. He very logically moved to another town and hung out a tin sign as attorney-at-law. A leading citizen of this town was a very bad man. He was running the town. With a gang at his back he would set forth every once in so often for a tour of the bars. He would line men up and make them drink at the point of a gun. Once in a while someone would resist or refuse and almost always this curmudgeon would get killed.

This man was increasingly regarded as a nuisance by almost everyone but to a young lawyer needing practice he was a boon. The young lawyer defended him repeatedly, successfully, expensively, and without a qualm. He not only needed the money and the practice but he believed in the law. By law every man is entitled to the best defense he can get and a bloody murderer has as good a right to counsel as anyone else. This young lawyer had observed that self-defense was popular in the West. He didn't believe in it himself. He never carried a gun. When he saw danger approaching he moved away just as he avoided stepping on rattlesnakes. But he capitalized the popularity of self-defense. Always the victims of his clients had guns. Always there had been an altercation. Always the other fellow got killed. Why? He was too slow, that was all. The reluctance of witnesses to testify against a man who was never too slow may have helped this rising young lawyer to win his cases. At any rate he cleared his client again and again and made a living and reputation out of him.

Naturally the client began to think of himself as immune to human vengeance. In a careless moment he killed an unarmed man. They put him in jail. He sent for his attorney and demanded to be gotten out. The young lawyer explained regretfully that it couldn't be done. His regret was genuine. It became acute when the populace broke down the door of the jail and took justice in their own hands. The young attorney saw his client, his income, his reputation hanged on the limb of a cottonwood tree. He must have viewed the corpse with painfully mixed emotions. There was ninety percent of his practice, dead as a kippered herring, aswing in the morning breeze. Yet that corpse was a monument to his ability too. They would never have needed to lynch the man if he hadn't had such a brilliant attorney. With a sigh of regret, perhaps, but with confidence in his heart, he packed his bag and moved to New Town. He had come home. There he became an attorney for the railroad. He had a client with unlimited money and an iron neck.

2

New Town briefly was a frontier town where men wore guns outside their clothes and life was hazardous. Bad men on horseback rode its streets but none of them rode far or long. From the first this town was marked as a home of law and order, a cradle of respectability, a place where life was relatively safe and property was absolutely sacred. It had its killings but these on the whole took the form of a rapid extermination of those who did not appreciate civilization. A cowboy named Fish rode into town one day and in accordance with the most approved traditions of this kind, went on a shooting spree. Actuated still by the most revered precedents, he rode his horse through sundry open doors and chased innocent bystanders into the street. Finally he rode through the door of the new stone court-house which had just been completed — an impressive monument to human justice. At the point of a gun he marched the judge and jury out of the door and around a block or two and then let them return to their judicial duties. It was just the kind of pleasantry that had been tolerated in wide open towns all over the West but it wasn't popular in New Town. Fish was caught by the sheriff and lodged in the jail. Next day they went to call him out for trial and found him dead, shot through the head. His death remains to this day officially a mystery but old-timers say the sheriff admitted the shooting. He was a Mexican but he had become imbued with the new ideas of order and thrift and had put his own interpretation upon them. Since Fish was undoubtedly guilty, why should the county be put to the expense of a trial and a hanging? That was the way he explained the end of Fish.

Yarberry was another misplaced romantic. He was a six-shooter man of skill and courage and on the strength of his abilities he got the job of town marshal. Many famous gunmen had been given jobs as town marshals and sheriffs and almost always their careers ran the same course. They usually discharged their duties in a manful and deadly fashion for a while. Almost always their power impaired their judgment. They began shooting errant citizens on small provocation or even for sport. One of them would rule a town for a while by the sheer might of his trigger-finger and finally perish at the hands of some man a fraction of a second faster on the draw. Yarberry ran true to type. He was an excellent officer for a while. Then some of his gun plays seemed a little unnecessary and finally he shot a man who had committed no crime whatsoever. He too went to the new jail in the hands of the sheriff. He was tried, convicted and sentenced to die. On the gallows he asked for ten minutes to make a speech. The sheriff gave him the ten minutes, timed him, watch in hand, and broke his neck in the middle of an eloquent sentence.

New Town was not a wild town for long, doubtless because the supply of wild men didn't last. They were given too much rope. Even Billy the Kid couldn't have any fun there. It is said that he once leapt on a table in a dance hall in New Town with drawn gun, whether to make speech or dance a break-down is not recorded. The sheriff of the new regime knocked his gun out of his hand and took him to jail. Some say Billy was a friend of the sheriff and didn't want to kill him. But just as likely he was astounded and overwhelmed by such unconventional treatment. Many men had tried to shoot him but no one had ever before knocked his gun out of his hand. It was unheard of. He served a peaceful term in the county jail and made himself useful by helping to sweep it every morning. Then he went back to Lincoln county where men had the manners to stand up and shoot at each other like gentlemen.

3

The railroad created New Town in 1881. By 1890 it was a peaceful place and by 1910 it was almost a model of what a small American town should be. In all essentials it was just like a town in Iowa or Kansas and not strikingly different from one in Pennsylvania or Michigan. Great and significant events took place in those peaceful years. The opening of the First National Bank, the organization of the Ladies Aid Society, the building of the waterworks, the coming of the bicycle and then of the automobile, the crusade of the ministerial Alliance against the Red Light district, the passing of the dry law under local option — all of these triumphs for progress and purity would be meat for a more leisurely historian than I am. And even more important than these epochal events was the steady spread of the little town into a neat and angular pattern of impeccable domesticity. The United States ideally is one vast community of cottages, bungalows and flats inhabited by virtuous couples engaged in raising babies, police dogs, gold fish and rubber plants, listening to radios, riding in automobiles, immune to every temptation save those of high pressure salesmanship and the installment plan. New Town has become perhaps as fair a sample of this vast fabric of felicity as can be found anywhere. To describe it in detail would be like a fish trying to describe water to other fish, for I am in it and of it and so are all the rest of us and it has an almost aqueous uniformity.

I would not represent it as perfect but its imperfections are those of its time. If the divorce evil has here and there marred the perfection of domestic life, it has not done so in New Town as much as in some other places. If the younger generation has substituted white mule for ice cream soda, moved from the parlor sofa to the back seat of the family limousine and misconstrued the petting privilege, this also has happened nearly everywhere. On the whole, respectability and progress have triumphed. The new Junior High School stands on the very spot where I used to shoot ducks when I was a boy. The road over which I painfully bumped my way to school on a primitive bicycle is now a paved thoroughfare filled with the purr of motors and the fragrance of carbon monoxide. They have leveled off the sandhills and filled the frog ponds, they have made a zoological park where the native fauna is impounded along with the inevitable monkeys and elephants. They have everything that a good town needs.

4

For a while it looked as though New Town would destroy Old Town, actually as well as symbolically. Here as elsewhere in pioneer America men lived in the dream of unlimited wealth and unlimited expansion. Its early newspapers refer to New Town repeatedly as a metropolis in the making. It was not only to grow — it was to boom. And it did share modestly in all the booms that swept across the West. It shared in the cattle boom when almost every railroad town became a shipping point for live-stock, fed by the long trails from the South. New Town itself was never much of a cow town but Las Vegas, a little way North, sent much beef to Chicago and enter-tained many a wild trail gang. It still holds a Cowboy's Reunion every Fourth of July but that is almost the only time any authentic cowboy is seen there. It is neither as large nor as prosperous as once it was and there are not as many cattle in the state as there used to be. For years British capital poured into the cattle business and New Mexico got its share. It had its cattle barons and its ranches as large as Balkan nations and some of these are still under fence, but cattle didn't thrive on most of the range. It was too rough in spots and too dry almost every-where.

The mine boom struck New Mexico during the period when Cripple Creek and Virginia City and the Comstock Lode and all the other famous names of mining history were being made. That was the gaudiest dream of all. Probably no one doubted that gold and silver and copper would work the final and complete transformation of wilderness into civilization. But the mining boom petered out more suddenly and more completely here than almost anywhere else, leaving the mountains littered with ghost towns and with pits and tunnels that became the haunt of bats and memories.

New Town grew but like everything else in this country it had only a slow and hardy growth. Chicago and Los Angeles and Denver and all the other great cities of the West are New Town grown colossal. They are the pioneer dream of progress become an overwhelming reality. They have obliterated everything that went before. But in New Mexico the seed of the machine fell upon a sterile soil. It encountered a peculiarly resistant environment. Fifty years of progress have left the face of the earth amazingly unchanged. Only a tiny fraction of it is cultivated. The mesas, made of sand and lava, stand as bare as ever and feed nothing but a few sheep. The government undertook to save the forests and it became in effect the keeper of the mountains so that they are almost as they were.

New Mexico towns, like other desert plants, tend to reach a certain modest size and then grow very slowly if at all. Taos is a place of inextinguishable vitality but it is about the same size now that it was when Kit Carson got there. Santa Fe has gained about two thousand people in two hundred years. Socorro, which boomed on silver, is only a fraction of its former self. Only Albuquerque and a few towns in the eastern part of the state, which rightfully belong to Texas, have grown substantially.

For dreams of wealth this country has surely been a graveyard. The drama of the seven golden cities has been enacted again and again. As Coronado followed a dream of unlimited gold and came away without even his coat of mail, so many another man has lost his shirt seeking wealth along the Rio Grande. The Southwest is perhaps the one large region in the United States where the great American dream of change and progress has most strikingly failed to come true. Here the persistence of primitive stocks and folkways has resisted social change as rock and sun have resisted the plow.

This finally has come to be its chief distinction — that here alone change has not wholly obliterated all that went before, that the past is present in patterns of life and types of men, that the face of the earth is not much altered. It remains, as it has always been, a place of destination, but most of those who come here now come seeking an elusive something they call color or atmosphere or romance or tradition. Whatever you call it, it is inadequately named and means many things to many persons but it surely represents some kind of a genuine need and value.

A man, to be whole, must not live too fast to think. He must reflect much upon his experience, accepting the worst of it, appreciating the best of it, making it all a part of his being, so that each moment is but the focal point of a long clear perspective. If he is too busy and if circumstance is too exigent he loses all sense of continuity, his life lacks significance. And surely it is not otherwise with peoples and nations. America in general has been too busy and the circumstance of change has been overwhelming. Chicago is not a plant with roots in the soil but a huge fungus of machinery and men, and it is a fair sample of industrial America.

A feeling of continuity in our experience as a people, a sense of the past as a living reality conditioning the present are what we have lost. I think even casual observers in New Mexico are aware of a richer and more living background, but to most of them it appears remote and irrelevant to the rest of America. They have dubbed it quaint, strange and picturesque and painted its costume rather than its soul. It is to many a place of romantic escape and they seem to look for the exotic rather than the significant. It has never seemed either strange or a place of escape to me, doubtless in large part because I was born there, but I think it is more intimately integrated with the whole American experience than most Americans know, and this whole book has been an effort to reveal what I believe to be its significant connections.

5

Many others have come here and worked at the same or at similar tasks. The latest invasion of this much invaded land has been an influx of painters and writers and of all those various types of men and women who are the camp followers of every cultural movement. This westward migration of the men with paint and ink on their fingers has given New Mexico a new type of society and a new spurt of life, just as the coming of the beaver trappers and the wagon traders did. It is a part of the region's social history, too important to be overlooked and too recent to be clearly seen.

Taos and Santa Fe now are art colonies whose life is shaped and colored perhaps more by the artists and intellectuals than by any other class. This, I think, is the distinctive thing about them. Santa Fe now has much in common with Greenwich Village, Carmel, Provincetown and all those other foci of cultural infection which pimple the fair face of our land. Not only the same types but many of the same persons are found in all of them.

In America the intellectuals tend to be the most exclusive and self-conscious class in the social aggregation. They tend to live in groups apart, consorting only with each other. The intolerance which they deplore in others is in them often exaggerated to the point of phobia. Doubtless this is inevitable in a country where the fine arts long have borne a measure of disesteem, where the social pressure has been toward material and practical accomplishment, where the life of the mind is traditionally suspect. Doubtless it is also regrettable, for surely the artist should leaven the social lump, should be a man among men of all kinds both for his own good and for theirs.

In New Mexico the painters and writers seem to be more a part of the society they have invaded than anywhere else I have been. They were drawn there in the first place by some felt affinity for the rich primitive background of the place. They have tried to make common cause with the Indians and Mexicans and if the alliance has not resulted in complete mutual understanding it has nevertheless been a genuine and fruitful social contact. Finding the Indians in danger of starvation because they were being robbed of their lands and in danger of losing their identity because of the government policy to make them over into good American farmers, the invading aesthetes have championed the red man. They have flooded the country with literature about their wrongs, have helped to force bills through congress and have caused senators and congressmen to engage in solemn and bewildered investigation of the aboriginal soul. This movement has been rich in absurdity and slow in result but I think it can fairly be said that the aesthetic group in New Mexico has created in the American public a new appreciation of the Indian as a unique and valuable survival who ought to be cherished for what he is rather than made over into something else. I think his extinction as a type of man has been postponed if not prevented.

Here too the painters and writers have more of a genuine and working relationship to the community life as a whole than elsewhere, chiefly because that community as a social organism is relatively small and weak. The literary group that gathered in Chicago a few years ago was widely advertised as a great cultural renaissance which was to move the literary capital of America across the Mississippi. But Chicago as a whole was no more aware of this spiritual phenomenon than a dog is aware of a flea which is not biting him. One by one the cornbelt poets migrated to Manhattan leaving Chicago to Al Capone and Big Bill.

Santa Fe and Taos were incapable of such magnificent ignorance. The artists have brought new life to both places. They have been followed by a troop of tourists with money in their pockets. They have boosted rents and bettered business. They are regarded with a tolerance which may have begun as no more than an appreciation of their cash value but has often grown into something more personal. I think this is one of the few places in America, if not the only one, where poets and painters have become prominent citizens, where hotels and other public places are decorated with the products of local artists and where the architecture of postoffices and movie theaters, as well as of residences, has been influenced by the artists of the community. The plaza in Santa Fe has been almost made over in the Pueblo-Mexican style and it is a daring soul who builds a house in Taos in any other mode. In summary, the artists here have become in some measure a part of society, have quickened the community life and produced a visible and physical effect upon it.

Even Albuquerque, the stronghold of prosperity and progress, the best business town between Pueblo and El Paso, the home of Rotary and Kiwanis, the obedient child of the railroad, has felt the renaissance a little. Recently an old adobe building in Old Albuquerque was made over, not to look like the first national bank, but to look as it had a hundred years ago. With a grand ball it was opened to the public as Albuquerque's Art Center. Here artists were to live and paint — at least so it was hoped and said. There have never been many artists in Albuquerque but the town at least offered them a home, as one might build a nest box in a tree to lure shy birds.

The opening ball was a costume ball and it was a great success. The daughter of an old Mexican family appeared in a ponderous wedding dress which had been worn in that same house half a century before. A promising young real estate man looked enough like an aboriginal Navajo to tempt the trigger finger of an unreconstructed pioneer. Buffalo Bill was there and Montezuma and more youths in tight Spanish trousers and girls in high Spanish combs than the floor would hold. This town, which has so long lived in its future, now for the first time shows a quickening awareness of its past.

When one turns from the long study of vanished types and cultures to survey the present, he enters a narrow and perilous place, where exaggeration threatens and speculation tempts. I say no more of New Mexico as it is today, except that here surely is a place where many kinds of men live and work, where one may dig or dream, make poems, bricks or love, or merely sit in the sun, and find some tolerance and some companionship. Here handicraft as well as the machine has some place in life, the primitive persists beside the civilized, the changeless mountains offer refuge to the weary sons of change.

Bibliography

I have not burdened this book with footnotes, nor with a formal bibliography, and this for several reasons. In the first place it is based upon observation and interview as much as upon documentary research, so that no complete accounting of its sources is possible. In the second place, although I have tried to be accurate in statements of ascertainable fact, the book is an attempt at interpretation rather than a record. Moreover, my researches have impressed me with the fact that very little besides a few dates, names and statistics can be surely known about the past. Whenever I have found several accounts of an event, almost always they have differed widely. I have had no choice but to accept the version that seemed most consonant with my knowledge of the kinds of men involved, so that the veracity of the book is necessarily more psychological than factual. It is true insofar as it is convincing. A good realistic novel, it has been said, is history that might have happened, and the same is very largely true of a good history.

My bibliography, therefore, is merely a partial acknowledgment of indebtedness and a brief commentary on some of the more interesting books that have gone into the making of this one.

I am deeply indebted to the New Mexico Historical Society and especially to the writings of Ralph Emerson Twitchell, the Reverend Lansing Bloom and the late Don Amado Chaves, who also gave me a great deal of valuable information in conversations a few years before his death. Twitchell's "Leading Facts of New Mexico History," while not an entertaining book is indispensable to anyone doing research in this field. The files of the magazine, "Old Santa Fe" published by the Historical Society, are full of valuable material, and so are the bulletins of the Society.

The work of Adolph Bandelier has been of great help to me in the early chapters. His remarkable archaeological novel, "The Delight Makers" is the most complete and vivid account of Pueblo life I know of, and it deserves to be much more widely known. I have accepted A. V. Kidder's excellent "Introduction to the Study of Southwestern Archaeology" as embodying the latest scientific findings about the origins of the Pueblos.

New Mexico history before the nineteenth century is based almost entirely upon archaeological research and the records and documents left by Spanish explorers, most of which have been admirably translated, paraphrased and summarized. As most of this material is of interest chiefly to scholars I give no account of it.

Beginning in the early nineteenth century there is a long list of records by Americans and Europeans who made the overland journey. The earliest and one of the best of these is Lieutenant Zebulon Pike's narrative of his expedition. Perhaps the most entertaining is the account of the Texan-Santa Fe expedition by George W. Kendall. Josiah Gregg's " Commerce of the Prairies " has been sufficiently noticed in the text. George Frederick Ruxton's account of his journey from Vera Cruz to the Missouri and his curious semi-fictitious book on the mountain men contain a great deal of information about the beaver-trapping period and are highly readable. So is Uncle Dick Wootton's autobiography, noticed in the text, and James Ohio Pattie's narrative. " A Campaign in New Mexico " by Frank S. Edwards is a revealing and amusing picture of New Mexico at the time of the conquest by the United States, and " El Gringo " by W. W. H. Davis is a careful and somewhat priggish description of life in Santa Fe in the fifties, indispensable for its picture of costume and manners. Inman's " Old Santa Fe Trail " is well known. Meline's " Two Thousand Miles on Horseback " will interest anyone who likes the old West. The " Personal Narrative " of J. R. Bartlett contains revealing information about the relations between Mexicans and Texans in the years following the occupation.

" The Conquest of New Mexico and California " by Philip St. George Cooke, James W. Abert's government report on his biological reconnaissance in New Mexico, and Richard B. Townshend's " A Tenderfoot in New Mexico " have all been of use to me and contain many revealing details.

" Recollections of a Western Ranchman " by William French is one of the best records of the six-shooter epoch in New Mexico and one of the most readable. " Law and Order Limited " by Kyle S. Crichton is a biography of

Elfego Baca written in collaboration with its subject, and
is a unique and highly entertaining little book. " A Vaquero of the Brush Country " by J. Frank Dobie and John
Young is a similar collaboration between an old timer
and a modern writer. It is the best book I know on the
origins of the cattle business in this country and very
readable. Emerson Hough's " The Cowboy " is also
valuable.

For the most part research is a long hunt through dull
pages for a rare and needed detail, but most of the books
mentioned above I read all the way through with pleasure
and I recommend them to anyone who shares my interest
in their subjects.

INDEX

i

A NOTE ON THE TYPE IN WHICH THIS BOOK IS SET

The text of this book was set on the linotype in Baskerville. The punches for this face were cut under the supervision of George W. Jones, an eminent English printer. Linotype Baskerville is a facsimile cutting from type cast from the original matrices of a face designed by John Baskerville. The original face was the forerunner of the "modern" group of type faces. ¶ John Baskerville (1706-75), of Birmingham, England, a writing-master, with a special renown for cutting inscriptions in stone, began experimenting about 1750 with punch-cutting and making typographical material. It was not until 1757 that he published his first work, a Virgil in royal quarto, with great-primer letters. This was followed by his famous editions of Milton, the Bible, the Book of Common Prayer, and several Latin classic authors. His types, at first criticized as unnecessarily slender, delicate, and feminine, in time were recognized as both distinct and elegant, and both his types and his printing were greatly admired. Printers, however, preferred the stronger types of Caslon, and Baskerville before his death repented of having attempted the business of printing. For four years after his death his widow continued to conduct his business. She then sold all his punches and matrices to the Société Littéraire-typographique, which used some of the types for the sumptuous Kehl edition of Voltaire's works in —————— seventy volumes. ——————

COMPOSED, PRINTED, AND BOUND BY THE
PLIMPTON PRESS, NORWOOD, MASS.
THE PAPER WAS MADE BY
S. D. WARREN CO.
BOSTON

THE RIO GRANDE NEAR TAOS

RUINS OF THE OLD CHURCH AT TAOS

A PENITENTE PROCESSION

PENITENTE MORADA, RANCHOS DE TAOS

THE RESTORED KHIVA IN THE CLIFF
DWELLINGS AT RITO DE LOS FRIJOLES
(By courtesy of the New Mexico Historical Society)

A MEXICAN DOORYARD

THE PUEBLO OF TAOS

THE KHIVA, SAN ILDEFONSO PUEBLO

(By courtesy of the New Mexico Historical Society)

A PENITENTE "CHARIOT OF DEATH"

(By courtesy of the New Mexico Historical Society)

COMANCHE DANCE, JEMEZ PUEBLO

AN OLD PICTURE OF THE RELAY RACE ON SAN
GERONIMO DAY IN TAOS

A NAVAJO SILVERSMITH

(*By courtesy of the New Mexico Historical Society*)

A BUSINESS BUILDING AND THEATER IN SANTA FE

A NAVAJO WOMAN

"UNCLE DICK" WOOTTON

(By courtesy of the New Mexico Historical Society)

JOSIAH GREGG

(*By courtesy of the New Mexico Historical Society*)

ARCHBISHOP JOHN B. LAMY

(By courtesy of the New Mexico Historical Society)

PADRE ANTONIO JOSÉ MARTINEZ

(*By courtesy of the New Mexico Historical Society*)

CICERO

and the end of the Roman Republic

W. K. Lacey

BOOKS

10 East 53d St., New York 10022
(a division of Harper & Row Publishers, Inc.)

Library of Congress Cataloging in Publication Data

Lacey, Walter Kirkpatrick.
    Cicero and the end of the Roman Republic.
    Bibliography: p.
    Includes index.
        1. Cicero, Marcus Tullius. 2. Rome—History—
Republic, 265–30 B.C. 3. Statesmen—Rome—Biography.
4. Orators—Rome—Biography. I. Title.
DG260.C5L25   937′.05′0924 [B]   78–1101
ISBN 0-06-494013-6

Published in the U.S.A. 1978 by
HARPER & ROW PUBLISHERS, INC.
BARNES & NOBLE IMPORT DIVISION

Printed in Great Britain

Preface

Cicero's biographers must begin with Cicero himself. How much of his testimony they believe, and which parts, will make them produce differing interpretations, but Cicero must himself always be consulted first about what he thought of the situation in the Roman *res publica* – a term which for convenience (but not for accuracy) is translated 'Republic'.

Naturally, Cicero was not always right in his diagnosis of what went wrong with the Republic, but we shall not be right either unless we bear several things in mind.

First, the speeches of Cicero we have were published by him, and in consequence what is in them has his imprimatur: they were put 'on the record', deliberately.

Second, Cicero was a politician: he therefore talked like a politician, he was prepared to have bedfellows of whom he did not fully approve, and he did not say in public exactly what he said, or would have said, in private. But he could not afford to tell lies; nothing destroys a politician's credibility like being caught lying. Cicero never lost his credibility.

Third, Cicero was a barrister. Most trials were overtly political, and judgment was given – and expected – not just on the question of 'guilty or not guilty on the evidence presented', but on whether the acquittal of the defendant was, or was not, to the advantage of the Republic as a whole.

Fourth, in the Republic it mattered whether you were well thought of or not; a man's influence amongst his peers depended on it, and so did his only hope of posthumous existence. Fame (or glory) really was the spur to the Romans, and men were expected to blow their own trumpets. Cicero overblew his, of course, and the Romans knew it, but not to the same extent that would be felt nowadays; and fame, not power or wealth, was the limit of Cicero's ambitions.

Fifth, Cicero had a mercurial temperament, and a pungent wit; we shall never understand him in an aseptic atmosphere of academic detachment, nor shall we if we cannot face the fact that some of the time he is being ironical or humorous at his own expense.

These two last points affect our understanding of the letters most; many of these were not meant for publication, but some were, and others were written in the knowledge that they might in fact become public; the fact that an opinion is in a letter does not necessarily mean that it was written only for the eye of the intended recipient.

An account of some recent books on Cicero and his times is in the bibliography. In this biography I have tried to illustrate Cicero's importance for the intellectual heritage of Rome as well as his place within the politics and society of his life-time. Other Romans, maybe, were more heroic, others reflected more fully the aims and aspirations of Rome's governing class, but Cicero was, and has always been, the most eloquent spokesman for those who believe that politics is the business of persuasion and the ballot-box, and not of coercion.

I wish to thank Mr D. Branch of the Geography Department of Auckland University for drafting the map of Italy; the sketch of Rome is based on that in Heinrich Kiepert's *Atlas Antiquus*, and the map of Cilicia is redrawn from *Res Publica* by kind permission of Oxford University Press. I wish also to thank my (now retired) colleague, Associate Professor L. W. A. Crawley, with whom I have had much profitable discussion since he read the whole of the first draft of the MS, and the Classics Department Secretary, Mrs Karen Staniland, who managed to fit the typing into an already very full programme. My own heavy teaching programme has long delayed the final publication of this work, which I was able to complete thanks to a period of sabbatical leave, for which I am most grateful to the University of Auckland.

Auckland, New Zealand   *September 1976*

Contents

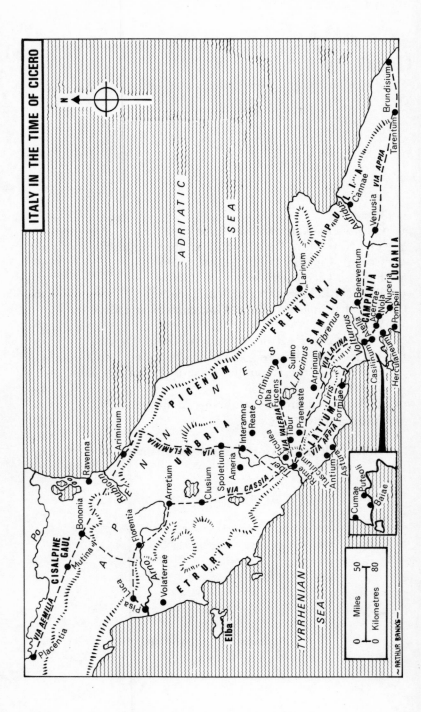

ITALY IN THE TIME OF CICERO

N

ADRIATIC SEA

TYRRHENIAN SEA

CISALPINE GAUL

VIA AEMILIA
Placentia
Po
Mutina
Bononia
Ravenna
Ariminum
Rubicon
A P E N N I N E S
Luca
Pisa(e)
Arno
Florentia
Arretium
FLAMINIA
UMBRIA
PICENUM
Volaterrae
ETRURIA
Elba
Clusium
Spoletium
Ameria
VIA CASSIA
Tiber
VIA FLAMINIA
Reate
Interamna
Ficulea
Tibur
Rome
Tusculum
VIA VALERIA
Praeneste
VIA LATINA
VIA APPIA
LATIUM
Antium
Astura
Corfinium
Alba
Fucens
L. Fucinus
Sulmo
Arpinum
Fibrenus
Liris
Formiae
Volturnus
Casinum
CAMPANIA
Larinum
FRENTANI
SAMNIUM
Aesernia
Beneventum
Acerrae
Nola
Nuceria
Pompeii
Herculaneum
APULIA
Aufidus
Cannae
Venusia
VIA APPIA
Brundisium
Tarentum
LUCANIA

Cumae
Puteoli
Baiae

0 Miles 50
0 Kilometres 80

~ ARTHUR BANKS ~

I
Cicero's Background and Education

Cicero we call him. His full name was Marcus Tullius, son of Marcus, grandson of Marcus, of the tribe Cornelia, Cicero; his name was thus identical with that of his father and grandfather, and his son bore the same name too; this was usual in Rome. The 'three names' were characteristic of the Roman citizen, and not to have the first two meant you were not a Roman.

Of these, the first, the *praenomen*, was the one that marked the individual member of the family – Marcus Tullius Cicero's younger brother was Quintus Tullius Cicero. The middle name (*nomen*) belonged to the *gens*, the group of families who had come into the Roman community through the same ancestor or family; many of these were ancient and contained both patrician families (aristocratic and priestly in tradition) and plebeian ones (non-priestly, and originally subordinate, but by Cicero's day frequently ennobled by political success). This was the case with Tullius; the Ciceros belonged to a plebeian branch, and Cicero regarded as faintly ridiculous the attempts of some of his contemporaries to find him a noble lineage. A woman, traditionally, was given only the feminine form of her father's *nomen*, like Cicero's daughter, who was called Tullia.

A man's last name, or *cognomen*, marked the family within the *gens* or clan; most of them, like many English surnames, originally had reference to some physical characteristic. Cicero meant 'chick-pea', a nickname given to one of his forebears who had had a mark of this round shape on his features. Tradition said that Cicero was urged to change it because it had never been heard of before in Rome, but he refused, saying he would make it as famous as any in Rome, and this, of course, he did.

Cicero was born on 3 January 106 B.C. in the mansion-house of his father's estate. This estate lay within the territory of the *municipium* (borough) of Arpinum, the modern Arpino, about sixty miles from Rome in a south-easterly direction among the foothills of the Apennines. His father was a landowner, a man of considerable wealth and cultured tastes. He was an invalid, who spent most of his life on his estate and rebuilt and enlarged the house. Cicero's grandfather was a public figure in Arpinum, a thorough-going conservative in politics, who disapproved of 'modern' trends, such as learning Greek. No member of the family had progressed outside the field of local politics into the national arena, so that when Marcus Cicero did so, he was, as the Romans said, a 'new man'.

In the same year, 106, on the other side of the Apennines, in the area known as Picenum, a son was born into the family of Gnaeus Pompeius Strabo. This child, Cn. Pompeius, a vain man, who dropped the family name of Strabo to assume the arrogant cognomen of Magnus (the Mighty), and who, thanks to Shakespeare, is known to all moderns as Pompey, was destined to be closely linked with Cicero, occasionally helping him, but more frequently frustrating and disappointing him in his political aims and aspirations. The family, however, was an important one in Italy, and Cicero himself always looked up to Pompey, who rose to a prominent political position much earlier in life than Cicero did.

Amongst the neighbours of the Ciceros was a family who bore the name C. Marius. There is no reason to suppose that the two families were closely connected, but they had some common kinsmen, and must have known one another. They can have had little in common, however, since Cicero's father was a man of culture and poor health, whereas the C. Marius of his generation was a man of great physical endurance and no culture, who had made his way from the rank of an ordinary cavalry-soldier to the highest magistracy in Rome, the position of consul. This he had achieved the year before Cicero's birth, in the face of stubborn opposition from the traditional governing classes. About the time when Cicero was born, C. Marius was setting forth to lead a new model Roman army he had created into the principal war then raging. This was across the Mediterranean in the area we know as Algeria, which the Romans called Numidia. The small town of

Arpinum must have been agog with excitement, since it was a place of strong local loyalties and of pride in its famous sons. It may well be that Cicero's father was fired by Marius' success to hope that his own son might also reach the top in Roman politics.

Roman politics were dominated by a group of noble families: noble because they were the descendants of the men who had held the consulship. They were extensively intermarried, and controlled the voting-mechanisms of the state through a system called *patronatus* (patronage). By this means they were able to manipulate the votes of the Roman equivalents of electoral wards or constituencies, which were known as tribes or centuries, and which decided every matter brought to the vote, including the annual elections to the magistracies. A patron looked after the interests of his 'clients' in their dealings with the state and its officers, and in return clients helped their patron and his sons in their political careers, by voting for them, and for their relatives and friends.

New men lacked any such ready-made access to the mechanisms of power; most were content to progress in politics under the sponsorship of some noble patron to whom they had attached themselves. Consequently they very seldom reached the consulship, which the nobles regarded as their own preserve, which would be degraded if a non-noble succeeded in obtaining it. Ambitious new men thus had to create their own following of clients in order to win the votes needed to get there. Military men like Marius created theirs out of their ex-soldiers, who stood in the same relationship to their general as the hereditary client to his noble patron. Cicero, the barrister, had to create his political following by services in the law-courts, and by pressing the interests of the *equites*, or knights: these were either landowners like his own father, who led the country towns, or business-men. Many of them were the state's contractors, who exploited the empire through their banking, moneylending, and commercial activities; but they could not enter politics, since, by a law passed more than a hundred years before Cicero's birth, contractors were not allowed to hold the magistracies or enter the state's deliberative and legislative council, the Senate.

Equites were very useful supporters in politics, however, since the principal electoral assembly, the assembly by centuries, was heavily biased in favour of the rich and the elderly; but their support was hard to muster continuously, since they were often out of Rome (where all voting took place) and they were generally not concerned with politics unless their own interests were affected.

The support – and the votes – of the common people of Rome was more easily mustered by a third class of politicians, the members of families which had once been noble, but had been squeezed out of the dominant group, and had become impoverished. Catiline, Clodius, and Caesar all belonged to this class; all were patricians and came from the city of Rome itself. They called themselves 'popular' leaders, perhaps because they based their political support on the popular assembly, known as the assembly by tribes, in which the common people had much more influence, and because they exercised political initiatives largely through officers known as tribunes of the people, who were elected by the popular assembly.

These 'popular' leaders organized their followers in clubs, to enable them to compete with the followings of the noble patrons, and, since they were on the spot in Rome, these clubs were able to put pressure on the political machinery of the state much more effectively than the equites and the country-based followings of leaders like Marius, Pompey, and Cicero, though they too could enjoy popular support at times when they were opposing the nobles.

We are accustomed to continuing, well-organized political parties with electoral programmes which touch almost every facet of national life. Roman political parties were totally dissimilar; they formed a kaleidoscopic pattern of changing alliances, and their programmes very seldom contained any aim apart from the election of one politician rather than another to the highest magistracies of the state. Magistracies were important to politicians not merely for the honour and the power that they brought, but also for financial reasons: magistracies were almost the only legal way in which a politician could make money, apart from the income from his estates. Once a man had held the lowest magistracy, the *quaestorship*, he became a senator, and was debarred from the business activities of the equites. Even a lawyer, or a barrister like Cicero, was not permitted to charge fees, though he could accept gifts from grateful clients. But politicians needed a great deal of money for political life; they often made cash distributions to their clients and the members of their own tribe (these were not bribes – bribes were cash distributions to other men's clients, and to other tribes). They also had to give entertainments to the people at large, mostly in the form of games and shows. In consequence, a man who entered politics often had to borrow money at the start of his career.

The two highest magistracies, the praetorship and the consulship, brought appointment to provincial governorships and army commands, and these enabled men to recoup their expenditures. This was not because governors were expected to take bribes and practise extortion and peculation (they often did, but both were illegal), but because the lump sum granted to governors for expenses was always grossly in excess of what they required to carry out their duties. Commanding an army was the most profitable activity of all, provided the general was successful, since the plunder and spoils of victory were at the general's disposal, and though the troops and officers expected a share, he usually took the lion's share himself. Almost all the fortunes of the leading families had been founded in this way, and in Cicero's lifetime first Pompey and then Caesar were to become multimillionaires out of their military successes. In a speech in 66 B.C., Cicero declared:

It is a hard thing to say, but we Romans are loathed abroad because of the damage our generals and officials have done in their licentiousness. No temple has been protected by its sanctity, no state by its sworn agreements, no house and home by its locks and bars – in fact there is now a shortage of prosperous cities for us to declare war on so that we can loot them afterwards. Do you think that when we send out an army against an enemy it is to protect our allies, or is it rather to use the war as an excuse for plundering them? Do you know of a single state that we have subdued that is still rich, or a single rich state that our generals have not subdued?

The sanction against extortion, or misuse of moneys or power, was prosecution, and the penalty for conviction was usually the end of a political career. The law-courts, however, were regarded as part of public life, and trials were almost always conducted on a political basis. As is very plain from Cicero's lawcourt speeches, a man's whole political career was brought into an indictment by

both prosecution and defence counsel, and one of the objectives
of a prosecution was often the weakening of a political opponent
through the conviction of one of his supporters. A prosecution
was often a young man's first political act; the victim he chose
and the zeal with which he pressed his case were often taken as
declarations of political intent.

In reaching their verdicts the jurors in the courts were often
swayed more by political considerations than by those of strict
justice; in consequence the senators fought a long, and generally
unsuccessful, battle against the equites for the senators' exclusive
right to be the jurors. For most of Cicero's public life, the senators
had to share it with the equites, but his two early triumphs, the
defence of Sextus Roscius of Ameria, and the successful prosecution of Verres, were before juries of senators. Juries were also
swayed by emotional appeals; Cicero excelled in this part of a
barrister's craft, in which his oratorical skill shone most brightly.

Oratory also played an important part in political life;
with a very fluid party-system, and vague (at best) party political
programmes, there were always a great many uncommitted
voters who could be persuaded by eloquence to choose one side or
the other. This was true in the popular assembly most of the time,
and also in the Senate. Although the popular assembly had the
right to overrule the Senate, and did so from time to time, the
Senate was the place where the state's policies were debated, and
formulated; since it was a very large body – a number of votes of
about four hundred are recorded – it had strict rules of procedure
which gave great weight to those who had held the consulship,
the consulars. Even so, the power of an orator was very great,
since issues were not normally settled by party caucuses before-
hand; we know at least one occasion on which a comparatively
junior senator by his oratorical skill persuaded the Senate to
change its line of policy. No politician could hope to progress far
unless he was a good speaker.

Roman education was therefore geared to producing good
speakers who had also a good knowledge of the law they hoped to
have to administer, and of the armies they hoped to command.
Some would specialize more in one than in the other, but the
leaders of Rome had to combine the talents of orator, lawyer, and
general.

Cicero's education began at home, in Arpinum. His father

was probably responsible for his elementary education; many Romans of a conservative outlook taught their own sons at least their reading and writing, and the rudiments of the law. Cicero learned by heart the Twelve Tables, the primitive lawcode on which the Roman civil law was based. Boys were also taught the history of their own country by stock examples, or stories which served as stock examples, of the virtues that the Romans thought peculiarly their own.

Cicero loved his country home. As a young man, in the hot, ardent chase for higher and yet higher honours, in the hectic turmoil of politics, and of briefs to prepare and present in court, he loved the Forum in Rome and the Senate-House; the bustle of the crowds, the swarms of callers who came to visit him when he held his morning levée in the fine house he bought in the busiest part of the city. Yet he never forgot his country home; he wrote in his speeches and poems of the rugged land and its mountains, and used to quote the *Odyssey*:

> 'A rugged soil, yet nurse of hardy sons,
> No dearer land can e'er my eyes behold.'

In his middle age, when he had tasted triumph and failure, he used to escape to Arpinum from the heat of the summer in Rome or from the society bores who plagued him, or in disgust at the behaviour of the military juntas which had taken over the Republic he loved. In his dialogue on the laws for his ideal republic, he placed the scene by the Fibrenus stream that flowed by his childhood home, fed by the mountain springs, icy cold even in the hot Italian summer, and bringing a welcome coolness. He wrote also of the shady trees, and of the small island riding like a ship in the waters that lapped all along its sides until they united again and plunged into the larger Liris River.

When Cicero was still a boy, that is, before he was fifteen, his father moved the family to Rome to further the education of his two sons. Plutarch, a Greek who wrote a biography of Cicero in the second century A.D., says that Cicero was a brilliant schoolboy, and much admired and envied by his fellows. Among these was T. Pomponius, whom we know as Atticus, the cognomen he was given because he lived twenty years in Athens; Atticus was three years older than Cicero, and his biographer says that Cicero was stimulated by Atticus' great abilities to try to rival him.

Cicero and Atticus became close friends, and though they saw little of each other while Atticus was in Athens and Cicero made his way to the leadership of the Roman bar, their friendship was renewed on Atticus' return to Rome, and Cicero's letters to Atticus give us our clearest impression of his mercurial and yet devotedly loyal character.

Cicero's first love was poetry; while still a boy, he wrote a poem called 'Pontius Glaucus', which was published, and known to Plutarch; also one about C. Marius, the national hero of his childhood years, which spoke about Arpinum, and a great oak tree that grew there. Plutarch says that Cicero's contemporaries rated him the best poet as well as the greatest orator. There is probably some exaggeration here; we know that some of his lines were made fun of in his lifetime, and he gave up poetry after the age of forty-five or so; but we should not underestimate his contribution to Latin poetry, which developed enormously in his lifetime.

Higher education was the prerogative of the rich; it required money as well as time free from the struggle to win a livelihood, but much of it was, by our standards, very informal. When a boy of the upper classes was about fifteen, he was ceremonially presented by his father with his man's *toga* (the citizen's robe). Thereafter he started to attend his father on many occasions, especially when he was called in by a friend or colleague for one of the informal councils of state which were a feature of the Roman Republic. These were held regularly by magistrates at, or before, their morning levée, also by the most prominent lawyers, and it was by listening to these experts that Roman boys got their practical training in the law. Cicero used to go and listen to the greatest civil lawyer of the day, Q. Mucius Scaevola, who, though he did not take pupils, used to teach all who cared to listen by the replies he gave to those who consulted him.

For studying oratory, Cicero began to frequent the Forum in 90 B.C., when he was sixteen, but as it was wartime there was only one court sitting. The war was the Social War: the communities in Italy allied with Rome had been driven by repeated frustrations to revolt in order to gain a higher status in their relations with Rome. Next year, 89, Cicero enlisted, probably in the cavalry, with Pompey's father as his general. Pompeius' campaign was successful, and he returned to triumph in Rome in

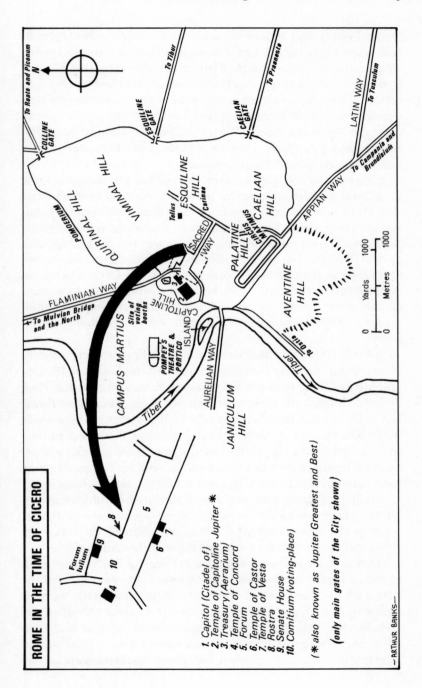

ROME IN THE TIME OF CICERO

1. Capitol (Citadel of)
2. Temple of Capitoline Jupiter *
3. Treasury (Aerarium)
4. Temple of Concord
5. Forum
6. Temple of Castor
7. Temple of Vesta
8. Rostra
9. Senate House
10. Comitium (voting-place)

(* also known as Jupiter Greatest and Best)

(only main gates of the City shown)

~ ARTHUR BANKS ~

December 89, and to face an acute political crisis. No elections had taken place for 88, and it was clear that the consuls chosen would probably have to fight Mithridates the Great, the King of Pontus on the southern shore of the Black Sea; and they would certainly have to arrange for the enrolment of thousands of new citizens, who had been rewarded for their loyalty or speedy capitulation in the Social War. The possibilities for acquiring wealth and patronage were enormous, and there were many candidates in a hard-fought election.

Pompeius Strabo tried to stand himself but was dissuaded; old C. Marius decided to stand for an unprecedented seventh term, though he was old for a strenuous campaign, with one of Julius Caesar's relatives as his running-mate, though he was ineligible. Strong feelings were aroused, and there was rioting and fighting in the streets, but eventually two nobles were successful, Q. Pompeius Rufus and L. Cornelius Sulla, the latter a patrician of impoverished family who had risen under the patronage of the great family of the Metelli, and now enjoyed their support. Strabo retired to Picenum without disbanding his army.

What Cicero did is uncertain; in his autobiographical account of his education, he says that he frequented the Forum in 88 B.C., and listened daily to one of the tribunes, P. Sulpicius Rufus. If so, he lived through the grim experience of Sulla's march on Rome late in 88, the first march against the civil government ever made in the history of the Republic. Perhaps he saw the fighting in the streets, and heard the threats of the consul to burn down the citizens' houses if they did not stop opposing his troops. He may have been present in the city when Sulpicius, one of the people's sacrosanct tribunes, was proscribed (declared a public enemy), hunted down and killed; and he lived, apparently in Rome, through the counter-coup of Cinna and Marius the following year, and the murders of leading citizens that followed.

He was again in Rome when the revengeful Sulla returned in 82 B.C., a savage battle took place outside the Colline Gate of the city, and the survivors of the battle were shot down without mercy in the Circus Maximus, where the games sacred to the gods used to take place. A new massacre of citizens had then followed, random at first, but soon turned into a proscription as everyone who had opposed Sulla was marked down for destruction. Towns were victimized, and so were wealthy land-owning equites, whose lands were needed to settle Sulla's veteran troops and satisfy the greed of his officers. All this was done in the name of restoring the nobles to their rightful place in the state. As these events occurred in 82 and 81, Cicero, who was eighteen in 88 B.C. when Sulla first marched against the city, was twenty-five when peace – now the peace of exhaustion – settled again on the Roman Republic.

Cicero was disgusted by the brutality and injustice of Sulla's proscriptions; throughout his career they are seen as the epitome of evil. In politics also he may have learned his dislike of the nobles, whose hereditary rights Sulla had claimed to be serving, and a personal dislike of certain profiteers like M. Crassus, whose vast wealth was founded on speculating in confiscated land. Perhaps he learned also that survival in a bitter civil war sometimes depends on being able (to use a yachting metaphor favoured by Cicero himself) to run before the wind, and reach one's destination by tacking instead of trying to fight a gale. He was also shocked at the economic crisis which followed the collapse of credit, and by the ruin of many equites which followed Mithridates' invasion of the Roman province of Asia in 88 B.C.; certainly he became a consistent upholder of the need to maintain financial stability and credit.

Moreover, at the time of Mithridates' invasion, the peoples of the province rose and massacred the Romans they found there. Our sources give a figure of 80,000 slaughtered, but even if the number is exaggerated the massacre itself showed what the Romans' subjects thought of their masters and their exactions. Cicero was one of the few who realized that the provincials must have been sorely provoked, and he constantly urged the need for justice and humanity in provincial government.

Mithridates' aggression, and his subsequent invasion of Greece, drove some of the teachers of philosophy from Athens to Rome. Cicero now took up philosophy, partly because he loved the subject, partly because the law-courts were closed, and therefore he could not go there to listen to the orators. He later maintained that in his day an orator needed to study philosophy, 'since M. Antonius [consul in 99] and L. Crassus [consul in 95] had brought Latin oratory to a peak where nobody could expect to add anything to it without a more extensive training than they had had in philosophy or the civil law or history'. Philosophy was thus a means to an end, and not an end in itself; the end was the production of a finished orator.

In his early twenties, Cicero wrote the work commonly called *De Inventione*; it is the first part of a treatise on rhetoric which he never completed. It shows however that Cicero always aimed at a political career based on the practice of oratory. As he himself put it: 'In a state as great and ancient as our own, where eloquence offers the greatest prizes, all men want to be speakers; not a great many have ventured to try to be orators, and only a handful have succeeded.'

In the course of his education, Cicero studied a number of Latin orations; one, a fine speech by C. Curio (praetor in 121 B.C.) in defence of Servius Fulvius, was then thought the best of all speeches, and he memorized the peroration delivered by C. Galba when he was prosecuted in 110, because it was so well thought of. During the civil war period he practised oratory daily 'most often in the company of M. Piso, Q. Pompeius and others, speaking in both Latin and Greek, but more often in Greek because the principal teachers could speak only Greek, and therefore could not correct faults in Latin orations'.

No remark could illustrate more clearly how far Roman culture had remained under Greek dominance; Roman contacts with Greece had been established for more than a hundred years, and Greece had been a Roman province since 146, which was forty years before Cicero's birth; but the most highly educated Greeks could not speak Latin despite the fact that they were living in Rome. Nor had Latin literature yet become fully adult even in Roman eyes. Technical terms for intellectual concepts simply did not exist for the most part. When Cicero later in his life wanted a vocabulary for oratorical and philosophical terms, he had to invent it; some of his inventions passed into normal Latin usage, some failed to become current, and disappeared into the limbo of obsolete words. By his inventions Cicero contributed notably to the enlargement of the Latin language, and to the value of Latin as a tool for literary composition, but he received much of his training in Greek, and was always a lover of Greek literature. It has been noted that in his writings Cicero quotes from 127 Greek authors, and only twenty-nine Latin ones; this reflects both how deeply impregnated with Greek culture he was, and how much richer was the fund of Greek literature available. As a young man he also made a number of translations from Greek writers (it is not certain that all were published); these included selections from Homer, a verse translation of the astronomical poem of Aratus of Sicyon, and, in a very different vein, Xenophon's treatise on home management.

2
The New Man:
Cicero's Rise to the Consulship

Cicero's entry into the political arena was unusual, in that he was ostensibly the defence-counsel in his first major case. This took place in 80 B.C., when Cicero was twenty-six. He later said that he had not wanted to enter the Forum until he was fully educated, instead of doing what most people did, and learning his trade by practice there, but the fact is that he took the first opportunity offering after the civil wars were over. The courts had newly opened again after their reorganization by Sulla, and Cicero's client, Roscius of Ameria, was the first person to be prosecuted before the new murder-tribunal.

The proscriptions had newly finished, but it was still not certain that no new names could be added to the list; the ruthless dictator was still in office, and the clubs of strong-arm men he had organized ruled the Forum; the peace was the uneasy peace of a dictatorial regime which had proclaimed the restoration of the constitution. Cicero's client, Roscius, had been accused by Sulla's henchmen in order to conceal the fact that they had themselves murdered Roscius' father in order to obtain his estates. They had assumed that there would be no adequate defence, and that no speaker would dare to attack Sulla's favourite freed slave, Chrysogonus. Cicero describes in a splendid passage how the prosecution were electrified when he introduced this name, because they saw that the defence would really dare to expose their machinations. To defend the case at all required some courage; to defend it in the way Cicero did – by an open attack on the profiteering elements in Sulla's retinue – required something more than courage; it required a belief in the sanctity of law and the need to establish any political settlement on justice.

Cicero had prepared his brief with great care; he was determined to make his debut in the arena of public life a memorable one. It is hard to be sure just how far the published speech represents what Cicero actually said. In his account of Cicero's methods, Quintilian, professor of rhetoric at the end of the first century A.D. and a fervent admirer of Cicero, tells us that he wrote out in advance the most vital parts of his speeches, especially the beginning, and memorized them. The rest of the speech he worked out in outline only, and extemporized where necessary.

Some of this is clear enough in *For Roscius*; the opening paragraphs are elaborately planned and particularly careful in expression and phraseology, while some of the body of the speech – the description of the opposition, for example – is much livelier, and has every appearance of having been made up on the spur of the moment.

Cicero's speeches were of course edited before publication; Cicero himself warns us that 'most speeches are written up when they have already been delivered, not with a view to delivery', and this suggests extensive editing. Editing however did not always involve expansion and elaboration; for example, the speech *For Murena* (spoken in 63 B.C.) is known to have been abridged for publication.

The publishing of the speech *For Roscius* illustrates Cicero's ambition; the unambitious did not trouble to write up their speeches. Cicero believed that there was nothing like writing for improving a man's oratorical talent, and he was determined to succeed in his career. He was always a tremendous worker, and at this time he was also training himself in public speaking by practising with the leading actor of the day; they used to compete in expressing the same sentiment in the greatest possible number of ways, the actor using a variety of gestures, Cicero changes of tone in speaking.

For Roscius was also a political manifesto, and the demand that Cicero made in it that the nobles should use the power they had won to uphold justice in government represents the standpoint of the critical, but uncommitted, politician. Cicero also published two other speeches; in one, he attacked the right of Sulla to deprive his opponents of their citizen status, in the other, the claims of the nobles as a class.

Cicero's publication of his speeches means that he intended them to be read; at this period of his life his writings were presumably directed at potential political supporters: politicians not in Sulla's noble circle, and equites. Twenty years later, when Cicero was famous, Atticus acted as his publisher, using teams of slave copyists; and we hear of bookshops where volumes of speeches and poetry could be bought. But we have very little idea how far down the social scale literacy spread in Cicero's day. If the level of literacy in Rome can reasonably be deduced from the scribblings on the walls of Pompeii some 150 years later, we may conclude that the ability to read was fairly widespread. At Pompeii, the plaster surfaces of the outside walls of all buildings were covered with writing: slogans and advertisements abound; at the height a child could reach, practice alphabets appear, also maxims and school exercises, some of them written backwards, or in mirror-writing, as children tend to do when they are learning to write. One wit even wrote: 'Everyone writes on the walls except me.' Scratchings on pottery, and occasionally on wood, where that survives, also show that quite humble people were literate, though evidence from papyri also shows that there were plenty of illiterates as well.

In 80 and 79 B.C., the success of the defence of Roscius may have caused him to overwork; he was very thin and weedy, with a very long, thin neck; his physique suggested that he could not stand too much physical exertion, or strain on the lungs. His friends urged him to abandon his career at the bar, but he refused to give up his ambition for fame as an orator, and decided to take a course in voice-control and learn to relax while speaking. He thought he might improve his style as well, and went to Greece to study. He spent six months in Athens, where, as well as studying oratory, he studied philosophy in the Academy in the company of Atticus. He went on to Asia Minor, where he practised with all the leading speakers and teachers of oratory, and thence to Rhodes, where he studied further under Molon, Caesar's teacher, whom he had already met when he was in Rome as an ambassador. A recent study has illustrated the truth of Cicero's own claim that Molon repressed the excesses of his youthful exuberance. So, in 77 Cicero returned to Rome a better speaker, with improved voice-control, more power in his lungs, and having put on some needed weight.

Shortly after he returned, he married, probably in the early autumn of 77 B.C. His wife was named Terentia; she was a lady of good family, with relatives among the nobles, though she was not herself of them. As was usual in Rome, Terentia brought her husband a dowry; according to Plutarch it amounted to 400,000 sesterces, the sum of capital which qualified a man for the status of *eques*, and hence was a substantial amount. Cicero himself became considerably richer at about this moment since he received a substantial legacy of 360,000 sesterces, not much less than his wife's dowry. We do not know the source of this sum, but it was probably the result of his court-work, which brought him in more than twenty million sesterces in his lifetime.

Terentia was a strongwilled and ambitious woman; Cicero once remarked that she was more inclined to take a share in his political concerns than to give him a share in her domestic ones. For an ambitious young politician, however, such a woman would be a good partner, and some of Cicero's restless ambition may have stemmed from her. They had two children, born some ten years apart; Tullia, the daughter, was born on 5 August 76 B.C., Marcus Cicero, the son, in 65. We know little about their life together; Plutarch, who derived much of his information from Cicero's secretary Tiro, who was then a slave in the house, speaks of their living in a manner that was generous but sensible, with a circle of literary friends both Greek and Roman. Cicero was something of a valetudinarian, submitting himself to a regime of massage and walking to help his digestion, which was weak; the constant concern for his wife's health in the earliest surviving letters to her perhaps owes as much to his own hypochondria as to any actual ailments she may have had.

Terentia evidently had a very different character from that of her husband; he admires her bravery in one letter from the time of his exile, which obviously she bore with much more fortitude than he. (She could afford to, since he would have to bear all the financial loss himself while her dowry would remain intact if she claimed it.) But she never appears in any literary context, and seems to have been quite without intellectual interests. Politics, no doubt, was the field she enjoyed, and Cicero's failure to maintain a position of political leadership may therefore have contributed to the estrangement which they underwent and which ended in their divorce after thirty years.

Cicero was unpopular with the common people when he first returned to his legal practice; uncultured people nicknamed him 'the Greek' and 'Egg-head'. He soon made them change their minds by the quality of his work in the courts. He had now mastered the art of projecting his voice, and set out to emulate Q. Hortensius, then the leading barrister in Rome, whose style he admired, because 'large meetings and the noise of the Forum call for an orator who is fiery, and has plenty of action and a resonant voice'.

In 76 B.C., Cicero stood for the quaestorship for the year 75, which was the first year in which he was eligible; he was successful, perhaps with a large majority, and obtained by lot the apparently unimportant post of quaestor at Lilybaeum, in the far west of Sicily. However, it turned out to be important; there was a shortage of corn in Rome (a recurrent event in this period), and Cicero had to cope with demands from Rome for corn. Despite the unpopularity which he incurred when he had to compel the provincials to send extra grain to the city, he won them round by his care for them, his justice, and his mildness, so that when he left for Rome they gave him an unprecedented farewell. At this ceremony he undertook to serve the people of Sicily as their patron if they ever needed an advocate.

Whether this was intended as a mere gesture in gratitude for the honours he was being paid, or whether it was a deliberate attempt to obtain a following of clients in a province which already had powerful patrons, we do not know; but it bore fruit some five years later when the Sicilians had been driven to desperation by the atrocious behaviour of C. Verres, whom the Senate had allowed to plunder the province for three years. They then invited Cicero to prosecute Verres for extortion.

The three qualities attributed to Cicero in Sicily are important, because they are the hallmarks of all that Cicero stood for in provincial government – conscientiousness, and strict justice, which are perhaps obvious enough, and others before him had no doubt striven to this end, but the Romans were usually arrogant in their attitude to their subjects. Cicero was not; he was himself humane and mild in manner, and made himself approachable to the people he governed. He also praised others who showed this attitude, such as Pompey, in a speech of 66 B.C., and urged it on his brother Quintus when he was governing Asia from 61 to 58. His model, he believed, was Scipio Aemilianus, the great conqueror, statesman, and cultured philhellene of the previous century, whom Cicero regarded as the epitome of Roman virtues.

On the way home, he visited Syracuse, on the eastern coast of Sicily, in order to visit the tomb of Archimedes, the famous scientist who had invented the screw-pump, and a planetarium which worked, and had made important discoveries about the displacement of water by mass and the formulae for calculating the surfaces of spheres and cylinders. To commemorate this, his gravestone had a cylinder and sphere on it. Cicero knew this, went and discovered the tomb in a disused graveyard, and recalled the Syracusans to honour their distinguished fellow-citizen. The whole episode shows Cicero in a role untypical of a Roman magistrate, enquiring and humane. It is paralleled by an action many years later, when he used his influence to enable the followers of Epicurus to save the house of the founder of their sect from 're-development', the greatest threat to all monuments of the past both then and now.

It was perhaps in Sicily too that he began his interest in works of art: he was an enthusiastic collector when he had the money to spare (and sometimes when he hadn't), but – again unlike many of his fellow-Romans – he paid for what he collected, and he collected selectively. He wanted his works of art to reflect his own cultural interests; he did not want a statue of Mars, for instance: 'What do I, a man of peace, want with a statue of the war-god?' he enquired – nor did he want a group of frenzied Bacchic maidens: he was 'no devotee of ecstatic cults or religions'.

Elated with his farewell in Sicily, Cicero returned to Rome, and on the way landed at the port of Puteoli. Here he had an experience which coloured the rest of his career; he told the story in a speech some twenty years later:

I am quite certain that no one would seriously claim that there ever was a more successful or popular quaestorship in Sicily than mine. And I must confess, alas, that I imagined at the time that all Rome was talking about it. . . . As a result, I left there fondly expecting that when I got home the people of Rome would grant my every wish almost without my having to ask. How wrong I was! On my way home from my province at that time I happened to pay a visit to Puteoli at the height of the season, when most of the fashionable and wealthy people are there.

You could have knocked me down with a feather, gentlemen, when someone asked me how long ago I had left Rome and if there was any news from there. I retorted that I was on my way home from my province. 'Oh! Africa I suppose', he said. 'Sicily actually', I replied rather loftily, upon which one of those people who know all the answers piped up and said, 'What! Didn't you know he was quaestor at Syracuse?' Well, after that I gave up and lost myself among the crowd of holiday-makers.

But I am rather inclined to think, gentlemen, that that little episode was more valuable to me than if I had been met with universal acclamation. For it brought home to me the lesson that the Roman people use their eyes, which are perceptive and alert, rather more than their ears. As a result, I gave up worrying about the effects of rumour on my reputation, and saw to it that men should see me daily in the flesh instead. I became a permanent fixture in the Forum, and kept open house, day and night.

In the Forum he worked hard, with many cases coming to the courts, though very little of the work of this period has survived. In 71 B.C. there was another upheaval when Pompey returned from a successful campaign in Spain and demanded a consulship, though he was qualified neither by age nor by the prerequisite offices. He also used a popular platform – the restoration to the tribunes of the ancient rights which had been taken from them by Sulla. He was elected consul with M. Crassus who had done most to suppress the slaves' rising under Spartacus. There was thus a 'popular' leadership of the state in 70 when Cicero became eligible for election to the *aedileship*, the next step on the political ladder.

The aedileship was a magistracy which offered great opportunities for self-advertisement. The aediles' work was in the city, since it was concerned with public services, and it gave ambitious men an opportunity to make a display of generosity in the way they carried out their duty of giving games and shows. Cicero was just preparing his election campaign when the Sicilians' invitation to prosecute Verres came. The moment could not have been more opportune; Verres was an ideal victim; his misdeeds had already been heard of in Rome, and had even been mentioned in the Senate. Though not a noble himself, he had risen under the wing of the nobles of Sulla's party, and this party was now falling apart as its failures became more and more obvious. A new war against Mithridates had started in 74 B.C., there were recurrent food-shortages due mainly to the pirates who swarmed in the Mediterranean, and a series of judicial scandals had disgraced the whole Senate. Public opinion had not been satisfied by the election of censors in 71, who had expelled sixty-four senators, most of them for taking bribes; and there was talk of a proposal to restore equites to the panels of jurors. The situation was ripe for new political groupings, and for the advance of new men to the higher offices in Pompey's wake.

Cicero thus welcomed his opportunity to attack Verres; he out-manoeuvred his opponents by his industry and determination, and when the nobles rallied to Verres' side, Cicero convicted them of intimidation and attempted misuse of power; when Hortensius, the leading advocate of the nobles' party, undertook Verres' defence, Cicero defeated him in court, despite the fact that Hortensius had just been elected consul for 69 B.C. Cicero's victory in this case set him at the head of his profession as a barrister, and this leadership became more conspicuous when Hortensius declined in his industry after his consulship, and consequently lost some of his skill, so that Cicero was left to dominate the scene. Moreover, his conduct of Verres' trial, and his subsequent publication of his speeches (the second of which was never in fact delivered because Verres abandoned all hope of acquittal after the first) established him as one of the ablest critics of the nobles' practice of government.

In these speeches, Cicero also proclaimed a political creed. He proclaimed that the Republic itself had a dignity and an honour which men ought to respect, and that every Roman citizen had full rights, wherever he lived and whatever walk of life he followed. The speech closes – amongst other assertions – with a challenge to the nobles of the day:

If there are any people who want to fix things or to take a bold stand or be perpetrators of corrupt justice in the case of this defendant, let them be ready to deal with me under the eyes of the Roman people. And if they have recognized me as a man of enough vigour, persistence and vigilance to succeed in dealing with this defendant with whom the Sicilians have made me cross swords, I bid them to bear this in mind: when it is for the sake of the preservation of the Roman people I shall be a much more severe and acrimonious opponent to any with whom I ever cross swords.

This stand against all noble factions who sought in turn to

impose their will on the Roman political machine by force or threat of force, was the basis for almost the whole of Cicero's subsequent political career.

During his prosecution of Verres, Cicero obtained the aedileship for 69 B.C. In his conduct of this magistracy he spent what he considered an appropriate amount on entertainments for the common people; he believed that most people did not in fact approve of vast expenditures, because they knew that those who spent would want to recoup, sooner or later. This upper class view was in fact not shared by the common people, who were impressed by men like Caesar who demonstrated their interest in them by extravagant games and other things. Cicero also thought that deeds of personal kindness made more of an impression on men's minds, and were longer remembered than games; in his work *On Duties* (*de Officiis*) he mentions ransoming the victims of brigandage and piracy, assisting those in debt and those who could not provide their daughters with a dowry, and helping men in business. He was also fortunate that in 69 the grateful Sicilians sent him all manner of goods and foodstuffs, including meat (a luxury food for the poor), which he was able to distribute generously, thus keeping the market prices down. From this he gained further popularity.

Cicero was also gaining support among the equites. His Sicilian quaestorship will have been approved by them, as will his support for their restoration to the panels of jurors, which took place in 70 B.C. In 69, in the speech *For Fonteius* he claimed to be a spokesman for the class as a whole; in another, *For Caecina*, he spoke for the peoples of Etruria whose interests had been attacked by Sulla. They were important, and numerous, in the electorate.

Domestic affairs were keeping him busy too. The stormy marriage between Cicero's brother and Atticus' sister Pomponia had begun; apparently Cicero had been largely responsible for it, and in 68 he found himself having to act as peacemaker. He believed he had succeeded – 'There is plenty of evidence', he wrote to Atticus, 'and besides, your sister is expecting a baby.' In the autumn too Cicero's father died; this made him head of the family, and changed his financial circumstances.

Under Roman law a son legally owned no property during his father's lifetime, and, however far he had ascended the political ladder, a son of the family (*filius familias*) remained financially in tutelage to his father; Cicero's father's death thus made him substantially better off. Plutarch says he left the family house on the Esquiline Hill to his brother Quintus and moved to the more expensive Palatine. He also bought a villa in the fashionable suburban resort of Tusculum; his letters to Atticus show him asking his friend to secure *objets d'art* with which to adorn it, and books for the library there, which Atticus helped him to design. His enthusiasm for these opportunities to indulge his cultural tastes is very obvious.

The year 67 B.C was an important one; Cicero was a political candidate again, this time for the praetorship. The year was a landmark too, as tribunes began to initiate policies for the first time since their powers were restored in 70. The most important of these initiatives was A. Gabinius' proposal to create a vast command at sea in order to suppress the pirates once and for all. Everyone knew that Pompey was the destined commander; the debate became stormy, riots broke out, and in the end Pompey's supporters forced the measure through; this devious politician thus became the commander of the greatest military and naval force in the Roman world. In three months he swept the pirates from the seas, assisted not a little by the fact that L. Lucullus had now chased Mithridates from Western Asia Minor, but probably even more by the generous terms he offered to those who agreed to give up their piratical trade. More than thirty-five years later Virgil wrote of one of them, as a happy and contented old peasant living in peace on an idyllic croft. In 67, Pompey's star was clearly in the ascendant, and Cicero now attached himself to Pompey's following, if he was not already attached to it; he later claimed he had always been a supporter of his. Pompey now provided strong leadership for those opposing the rule of the nobles, and by reopening the lines of the corn-supply to Rome he became a popular idol.

Another important political event was a new attack on electoral bribery. A tribune, Cornelius, initiated the movement, but the law when passed was in the name of the consul, Calpurnius Piso. Since the Roman assemblies decided questions by the votes of a majority of voting-units based on the tribes, there had risen a class of men who distributed to the members of their own tribe the money for bribes received from candidates for election. In this way a candidate could secure the votes of enough tribes (or other units) to win success. These people, known as *divisores* (dividers), were of course engaged in an illegal activity, but their existence was well enough known, as the technical term for them makes clear. They were important too, as they increased the cost of public life, by persuading rival candidates to raise the stakes.

It has been plausibly conjectured that the struggle over the new law on bribery, and perhaps counter-pressure from the *divisores*, was responsible for the praetorship elections having to be held three times. Cicero, however, finished at the head of the poll every time, a sure sign that he had made his mark among those whose votes counted in the electoral assembly – the rich, among whom he had many friends and connections.

Early in 66 B.C. the new praetor had a chance to show his political hand; Pompey's command against the pirates had brought him to the Black Sea, where he found the forces of L. Lucullus in disarray. Mithridates had proved unbelievably resilient; defeated and driven from his kingdom in the initial stages of the campaign, he suddenly reappeared in his kingdom in 67 B.C., raised a new army, and defeated Lucullus' lieutenant Triarius. In 66, Lucullus' army was mutinous, and had begun to demand their discharge when Pompey appeared, with an army and a naval force and the right to exercise command up to fifty miles from the coast. Pompey's friends proposed that he should take over from Lucullus the war with Mithridates. The mover was one of the tribunes for 66, C. Manilius, who brought his proposal before the popular assembly. It was vehemently opposed by the nobility, whose leading orators, Hortensius and Catulus among others, spoke against it.

Here was a chance for Rome's leading barrister to take a political stand; Cicero now delivered what he claimed was his first political harangue, the speech *On Pompey's Command*. The tone of the speech contrasts with that of the speeches against Verres: no longer is it one of rancorous hostility towards the nobles; the panegyric of Pompey and his career is combined with respect for Lucullus' remarkable achievements, and there are compliments to spare for Cicero's own original order, the equites, and for the business community, whose management of the revenues provided the sinews of the Republic. But important and familiar themes recur: the need for Roman commanders to consider their subjects, to be not merely just, but approachable, and to combine mercy with the maintenance of law and order. In this, Pompey's attitude is contrasted with the arrogance and brutality of other (unnamed) commanders, of whom contemporaries might recognize easily enough Q. Metellus Creticus, and Mark Antony's deceased and discredited father. Moreover, the speech is a masterpiece of tact – 'I mention no names', Cicero says, 'so that nobody without a guilty conscience will be able to criticize me.' It is a brilliant demonstration of that more relaxed style appropriate to popular speeches which he was to analyse in his great work *On the [making of an] Orator* some eleven years later (55 B.C.).

Manilius' law was passed, and Cicero had established a political position in the state. Shortly afterwards, the praetor had to face an important decision; he was in charge of the extortion court when a notable popular leader of the previous decade appeared before him, one Licinius Macer. Macer evidently expected Cicero to be prejudiced in his favour, but Cicero remained judicially impartial; Macer was condemned, and Cicero, to his surprise, found that his stand for justice had won him the respect of ordinary people.

Being a magistrate did not debar an advocate from practising at the bar – indeed it was an aid, since pleading in the courts was regarded as much a public act as being a magistrate – and several of Cicero's speeches from this year survive. The most notable is that *For Cluentius*. In this speech he afterwards said he had 'thrown dust in the eyes of the jury'; for us its main interest is a passionate defence of the majesty and validity of the laws. In this belief Cicero appears in sharp contrast to his great contemporaries, Pompey and Caesar, who showed themselves contemptuous of the laws when they inhibited their own political schemes.

The other speeches Cicero published this year are lost, as are the three published in 65 B.C. A commentary on the defence of Cornelius, the tribune of 67, however, reveals Cicero's extraordinary rhetorical skill as he contrived to defend a tribune while criticizing the tribunate, and to speak in favour of Pompey while accepting the historical interpretation of the tribunate held by Pompey's critics.

Most ex-praetors left to govern a province for at least a year.

Cicero did not; his heart was set on the consulship, and he judged that he could do more to forward his chances by remaining in Rome than by quitting the centre of public life for a province. We must conclude that Cicero could afford not to go – many men had to go to recoup their election-expenses – and this lends powerful support to the view that Cicero was not like Caesar, a politician who purchased his way into the highest magistracies; the support he obtained was honestly gained, as he himself claimed, by his hard work in the Forum, and the services he did for his friends.

It is hard for us to grasp how audacious was Cicero's ambition not merely to be elected consul, but to be elected in the most honourable year, the year he was first eligible for the office. The noble families virtually monopolized the consulship in normal times; the honour of the family demanded that consular families should hold it every generation, and there were barely enough consulships available to satisfy this demand. As the nobles were also the priestly families (at Rome the chief priesthoods were the rewards of distinguished public service), they felt the consulship's sacred character was injured if a new man held it, since the consuls guarded the auspices, the means by which the Roman state maintained its treaty with its tutelary gods, the *pax deorum* as they called it. Pious Romans (and in this respect perhaps most Romans were pious) believed that this treaty was what ensured their success in international affairs. Moreover, only two consuls were elected every year, compared with eight praetors, and twenty quaestors, the only two necessary prerequisite offices; three-quarters of the praetors therefore, and nine-tenths of the quaestors who held office together, would never become consul. It is no wonder that an outsider like Cicero, none of whose ancestors had even sat in the Senate, believed that the nobles would close their ranks against him, and that, to obtain the consulate, he would have to strain his resources to the utmost, and gain political support from every available quarter. Fortune however favoured him. Thinned by the Civil War and by Sulla's proscriptions, the ranks of the aristocrats of Cicero's age (he was eighteen in 88 B.C.) contained few men of merit, and none from the most important families. The election was due to be held in 64 B.C., and already in 65 Cicero was writing to Atticus about the prospects.

The rivals he could see in the field were either putting voters' backs up, like the patrician Galba, or had little influence, or were men of tarnished reputation like C. Antonius, Mark Antony's uncle, who had been thrown out of the Senate in 70 for rapacity and debt, and L. Catilina, whom we know as Catiline. Both these men belonged to the lower ranks of Sulla's supporters, and had made large sums of money, which they had now lost. Catiline had also behaved with great brutality to those whom Sulla had proscribed, and had later been accused of seducing Cicero's wife's half-sister Fabia, a Vestal Virgin. Though he was acquitted of this, when he returned from governing Africa in 66, he again came under threat of prosecution, this time for extortion. He was, in Cicero's view, manifestly guilty, but the prosecutor, a young patrician called P. Clodius, was persuaded (no doubt for money) to compromise the case, and thus declared his political position.

There was nobody in sight with a manifestly better claim than Cicero himself, whose only handicaps were his lack of pedigree, and his birth in a country town. Cicero feared that Pompey might send one of his officers to stand against him, but in fact he did not do so; he had no cause to be unsympathetic to Cicero who had defended both the tribunes who had proposed his great commands.

In the event, only C. Antonius and Catiline were serious competitors. In the past, Cicero had helped Antonius to become praetor for the second time in 66 B.C., and thus recover his place in the Senate, and be qualified for the consulship, and in the following year had offered to defend Catiline, guilty though he knew him to be. For some unknown reason, most probably because Catiline decided that he did not want to be obliged to Cicero and felt that he could get off without the aid of the orator, Cicero did not take the case.

Something of the stormy character of politics in this period emerges from the history of the consulships of 65. The successful candidates, P. Sulla, nephew of the dictator, and P. Autronius, were indicted for electoral bribery by those they had defeated, and were deposed; their rivals, both men of noble family, were then declared elected. Autronius at least was ruined, and both were later accused with Catiline of having planned to occupy the Forum on January 1st and kill the new consuls, though the plot miscarried. Many modern scholars disbelieve the allegations,

though they are made by both Cicero and Sallust, the contemporaries in the best position to know, but in any event a belief
in a plot at this time was at least as important as its existence.

Throughout 65 and 64, the political temperature remained
high; there is very little concrete evidence of legislation, but two
sets of censors went out of office without doing their job, the first
pair, Crassus and Catulus, because of their quarrels, the second
pair because of the vetoes of tribunes. The most important event
of 65 B.C., however, was the aedileship of Caesar. It showed that
he was determined to bring himself before the public eye, and to
gain a substantial following among the common people. His
games, and the gladiatorial show which he gave in memory of his
father, were extravagant even by the standards of the late
Republic, and the latter even provoked a vote of the Senate to
limit the number of gladiators exhibited. For politics too Caesar's
aedileship was important, since he also proclaimed the revival of
the party of Marius by restoring the latter's trophies, and by
proclaiming the following year that he would revoke the
immunity granted to those who had received money for killing
men in Sulla's proscriptions. He thus established a new 'popular'
party, to rival that of Pompey and his friends in criticizing the
nobles and trying to win the support of the popular assembly; and
thus in a sense founded the party which was victorious in the Civil
Wars of 49–45 B.C. and formed the basis on which his heir built
the Roman Empire.

A pamphlet on electioneering survives, supposed to have been
sent to Cicero by his younger brother Quintus. If genuine, it
reveals much of the situation in 64, and of the character of
Roman politics: Cicero's chief claim to the consulship is said to be
his oratory, since, new though he was, an orator who had spoken
for men of consular rank could not be thought unworthy of
consular honours. Moreover his speeches had attached many
groups to his support: equites, the financial world, many of the
towns of Italy and of the Po Valley which he had himself visited
in his canvass, and a number of associations of working men. But
being a new man was against him; the aristocrats would resent
admitting an outsider, and even men of his own standing who
had not thought to advance beyond the praetorship would be
jealous of him. He must muster every connection, and get anyone
whom he had ever served to muster their friends; plans must be

made to cover everyone, anyone must be granted an audience, and promises must be made, even ones which he knew he would not be able to keep.

Cicero's rivals canvassed vigorously too: Antonius and Catiline campaigned together, with a view to being elected as a pair, thus excluding Cicero; they launched vigorous attacks on the wealthy, and on the financial interests who were backing Cicero, and raised such large forces of supporters to escort them in their canvassing that the Senate tried to limit the numbers of such attendants, and made illegal the clubs through which these forces were organized.

A further decree, aimed at curbing their overt and rampant bribery, was vetoed by a tribune, whereupon Cicero rose in the Senate and delivered a scathing attack on his rivals. He published it, though it has not survived except in excerpts with a commentary. The excerpts range over the characters and past records of both his rivals in all their salacious details. Whether the speech also exposed their intention to decree a general cancellation of debts if elected is not known; but it was instrumental, if not fundamentally important, in bringing over to Cicero's side such a large proportion of the property-owning classes, and even the nobles, that in the election he was returned by a unanimous vote of all the centuries who voted (for an election ended when a majority of all the centuries was achieved). Antonius narrowly defeated Catiline, and became Cicero's colleague.

3
Consul:
Cicero's Political Leadership

Cicero's election provoked a sharp reaction; to Catiline's party it represented a victory for the financiers over the nobility; certainly Catiline's own finances were thrown into jeopardy, since he had now no certain prospect of recouping from a province the vast sums his vain canvass had cost; his young friends resented his defeat, and there was wild talk; perhaps threats were uttered. It was a defeat for Caesar's 'popular' party too, since they had also backed Catiline; Caesar had wanted a friendly consul since he would be a candidate for the praetorship in the elections to be held in 63 B.C. Two of the tribunes elected for 63 were Caesar's friends, however, P. Servilius Rullus and T. Labienus, who later became Caesar's right hand man in Gaul. They entered on their year of office (as was usual) on the preceding December 10th; Rullus put forward a grandiose scheme for allotting lands to the city poor and to veteran soldiers, and Cicero's first speeches as consul were against Rullus.

In them he painted a vivid picture of the political scene:

I have taken over from you [Rullus] a state seething with suspicion, harassed by fears, and driven to distraction by all your legislation, propaganda, and colonial enterprises. You have boosted the morale of every crook in Rome, and frightened the life out of every man of standing; you have destroyed confidence among business-men, and subverted the respect men feel for the Republic. The situation, in fact, has been so chaotic, and men's expectations so confused that to the ordinary man in the street it came like a breath of fresh air suddenly to hear the voice of a consul firmly in control of things explaining that all is well . . . and that as long as he was consul peace and good order would be his absolute priority.

This he said in the Senate; to the people:

I have only to look at the Republic on the 1st of January, when I
entered office, to realize that alarm and despondency were everywhere. . . . Rumour had it that there were conspiracies against the
Republic, and against public order; some plots were started, others
were hatched the moment it was known that I was to be the next consul.
Business confidence was shattered, not by any national disaster, but
because opinion was so sensitive, and it was thought that the law-courts
would be in chaos and verdicts overruled, and that a new breed of rulers
would arise and seize the powers not of mere dictators, but of kings.

Cicero however was not content merely to criticize Rullus. In
his jubilation at his electoral success, he thought fit to expound
the theme that all the traditions of the nobles were out of date;
patronage and family connections no longer mattered in politics;
a plebeian 'new man' from outside their order would give Rome
a new and better government; the way to the consulship in future
would lie in imitating Cicero in hard-work and conscientious
application to public affairs. This was unnecessarily tactless, and
he aggravated the offence by making insinuations against the
nobles' patriotism: 'I am troubled night and day about how to
defend my consulship', he told a popular audience. 'It is a hard
task for anyone, but especially for me. I shall receive little mercy
if I fail and only grudging praise if I succeed. You see, when I am
in doubt, none of the nobles will give me honest counsel, nor will
any give me reliable support if I am in trouble.'

However, he had tried to forestall trouble. He had managed to
reconcile Antonius to himself, a considerable feat in the light of
what he had said about him in the speech preceding the election.
Probably he, or Atticus, had lent Antonius money – quite likely a
large sum, without interest, or at a low rate. Since Antonius had
spent heavily on his election this would have been a considerable
service. It was unacceptable behaviour to oppose a man to whom
you owed money; so Antonius supported Cicero in 63 B.C., at
least passively, by not opposing him, and we know that Antonius
paid money to Cicero through an agent while governing his
province after 63; it is not unreasonable to see a connection.

Cicero had also decided not to govern a province after his
consulate. This may have been part of the programme to
conciliate Antonius, who thus got his pick, but Cicero said that it
was to prevent tribunes having a hold on him. He may also have

felt that if he did not go to a province nobody could trump up a charge of misgovernment against him, and he was well aware of enemies. It was also perhaps a tacit claim (and one which contemporaries could not have failed to see) that he had no vast election-expenses to recoup; his hands were clean, and men could not deny it.

It would be pleasant to believe that Rullus' scheme reflected a genuine social conscience, but several elements in it make such a belief implausible. Cicero undoubtedly misrepresented the proposers' intentions and proposals, but the overwhelming powers proposed for the commission, the pre-empting of the lands Pompey was engaged in settling in the eastern provinces, and the dubious mechanism for choosing the commissioners, all smacked of a party deal, an attempt to create jobs which would enable Pompey's rivals (or possibly Pompey himself) to enjoy a wide patronage and thereby gain profit and power.

Such special commands and extensive opportunities were characteristic of the end of the Roman Republic. After Sulla, ambitious politicians were not content to govern a single province for one year at a time; they demanded longer tenures and control of several provinces. The extended commands given to Pompey in 67 and 66 were the forerunners; Rullus' proposal foreshadows the special commissions created for Caesar and others which destroyed the Senate's general control of the provinces and created the class of dynasts whose struggles killed the Republic.

Schemes of this sort could not be set in motion through the normal channels of debate in the Senate; they were hatched in private by small cliques, often on social occasions; these cliques were in ancient political language 'the few': oligarchies in the strictest sense.

Cicero always opposed such schemes. In this he was perhaps not entirely altruistic; lacking an entry to the nobles' social circles by birth, he lacked the charm (and tact) to obtain it by social graces. His intellectual (and Greek-oriented) interests were not shared by many of the nobles, who tended to be more interested in military affairs, and in intrigues, amorous and political. While Cicero spent his leisure in reading, writing and intellectual discussion, most Roman nobles preferred to spend theirs, and their money, on pets, such as the fish they trained to feed from their hands, on fashions in houses, clothes and hair styles, and on developing an exquisite palate in food and wine, and other refinements which leisured and prosperous societies have often pursued.

In contrast to his social inadequacy, Cicero's public performance was outstanding; with his intellectual range and quick wits, constantly sharpened by practice, he was a formidable opponent in debate. His devastating wit and crushing repartee were often resented by his victims, but they were extremely effective in meetings to which men had come with open minds. His power was always likely to be greatest in fact when there was least prearrangement and the largest number of uncommitted voters. As consul, leading their debates, he must have dominated the Senate in 63 B.C., and this very dominance may itself have contributed to the growth of political activity in private amongst those who resented Cicero's leadership.

In attacking Rullus, Cicero was able to attack the nobles' faction-politics, and at the same time to put forward his own claims to popular leadership. 'What is so "popular"', he asked, 'as peace, freedom, and a quiet, ordered state?' All who advocated revolution, he said, were in reality grinding their own axes, however fair their pretensions; it was only those in a revolutionary party who would profit from upsetting the established order in the state. In the Senate he said the same, substituting 'harmony' for 'freedom', and this is the practical policy – peace at home, and harmony (or concord) among the various elements in the Republic – which forms a consistent theme in Cicero's outlook from now till almost the end of his life.

Cicero procured the rejection of Rullus' bill, but he could not prevent further proposals. Caesar's 'Marian' party proposed a bill to restore full political rights to the children of the victims of Sulla's proscription; Cicero opposed this proposal too, fearing that it would renew dissension, and it also was dropped, as was a proposal to restore to the Senate the two consuls deprived of their office in 65 B.C. The reason given was presumably that the court was corrupt; if this is so, the proposal was an attack on the financial class, the equites, who had provided most of the jurors. There was also an overt attack on them this year. As tribune Roscius Otho had granted them the privilege of occupying fourteen rows of the best seats in the theatre. He was probably praetor now, when a demonstration was staged against him in the theatre. Cicero arrived at the performance, and, seeing the disturbance, summoned the demonstrators to a meeting outside the theatre at the Temple of Bellona. By his speech he persuaded them all to return to the theatre to watch the play in a spirit of harmony. Unfortunately the speech, though published, is almost entirely lost.

There were also various projects to reduce debt and relieve the insolvent, but there is no clear evidence about these, though the relief of debt was undoubtedly an important element in the programme of Catiline. Scholars have debated at length how much altruism there was in Catiline's programme, and how much sheer self-interest. Most modern minds have little sympathy to spare for great landowners who lived lavishly and borrowed far beyond their means for political purposes and then were unwilling to pay their debts, and no more for financiers whose rates of interest were sometimes exorbitant – we have evidence of 48% per annum being demanded in one province; on the other hand, the poor of Rome were very poor, and were exploited by money-lenders, by unscrupulous landlords, and by merchants who made as much profit as they could out of the necessities of life. It is doubtful, however, if the great banking houses of the equites dealt with the debts of the poor, and though cheap – and even free – food became one of the programmes of 'popular' politicians, the plans of Catiline do not seem to have embraced this feature.

Shortly after the defeat of Rullus the 'popular' tribunes arraigned an elderly senator called Rabirius on a charge of high treason; the offence alleged was that he had struck the blow which killed the 'popular' tribune Saturninus in 100 B.C. (thirty-seven years before). Rabirius was undoubtedly one of those who had paraded under arms when ordered by the consul C. Marius to do so after a state of emergency had been declared; this occurred when the Senate passed the 'Senate's Last Decree', a form of words which bade the magistrate and other persons named to 'see to it that the Republic comes to no harm'. Cicero appreciated that the real aim of the prosecution was not to have Rabirius flogged in the Campus Martius (the penalty proposed by the prosecution), but to warn the consul Cicero and his supporters that they could not take strong action with impunity if the Senate should again pass the 'Last Decree'. Had the use of the 'Last Decree' been threatened, or did they intend to provoke a confrontation which would make the Senate (or Cicero) want to use it? Such a confrontation might occur if the assembly was coerced at the coming elections at which Catiline was determined to become consul, and Caesar praetor. We do not know what was in their minds, but Caesar's is the hand usually seen behind the prosecution.

In his defence Cicero made no attempt to deny Rabirius' responsibility; instead he challenged Labienus, the leading prosecutor, on his party's right to claim to be 'popular'; a popular party, he declared, is one which seeks to save the lives of citizens, not to punish those who have done their patriotic duty.

The trial never reached a verdict. Perhaps it was never meant to, but we do not know whose hand caused the meeting to be dissolved – was it the 'Marian' party wanting to be saved the embarrassment of having to carry out an execution, or was it Cicero's friends wanting to prevent by a ruse what they could not prevent by argument? The former seems more probable, in the light of their failure to revive the case. Certainly the 'Marian' party was not ruined by the trial, nor was Cicero intimidated.

Shortly afterwards, Caesar proved what great popularity he had achieved by winning the coveted post of *pontifex maximus* which fell vacant on the death of Metellus Pius. His opponents in the election were his elders by far, the stalwarts of the old nobility, Q. Catulus, its leader in politics, and P. Servilius Isauricus, its leading general. One of them ought to have been elected, but Caesar won easily, spending lavishly, not to say recklessly, in his election campaign. The sign was not unnoticed. The nobles now closed their ranks behind Cicero the consul: his election could not be undone, they may have thought, and his arguments for peace and the existing political order, and for the maintenance of credit, were such as to appeal to their sense of values. It is often said that in the course of 63 B.C. Cicero joined the conservative nobles; it is much truer to say that they joined him, or at least gave him their support for the time being.

Some evidence of Cicero's independence of the nobles lies in the only two pieces of legislation known to have been passed by him. Neither can have been welcome to the nobles: one was concerned with strengthening the laws about electoral bribery,

the other concerned the welfare of the provincials. Noble
Romans used to make tours of the provinces, often in pursuit of
their personal profit, under the guise of roving envoys sent out by
the Senate; this meant that they could demand that the provincials provide them with the supplies in kind to which
governors and their staffs were entitled, and they usually did not
hesitate to take advantage of their position. Cicero regarded
these tours as an unwarranted imposition, and tried to get them
abolished altogether; he was opposed by a tribune's veto, but
eventually succeeded in getting them limited to one year's
duration.

He was equally independent of Pompey, and of his opponents;
under his presidency Lucullus was at last enabled to hold the
triumph he had earned but had been prevented by Pompey's
supporters from celebrating, while later in the year Cicero
proposed that the gods be thanked for Pompey's success in
procuring the death of King Mithridates. In these actions he
proved he was no party hack.

Towards the end of the year, his major problems were with
Catiline, who tried once more to become consul, using a mixture
of bribery and intimidation in his campaign. As with all secret
faction-politics we cannot know exactly what was planned;
before the election wild talk certainly took place, perhaps
promises of proscriptions and annulment of debts (though these
can hardly have been publicly advertised). Cicero was certainly
aware of much that other members of the Senate were ignorant
of, since one of Catiline's associates was unbelievably indiscreet,
and his mistress kept Cicero informed of what was said and
planned. Catiline raised a strong force of supporters from
Etruria, who accompanied him within the city: an escort some
might have called it, a bodyguard or gang to intimidate
opponents might be another description; Cicero raised a similar
force from Reate in the Sabine country. Rumour said that an ex-
officer of Sulla's called Manlius was gathering recruits in Etruria,
though at this stage his purpose was unclear. Cicero got the
consulship elections postponed, and when he challenged Catiline
to give an account of himself in the Senate he was met with an
ambiguous but threatening reply; when Cato threatened to
prosecute Catiline for bribery, he was also menaced.

When the elections took place, Cicero, as presiding officer, came down with a breastplate clearly visible under his civilian toga, whether in genuine fear of violence, or as a symbol of protest against the violent talk of Catiline we do not know. This act, however, and his bodyguard were later held to have been responsible for Catiline again being defeated, and it is probable that it strengthened Catiline's determination to get rid of Cicero.

The first plan to assassinate Cicero was exposed when other senators, like M. Crassus, informed Cicero that they had been warned by letter to leave the city. When Cicero brought these letters to the Senate and revealed all he knew about the planned assassinations, the Senate was alerted, and when Manlius' activities were reported, the 'Senate's Last Decree' was passed. On the authority of this decree Cicero raised forces of volunteers, who garrisoned many places in the city and throughout Italy, and frustrated an attempt to seize Praeneste on 1 November, of which Cicero was forewarned. An incipient financial panic was allayed, thanks to the support Cicero received from the equites, but Rome was evidently very uneasy. There was good reason, for it was now plain that there was a conspiracy afoot with unknown but certainly violent and probably extremist aims. Catiline and his associates agreed to assassinate Cicero at dawn on 7 November; again forewarned, Cicero refused the assassins admittance to his house.

He convened the Senate the next day in a temple surrounded by armed equites, and, seeing Catiline present in the house, delivered the *First Speech against Catiline*. As Cicero revealed the details of his conspiracy the benches around Catiline emptied of the few supporters who had sat beside him when the consul began. Catiline attempted to reply, and insulted Cicero, calling him an alien lodger in Rome, but was shouted down by the rest of the senators. The same evening he left to join Manlius' force, and made it clear that he and they were traitors planning a coup d'état, or civil war.

A propaganda battle began; Catiline wrote letters claiming that he was not bankrupt, insulting Cicero, and complaining that he had been cheated of the offices to which his birth entitled him; other letters put all the blame on the equites, the financiers of Rome. The next day Cicero delivered the *Second Speech against Catiline* to a public meeting in the city (sufficient proof that the city populace was not strongly opposed to him), reassuring them, predicting the conspirators' next moves and (significantly enough) admitting that many senators were not yet convinced of the guilt even of Catiline.

This last soon changed when news came that Catiline was in Manlius' camp, using a consul's insignia. He was proclaimed a public enemy, and Antonius, Cicero's colleague, was instructed to suppress the rebels as soon as possible. Most men no doubt thought that the conspiracy was over, but Cicero knew better. He was told that a new attempt on his life, and an attack on the financiers, was planned for mid-December when one of the new tribunes would attack him for having accused innocent men. The opportunity afforded by the merry-making of the Saturnalia (the Roman Christmas) on 17 December would be taken to start assassinations and arson in the city; this was to open the way for Catiline who, it was planned, would move on Rome and take control.

Evidence that others thought that danger was over comes from the fact that M. Cato, now a tribune-elect, and Servius Sulpicius Rufus, a lawyer of the greatest distinction, decided to indict Murena, one of the consuls-elect, under Cicero's new bribery law. Murena was undoubtedly guilty, but Cicero was determined that there should be two consuls in office on 1 January, and used all his oratorical skill to mingle urgent pleadings on this score with a witty skit at the expense of Cato on the effects of applying Stoic maxims to Roman politics. This persuaded the laughing jurors to return a verdict of 'not guilty'. The defeated and disgusted Cato is said to have exclaimed, 'What a wit we have for a consul.'

Having secured the acquittal of Murena, Cicero suddenly found in his hands the means of smashing the remainder of the conspiracy. Searching for allies, the conspirators had contacted an embassy of Gauls, who had come to Rome to complain about their governor and the Roman financiers. They were persuaded to extract treasonable letters from the conspirators and then betray them to the government. The letters were written, and the Gauls carrying them were duly captured and brought to Rome on the night of 2/3 December.

At dawn on 3 December Cicero summoned the conspirators to his house; leading senators called too, before the Senate met, and urged him to open the letters in case there was nothing in them.

But Cicero was supremely confident that he had incontrovertible evidence, and convened the Senate for an emergency session which was to last three days. It met in the guarded temple of Concord. Cicero began by introducing a certain Volturcius, who had acted as escort of the Gauls; on a promise of immunity he turned state's evidence and revealed all he knew. Cicero next cross-examined the Gauls and secured from them an admission that they had conspired to support Catiline by force against the government in Rome. One by one the conspirators were called and forced to acknowledge their handwriting and seals; their letters were opened publicly and they confessed their guilt in turn. A raid on one of their homes produced a large cache of arms; no one could any longer doubt that there was a treasonable conspiracy afoot. Cicero invited the Senate to debate the affair.

The Senate resolved to thank Cicero 'for the courage, skill and foresight with which he had saved the Republic from the most terrible dangers'; it thanked the praetors Flaccus and Pomptinus for their courage and loyalty in apprehending the envoys. It then decreed that nine men should be arrested: Lentulus as soon as he had resigned the praetorship, those present in the Senate forthwith, those who had gone to organize insurrection in Italy, when possible. A thanksgiving was then decreed to the gods in honour of Cicero 'because he had saved the city from fire, the citizens from slaughter, and Italy from civil war'. It was, as Cicero records, a unique occasion, the first and only time in the Republic's history when such a thanksgiving was made in honour of a civilian. If he was proud of his achievement, it was one that any man might have been proud of. In the evening, in the *Third Speech against Catiline*, Cicero told a meeting of non-senators what had transpired. At the height of the crisis too Cicero did not fear to face the common people.

Next day the Senate met again: an informer accused M. Crassus of complicity, but after debate he was cleared; two nobles urged Cicero to have Caesar arrested, but he refused. Though both men had supported Catiline at one time it is not credible that the richest man in Rome should support the cancellation of debts, and Caesar, who had now secured the praetorship and the prospect of a province, was unlikely to lose his political acumen in a venture as desperate as Catiline's. Cicero's disbelief was surely well-founded, but neither man showed him gratitude for long –

Crassus even accused him later of having instigated his accuser.

In the evening the Senate declared that the conspirators had 'acted contrary to the interests of the Republic'. This was probably a new formula, whose implications were therefore unclear. Certainly it did not mean that they were declared public enemies whose lives were automatically forfeit. Threats against their lives must have been made, however, and counter-threats against Cicero if he were to put them to death. As night fell, a crowd, incited by Lentulus' freed slaves, tried to set him free, and forcible attempts to rescue other conspirators were also made. Cicero posted stronger guards, and parts of the city resembled an armed camp. Next day, 5 December (the Nones), Cicero called on all citizens to take the military oath, as Marius had done thirty-seven years before; armed volunteers occupied the Forum, and equites the approaches to the Temple of Concord to which the Senate was summoned. When they met, Cicero asked the senators to advise him how to deal with the imprisoned conspirators. D. Silanus the consul-elect was asked to speak first, and advocated the death-penalty. Fourteen of the consulars, the senior senators, supported him when their turn came to speak. Caesar, as praetor-elect, was called; he proposed a form of life-imprisonment in the country towns of Italy, with safeguards against premature release. His speech was persuasive enough to alter the direction of the debate, and men stopped demanding the death-sentence.

Tiberius Nero, ancestor of emperors, proposed imprisonment till the forces of Catiline were defeated, then trial by law; Silanus recanted his earlier severity, and it appeared that Caesar's proposal would win the day. Among the tribunes-elect, however, was M. Cato, whose speech on this occasion was so powerful that he converted the whole Senate back to Silanus' original view, and he rephrased it so effectively that Cicero eventually put the motion to the Senate in Cato's words.

During the discussion, apparently on resuming after a break, Cicero delivered the *Fourth Speech against Catiline*. The speech had two main themes, that the people were solidly behind the Senate whatever they did, and that he himself was not afraid of carrying out the death-sentence if the Senate advised him to do so. This latter theme was presumably prompted by the sort of argument familiar in modern debates in which the speaker presses his own view in the guise of looking after other people's interests; probably, too, threats had been uttered against him if he executed the prisoners.

In his speech Cicero also demanded a vote that night, before the Senate adjourned. When it eventually took place, Cato's motion was passed, and the Senate thus advised Cicero that the penalty of death was appropriate. Cicero decided to act on the advice, and personally supervised the execution that same night; 'They have lived', he reported laconically to the crowd who met him as he emerged from the prison building. He was escorted home amid tumultuous rejoicings. It was the apex of his career; he was not quite forty-four years old.

Cicero's action in executing Catiline's fellow-conspirators provoked a storm of argument which has not yet ended. In 63 B.C. Catiline's young noble friends swore vengeance on Cicero and all his supporters; Cato and the senior senators hailed him as 'Father of his Country' and said he deserved the wreath presented to soldiers who saved the lives of citizens. Later in his life, Cicero wrote that 'the safety of the people is the highest law', and that therefore 'to have acted against the Republic' was rightly interpreted as 'to have put themselves outside the protection of the law'. Caesar, according to the historian Sallust, argued that it was a most dangerous precedent for a consul to take the power to put citizens to death on the strength of a Senate's decree – another time the Senate might be intimidated, as it was by Sulla. That way led to legalizing proscriptions.

Immediately, the executions extinguished the threat within the city, and a military force was sent to deal with the armed forces of Catiline and Manlius which now began to suffer desertions. The propertied classes breathed more freely again, but suspicions still flourished. Caesar became the centre of controversy; he was again accused and again exonerated by Cicero. It says much for Cicero's integrity that he refused to use his position to get rid of a formidable opponent of the Republic he cherished. He could easily have done it, and it may well be that the respect which Caesar always had for Cicero, and the consideration which he later showed for the orator, stemmed from Cicero's actions at the end of 63 B.C.

Others, like Caesar's personal enemy, M. Cato, were determined to get rid of him. In his biography of Caesar Suetonius declares that he did not dare to attend the Senate until 1 January 62 B.C., when, being praetor, he was immune from attack. Other sources say that Caesar tried to clear himself, but the interruptions in his speech were so numerous and so violent that a riot nearly ensued.

On 10 December new tribunes entered office; among them was Metellus Nepos, who had been sent home by Pompey, perhaps to promote his interests. Metellus immediately launched a violent attack on Cicero, giving notice of an impeachment for having put citizens to death without an appeal to the assembly, and forbidding him to address the people. Even on 31 December, when outgoing magistrates took an oath that they had not broken the laws, he would not allow Cicero to make the customary speech. Cicero thereupon mounted the rostrum and swore that he and he alone had saved the Republic. His audience burst into applause and escorted him home triumphantly: another 'popular' leader found himself exposed as only a member of a clique of nobles.

M. Cato became tribune the same day as Metellus; he had only stood at the last moment in order to be able to frustrate him. It is evident that the common people's hopes of some relief from the burden of debt had been aroused by Catiline, and that his defeat had led to disappointment, and indignation. Either at the end of 63 B.C., or early in 62, Cato persuaded the Senate to renew the ration of corn at subsidized prices which had been discontinued, probably since Sulla's regime. There was now a scarcity again, and this had led to high prices, no doubt because in the uncertainty caused by Catiline the merchants had not put their money into stocks of food which might be looted.

On 1 January 62, Cicero became a private citizen again. He had a position of honour, for the new consuls made him the leader of the Senate, whose opinion was asked first when matters came up for debate, and he had a strong following of supporters who were grateful for what he had done to defeat Catiline, but he was a private citizen without actual powers. His position provoked much jealousy, especially among the nobles whom he had grievously insulted: 'I rose to a pinnacle of glory', he wrote to Atticus in 60, 'and met the envy and political enmity attached to it', and later in the same letter he wrote of 'the enmity' his position stimulated 'in the minds of the envious and luxury-loving young nobles'.

For the time being, 'Catiline's mob', as Cicero called them, could not touch him, but they could insult him. Someone proposed that Pompey should be recalled 'to save Rome from domination by Cicero'; a rival barrister called him a 'foreign tyrant' and spoke of his 'overlordship of the law courts'; 'how far shall we endure this regal personage?' P. Clodius asked in an altercation in the Senate-House. In 62 Metellus continued his attacks; through the influence of the women-folk of his family Cicero tried to persuade him to moderate his language and his conduct, but to no avail. On 3 January Cicero delivered a strongly worded speech against him; though he published it, this has not survived.

This speech provoked a coarse and abusive letter from Metellus' brother who was governor of Cisalpine Gaul (the Po Valley), to which Cicero replied in a forthright but dignified letter of self-defence. Both letters have survived, the earliest in the collection known as *Letters to his Friends* (V. 1 and 2). Cicero appears in a favourable light compared with the boorish aristocrat: 'I understand your feelings towards your brother', Cicero said in effect, 'and I have no wish to quarrel with him. I have not provoked him, but if he insists on making violent attacks on me, I am obliged to reply to him in self-defence.'

Metellus the tribune persisted in his attacks, however, attempting to impeach Cicero until frustrated by the Senate, who passed decrees indemnifying all who had taken action against Catiline and his fellow-conspirators, and declaring that to try to prosecute them would be to act against the Republic.

Metellus next proposed that Pompey be commissioned to return to save Rome from Catiline; this was just what Pompey will have wanted, but Cato and other tribunes were determined not to bring Pompey back into Italy with a military commission. Uproar broke out as Cato pressed his veto, and in the end Metellus left for the camp of Pompey in defiance of his duty as tribune to remain in the city. Caesar supported Metellus, and was suspended for a time as praetor, but when he decided that things had gone far enough and curbed a demonstration, he was formally thanked by the Senate and reinstated.

The departure of Metellus restored peace to the city, but Pompey remained a threat; he had made a regal progress through the Asiatic provinces, making agreements with client kings in the name of the Roman people, acquiring enormous resources of patronage, and handing out donatives to his troops vastly in excess of those customarily given. Was he planning another coup d'état?

Crassus went to Asia, almost certainly in the interests of the equites; Cicero wrote Pompey a letter 'as big as a book' outlining the achievements whereby he had secured the leadership of the Senate; he later admitted it was rather high-handed, and it is not surprising that Pompey's reply was chilly. Unfortunately neither of these letters has survived, but a second letter from Cicero has done so; after expressing disappointment that Pompey will not reciprocate his congratulations Cicero adds that the interests of the Republic will bring them together – Pompey had established abroad that peace which Cicero always cherished, and at home, 'Let me tell you that what I did is approved by the verdict of everybody; when you return, you will find that I acted with a judgement and courage which will make you happy enough to be associated with me in public life.' He had always supported him, he claimed, whereas Pompey's new friends were his old enemies who had been shattered by his successes.

In 62 B.C., Cicero also found his new friends among his old enemies, the conservative nobles. They had given him their backing in the Rabirius affair, and again against Catiline, and Cicero had given them his support in promoting Lucullus' triumph. He supported them again in 62 in defending Archias, a Greek poet who was a client of Lucullus', and had influenced Cicero as a young man; he was now arraigned for usurping citizenship. The case was heard before Quintus, Cicero's brother, who was praetor this year, and it provided Cicero with an opportunity to pay a debt of gratitude, while expatiating on the meaning and benefits of a liberal education, and of the place of writers in society. The speech survives, a gem of its kind.

In his new position of political leadership Cicero decided that he should own an appropriate house, and purchased one from M. Crassus, the millionaire, for a sum so large that he had to borrow to pay for it. He was criticized for the purchase, and he was more criticized when P. Sulla, from whom he had borrowed the money for the purchase, was charged with complicity with Catiline, and Cicero was asked to defend him. The request was very embarrassing: Cicero had provided the evidence that had caused other suspects to be convicted, he had probably talked too much already about Sulla's part in the supposed conspiracy of 65 B.C., and the prosecutor was a personal friend, L. Manlius Torquatus, who decided that the only way to conduct his case was to make a direct attack on Cicero, in order to weaken his defence by destroying his authority. 'Torquatus says he cannot bear my tyranny', Cicero said; 'it is hard to see what he is referring to; I can only assume he means my consulship, in which so far from giving orders like a tyrant I actually took my orders from the Senate. . . . Or perhaps he calls me tyrant . . . on the ridiculous grounds that all those against whom I have given evidence have been convicted, while my client hopes to be acquitted. Of my evidence, all I can say is that if my evidence was false, so was Torquatus'; if it was true, it is hardly characteristic of a tyrant to vindicate the truth of evidence given under oath.' Torquatus also charged Cicero with cruelty, to which he replied that 'in the days when the Republic was falling I was implacable and courageous, but once it was preserved I was willing to show mercy, and to pardon'.

Sulla was acquitted, but the truth about Cicero's loan leaked out, and Cicero became more embarrassed than ever, and he is found in 61 B.C. pressing his agent known in code as Teucris to hand on the money she was being sent, probably by C. Antonius in Macedonia.

Antonius' extortions became notorious; they were reported in Rome, and Cicero had to defend him in the Senate. Early in 61, Cicero heard a report that whenever Antonius demanded money he said that part of it was for Cicero. This he resented (though it was probably true, since Antonius would have had to repay Cicero's loan), and in a letter of early 61, Cicero sharply accused Antonius of ingratitude; and though he implied that he intended to defend Antonius if he were tried, he wrote to Atticus that Antonius' behaviour was too shameful to defend.

Antonius provided Pompey, opportunistic as ever, with a 'cause' to advertise on his return from Asia. Late in 62 he crossed with his army to Brundisium, where, to the general amazement, he disbanded his legions and proceeded on foot towards Rome without any troops at all. He had returned feeling hostile to Cicero, but when he arrived and found the general sentiment in Rome strongly in support of Cicero, he proclaimed himself very well-disposed to him, and on one occasion at least, went and sat next to him in the Senate. Atticus was not deceived – 'he began to praise you only when he dared not criticize you any more' was his sarcastic comment, and Cicero's own assessment – 'awkward, tortuous, never unequivocal in politics, shabby, timid, disingenuous' – sums him up well. Pompey was indeed one with whom to sup with a long spoon, and Atticus warned Cicero over and over again against trusting him.

Cicero led the Senate throughout 62; we know no details of the business transacted but they heard plenty about 'fire and sword – you know my palette and the scenes I'm always painting in my speeches', he wrote to Atticus.

At the end of the year, there occurred a famous scandal which was to have tremendous repercussions. The festival of the 'Kindly Goddess', to which only women were admitted, was celebrated in Caesar's house (Caesar was praetor this year as well as *pontifex maximus*); a man disguised as a woman was discovered in the house; he took to his heels and escaped apprehension thanks to a female slave. The whole festival was repeated, the augurs declared a sacrilege had been committed, and when Caesar heard the man was there in pursuit of an intrigue with his wife, he divorced her, saying his wife must be above suspicion. This remark, from a notorious libertine, must have been seen as a good joke.

When Cicero first mentioned the affair to Atticus he named P. Clodius, with the comment that Atticus would know all about it already, and feared, quite justly, that the incident would escalate into a major political struggle. At first he was for taking a hard line, but later he began to soften in his attitude; finally he became the chief spokesman for severe action because the authority of the Senate in dealing with the offences of senators was brought into the case.

Certainly, Pompey understood this to be the issue when he was questioned about the case shortly after his return, both in the popular assembly and in the Senate. His recorded remark that 'he hoped he had given enough answers about these questions', suggests that he found the case tiresome compared with what he wanted discussed: his settlement of the East and lands for his army veterans. However, it occupied, apparently, the whole time of the Senate from late in 62 B.C. till May 61.

What the Senate did was to ask the consuls to promulgate a law to be based on a decree setting up a court to try a case of sacrilege which had been committed; the court was to be presided over by the urban praetor, and the jury hand-picked by him, to ensure that the trial was not vitiated by bribery. The draft decree was attacked in the Senate by a number of people including Pupius Piso, the consul, while Clodius used his influence, supplemented by personal appeals, to get it defeated. It was passed, however, and taken to the popular assembly for ratification as a law. There an attempt was made to intimidate the voters by not issuing the 'aye' tokens, and by stationing parties of strong-arm men around the Forum, but the voting was broken off when some of the senators present, led by Cato, attacked Pupius Piso and got the bill returned to the Senate. Here a motion that it be not approved by the Senate was defeated by about 15 to over 400, but the approval of a motion that the consuls urge the people to accept it was vetoed by a tribune.

When the Senate had given a clear vote in favour of setting up a court under the terms of the consuls' law, Cicero was determined to uphold the Senate's expressed will, and fought as hard as he could to prevent it being nullified by the opposition. He became identified as the leader of the senatorial majority demanding that the Senate's decree be implemented, whereupon Clodius turned this basically legal struggle into a political one on the question of the Senate's authority and rights, and we can hardly doubt that the old issue of the Catilinarian conspirators was fought all over again. Cicero says that Clodius used his name to stir up the hostility of the common people, and he himself replied in vigorous, not to say violent terms, attacking all who were defending Clodius. Deadlock ensued. In about April, an unwise compromise proposed by Q. Hortensius was accepted by the Senate, whereby the jurors were not to be hand-picked, but chosen by lot – which, as Cicero says, vitiated the whole point of the consuls' proposal; Hortensius was quite certain that no jury, however empanelled, could possibly acquit Clodius, whose reactions to all proposals to deal with the sacrilege had clearly shown a guilty conscience. 'A sword made of lead is sharp enough to cut his throat', Hortensius is said to have declared.

Cicero was wiser than Hortensius. When the trial came on he contented himself with saying in evidence only what was already familiar to everyone in court; 'I did battle less than usual', he wrote to Atticus, despite the fact that the jurors staged a demonstration in his favour when Clodius' friends tried to intimidate him and the court. Another demonstration took place in support of Cicero the next day, so great a crowd of supporters escorting him to the court that the jurors asked the Senate for a guard, which they were granted. 'Why did you want a guard?' Catulus asked one of them afterwards, 'Were you afraid of a pay-snatch?'

The bribery by which Clodius was acquitted was so flagrant and so notorious that it became the subject of debate in the Senate, and Cicero claimed that it nullified any reflection that might be cast on him by the fact that his evidence on oath (which destroyed Clodius' alibi) was rejected by the verdict. Consequently, he was able to denounce the jurors and urge the Senate to ignore the insult to its prestige and policy. This was combined with a personal attack on Clodius and his defence-counsel, C. Curio, in a set speech *Against Clodius and Curio*, which had the odd fate of being published at a moment when Cicero had intended not to publish it; it is now almost entirely lost.

In 61 B.C. Cicero was no longer leader of the Senate, Pupius Piso, the consul, preferring his relative, the Piso who was consul in 67. Cicero consoled himself with the thought that the second place 'conveys nearly as much honour, and leaves you less beholden to the consul', thus more free to criticize.

Piso gave Cicero cause for criticism too, for, apart from witty or sarcastic remarks against him, he took Clodius' part in the business of arranging the trial for sacrilege.

Clodius was overjoyed by his acquittal, and attempted to reply to an attack by Cicero on 15 May; this led to an altercation which Cicero related to Atticus. It reveals something of the intensely personal character of Roman politics. 'You were at Baiae', said Clodius (Baiae having a reputation for immorality); 'Is that like saying I was at a secret ceremony?' Cicero replied (a reference to the 'Kindly Goddess's' festival). 'What has a man of Arpinum [a country bumpkin, that is] to do with a spa?' (a place of culture), said Clodius; 'Tell that to your counsel Curio, who was keen enough for an Arpinum man's house at the spa', Cicero replied – a reference to Curio's family's purchase of Marius' house at Baiae. 'How long shall we put up with this king?' said Clodius. 'You call me "King" when you were ignored by King' (the name of

Clodius' brother-in-law, who had failed to mention him in his will). 'That was some house you bought', said Clodius (a reference to Cicero's new mansion, p. 44). 'You'd think', Cicero replied, 'he was saying I'd bought a jury.' 'You gave evidence on oath and they didn't believe you', said Clodius. 'I was trusted by twenty-five of them', Cicero replied, 'but thirty-one of them didn't trust you – they'd got their pay in advance.' The shouts of laughter compelled Clodius to sit down and say no more. Popular opinion was on Cicero's side, he felt; the ordinary Roman was as disgusted as Cicero with the way the nobles had behaved, and Cicero believed that the battle over Clodius' trial had resulted in a diminution of the ill-feeling against him for his actions against Catiline and his followers.

The trial itself split the solid front of Cicero's coalition; Cicero describes Clodius' supporters as 'the flock of Catiline', but some – the consul Pupius Piso, for instance – were not in that category at all. Its aftermath was to alienate the sympathy of the equites from the senators, and destroy Cicero's 'Harmony of the Orders' and his leadership of the Senate. There was a senatorial proposal to bring equestrian jurors under the bribery law. It was ludicrous of course that they were immune, but they not unreasonably resented the imputation that they were principally responsible for the scandal of Clodius' acquittal (which was entirely organized and paid for by senators), and Cicero became one of their spokesmen, opposing the proposal in order to retain their political support.

The equites were further antagonized when the Senate refused to accede at once to their request for an alteration to the tax contract they had made with the Senate. The collection of taxes in Roman provinces was normally let out to syndicates of contractors, or publicans (usually equites): they used to pay a lump sum of money for the privilege of collecting the dues, and would then keep as profit whatever they were able to collect over and above the agreed price. In this instance they claimed that they were going to suffer a loss, since for some reason unknown to us they had overbid. It has been suggested that they expected the contract to include the revenues from Pompey's new conquests, but there is no clear evidence for this; Cicero merely attributed it to their greed. He thought their demand was impudent, but believed that their political support was more important than the money or the principle involved. Cato disagreed, and fought with an unshakeable tenacity of purpose until the Senate was persuaded to reject the request in 60 B.C. Cicero admired Cato's unflinching rectitude but recognized that politics is the art of the possible: 'He talks as if he was in Plato's *Republic*', Cicero wrote, 'and not in Rome's midden; he has the best of intentions but the damage he does to the Republic is appalling.'

Cicero's defeat on these two issues caused him to be supplanted by Cato as leader of the traditionalist nobles (who were probably glad to rebuff Cicero); he had a brief alliance with Crassus over the equites' contract, and Crassus, probably merely to spite Pompey, delivered a passionate eulogy of Cicero early in 61, but their alliance was of short duration only, and by the end of the year Cicero felt very isolated.

Cicero's brother Quintus left to govern Asia in 61; on the way he quarrelled with Atticus his brother-in-law. His stormy relations with his wife probably played a part, but the prime cause seems to have been that Atticus declined an invitation to join his staff. Cicero intervened, found himself involved, and had to try to soothe Atticus' feelings. In a letter dated 5 December 61, he wrote:

In the things that really matter – uprightness, integrity, conscientiousness, fidelity to obligations – I put you second neither to myself nor to any other man, while as to affection towards me, leaving aside my brother and my own home circle, I give you first place. I have seen with my own eyes and noted in detail your anxieties and your joys in the ups and downs of my career. Your congratulations have often given me pleasure in success, and your comfort consoled my apprehensions. Indeed, in your absence at the present time I badly miss not only your excellent advice but also our habitual exchange of talk, which is such a delight to me. I don't know whether I miss it more in public affairs, which I am in duty bound not to neglect, or in my court work, which I formerly undertook for advancement's sake and still keep up in order to maintain my position by the personal influence so acquired, or in my own private concerns, in which I have felt the want of you and of our talks together, more especially since my brother's departure. In short, whether working or resting, in business or in leisure, in professional or domestic affairs, in public life or in private, I cannot for any length of time do without your affectionate advice and the delight of your conversation. Diffidence has often kept both you and me from putting these things into words, but it has now been necessary to do so because of the passage in your letter in which you have set out to justify yourself and your manner of life to me.

Atticus accepted Cicero's explanation unreservedly, and Cicero expressed his delight in a letter written in the second half of May. On 20 January 60 B.C., he told Atticus how much he needed his company in Rome:

> I must tell you that what I most badly need at the present time is a confidant – someone with whom I could share all that gives me anxiety, a wise, affectionate friend to whom I can talk without pretence or evasion or concealment. My brother, the soul of candour and affection, is away.... And you, whose talk and advice has so often lightened my worries and vexation of spirit, my supporter in public life and the intimate of all my private concerns, the sharer of all my talk and plans, where are you? I am so utterly forsaken that my only moments of relaxation are those I spend with my wife, my little daughter, and my darling Marcus. My brilliant, worldly friendships may make a fine show in public, but at home they are barren things. My house is crammed of a morning, I go down to the Forum surrounded by droves of friends, but in all the multitude I cannot find one with whom I can pass an unguarded joke or fetch a private sigh. That is why I am writing and longing for you, why I now fairly summon you home. There are many things to worry and vex me, but once I have you here to listen I feel I can pour them all away in a single walk and talk.

Atticus was indeed an ideal foil to one of Cicero's mercurial temperament.

4
Failure:
Cicero Driven out of Politics

The years 62–60 B.C. showed the fragility of Cicero's political party; they also showed how few of the senators were continuously active in politics. Only those who aimed at long-term political leadership troubled to participate in the formulation of policies when their own immediate interests and careers, and those of their relatives and friends, were not directly affected. Cicero had noticed how Q. Hortensius had declined in his oratorical vigour after his consulate in 69; he now noticed how many nobles withdrew from active politics after achieving what they wanted – as Lucullus did after his triumph in 63; Cicero thought they were jealous of him and sneered indignantly at their passion for their fish-ponds. Many hints in his letters suggest that men expected him to retire after his triumph in 63, but he had no intention of doing so; he believed that he was cut out for leadership, and that the Republic needed him. The next phase in his career was to see him driven out of the state and, when he returned, out of political leadership again.

In December 61, Cicero was looking for political allies, and found Pompey in a receptive mood. His offer of a marriage-alliance with Cato's family had been rejected, and Cicero must have appealed to him as a politician who had aided him before and now had a strong following, and who had also been rebuffed by the conservative nobles. Pompey therefore let it be known that he and Cicero were to be associated; this produced demonstrations of popularity which pleased Cicero very much, and Pompey's speeches in the Senate in praise of Cicero pleased him even more.

Atticus warned Cicero repeatedly against allying himself with

Pompey, but Cicero assured him that such an alliance was the best way to protect his influential position. He proved unable, however, to help Pompey to achieve what he wanted, the ratification of his settlement of the eastern provinces, and lands for his troops. Pompey's old officer Afranius, whose election as consul he had secured by overt bribery on a huge scale, proved a broken reed, nor was a tribune called Flavius successful in starting a new scheme for land-allotments for veterans. The nobles suspected Pompey wanted another big commission, and Metellus Celer, the other consul, opposed Flavius tooth and nail, and dominated Afranius his colleague in the Senate.

In the wider political field, the most important development in 60 B.C. was Pompey's failure to get what he wanted from the Senate despite his alliance with Cicero. Cicero did not tell Atticus his views on Pompey's eastern settlement, but he criticized Flavius' bill, except for the establishment of a commission to purchase lands with the money won in Pompey's conquests: this would satisfy Cicero's 'army' – the prosperous. The Senate however allowed Cato's attack on the tax-farmers to take up two months of their time, and then before 15 March news came of disturbances in Gaul, the first stirrings of the folk-movements which were to give Caesar his great chance of military glory; the consuls were told to draw lots for the province of Transalpine Gaul, where the Roman allies were under pressure. A levy was called, and ambassadors were to be sent, one consular, one of praetor's and one of quaestor's rank. When Cicero's name was drawn first as ambassador, the Senate voted that he must be kept in Rome; the same happened to Pompey whose name was drawn next. Cicero took this as a compliment, but we might perhaps wonder if other feelings did not play a part too; Cicero had no experience in this field, Pompey's experience was bellicose.

For Cicero, Clodius' acquittal on the sacrilege charge brought a threat, since Clodius proved vindictive. It has been suggested that Cicero injured Clodius' patrician pride in the fierce debates over the court to try him; Cicero has also been accused of ingratitude to Clodius, since Clodius had supported Cicero against Catiline but Cicero gave evidence against him. Both these may be true, but to Cicero the most important issue in Clodius' trial had been the political one of the Senate's standing in judicial and quasi-judicial cases. There was an irreconcilable clash here, since Clodius' interest in his acquittal conflicted with Cicero's interest in maintaining the Senate's authority. Clodius determined to be elected tribune and thus able to attack Cicero and perhaps the whole Senate under the ancient law that guaranteed to all citizens the right to trial by the people. To become a tribune the patrician Clodius had first to become a plebeian by means of a popular vote and a religious ceremony. A bill was first proposed in 60 B.C., and supported by Metellus Celer the consul, Clodius' brother-in-law, but it failed. Clodius persisted; his agent was a tribune called Herennius, son of one of the *divisores*. Atticus could not believe that Clodius was serious; Cicero assured him that he was, and that he might have to summon Atticus home urgently if Clodius made any progress. Clodius' threats were another reason for Cicero to want to ally himself with Pompey. Under the shadow of that mighty popular leader tribunes could hardly touch him, or so he thought.

In May 60, Caesar returned to Rome, fresh from his province in Spain, claiming a triumph for his work there and announcing his candidature for the consulship of 59. Cicero expected a visit from him early in June when he was at the seaside in his villa at Antium to avoid having to attend the gladiatorial games which he disliked. Caesar had a fair wind in his sails and was doubtless canvassing Cicero's support for his consulship. Cicero hoped that he could 'improve' Caesar. Atticus warned him against damaging the Republic by associating with such a firebrand, but Cicero felt that there was much to be said for trying to treat the unsound members of the body politic by healing rather than amputating them – that is, to secure concord rather than to procure the exile of political enemies. Concord was what the Republic needed; with the equites estranged and the leading men concentrating on their fish-ponds there was no way of dealing with extremists except to persuade them to become more moderate. Since Caesar was campaigning with L. Lucceius, an extremely wealthy man with literary tastes, he was hardly likely to propose drastic measures to cancel debts.

The collapse of Cicero's political front caused him to withdraw somewhat from public life, and he published only one law-court speech in 60 B.C. He decided to put his achievements on record: he wrote an account of his consulship in Greek, which was finished by the middle of March. He clearly regarded this as the definitive work on the subject, and contemplated a Latin version. He also began a poem on the subject, published by the end of the year. For us the most significant literary work, however, was the preparation of his consular speeches for publication; he told Atticus that this was in response to the demands of the young men who crowded his house to listen to him practising, as Cicero himself used to listen to the leading orators of his youth. Many of these speeches survive in whole or in part, and have been referred to above.

He also wrote his brother a long letter, almost a manifesto, on the ideals of a provincial governor. Reading between the lines we can see that Quintus Cicero had been criticized, and his brother wanted to ensure he was not prosecuted. Cicero was also delighted by a gift of books from his friend L. Papirius Paetus in return for legal services. 'Do make every effort', he wrote to Atticus, 'to see that not a page goes astray. . . . Every day, in whatever time I have over from my legal work, I find greater relaxation in these intellectual pursuits.' Atticus also sent Cicero an account of his consulship in Greek. 'I'm glad', he wrote, 'that I had already sent you off my version, or you'd be accusing me of plagiarism. . . . Your piece is embellished by its very lack of ornamentation – just as women seem more fragrant when they've not put on any scent.'

When the elections for the consuls of 59 B.C. came on, Caesar was a candidate; his troops in Spain had hailed him as '*Imperator*' (General) and he was thus entitled to ask for a triumph which would make his election an absolute certainty. To triumph involved remaining a soldier, to stand for the consulship involved becoming a civilian. Caesar requested a dispensation from the laws to allow him to remain a soldier till after nomination day. Left to themselves the Senate might have agreed; Caesar had many friends, but Cato was unrelentingly vindictive against his enemy and conducted a successful filibuster, talking against the proposal until the time for it to be of any use had expired. With his usual grasp of political realities Caesar let his triumph go, and became a candidate.

The other candidates were L. Lucceius and L. Calpurnius Bibulus. Bibulus was an aristocrat and the ideal man for the role of obstructionist; narrow-minded and unrelenting, he was a man with whom there was virtually no chance of compromise. Caesar and Lucceius joined to campaign together, spending lavishly out of Lucceius' funds and Caesar's promises. Determined to clip Caesar's wings, the Senate chose as provinces for the consuls of 59, tasks which would give no opportunity to recoup election-expenses, or to gain a military name. Cato's circle also organized a fund from which to match in bribes everything that Caesar and Lucceius promised; Cato, the incorruptible, contributed; Cicero did not. The impossible happened; Caesar and Bibulus were elected.

Though Cicero was no friend of either consul, he felt no deep foreboding for the future: 'I shall argue on both sides', he wrote, 'like Socrates, but in the end I shall declare my choice.' There was no obviously clear-cut issue between good and evil. Caesar had an agrarian law to promote; he had announced the fact in advance; land was to be bought for settlements of veteran soldiers, and also for the city poor. He was confident that Cicero would support him in proposing the purchase of lands, as he had supported Flavius. Caesar also sent messages through an in-termediary, Cornelius Balbus, who assured Cicero that he would follow his advice and that of Pompey, with whom Cicero had been associated in 60 B.C., and would try to get Caesar's old ally, Crassus, to unite with Pompey. It was to be a new party, a combination of all who were opposed to the leadership of Cato and his narrow-minded circle of nobles.

In later years Cicero declared that he had tried to persuade Pompey against this partnership with Caesar, but there is no trace of such an attempt in his few letters of the end of 60 B.C. However, when Pompey was persuaded to join Caesar, Cicero could see the attractions of Caesar's invitation to him; he would stand alongside the Pompey he admired, recover some of the popularity for which he longed, and even become reconciled with his enemies. But to support Caesar would have involved violating one of his most dearly-held principles – the principle that government should be by and through the Senate, which should initiate policies of this sort. Cicero was not prepared to do this without seeing the Senate's reactions to Caesar's proposals; he decided to wait and see.

The year 59 began, and Caesar brought his bill to the Senate. Cicero, who will have spoken early in the debate, probably spoke in favour of the proposal, but the faction of Cato, with the aid of the consul Bibulus, proved immovably obstructive. According to the later historian Dio (who is not usually prejudiced in Caesar's favour), they were unable to find specific fault with it, but prevaricated and argued and merely wasted time until Caesar lost patience with Cato, who was arguing that things were all right as they were (which they manifestly were not, because of the vast unemployed and miserably poor urban proletariat). A threat to imprison Cato brought a demonstration of sympathy for him, and Caesar announced that he would waste no more time on the Senate, but appeal to the people. In the assembly Bibulus continued his unreasoning opposition; he swore he would oppose all measures for reform, and when the bill came to the vote he appeared with three tribunes and tried to interpose a veto. All, however, were roughly handled and the bill was passed.

Bibulus' attempt the next day to get the Senate to repeal the measure got no support, and he therefore resorted to obstruction by religious means, declaring every day a holy day, or that he was seeking the will of heaven, for the rest of the year. The object of this was to render all Caesar's acts technically invalid, and thus able to be annulled at a later date. Caesar simply ignored him and proceeded to carry out his intended programme, ratifying Pompey's eastern settlement, granting the equites their concession in respect of the taxes of Asia, recognizing the claimant to the throne of Egypt (for which rumour said he was paid 6,000 talents), revising the laws on provincial government so as to make them more stringent, and providing that the Senate's business should be made public (thus frustrating secret decision-making). A tribune, P. Vatinius, had the allocation of provinces to the consuls changed to give Caesar a large province, Cisalpine Gaul and Illyricum (the Po Valley and Jugoslavia on modern maps) with a large army for five years, and when by chance Transalpine Gaul (Provence) fell vacant, the Senate added that too, on the proposal of Pompey. Thus was Caesar given the command which was to make his name a household word.

During the course of the spring Caesar lost the general measure of sympathy and support he had at first enjoyed. His loss of patience with Cato alienated some sympathy, possibly his ally Pompey's unwise threat that he would counter force with force alienated more. When the first agrarian measure failed to produce the necessary land, another bill was hastily drafted in mid-April, taking over the ancient rich lands of Campania, and establishing colonies at Capua and Casilinum among other places. To pass this, force was used, and, not improbably, open military force. Troops were certainly in evidence by the middle of the year, and this alienated all sympathy. Caesar was accused of using the consulate like a tribunate, serving the purposes of a powerful politician, and not acting independently as consuls ought. Pompey was bitterly criticized too, as it was his old troops who were Caesar's instrument of coercion, recalled to the ranks ostensibly for a Gallic war. The gratitude of the equites was quickly dissipated by the annexation of Campania, whether because they had interests in the area (which is probable) or because they were strongly opposed on principle (the compelling one of self-interest) to the state resuming control of its lands.

In the light of after-events it is hard to remember that in 59 Pompey was seen as the leader of the coalition; to Atticus Cicero usually calls him by names like 'Nabob', or 'Pasha'. The opposition forced Pompey further and further into the open as the power behind Caesar, and his marriage in May with Caesar's daughter, who had been betrothed to a member of Cato's circle, exposed the realities of their association for all to see.

Cicero found his position more and more intolerable. He had associated himself with Pompey and with land purchase; he had been approached by Caesar in 60 B.C., and had not rebuffed him; Caesar made him a stream of offers, a place on the land commission of twenty, a staff appointment in Gaul – which would clearly be honorary as Cicero was no soldier – and missions overseas, including a roving commission of the type he himself had tried to abolish. He may have tentatively accepted the roving commission for a later date – a chance to visit Egypt on an embassy was very tempting – but he dared not face the criticism he knew would result; even as it was, he felt he could not face the people he knew, since he was seriously compromised by Caesar's activities. However, during the spring he spoke out strongly against Caesar in his defence of his old consular colleague C. Antonius, who was accused either of extortion or (more probably) of treason, having left his province without authority. Cicero not only lost the case, but suffered reprisals, in that Pompey and Caesar immediately arranged for Clodius the adoption into a plebeian family which he had been trying to secure for two years. Clodius made it clear that Cicero was one of the targets for his programme as tribune; Catiline's old circle celebrated the conviction of Antonius with a banquet, and decked the tomb of Catiline with flowers.

To be both criticized for Caesar's actions, and also deprived by him of the right of independent speech, was intolerable. Cicero left Rome, sick at heart: 'I wish I had never taken up politics', he wrote to Atticus from his seaside villa at Antium. He tried to compose; a geography was projected, but his heart was not in it; 'the subject is hard to set out and monotonous, and does not lend itself as easily as appears to stylish writing', he felt. He decided to be idle, not even to go fishing – it was the wrong season – or perhaps to write a scurrilous history not for publication. Atticus kept urging him to write, but in fact he could not tear himself away from politics in Rome: 'who will be the next consuls, do you suppose?' he asked, and the next letter looks to see the highwaymen falling out over their spoils. When Cicero composed he wrote up two of his political speeches; and he was glad enough to receive political callers in Antium.

Meanwhile, he heard a great deal about what was going on. Atticus was busy behind the scenes as usual, having a talk with Bibulus, negotiating with Clodius through the latter's sister Clodia, finding out what Pompey felt about Cicero through his confidant Theophanes. The political currents were swift, deep and confused, and we can only glimpse movements. A bargain about Cicero was struck, but Cicero had no idea whether it would be kept or not; Clodius appeared to have quarrelled with Caesar and to have threatened to undo his legislation; Caesar had retorted that Clodius wasn't really a plebeian – an attitude of indifference to the niceties of religion which seems typical of Caesar.

Cicero revelled in Atticus' letters; his mercurial temperament is vividly reflected in his replies, as now he grasped at every hope of a return to political life, now despaired of the Republic, now jeered and mocked at Pompey, now at the infuriated and frustrated nobles – they had let him down, let them stew in their own juice, Cicero would not return to the firing line. But in his more optimistic moods, he thought the unpopularity of the dynasts (usually, but wrongly, called the first triumvirate), and the recognition of Cato's folly would make men happy enough to recall the period of his own leadership with pleasure. He might have been right, but in May, or at latest in June, Caesar abandoned any pretence of legislating in accordance with the popular will and brought troops into the Forum. Force now became the arbiter of politics, sometimes military force, sometimes para-military, and the caucus-decisions of the pay-masters of these organized forces supplanted, except for rare intervals, the deliberative machinery of the Senate.

In April, Cicero moved to Formiae, where he found himself plagued by boring neighbours who came to talk philosophy all day. He moved to Arpinum early in May. He and Atticus then met and remained together till the latter returned to Greece, leaving Cicero in Rome in the month of June.

In Rome Cicero felt helpless; he anxiously looked for every sign of the unpopularity of the dynasts, whether in public life in the Forum or at the games, and reported them with delight. Caesar continued to tempt Cicero with offers, but he was unwilling to enlist under Caesar's banner, or to be intimidated by Clodius into a virtual admission that he had done wrong in 63 B.C. – to do either would reflect upon his honour. Nor did he wish to be away from Rome when Quintus returned from Asia, since this would leave the latter open to prosecution without Cicero's defence, and Quintus might be made a scapegoat. Indeed, Quintus' return was a problem which exercised his brother a good deal. Almost all Cicero's letters to him are lost, but it is clear from the one that survives that many were critical, and one even angry. He told Quintus he had tried to mollify many people by admitting them to his social circle – 'not because I like either these individuals, or the people of Asia as a whole; I'm disgusted with their fickleness and timeserving servility and lack of principles'. Quintus had foolishly put his seal on letters written by others; there was a whole volume of them in circulation; others of his letters had been joking but liable to misinterpretation, others abusive: 'I beg you not to write letters which are either arbitrary or contradictory or contain ridiculous or eccentric usages or insults to anyone.' It was no use pleading that he was better than his neighbours in Cilicia and Syria; the higher reputations of Vergilius in Sicily or Octavius in Macedonia should be what concerned him. A man's reputation was what mattered above all; 'the concerns and careers of all of us who have taken to public life depend not only on what is true but also on what is rumoured, ... so, on your return home, do please try to leave behind as pleasant a memory as possible.'

Moreover, Cicero was not willing even to seem ready to throw his brother to the wolves. He was in a fix, and, as was his way, he temporized, now seeming inclined to accept Caesar's offers, now deciding that he had enough support to defy Clodius, especially if Pompey gave his backing. He had promised Cicero he would, but even Cicero recognized that he promised more than he could perform:

> He asserts that Clodius won't say a word against me, but in this it's not I who am taken in but Pompey himself ... Pompey is my friend, holds me close to his heart – 'Do you believe him?' you may ask—; yes I do, he has me convinced, but it's because I want to be. Men of the world bid me in every history-book and hand-book and poem, 'Be wary, don't trust anyone.' One part I do, I'm wary, but I'm incapable of the other part, not to trust.

Cicero was as helpless as iron near a magnet. He could not rid himself of Pompey's power to attract, though Pompey let him down again and again, and now, even in his indignation at the dynasts' proceedings, he was sorry for Pompey, who was always deeply hurt by demonstrations of unpopularity. 'I could not keep back my tears when I saw him addressing a meeting on 25 July about the edicts of Bibulus ... he was so humbled, so downcast that he seemed to dislike himself as much as his audience disliked him.'

So Cicero would not join the dynasts, nor would he join Cato's party – he did not like them, and they snubbed him, and in his view had betrayed him through jealousy; 'Bibulus is a star', he said, 'I've no idea why, but he's regarded like Fabius, who by his delaying alone saved our all from Hannibal. ... They take down his edicts and harangues and read them out aloud ... I don't like them, I must say, they put him I have always loved [Pompey] too harshly on the rack.'

Such manifestations of popular displeasure became common. Cicero became nervous of what the dynasts would do: Caesar had already shown he could lose his temper; Pompey, 'a man so unaccustomed to abuse, of such impetuosity, such a determined warrior, might give vent to his resentment and anger with the full force of his temper'. When there were demonstrations in the theatre the dynasts threatened to deprive the equites of some of their privileges, and to cut off the common people's food-supply at concession rates. Caesar could not provoke a demonstration against Bibulus in August, even when the latter postponed the elections, always an unpopular move. But Cicero undoubtedly exaggerated Pompey's unpopularity, at least later in the year, for a young noble who dared to call Pompey 'an unofficial dictator' publicly was almost lynched.

The violence of the dynasts produced a sense of insecurity. When Cicero wrote to Atticus he felt he could not say openly what he thought; he used pseudonyms, wrote in Greek, expressed himself in riddles, or employed an amanuensis to try to conceal his identity in case the letter got into the wrong hands. There was talk of counter-violence and assassinations, and wild allegations were made against Curio, the leading opponent of the dynasts, Cicero and others. Whether true or not – and even in 59 B.C. it was never proved whether they were – they succeeded in alienating Pompey from Cicero, at least for a time. Cicero felt very insecure, and constantly urged Atticus to come to Rome, for he had an entry to the social circle of the nobles, and could find out through Clodia what her brother had up his sleeve. 'Oh dear, why are you not here? There's nothing that would escape you – maybe I'm blind and too trusting that all's well.' Cicero knew himself too well.

Till Atticus returned, Cicero stayed out of politics; he frequented the Forum, and resumed his legal work; he found people friendly and sympathetic, and remembered the kind words he heard about his own government of the Republic. He conducted at least three defences, two of A. Thermus, which are now unknown, and one of the Valerius Flaccus who had assisted Cicero in 63 by arresting the Gauls as praetor.

Cicero's fellow-advocate, Hortensius, had delivered a splendid eulogy of Cicero in the course of his speech. Cicero followed him; he argued very forcibly that to condemn Flaccus would be to comfort the survivors of Catiline's party; Flaccus was intended as a sacrificial victim to the ghost of Lentulus, as Antonius had been to Catiline's; if Flaccus were convicted, Cicero himself would be the next target for attack. He combined this theme with ridicule of the Greeks of Asia and with an appeal to the Romans' imperial consciousness and their contempt for lesser breeds of men; it was sufficient to secure the acquittal of Flaccus, though he was almost certainly guilty of the extortion of which he was accused. Some modern critics of Cicero have mocked this final Catilinarian oration, but it was timely in its context at the end of the dynasts' year of violent and arbitrary rule, and when Cicero recalled the days when the Senate was in control and violence and rioting were checked he clearly won the sympathy of the jurors, and demonstrated yet again the unpopularity of the self-styled 'popular' leaders. The speech could well have been taken as an announcement that Cicero intended to return to politics in 58 B.C.

At the elections for 58 the dynasts had succeeded in getting two sympathetic consuls, Gabinius, who had long supported Pompey and was heavily in debt, and Caesar's father-in-law, the aristo-cratic L. Calpurnius Piso. However, among the praetors were L. Domitius Ahenobarbus and C. Memmius, who were hostile to the dynasts, as were at least three tribunes. Domitius and Memmius proclaimed that they would have all Caesar's meas-ures annulled and Caesar himself recalled from his province, and they were backed by Cato and others of his circle.

Caesar had to do something to protect his position, and Clodius was the only instrument in sight. Since he had not been able to win Cicero by any of his offers, the latter had to be stopped from leading a revival of his coalition of Senate and equites, which could hardly fail to support Domitius and Memmius, and would certainly separate Pompey from Crassus. Caesar therefore abandoned Cicero to Clodius. Crassus was already behind Clodius; he was reputed to have been the paymaster of the court which had acquitted him in 61, and is the only likely source (apart from Caesar) of the funds necessary to hire a gang of strong-arm men. Crassus had also been putting pressure on Pompey as early as August 59 B.C., and so Pompey turned his coat yet again and a bargain was struck: as tribune, Clodius would silence the opposition, especially Caesar's enemy Cato, and deal with his own enemy, Cicero.

We do not know exactly when Pompey and Caesar abandoned Cicero. Unless they deceived him, or he deceived himself, they were still promising him what he asked some time after Clodius' election; then Cicero still believed he could face Clodius with the

support of the Italian towns which would put at his disposal
sufficient force to counter any violence Clodius could organize.
Most probably the dynasts' decision was taken – as Cicero later
stated – when the praetors-designate announced their all-out
attack on Caesar's work. It was evidently a sudden decision; two
years later Cicero told Atticus it was a surprise. But this now
became the pattern of politics as established in the consulate of
Caesar. Dominant dynasts made their decisions and bargains
behind locked doors, and employed naked force to see that they
were implemented; other people had to comply or become the
victims of personal vendettas or violent intimidation. Cicero's
ideal of policy-making by public discussion was discarded
openly; when he ·declared, 'there is no Republic', he spoke
nothing but the truth.

When Clodius' tribunate began on 10 December 59 B.C., he
lost no time in showing his colours; as Metellus Nepos had done to
Cicero in 63, he prevented Bibulus from addressing the people on
31 December. He then proposed new legislation which was as
irresponsible and damaging as could have been devised. The two
worst enactments were the revival of the clubs established by
Sulla for coercing the assembly, and the conversion of the ration
of corn at subsidized prices into free rations. Superficially there
was nothing wrong with the latter – the poor were very poor, and
relief was both welcome and needed – and not much with the
former if the clubs were kept in check, but the results were
catastrophic. Determined politicians who had not too many
scruples liberated numbers of slaves whose sole asset was their
brutality and discipline, and organized them into para-military
gangs, who, as free men, would be subsidized with food from the
state. Such gangs had no claim to represent the Roman people;
many of the individuals, if liberated slaves, were likely to be
foreigners who had had no contact with, or sympathy for, the
Romans' traditions of government, and had neither loyalty to
Rome nor interest in the welfare of the Republic.

The historian Dio (who is seldom sympathetic to Cicero) says
that Cicero and the tribunes who supported him were double-
crossed by Clodius. The latter agreed, so Dio says, not to indict
Cicero if he and his friends did not veto any of Clodius' measures.
When Clodius had gained his following, and by means of two
more measures, had removed the possibility either of censorial

action against him or of religious obstruction, he proposed a revival of the ancient law which forbade the putting of citizens to death without appeal to the people, and made it retrospective. Cicero was not named, but it was a clear and obvious attack both on him and on the Senate's right to declare that a man had forfeited his right to the protection of the law. Naturally, those who sympathized with Cicero opposed it; Clodius thus could claim that he was free to indict Cicero.

Cicero lost his nerve; afterwards he said that if he had chosen to support the bill, or to ignore it, he would have come to no harm. But he did not do so: he assumed it was aimed at himself, and thus convicted himself. He rallied all the support he could; the equites demonstrated by donning mourning garb, as did some of the young nobles who admired him; the senators tried to do the same until they were intimidated by the consul's order to take it off. Senators who tried to address meetings of the people were beaten up, and one was so severely injured that he died. Cicero appealed to Piso the consul, who said that it was useless to appeal to him and Gabinius, as Clodius would deprive him of the province he needed to enable him to get rid of his debts.

Clodius summoned the dynasts to appear at meetings; at one held outside the city Caesar said the execution of Catiline's supporters was wrong, but that he disapproved of retrospective legislation. Pompey avoided the issue by retiring to his country villa; when visited there he now blamed Caesar and now said he could not act against an armed tribune without a senatorial decree sponsored by the consuls. According to Plutarch, he once avoided Cicero by sneaking out at the back door as Cicero entered by the front. Crassus backed Clodius, and this fact casts an interesting light on Roman family politics, for P. Crassus, Crassus' own son, was among those who demonstrated in Cicero's favour and then went to Gaul on Caesar's staff.

Cicero's friends gave him conflicting advice, but in the end he left Rome; he afterwards more than once claimed he could have fought, and should have fought, but on other occasions he claimed that he had preferred civil peace to his own personal safety. The day he left, Clodius proposed another bill, naming him directly and 'interdicting him from fire and water' (the Romans' phrase for outlawing a man), confiscating his property, and destroying his houses. Cicero's friends succeeded in getting this latter bill modified to an exile at least 400 miles from Italy. After hanging round southern Italy for a few weeks he left for Greece, and settled at Thessalonica, where he was befriended by the quaestor Cn. Plancius. Indeed, in this melancholy moment of his life Cicero found some good friends, Sicca at Vibo and Laenius Flaccus at Brundisium, and he lived to repay them all for their kindness.

He planned at one time to kill himself, or so he wrote to Atticus; he also wrote that Atticus persuaded him not to do so. How serious the intention ever was we do not know, but during the period of his exile Cicero appears in a poor light; he did not endure his adversity with fortitude, and showed an unattractive (but very human) inclination to blame other people for his predicament, even suggesting that some of the advice that did not turn out well had been given treacherously. This applied particularly to the nobles whom Cicero had always believed to be jealous of him.

Perhaps the one redeeming feature of his melancholy letters is the fact that, even in his distress, Cicero was still capable of thinking of others, of his wife and children, and of his brother in particular, who might be indicted on his return from his three-year government of Asia. Atticus showed himself a friend indeed; he put up with all Cicero's complaints, and tried to console him, reproving him for his extreme depression. He also supported Terentia and Cicero's family in their distress, and used his influence to work for Cicero's return. He kept Cicero informed about how things were going, telling him whom he should write to, to ask for favours or to thank for support.

Many supporters rallied round; Tullia's husband Piso tried to influence the consul to whom he was related, and refused an invitation to go with him to his province; Quintus Cicero was warmly received when he returned from his province and also worked for his brother; another young friend and orator, P. Sestius, stood for the tribunate, was elected, and went on a mission to Gaul to see Caesar. Varro, the most learned man of the day and perhaps a relative of Terentia's, also got in touch with both Caesar and Pompey.

By the time the elections were held Pompey had become sympathetic; one of those elected consul for 57 B.C., P. Lentulus Spinther, was in Pompey's pocket, or so Atticus assured Cicero,

and only one praetor, Clodius' elder brother, was hostile. Eight of
the ten tribunes gave notice of their intention to move a bill for
Cicero's recall, though of course Clodius and his allies vetoed its
discussion in 58 B.C.

After the elections Pompey withdrew to his country estates,
saying he feared assassination by Clodius; this may have been
mere propaganda, for Pompey, the greatest general of the day,
was not easily intimidated, but it is a measure of Clodius'
violence that the allegation could have been made. At some time
in the autumn a bargain was struck; the details are not quite
certain, but the most likely terms are that Caesar would not
oppose Cicero's recall provided that Cicero did not attack what
Caesar had done in 59. Quintus Cicero would stand surety for his
brother, and probably was promised immunity from prosecution
if he kept him in line. Pompey was the prime mover in this
bargain; Quintus Cicero's undertakings were made to him, and
he clearly was responsible for obtaining Caesar's consent. Cicero
afterwards always recognized Pompey as the author of his
restoration.

The proposals were drafted before October 58; Cicero became
very anxious to ensure that the measure recalling him restored his
property and his honour as well as his civic rights. He criticized
some of the proposals quite severely on this score, and became
very difficult to please. In the autumn of 58, he moved to the
Adriatic port of Dyrrhachium where his spirits rose and fell like
the mercury in a thermometer according to the news that came.

Cicero's recall illustrates the extreme difficulty of getting
anything done in Rome against determined opposition; as Cicero
wrote to Terentia: 'It was a hard job to get me thrown out: it is
easy to keep me out . . . It was much easier to stay in Rome than to
get back.' Lentulus, the new consul, proposed on 1 January that
Cicero should be recalled; his colleague did not oppose him;
Clodius' brother, Appius Claudius, the only unfriendly praetor,
said nothing; eight of the ten tribunes were on Cicero's side;
senior senators spoke in his favour. Despite all this weight of
opinion, however, no progress was made for the whole of
January, since one of the two unfriendly tribunes succeeded in
obtaining successive postponements, and before the end of the
month violence erupted.

It seems clear that Clodius and his associates began the

violence; as tribune he had been able to disguise his strong-arm men as a tribune's posse, but now they were an overt bodyguard, and their weapons were an open defiance to the magistrates. The tribunes Q. Fabricius and P. Sestius were attacked and the latter was left for dead in the Temple of Castor. On 25 January when Quintus Cicero tried to make a speech he was thrown off the rostrum and nearly murdered; in the riot that followed, the blood that flowed in the Forum had to be swabbed up with sponges, and the corpses choked the Tiber and the sewers. So we are told – with some exaggeration, no doubt.

Cicero's spirits fell to a new low level as it became obvious that those who opposed Clodius had to submit to intimidation or meet force with force. One of the new tribunes, T. Annius Milo, decided that the latter policy was preferable; so did Sestius, and both raised gangs to counter those of Clodius. Clodius was overawed or overwhelmed, and submitted, contenting himself with the sneer that Cicero's recall had been procured by force. Some modern critics of Cicero have accepted this as a fact, but the truth seems to be much nearer Cicero's contention that his return was the will of the vast majority whom Clodius had been forcibly preventing from exercising their right to express their opinion.

Eventually, the proposal to recall Cicero was able to be discussed; the Senate prepared the ground for the assembly with a formal vote of thanks to Cn. Plancius, Cicero's host at Thessalonica, and another vote commending Cicero to the protection of the governors of all provinces. It then summoned the citizens of the Italian country-towns to come to Rome and vote, and Pompey travelled from town to town encouraging them to do so; there were demonstrations in the theatre in favour of Cicero's patrons and against Clodius and his friends; special decrees were made to prevent religious obstruction, and to declare that to prevent Cicero's return was to act against the Republic. The men from the country towns flocked in; when the bill was put to the vote on 4 August there was a huge and almost unanimous crowd present. On 5 August Cicero himself landed at Brundisium, where his daughter Tullia, recently widowed, came to meet him; it was her birthday. All the way through Italy he was met by welcoming crowds. The men of rank and standing in Rome streamed forth from the city to welcome him on 4 September when he arrived, and his progress through the city to the Forum and Capitol was that of a triumphant hero. It is hardly surprising that he told both the Senate and people that he felt that he had been fully restored to his former position, his honour in no way tarnished by his exile. His restored position was perhaps symbolized by the fact that he was chosen to move a proposal to put Pompey in charge of the city's corn-supply since there was a shortage. This was blamed on the huge numbers of Cicero's supporters in the city – a certain indication that there were some influential people in fact opposed to Cicero's return.

How great was the wave of popularity on which Cicero swept back to Rome? Was it a tide which moved the whole Roman people, or did it affect only the upper classes and the people from the country towns? The latter seems more probable; in the late Republic the common people of the city lost interest in the rivalries of the political classes, and felt a jealousy and fear of the ex-soldiers who represented a fairly numerous element among them, and who were a ready instrument for coercion.

The ex-soldiers were, in a sense, only temporary members of the urban proletariat. For the most part, they were frustrated peasants who wanted to stay in the city only until they were able to obtain a croft on which to settle. They wanted the state's revenues to be used for setting up colonies, and dividing up the state's lands among them, and they gave their support to 'popular' politicians who proposed these things. They were thus enthusiastic supporters of Caesar, and of people like Cicero when they were prepared to finance settlements. But the city-born-and-bred urban proletariat, whose skills, if they had any, were in a craft, had learned from their earliest youth to pick up a living in the city, and not how to farm; they were interested in the price of food. They took the view that the proper use for the revenues of the state was to subsidize and stabilize the cost of grain; consequently they were enthusiastic supporters of Clodius, who had made it free altogether, and hostile to people like Cicero and the property-owning classes, who resented the money spent on this, and to the bankers and moneylenders whom they regarded – rightly or wrongly – as the cause of their own impoverishment.

Clodius also, by re-organizing the *collegia* (the political clubs), had given these people a new opportunity for earning an income, and this was no doubt welcome too. Whether they regarded with favour the additions to their number from the liberated slaves we do not know, but it is likely that they were not resentful (at least at first) of the admixture of new foreign elements into what was already a pretty heterogeneous body. They may have felt more satisfaction in that now they too had a means at hand for coercing the organs of the Republic.

When Pompey and Caesar had introduced – or perhaps reintroduced – the use of coercion into politics in 59 B.C., it had made them extremely unpopular, especially Pompey. Clodius' use of force in 58 made him also unpopular for a time, but his unpopularity was not so deep-seated, it seems, and perhaps never spread all through the urban proletariat; it must be significant that the people could be stirred up by agitation over a corn-shortage almost on the morrow of Cicero's triumphant return, and that it was certain only a month or so later that Clodius would be elected aedile if he stood.

Whether Cicero and his friends did not appreciate this, or whether, in the flush of victory, they thought they could avenge themselves, they made the mistake of attacking Clodius personally. This split the forces which had promoted Cicero's return from those who had only accepted it. Clodius' numerous relatives rallied round him, and when Milo tried to bring him to trial for riotous behaviour he replied by standing for the aedileship. A struggle then ensued whether the elections should be held first or Clodius' trial. Milo used his tribune's veto to postpone the elections. When the Senate tried to debate the case, Cicero made a long and vigorous attack on Clodius, to which the latter replied, but the meeting was intimidated by a demonstration, and broke up with nothing done.

The postponement of the elections led to great unpopularity for Milo, and for Pompey who was thought to be behind him. When Milo's tribunate ended on 10 December 57 B.C., the elections were held, Clodius was successful, and in 56 as aedile he prosecuted Milo for riotous behaviour. The case came up on 6 February, and it resulted in a pitched battle in the Forum. Cicero saw the scene and sent a description of it to his brother, who was serving Pompey in Sardinia as a commissioner for procuring corn:

Milo appeared in court on 6 February. Pompey made a speech – at least he tried to. When he got up, you see, Clodius' gangs began to shout; they kept it up all through his speech – not just shouting, but

cursing and swearing too. Pompey refused to be stopped, he's got
courage. He said all that he had to say, sometimes even getting a bit of
silence.... Anyway, as he finished, Clodius got up. He was greeted with
such a roar from our chaps (for we'd decided to return the compliment)
that he completely lost control of himself and couldn't speak. Pompey's
speech ended about an hour after noon; the din went on for two hours,
swearing and the filthiest ditties about Clodius and his sister being
bandied about. Pale with fury, he began to shout to his supporters
through the din, 'Who's starving the people to death?' 'Pompey', the
gangs replied. 'Who wants to go to Alexandria?' he asked; 'Pompey',
they replied. 'Whom do you want to go?' 'Crassus' came the answer – he
was there too, not wishing Milo any good. About an hour later, it
seemed as if someone had given Clodius' men an order to start spitting
at us; our men's tempers rose. They began to jostle us to make us give
ground; our men charged, the gangs took to their heels, Clodius was
thrown off the speaker's platform. I took to my heels too, in case
anything happened in the crowd. Pompey went home. I didn't go to the
Senate either, to avoid having to hold my tongue on such an important
question, or having to tread on the toes of the men of quality in a defence
of Pompey. Bibulus, Curio, Favonius, young Servilius were all criticizing him.

These were Cato's circle. The tone of triumph in Cicero's letter
suggests that he was personally involved, and aware that violence
was expected.

The para-military nature of the forces on both sides needs no
elaboration; the split between Pompey and Crassus seems equally
clear. Pompey was violently attacked in the Senate for his part in
the affair, and it seems that another attempt to intimidate him
with a threat of assassination was made. Cicero told his brother
that Pompey believed that Crassus was behind the plot. This
time, however, Pompey was resolved not to be intimidated, and
said that he was going to recruit some henchmen of his own from
the countryside. Such a force would render him quite independent of Milo, and independent of Crassus and Caesar too.
Crassus cannot but have been alarmed.

Immediately after his recall, Cicero was largely concerned
with clearing up his private affairs. As he remarked to Atticus, his
private property had been wrecked and scattered and plundered,
and he was in trouble financially. Clodius had consecrated the
site of his great mansion on the Palatine Hill for a temple to the
goddess Liberty; Cicero later maintained, in an amusing passage

of mockery, that the fine statue of Liberty was actually the funeral monument of a Greek courtesan, a 'Kindly Goddess' of course, like the one at whose festival Clodius had been caught in his amorous adventure and sacrilege. The land could be restored to Cicero only by the College of Pontiffs, one of the two most distinguished of the state's priesthoods, which were always recruited from patricians and the leading political families. Cicero therefore felt he must watch his step in politics till the question was decided. He appeared to plead his case before the Pontiffs on 29 September, and delivered the speech *On His House*, which he published almost at once, by popular demand. He also published the two speeches *On His Return*, one delivered to the Senate, the other before the people. The Pontiffs decided in his favour, whereupon the Senate voted him compensation from the treasury for his losses, though he complained that the amount was very inadequate. 'Those who clipped my wings', he wrote to Atticus, ' – you know who I mean – don't want them to grow again. But I hope they are starting to grow already.'

His financial difficulties caused trouble with his wife. His letters to her in exile are affectionate in the extreme, but there had been signs of her lack of financial acumen, or irresponsibility, which he had criticized, and now he hinted to Atticus that all was not well: 'My other worries are more private,' he wrote; 'My brother and daughter love me'; this surely contains an important omission. Perhaps indeed his exile was the start of the disagreements with Terentia which eventually led to their divorce. Further traces of estrangement appear, if rarely: when Cicero was to entertain Atticus and his young wife Pilia in 56 B.C., Tullia acted as his hostess; she was the intermediary in a business deal in 55; when she was ill in 54, she was worried in case her father again provoked Clodius. Terentia is never mentioned.

In public life Cicero thought he could detect signs of the old dislike of him which he had always attributed to jealousy – he was never a popular man – but the Senate as a whole certainly welcomed him. The senators shouted Clodius down when he tried to filibuster by talking for over three hours on restoring the site of Cicero's house; a tribune's attempt to veto the motion was met with strong language, and the tribune was intimidated into withdrawing.

In November 57 B.C., when Cicero began to rebuild his house,

Clodius and his gangs attacked the workmen and drove them off the site; those building Quintus' house next door were also attacked and the house was set on fire. Milo's house was attacked too, in broad daylight; even to walk about became unsafe: Cicero was attacked on the Sacred Way; luckily he had a bodyguard and they successfully defended themselves by taking refuge in a friend's house nearby. On another occasion Clodius had to take refuge under the stairs in a bookseller's shop when he was pursued. Rome was chaotic, but the consuls either could not, or would not, restore order.

Pompey had offered Cicero a job as chief lieutenant on his corn commission, but Cicero declined it. To Atticus he explained that he wanted to be free to stand if there was an election to the censorship next year – and besides, he wanted to be in Rome – 'to be in the sight of my fellow-citizens to whom I owe so much' as he put it. But by November he had got sick of the chaos: 'I want to cure the state by treatment now,' he wrote, 'I'm fed up with surgery' – by which he meant he wanted to come to terms with Clodius, not simply to get rid of him.

Early in 56 B.C. Cicero returned to the scene in the Senate; his main object was to defend P. Lentulus Spinther, now governing Cilicia, who had been commissioned to restore to his throne the Ptolemy known as 'the Flautist' whom Caesar and Pompey had caused to be recognized as King of Egypt in 59. The commission promised rich rewards, and many coveted Lentulus' fortune. His championing of Cicero had made him enemies, and now, when a fortunate stroke of lightning caused the Sibylline Books to be consulted, a text was discovered which forbade 'helping the King of Egypt with a crowd'. A 'crowd' was declared to mean an army; Lentulus' commission was cancelled and the Senate had to deal with a variety of proposals to meet the situation. As the debate dragged on, Cicero claimed to be working hard for Lentulus; he made at least one long speech in the Senate and kept him informed on the progress of the debate. Perhaps the most important result, however, was that the affair again exposed a clash of interests between Pompey and Crassus.

In the spring of 56, Clodius and his friends found another religious excuse to disturb the Republic. A strange noise was heard in the countryside (it is a mark of troubled times in Rome that portents in large numbers are reported); the question was taken up by Clodius, and referred to the *haruspices*, a college of non-senatorial soothsayers who claimed to foretell the future by studying the entrails of sacrificial victims. Their reply, characteristically, was ambiguous, but, as it included a reference to 'the use for non-religious purposes of places consecrated to the gods', Clodius used it to criticize the restoration of the site of Cicero's house. Cicero's reply was made in the Senate; it contains a number of interesting themes – he argued, for example, that the Romans were a particularly religious people – but the most interesting is his seizure on another passage in what the *haruspices* said: 'Let not the discord and dissensions of the men of standing bring death and danger upon the senators and leaders of our state.' He used this to deliver a passionate plea to end the quarrels of the senatorial order which, he maintained, were what gave riotous popular leaders like Clodius their chance: 'At long, long last let there be an end to our strife; let us rest from our everlasting quarrels.... There was once a time, long ago, when this Republic of ours was so safe, and so secure, that neither senatorial incompetence nor the wicked actions of individual men could disturb it. But this is no longer so, ... we shall only be able to preserve our present position if we unite.'

The Senate was more concerned in the long run with the chaos and gang-warfare in the city, and scenes such as that at Milo's trial. Clodius next turned on Sestius and indicted him also for riotous violence. The trial took place on 11 March, and gave Cicero an opportunity to defend a supporter. It was a triumph for Cicero when the defendant was acquitted unanimously.

In his speech *For Sestius* Cicero repeated the need to create some sort of concord within the governing class, and to re-establish civil peace. He gave an interpretation of the events since 58 B.C. which exonerated Caesar from responsibility for Clodius. Caesar had been compelled to rely on Clodius because of the noble politicians' attacks on his actions as consul; ... Clodius' political prominence was entirely due to force. Civilization is based on the replacement of violence and force by law, so that Clodius' coercion was a basic denial of civilization.

Cicero then launched into what he called 'a political lesson for the young', in which he expounded the theme of the breed of the men of quality (*natio optimatium*), evidently a new phrase, which one of Clodius' supporters, P. Vatinius, had demanded to know the meaning of. *Optimates*, Cicero replied, were everyone who was sound in mind, morals, and financial standing, regardless of rank and position; there were *optimates* in the Senate, and among the equites and common folk as well, and all of these repudiated violence. Violence was the resort of those who were unable to achieve their political ends without it; it was the only means by which the 'popular' politicians could enjoy any power and influence.

This was, of course, a fundamental attack on their position, since it denied the truth of their basic pretension, that they spoke for the common people. It marks the start of a new phase in Cicero's thought on politics, a train of thought which led to his *Republic* and *Laws*, but it is important to remember that it was not born in a moment of triumph, but out of the chaos caused by gang warfare in 57 and 56 B.C., of which Cicero had already claimed to be sick.

This trial showed again the split between the dynasts: Vatinius, the tribune who backed Caesar in 59, supported the prosecution and was mercilessly attacked in Cicero's interrogation (which he subsequently published); whereas Pompey supported the defence.

Early in April the noble circles again came under bitter attack when Cicero was called to defend M. Caelius Rufus, a young man who had come to Rome to study with him and had turned out rather wild. He had got mixed up with the circle of Clodia, Clodius' sister with the lovely eyes, who may possibly also have been 'Lesbia', the mistress of the poet Catullus and the subject of his most passionate amatory poems and the object of his vilest hymns of hate when she proved untrue to him. Caelius became Clodia's lover, but their affair too ended in a quarrel, and he was accused of defrauding her, and procuring poison to use on her. The prosecution evidently made much of the fact that Caelius was Cicero's pupil, and attacked him for the conduct of his circle. Cicero's reply was to destroy the name of Clodia's circle. Starting with a defence of youth, and a feigned nervousness at criticizing a Roman lady, he builds up his attack on her, calling her 'a Medea sick with love', cracking a joke about her supposed incestuous relationship with her brother, and making an epigram about her 'being no man's enemy, but loving them all'. By impersonating her great ancestor Appius Claudius the Blind he then accuses her

of gross promiscuity – accusations repeated in connection with
her seaside villa at Baiae ... 'parading herself in provocative
dresses, keeping loose company, making eyes at one and all,
flirting too, and (still worse) kissing, cuddling, importuning men
everywhere – picnics, boating-parties, dinners, till everyone
would think her the most brazen harlot in town' – though Cicero
pretends he was not speaking of her. Caelius was acquitted and
Clodia's circle never recovered from this devastating attack.

The dynasts' party was clearly falling apart; divergences on
minor questions did not matter, but Pompey's declaration that
he would make himself independent by recruiting his own
followers was serious (p. 71). Threats to Caesar were in the air
too: Cato, his enemy, was on his way home from a mission in
Cyprus which he had not been able to avoid; Domitius, who had
been hostile in 58 B.C., was now a candidate for the consulate of
55, swearing he would do as consul what he had failed to do as
praetor; Cicero had again proved what a force in politics he was –
for the trial of Sestius was a political trial; 'My house is as full as
ever', he wrote to Quintus. Meanwhile, Caesar crossed the Alps,
and was at Ravenna, on the northern border of Italy as it then
was. Seekers of patronage and promotion went to see him there.
Crassus went too, to discuss the political situation no doubt;
Cicero later said Crassus had inflamed Caesar's feelings, and
had urged Caesar to go and meet Pompey. Others came too,
including Clodius' brother from Sardinia, and Metellus, consul
in 57, on the way to Spain.

After these meetings were arranged – there hardly seems time
for it to have happened before – Cicero took up a proposal first
mooted in the Senate late in 57 by a tribune called Rutilius. This
was that the arrangements made for the public lands in
Campania by Caesar in 59 should be reviewed. On 5 April, he
moved that the Senate discuss it in full debate on 15 May. There
was a heated debate in the Senate – 'it was almost like a popular
meeting', he told his brother – and the more so because money
was short and grain expensive; but the notice of motion must
have been accepted by the consul who had said, when the
question was first raised, that he would not allow any debate on
the subject in Pompey's absence. It is clear that there was a real
problem caused by the free issues of corn, since Pompey asked for
(and got) a grant of 40 million sesterces for his commission at this

time, and Dio declares that this year Pompey had trouble with regulating the supply of free grain because of the number of ex-slaves, freed presumably for political purposes.

A few days later, both Cicero and Pompey were leaving Rome, Cicero on 8 April for three weeks, Pompey on the 11th, for an uncertain time, but since he planned to visit Sardinia and Africa it is not likely that he planned to be back before 15 May, five weeks away. Cicero went to call on him the night before he left and asked him to send Quintus back to Rome, to which Pompey agreed. Cicero then went to visit his country estates where he was delighted at the work which had been done by Atticus' servants to restore his books and library at Antium.

When Pompey set out, he went north, and near Florence, at Luca, he met Caesar, and presumably also Crassus and the 200-odd others who had gathered there. This meeting, the Conference at Luca as it is usually called, set out to determine the course of politics for the next quinquennium. It was agreed that the actions of 59 must all be defended, Domitius humbled, Cato frustrated, and Cicero reminded of the terms of his restoration. If he did not agree, he would be exiled again, and Quintus attacked too; if he did agree, Clodius would be called off. Cicero had no choice; he wrote a letter or letters renouncing his previous policies, and announcing his adherence to the party of the dynasts.

The ultimatum was delivered by Pompey through Quintus: he also sent a letter of his own and a messenger demanding that Cicero should not raise the question of the Campanian land in his absence. Cicero complied; 'The subject was not raised on 15 or 16 May', he wrote to Quintus. 'My right to speak on that subject has been cut off.' Cicero has often been accused of abandoning his principles, but for him in 56 there was little to choose in terms of legality between the dynasts and the nobles who backed Clodius. Moreover, Atticus was advising him to side with the dynasts, and had for some time been doing so; if Atticus did not think them ruthless desperadoes, why should he? Cicero decided that those who sought his help should be prepared to defend him: 'Since the powerless won't be my friends, let me see to it that I'm friends with the powerful.'

5
Political Eclipse and Political Treatises

At the conference at Luca it was also determined that Pompey and Crassus would be consuls next year, 55 B.C.; they would then both be granted long-term commands, and Caesar's command in Gaul would be renewed. Crassus would go to Syria to take over from Gabinius, and defeat the Parthians on the eastern frontier, Pompey would have charge of Spain – at least in name. He was still corn-commissioner, so he had an excuse to stay in Italy where he could watch the political situation.

If Caesar's command were to be renewed, it was necessary that Gaul should not be allocated to next year's consuls. To secure this, Cicero was persuaded to make the speech *On the Provinces for the Consuls*; he also supported a proposal to pay Caesar's four new legions. In the published speech, he again spoke for harmony, and for dropping old feuds and dissensions in the interest of the Republic. He made no attempt to deny that he had had a feud with Caesar, but claimed that the needs of the Republic were paramount. This theme – of reconciliation – he repeated in the speech *For Balbus*, a man of Spanish origin, given citizenship by Pompey for valuable military services, and now acting as head of Caesar's rear echelon. Balbus was accused of usurping Roman citizenship. The accusation was really an attack on Caesar, though Balbus himself, like Cicero, had aroused envy by the fine house he had bought at fashionable Tusculum. Unlike many of Cicero's noble clients Balbus remained grateful to him for his successful defence, though Cicero like many other freeborn Romans strongly resented the power Balbus subsequently obtained as one of Caesar's righthand men.

Recognizing that 56 B.C. marked the end of another epoch in

his life, Cicero decided to put on record the honours he had received in his brief second hour of glory. He published ten of the speeches he had made, from his thanks to the Senate and people for his recall to the great political manifesto of the speech *For Sestius*, and he set to work on a poem in three books on his rise and fall. The poem took some time to write; it was still not published in full by the end of 54, perhaps because Cicero was afraid of giving offence to those not named in the list of his defenders. Parts however were in circulation, and these included one line which became a joke in his life-time but which nevertheless contains the essence of his political creed – *'cedant arma togae, concedat laurea laudi'* (let arms give place to civil garb, laurels of victory to words of panegyric). It is not great poetry, but it was a salutary – and much needed – recipe which could have saved the Roman Republic. He also wrote to L. Lucceius, who had taken to writing history after his unsuccessful bid to be elected consul with Caesar in 59 B.C, and in 56 was approaching Cicero's consulate. Cicero asked him for a monograph on the period of his political leadership and fall for insertion into the framework of the history – it had all the tragic qualities necessary, he said. Should Lucceius not oblige, Cicero would have to write it himself. Lucceius was also earnestly asked to make it sympathetic – more than an historian would – thereby implying that writers of monographs were thought to have more scope for dramatic presentation than historians. Lucceius agreed, Cicero sent him materials, but all traces of the work are lost.

Cicero next wrote the first of his dialogues, *On the Orator*; he modelled it on Aristotle's (now lost) dialogues, and put it in the historical context of his own first appearance in the Forum, just before Sulla inaugurated the first age of coercion by military force, in 88 B.C. Its subject is the training of an orator, and the leading parts are played by the orators whom Cicero most admired as a young man, L. Crassus, uncle of M. Crassus the millionaire, and M. Antonius, grandfather of Mark Antony. Crassus is made to expound Cicero's own views.

'Crassus' argues that oratory is the most difficult of all pursuits, requiring a wide general education as well as a knowledge of techniques; it is so difficult that though it is the most widely studied subject it is the one in which the smallest number of men succeed. An orator requires to know the (Roman) civil law, and

to study history and philosophy. The civil law needed a systematic overhaul which would set it within a framework of
simple principles; these would divide it into general headings each
subdivided into branches with its own special significance and
sphere. However, though Cicero may have contemplated doing
this work himself, and actually wrote a (now lost) work *On
Systematizing the Civil Law*, nothing came of it.

History was requisite because an orator had to be able to quote
examples to illustrate his theme, but Roman History was still in
its infancy in Cicero's day. Nobody, says 'Crassus', had yet
written with the stylistic grace that distinguishes an historian
from a chronographer; Coelius Antipater had tried, but Coelius
too had failed to write in a distinguished way, or to introduce
some variety into the different parts of his work, or to give it a
high polish by stylistic arrangement of the materials or a smooth
flowing style. A finished orator however could write history, since
he is master of every type of writing, and could write it as well as
he could write panegyric or official despatches or accounts of
campaigns (such as Caesar's *Commentaries*, which Cicero much
admired).

Cicero never published a formal history in Latin, though he
published an account of his consulship in Greek, and 'commentaries' on it in Latin,which he offered to bring up to date for
Lucceius' benefit in 56 B.C. He also wrote a 'secret history' not to
be published till after his death, in which he said what he really
thought about his famous contemporaries, but none of these are
quite the same as publishing a formal history.

An orator could also write on philosophy, and philosophy too
was a suitable subject for training an orator; but it was a subject
which an orator should not pursue beyond the sphere of the
practical – Socrates, for example, was blameworthy for 'deliberately neglecting public affairs and those of his friends, and
thus scorning the practice of oratory'. This too is an idea not
perhaps original to Cicero, but fundamental in Roman thought –
that philosophy is un-Roman if you have the talent for public
affairs. But it was philosophy that Cicero turned to when he was
excluded from government under Caesar's dictatorship.

Cicero then argues that real eloquence requires some elaboration of style, and he offers rules for this, showing how to
ornament a speech by choice of appropriate vocabulary, now

choosing archaic words, now inventing new ones, employing simile and metaphor, rhythm and tone, and appropriate gestures which must be learned, as an actor does. But an orator's most important talent was the ability to win the favour of the hearer, 'and to have him so moved that he is governed by a sort of impulse or emotion rather than by any deliberate choice or plan. Men make up their minds on far more things through hatred or affection, greed, anger or indignation, happiness or hope, fear or confusion, or by some other impulse, than they do by truth or authority or any standard of right, or formula for judicial action, or legal enactment.'

It is probable, though since we lack writings other than Cicero's we cannot be certain, that this treatise advocating an elaborate style of oratory designed to sway men emotionally – Cicero's own style – played an important part in the argument which took place in Cicero's life-time between the advocates of the simple 'Attic' and the florid 'Asianic' styles of speaking; most of Cicero's later rhetorical writings refine and elaborate, or defend the points of view set out in this great work.

Cicero did little at the bar in 55 B.C.; Rome was in disorder or under military control most of the year. One case was undertaken unwillingly, at Pompey's request, and Cicero wrote to a friend, M. Marius, complaining that he 'had to defend those who had not deserved well of him at the request of those who had'. Nor did he gain any profit from his work as he had no place in politics. He wrote to Atticus:

What could be more degrading than our present life, especially mine; you may be a political animal by nature, but you don't have your own private brand of slavery.... But I am regarded as a madman if I say what I ought on public affairs, as a slave if I say what I have to, as a prisoner of war if I say nothing – what do you think I feel like? I'm as miserable as you'd expect – and the more so because I can't be miserable without ingratitude to you; I can't even withdraw into retirement if I want to; I must be in the firing-line ... and since you want me to be a camp-follower [of the dynasts] and not a [rival] commander, that's what I must be.

His only independent political actions in fact were attacks on Gabinius and Piso, the consuls of 58 B.C.; Gabinius had not yet returned from Syria, but Piso complained in the Senate about Cicero's criticisms. An impromptu altercation ensued, which

Cicero wrote up and published as the speech *Against Piso*. It is a masterpiece of invective, whose range and power is nowhere surpassed; as Cato had been teased for his Stoicism in 62 B.C., Piso is now mocked for his Epicureanism, besides being treated to a stream of epithets: beast, fury, pest, blot, hangman, filthy mud, funeral pyre of the Republic, wrecker of the ship of state, foul-breath, dumb animal, log, foreign Epicurus, shame on your breeches-wearing relations, donkey, carrion thrown away, and a number of others. Piso, replied, in a work now lost; Quintus Cicero urged his brother to reply to him again, but he scorned the task: 'Nobody is going to read that stuff of his if I don't reply, whereas every schoolboy gets off by heart my attack on him as a school exercise.' Clearly the speech soon became famous. Oddly enough, there is no sign that Caesar resented this violent attack on his father-in-law.

Though he remained out of public life, Cicero watched it, and wrote about it to Atticus, Quintus, and Lentulus Spinther, who had procured his recall in 56. When Domitius was deprived of the consulate of 55, Cicero reported a rumour that the dynasts had the consular elections settled for a decade, an interesting rumour in the light of the results, which were that the nobles monopolized the consulship from 54 to 49 – to the Civil War that is – except for the third consulship of Pompey in 52. Cicero felt humiliated, but determined to accept the situation; 'Public affairs are so much in our friends' power', he wrote to Lentulus, 'that there'll be no change in our day. Our choice lies between undignified assent to the dynasts or wasting time in opposition to them. Our hopes must be for civil peace (law and order), and our masters seem likely to give us that, if some people I could mention could bear their rule a bit more tolerantly.' 'Some people' meant the party of Cato and Domitius.

This was the party whose inextinguishable hatred for Caesar lay at the root of the next civil war, as they gradually first out-manoeuvred Pompey, and then won him from his alliance with Caesar after the deaths of Julia (Caesar's daughter), whom he loved, and Crassus, who had been able to act as a counterweight to both. Cicero took no part in this; he had made it clear he was Pompey's man, and Pompey's man he remained, enjoying at times a social familiarity with him, but not uncritical of him. He even accepted a commission to go with him to his new province of

Spain, but, as Pompey did not go, neither did Cicero. Quintus Cicero was more closely associated with Caesar, under whom he served in Gaul, in one action distinguishing himself by his coolness and tenacity when under heavy attack in his camp; this was in the winter of 54–53 B.C.

In his family affairs, Cicero was now concerned with his daughter's re-marriage; Tullia was now twenty-one and had been a widow since 57 B.C. Her new husband, Furius Crassipes, was a man of patrician family of no special note. The marriage was not a success, the couple parting quite quickly, but not so rancorously that Cicero and Furius could not correspond courteously enough.

As consuls in 55 B.C. Pompey and Crassus were allotted their provinces by a tribune, Trebonius (who afterwards was one of Caesar's murderers); they then extended Caesar's tenure in Gaul to a term concurrent with their own. During the year they became extremely unpopular despite the elaborate shows at the opening of Pompey's theatre. Cicero had to attend, and did not enjoy them; the plays were turned into spectacular extravaganzas of the sort familiar enough to us from the Hollywood studios. Six hundred mules appeared in *Clytaemnestra*, and three thousand wine-bowls represented the spoils of Troy in *The Trojan Horse*; there were also Italian farces and Greek plays on which Cicero did not comment, athletic games (the professional performers were poor), and wild-beast hunts (two a day for five days): 'spectacular, nobody denies it, but what pleasure can a cultured person have in watching either a puny man being torn to pieces by a powerful animal or a noble animal transfixed by a hunting spear?' Even the audience sympathized with the hunted elephants when they were trapped.

In the autumn of 55 a tribune tried to stop Crassus leaving for his Parthian campaign, and solemnly cursed him as he set out. Cicero had entertained him to dinner the night before he left, and later defended him in the Senate in a speech he published in 54. He also wrote him one of the most unpleasantly insincere letters in his correspondence, assuring him of his goodwill; he expressed his real opinion to Atticus in a note – 'What a scoundrel.' In the work *On Duties*, finished long after Crassus was dead, Crassus appears as the epitome of avarice: 'If you offered Crassus a chance to get his name put in a will as that of the true heir when he wasn't, he'd take it if it meant snapping his fingers – why, he'd do it, I tell you, if he had to make an exhibition of himself by dancing in the Forum.' Crassus is also bracketed with Sulla as one of 'those people who will stoop to anything or grovel before anyone to get what they want'. It is an unattractive picture of an unattractive person, a millionaire.

Clodius' elder brother Appius and Caesar's enemy Domitius became the consuls for 54 B.C. Cicero was active in the Senate early this year, and though he was defeated in his plea for freedom from taxation for the men of the Greek island of Tenedos, he succeeded in demolishing the pretensions of the client king of Commagene on the Euphrates to the town of Zeugma which guards one of the few fords on that mighty river; this was in February, the month set aside for hearing envoys from foreigners and communities within the Roman Empire. 'My performance here', he told Quintus, 'has made Appius most anxious to be on good terms with me' – in case Cicero exploded the other proposals for favours to client princes he had in mind (expecting payment, naturally). Cicero let the other proposals pass; he would not antagonize Clodius' brother unnecessarily.

In May, Cicero went to the seaside, Atticus to Epirus. Cicero remained out of Rome till July, and began his next major work, his *Republic*. It was modelled on Plato's work of the same name, but was very different in character and content. When he wrote to Atticus he was very busy with it: 'I've taken on a big task, as you know', he wrote, 'and it needs a very great deal of spare time, which I haven't got.'

During the summer he received friendly advances from Caesar and replied asking him to give a position in Gaul to C. Trebatius, a young friend. Trebatius was not a great success, as he pined for Rome and then seemed disinclined to work. 'You will never find a more ideal opportunity for cementing a friendship with a most distinguished and generous man, nor will you get a richer field of activity nor a better moment in your career for it', Cicero wrote; later Cicero warned him, if he did not get on quickly and make a handsome profit from his post, he should come home, or there'll be a farce put on called *The Lawyer in Britain*. Those who went out in the train of great men were expected to do well, or come home quickly.

In July, 54 B.C., Cicero reported to Atticus that he found

himself welcomed by the people in the theatre. He was extremely busy; apart from his *Republic* he had another spate of court-work. Some of this was undertaken voluntarily, as when he pleaded the case of the men of Reate against those of Interamna in a law-suit about the floodwaters of the River Nar, others by request of his leader Pompey. He spoke for Messius, Drusus and Scaurus, all of whom were acquitted, as was Vatinius, on whose case he remarked to Quintus that it was an easy one; it was extremely hot late in August, and he had never been busier with cases and trials.

Early in September he escaped to Arpinum, revelling in the cool air there while the Roman Games were on in the city. On his visit to the country he inspected some properties of his brother's which had recently been purchased – rather extravagantly it appears, as another letter suggests that Quintus had to stay in Gaul with Caesar to restore his financial position. He put right some architect's mistakes, such as the main flue to the hot bathroom running under the bedroom floor, and those of the builder, who had omitted to align his pillars properly, and gave some orders for ornamental stucco-work, and for some unsuccessful ceilings to be re-done. There were negotiations about water-rights and roads, but Cicero assured his brother the place was a good investment. Work at another villa had stopped, he reported; Quintus had added items to the contract but failed to agree a revised price.

He was also concerned about the education of Quintus' son; earlier in the year he had offered to teach him himself along with his own son, since he had plenty of time in his retirement from public life, but Pomponia had prevented him from going with his uncle to Arpinum – 'Please write to her and say that whenever I leave town she is to come along and bring Quintus'; out of town he had more time to give to the boys. Quintus was quite a diligent student of rhetoric; his teacher, Paeonius, favoured a different style from Cicero; he would not interrupt Paeonius' course with his own ideas, he wrote, but put them over when he and the boys were out of town on holidays, for which games in October provided another opportunity.

Letters to Quintus show the brothers' literary interests; Cicero read Lucretius' great poem – 'many flashes of genius', he commented, 'but much is artificial too'. Quintus was reading Greek history and filling in time in Gaul by composition. He thought of a poem on the Invasion of Britain, but he got stuck; he wrote some tragedies of which one at least got lost on the way to Rome. Caesar showed Quintus many kindnesses, but Quintus showed a lack of discretion in choosing those to whom to give favours. Cicero now asked Caesar for a post for a certain Curtius, but would accept a refusal cheerfully if it came – not like some people. Quintus was getting on well with T. Pinarius: 'he is delighted with your love of letters, and your company – and of course your dinners. I've always liked him.' But Cicero would not write to Quintus on public affairs; letters were not private, and in any case Caesar knew everything as he kept in close touch from Gaul.

In 54 B.C. Gabinius returned from Syria having antagonized the equites, whose operations he may have curbed, though a failure to stop piracy was also alleged as a cause for their lost profits. He had also antagonized many people by restoring 'the Flautist' to Egypt by force despite the religious objection and the Senate's decrees. Cicero, who hated him, swore he would not be reconciled to him as long as he retained 'a single particle of freedom'; he would much rather lead for the prosecution. However, Pompey decided Gabinius must be defended, and procured his acquittal on the charge of disobeying the Senate – of which he was manifestly guilty. He then demanded that Cicero defend him on a charge of misgovernment; Cicero had to submit. He did not win the case – it is hard to believe that he gave of his best – and he did not publish the speech, but he was humiliated by it, and by the criticisms he met with. He tried to make the best of things in a speech *For Rabirius Postumus*, a moneylender through whose hands the money-transactions with 'the Flautist' passed, when he argued that it was no disgrace to be able and willing to be reconciled to opponents, but he wrote his true thoughts to his brother Quintus:

I am being tortured, my dearest brother, positively tortured; the Republic is non-existent, justice does not exist. Now is the time when I ought to be at the peak of my authority in the Senate, but my life is dissipated in the courts or made tolerable by literary activity. My life-long ambition 'to excel all men and be pre-eminent' (as Homer said) is in ruins. I've not attacked my enemies: I've even defended some of them; I'm not free to think, not even to hate.

When he wrote that, he had not yet suffered the humiliation of Gabinius' defence.

He was glad, however, to defend Cn. Plancius, who had been his host at Thessalonica during his exile. Plancius was accused of electoral bribery when he won the aedileship. Cicero's speech contains another passage of self-defence:

I do not want, on this occasion, gentlemen, to refer to Pompey as the champion who organized and inspired my recall from exile – that would be to confuse the debt of gratitude I shall always owe him for a personal favour with the question of the safety of the Republic, which is my present topic. But surely he does deserve my sincere respect because he is universally regarded as the leading citizen of the state? The same goes for Caesar – should I begrudge him my admiration, when I know very well that first the Roman people, and now the Senate too, whose authority I always regard as paramount, have honoured him with many a generous vote of confidence and gratitude? That surely would be tantamount to a confession that I regarded the interests of the Republic as subordinate to personalities when it came to deciding my friends and enemies. If I found my ship running before a gale and heading for a harbour different from, but no less safe and sheltered than my original destination, I would be mad to insist on beating against the wind to reach the latter at the peril of my life rather than submit to the need to alter my course, especially to one which was likely to ensure my safety. The lessons of history, of my own experience and reading, the records and writings of the wisest and most distinguished statesmen of our own country and elsewhere, all point the same lesson to us, that no one's political views remain immutable, but that they are always adapted to the political situation, the mood of the times, and the cause of harmony within the state. And that is my policy too, and always will be. You taunt me with not being a free agent – but you are wrong. I am a free agent, always have been, and ever shall be, but I believe that freedom does not lie in being obstinate, but in being willing to accept compromise where compromise is necessary.

This theme was elaborated in a long letter on public affairs addressed ostensibly to Lentulus Spinther in Cilicia in December of 54 B.C., but consisting largely of a defence of Cicero's own public career since 57. He explained that he now backed Pompey and Caesar because the nobles had forced him to do so by their jealousy, and because they insisted on protecting Clodius against his attacks. Nothing would have induced him to join a party of scoundrels like Cinna, but Pompey and Caesar were great men honoured by the Senate for their services. Pompey moreover was an old political ally of Cicero's while Caesar had shown that he was a man who believed that one good turn deserves another, unlike the nobles. It was true that Cicero had quarrelled with Crassus, but the quarrel was started by Crassus and Cicero had then said more than he meant to; he was more true to himself in being reconciled with Crassus than in antagonizing his other friends Pompey and Caesar. For the same reason he had defended Vatinius; he had eulogized him as a way of getting his own back on the nobles for the way they supported Clodius. No mention is made of the defence of Gabinius; perhaps Lentulus had not heard of it.

Cicero was conscious of Caesar's kindness to him and his brother, and fully recognized the political importance of Quintus' presence on Caesar's staff: 'Remember why you joined Caesar's staff', Cicero wrote; 'it was no petty profit we were after, but to gain the maximum reinforcement possible for our political standing out of a most excellent and powerful person's goodwill.' Standing, and reputation, still mattered.

Appius Claudius and Domitius besmirched the end of their consulship by a shameful electoral bargain with their would-be successors, which was exposed in the Senate. Everyone knew about Appius, says Cicero, but Domitius, stalwart of Cato's party, was in ruins. Cicero was wrong; Domitius was unabashed. Caesar apparently was party to the plot as well, and was very angry at its exposure. All that Cicero did in public was to protest when the Senate decided to reverse its own policy in the affair. The year 53 B.C. began, and long continued, without consuls, who were not elected till July; even then they may have been elected only because Pompey saw to it that they were.

The strongest link between Pompey and Caesar broke when Julia died after childbirth late in 54 B.C., and in 53 Crassus, the third dynast, was treacherously murdered after being defeated by the Parthians. His son Publius Crassus, who was devoted to Cicero, was killed with him; Cicero was saddened by his death, though it brought the consolation that he himself was co-opted into a senior priesthood, the college of augurs, in Publius' place; Pompey proposed him and Hortensius seconded the motion. It was an important honour, for it meant that the nobles had accepted him, since augurs were supposed to be on good terms with their colleagues in the College. His election was one of the things that now turned Cicero's intellectual interest towards divination and the nature of the gods – subjects on which he later wrote treatises.

Cicero had also become friends with C. Curio, whose father he had attacked in 61 B.C. as an ally of Clodius. The son had changed from being a strong opponent of the dynasts in 59 to supporting Pompey's party. In 53 he was quaestor in Asia; Cicero was charming and complimentary to him: 'As I have nothing to tell you', he wrote, 'I will just close in my usual way by urging you to come first in the competition for honour, though you have a serious rival in the field – I mean the exceptional attainments everyone expects from you.' Yet Curio too could not hope for much from the Republic: 'I'm afraid you won't find any Republic to preserve when you return: its life is so feeble now all round, it's virtually wiped out.'

Cicero was again afraid to write letters on politics, he told Curio; the only real political concern he had was to get Milo elected consul for 52 B.C.; one letter asks Curio to help the cause. Cicero told Quintus that Pompey was against Milo, who might use force to support a tribune if he vetoed a dictatorship for Pompey – but Milo feared Pompey's enmity if he did. The impasse worried Cicero: Milo, he said, was 'his one worry'; 'I hope he'll end my worries by getting the consulship' he wrote at the end of 54; but he criticized Milo for spending vast sums he could not afford on lavish games which nobody expected of him, and later defended him when he was accused of minimizing his indebtedness in a statement to the Senate.

Milo, however, never became consul. In January 52, his escort and that of Clodius happened to meet outside the city; Clodius was wounded, and then killed at Milo's order. The city populace, stirred up by political opponents of Milo's, went berserk, demonstrated violently, used the Senate-House as a funeral pyre for Clodius, and completely destroyed it; they then attacked Milo's house and had to be repelled by archers.

The Senate decided that law and order must be restored; they voted that all men between seventeen and forty-six should be put under military discipline, and passed a 'Senate's Last Decree' to restore order. Pompey was then invited to become sole consul; he accepted, and immediately set up a court to deal with the outbreak of violence, choosing a special panel of jurors. Milo was the first defendant.

The trial opened with demonstrations by Clodius' friends; Pompey put the court under guard. On the final day, when Cicero was to speak, shopkeepers shut their shops as a precaution;

the Forum was packed. When Cicero rose to speak Clodius' followers raised an angry chorus. Cicero was unnerved (he was always nervous at the start of a speech, as he himself said), and failed miserably; whether the cause was the angry shouts (which he had met before), or the swords and javelins of Pompey's legionaries (which he had not), we do not know, but Caesar in Gaul read accounts of what happened and decided that a Rome guarded by Pompey's troops was unsafe for an opponent of Pompey.

Milo was found guilty; no other verdict really was possible, and he went into exile. Cicero, whether in shame for his poor performance, or as a political testament, wrote the magnificent speech *For Milo* which survives. 'Had the court heard that', Milo is said to have commented, 'I'd never have found the delights of the sea-food at Marseilles.'

The case of Milo, like that of Sestius, illustrates one of Cicero's more attractive characteristics, his loyalty. Although he disliked Milo personally, he had worked for his consulate enthusiastically, and now defended him in defiance of Pompey's wishes, and defied Pompey again in prosecuting a certain Munatius Plancus Bursa who had been amongst Milo's most bitter opponents. His loyalty is all the more remarkable in an age in which it was conspicuously absent in others, like P. Sulla, whom Cicero defended and who then supported Clodius, or Pompey, who repeatedly abandoned his political allies.

So ended the era of Clodius, a patrician left almost penniless when his father died, who gained vast wealth in the role of defender of the poor. This year also ended Cicero's close connection with Caesar, since Quintus' term of duty ended in a severe rebuke for carelessness.

This rupture may also help to explain Cicero's increased independence; he was busy in court again, defending Saufeius, a henchman of Milo's, on two occasions, and perhaps helping in the trials to punish many of Clodius' associates. He also defended P. Dolabella on two occasions; this had unexpected results, for Dolabella fell in love with Tullia (or Tullia with him, for he was a man of great attractiveness to women); while Cicero was abroad in 50 B.C., Dolabella obtained the consent of Terentia, Cicero's wife, and he and Tullia were married, though Cicero had promised to marry his daughter to Tiberius Claudius Nero, a distinguished patrician who came to see Cicero in Cilicia to obtain his consent. Dolabella was a disastrous choice; he was dissolute and promiscuous and caused the Ciceros great unhappiness. He may have contributed to the break-up of Cicero's own marriage too, since Cicero will hardly have refrained from blaming his wife for a match for which she and Tullia shared the responsibility.

The year 52 B.C., 'when Pompey began to become a defender of the Republic' as Cicero later described it, was a turning point in politics. His sole consulship, which was promoted by the party of Cato, won him from Caesar, and he confirmed his new alliance by marrying the daughter of Metellus Scipio, who became his consular colleague later in the year.

Caesar also lost touch with politics this year; the general revolt of the Gauls under Vercingetorix required all his energy and skill, plus some luck and a good deal of brutality. Caesar was thus unable to prevent the election of hostile consuls for 51, and Pompey's new laws on provincial government. These laws undermined Caesar's position at the end of his tenure in Gaul, and though Pompey supported a law of the Ten Tribunes of 52 to protect Caesar, its validity was dubious. Whether Pompey deliberately threw Caesar over this year, or whether he was outmanoeuvred by Cato and his circle, is hard to say. It would be more pleasant to believe the latter, but Pompey's own record in politics must make it an open question whether this was really so. Cicero however supported the Law of the Ten Tribunes and, having supported it, continued to maintain its validity.

Pompey's new laws compelled any ex-consuls who had not already governed a province to do so. Cicero thus had to go. Almost certainly his new allies were glad to have Cicero out of Rome, and the orator's pathetic desire not to be left in his province more than one year suggests that the possibility was a real one. While Cato's party prepared to crush their enemy, Caesar, nothing was more natural than that they would want out of the way the man who had declared that harmony should be everyone's prime object. Ten years before, the Senate had voted that Cicero was indispensable in Rome in a crisis; now they were anxious to have him away; Cicero felt the contrast. It is probably more than coincidence too that Appius Claudius, Clodius' brother, who was making a fortune in Cilicia, and, as Cicero subsequently said, behaving 'more like a wild beast than a man', now decided to write politely to him. No doubt Appius knew who was going to succeed him, and wanted to prepare the ground.

The commission to go to Cilicia came on Cicero like a bolt from the blue, He did not want to go. He was past fifty-five, some twelve years older than most proconsuls, and no soldier, and, though he knew the law well enough, his experience in the courts had mostly been as a barrister not as a judge. Having been appointed, however, he was determined to do a good job; to help him with the army, he recruited Quintus his brother who had learned much about campaigning from Caesar in Gaul, and C. Pomptinus who had also distinguished himself in the field since he arrested the Gauls at the Mulvian Bridge in 63 B.C. For his administration, he tried to select men who would uphold the standards of conduct which he had always advocated in his writings and speeches.

Provincial government, he had said, was part of the life of the Republic and not (as so many of his contemporaries thought) an interlude in a public career which gave an opportunity to recoup election-expenses. Moreover it was hard work, requiring integrity and self-control and the ability to be consistent as well as honest in deciding legal cases. Leadership was required too, to control the staff, both those who had come out with the governor and any provincials who were employed by him – especially the latter who had little concern for the governor's reputation. Slaves too must be strictly controlled, and never employed on public service, since to have to obey a slave must humiliate a free man.

The governor himself must be not merely honest (though a good reputation must be founded on honesty), and consistent in administering justice, but also humane, courteous and approachable. The ideal of humanity was perhaps peculiarly Cicero's own; popular opinion tended to represent Roman governors of provinces as haughty and reserved. Cicero had, moreover, spoken much of humanity during his laudation of Pompey when speaking for Manilius' law in 66 B.C., and repeated it in his letter of advice to Quintus, published in 60. There he said that while you must be strict on the bench, and impartial, you must also be ready to listen, cross-examine in a kindly way, and try by discussion to satisfy both parties to every case that they have had a square deal. 'In my opinion, the aim of all who govern others is that their subjects should be as happy as possible.' The interests of the provincials have prior claim; they should be helped to keep their finances straight, and disorders, party strife, and brigandage should be prevented. The provincials are then more content to pay taxes to Rome as the price for peace and the suppression of riots. The governor should be approachable at all times by men of every rank and station both while holding court in public and at home.

More recently too Cicero had written about provincial government in his great work on politics, the *Republic*, published in six books just before he was appointed to govern Cilicia. The name *Republic* indicates Cicero's consciousness of his debt to Plato's *Republic*; in a letter to Quintus he had called his work 'On the Best Form of the State and the Best Citizen'. With *On the Orator* (that is, the training and education of the Best Citizen, already published in 55 B.C.) and *On Duties* (that is, the ethics of the Best Citizen, published in 44) it forms a trilogy on Roman public life. Cicero's *Republic* was clearly intended to influence his contemporaries, and is very far from a work of retirement; it tries to say in dialogue form what Cicero would have said in his speeches had he been free to do so. Though the scene is removed in date to the age of Scipio Aemilianus (about 129 B.C.), the problems dealt with are those of the harsh years of 56–52 B.C., and their discussion is infused with a passionate earnestness arising from the pain and humiliation Cicero suffered in this period.

The dialogue opens with the typically Roman view that public life is greater and more important than intellectual pursuits like philosophy, and that the study of society is more important than (say) astronomy or mathematics. A Roman's best training, therefore, is in the experience of politics in Rome. 'A Republic', Cicero declares, 'is the common property of a people, and a people is not a haphazard collection of men, but an organized group associated by their assent to a common code of justice, and a common utility [or advantage].' It is, moreover, a natural association because man is by nature a social animal. The best state is not a monarchy or an aristocracy or a democracy, but a mixture of the three; a blend can prevent any of these three simple forms degenerating into its corresponding 'debased' form, tyranny, oligarchy or mob-rule. Monarchy, under a benevolent ruler, is the best of the simple forms, while mob-rule, because it has no regard for discipline or justice, is the worst perversion. The merits of democracy are that it produces liberty and equality – equality before the law, that is, because you cannot equalize men's talents – and harmony is easiest to maintain in that state in which everyone's interests are the same. The merits of aristocracy are that it is a law of nature that the superior in talents and spirit should rule the inferior, and they in turn want it so: therefore an aristocracy gives the common man the civil peace he wants, and the belief that his interests are being served – provided that the aristocracy is one of merit, not of birth or wealth. Thus, the traditional Roman constitution is the ideal.

Book II passes to a history of the Roman constitution down to the establishment of the Twelve Tables of the Law, and from there to a consideration of the prime quality needed in rulers, which is justice. Justice is the subject of Book III; it exists *per se*, Cicero argues, for there is such a thing as a true law, which is right reason in agreement with nature and is universal in its application, permanent and unchanging; by its demands it calls men to do their duty, and by its prohibitions deters them from wrong-doing. A society worthy of the name, therefore, cannot exist without justice, which is necessary for the noblest function of man, practical statesmanship.

Book IV, now almost all lost, dealt with the creation of moral standards by education and their maintenance by law; it was a characteristic Roman weakness to think that men can be legislated into virtue, and Cicero approved of the Roman censors' right to punish non-conforming citizens.

Book V (also lost) dealt with the law and its enforcement, and it was probably in this book that Cicero dealt with provincial government. He also sketched the ideal statesman, or best citizen, 'whose aim is to see that the citizen's life is happy' – an echo of what he had written to Quintus in his letter on provincial government.

The final book was concerned with the ideal statesman's work and his reward. A man's noblest reward is said to be the consciousness of the value of his work, but a statesman longs for something more enduring, not merely triumphs or statues. What this was is lost, but the dialogue ends with *Scipio's Dream*, written in imitation of Plato's *Vision of Er* at the end of his *Republic*. In this dream, a blessed haven of rest in an after-life is promised to those who live and practise a life of justice in the Republic, and help to save it (the aim of the leaders of the *optimates* as stated in the speech *For Sestius*).

Publication was just before Cicero went to Cilicia: his young friend Caelius wrote that his books had made a big impact on everyone, and Cicero told Atticus that these books were the surety for his good behaviour in Cilicia. He was delighted that Atticus approved them, though, like an acute reviewer, he had found a slip, on a point of Greek geography. Cicero blamed his source.

Following Plato's example, Cicero went on to write the *Laws* for his *Republic*: these he placed not in Scipio's lifetime but in his own, and presented himself, Atticus and his brother as the speakers. This work was written over a fairly long period, being begun possibly even before the *Republic* was issued, and was not certainly finished in Cicero's lifetime. The first book is closely linked in thought with the *Republic*, and the argument that Justice is absolute – 'surely there is nothing more valuable than the clear realization that we are born for justice, and that right is not established by men's opinions but by nature'. In Book II Cicero formulates the religious laws for his ideal state, and in Book III he starts on those for its officials, and for the legislative and judicial organs of state. Many of these are quite original, and this may explain why this work progressed much more slowly than his more derivative works. Cicero himself also seems to have regarded it as a political manifesto, as he abandoned it while he was in Cilicia and again in the periods of civil war before and after Caesar's murder. Only the first three books have survived.

6
Out of Rome:
Provincial Government and Civil War

When Cicero left for Cilicia in the early summer of 51 B.C. he had laid down standards; his attempts to maintain these, and Atticus' encouragements to do so, form a recurrent theme in his letters from abroad. In his anxiety to appear not to have made a profit out of his province he wished to repay a small debt to Caesar before he left for Cilicia; the matter was left in Atticus' hands. For political reasons too, Atticus wanted him not to be dependent on Caesar any more; always close to the centres of power and influence, Atticus probably knew that Pompey was planning to resist Caesar on his return from Gaul; Cicero himself discovered as much when he met Pompey at Tarentum on his way to Cilicia.

Cicero travelled slowly accompanied by Quintus, and witnessed his parting with his petulant wife; their two sons were with them, and a Greek tutor name Dionysius. Terentia and Tullia did not go; Tullia's remarriage was in hand (pp. 90–1); she was proving difficult about one of the candidates, and the great political ladies were taking a hand, since Cicero's only daughter, who was now about twenty-five, would be a good match.

Cicero stopped in Athens where he waited for Pomptinus from 24 June till 6 July. He enjoyed the city and the reminders of Atticus there, as he told his friend, but he could make nothing of the philosophers. Indeed, his mind was not on philosophy – it was on his private affairs and his finances, and on public affairs in Rome, especially his command, and preventing it being extended: 'fight against the extension of my command', he wrote to Atticus, 'or I may become a rascal after all'. As he forgot to add '(joke)', some modern critics take him seriously. He was also deeply concerned about his reputation: 'None of us even demand what Caesar's law (of 59 B.C.) allows', he wrote from Athens; and from Tralles in Asia: 'My arrival in Asia' (where he landed at Ephesus on 22 July) 'has not cost anyone even the smallest sum.' News of his intended policy had preceded him; he was welcomed at Ephesus by a huge crowd of provincials and agents of the tax-contractors; 'You'd think I was plenipotentiary in Asia, not in Cilicia', he declared. The same happened as he travelled east from Laodicea, the most westerly town in his province: 'We don't even accept the hay and the usual demands under Caesar's law, not even wood, nothing but a roof and four beds, and in many places not even a roof, as we camp out.' The only exception was his lieutenant L. Tullius, who had requisitioned some supplies under the provisions of Caesar's law, 'But only once a day, and not at every village as others used to do.' Apart from Tullius, nobody had blotted the copybook. The provincials responded to his treatment; grain hoarders, for example, were induced to disgorge their reserves when the crop totally failed. Not many governors could welcome a famine because of the chance it gave them to show their influence for good.

Cicero had reached Cilicia on 31 July; he assured the Senate in a dispatch that he could not have arrived sooner. He received good news there: the tax-contractors and the communities had agreed on the amounts due for Cicero's year; Appius had suppressed a mutiny in the army and given the troops their arrears of pay (presumably the cause of the mutiny), and there was no sign of a Parthian invasion. 'I have it in mind to go straight to the army', he wrote, 'spend the rest of the summer in campaigning, and the winter in the administration of justice.' Frontier defence, internal security and justice were the main spheres of activity of every provincial governor.

Surprisingly, Cicero found the military side the simpler; he marched across Asia Minor, hearing about Appius Claudius' extortions and injustices on the way and rectifying them when possible. Appius had ruined the provincials, imposing new taxes. Cicero's arrival, and his refusal to make any demands at all, began 'reviving them marvellously', and they flocked to visit him. He also found the neighbouring petty client kings much more helpful than they had been. The King of Galatia, Deiotarus, a client of Pompey's, acted as host to the two young Ciceros while their fathers were on campaign, and he and others

sent troops when Cicero requested them in the belief that there
would be a Parthian invasion. The King of Cappadocia,
however, was 'the world's most threadbare character; he was
helpless; he had neither treasury nor income to call his own'. His
debt to Pompey was so enormous that his whole kingdom's
revenue could not meet the interest, nor could he pay the interest
due on the money he owed to Marcus Brutus, Cato's nephew. Yet
Brutus got proportionately more of what he was owed than
Pompey – 'about a hundred talents this year', Cicero calculated;
Pompey got thirty-three Attic talents a month. 'I hope the other
kings who have already sampled my policy of mercy and
integrity have become better disposed towards the Roman
people, and that [eastern] Cilicia too will become more depend-
able after a taste of my rule'; so he wrote to the Senate. He also
warned them of the dangerous situation: 'if you do not send a full-
sized normal expedition you are in real danger of losing all the
revenue-producing provinces owing to their harsh treatment and
the injuries our allies have suffered at the hands of our empire;
they are either so weak that they cannot help, or so disaffected
that nothing can be expected from them.'

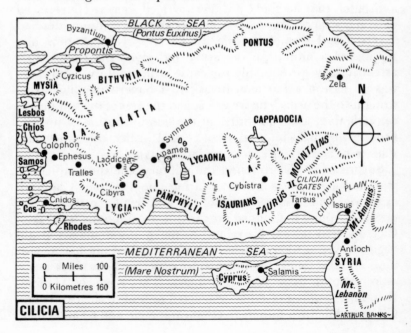

Hearing of a Parthian advance, he marched into the Cilician plain, arriving at Tarsus on 5 October; from there he launched a sweep on Mount Amanus, which separates Cilicia from Syria (and the Orontes Valley), and which was full of hostile tribes. Some enemy troops were trapped and killed, a night attack by Pomptinus followed by a morning attack by Cicero himself resulted in the capture of some fortified posts, and the troops greeted him as '*Imperator*'. But Cicero acquired no illusions about his military competence; he commented to Atticus when he wrote from the site on which Alexander the Great had camped before the Battle of Issus: 'Alexander was a better general by a long chalk than either you or I.' He then moved on some dissident subjects in 'Free' Cilicia, besieging and capturing Pindenissum after fifty-seven days. As luck would have it, the town fell on the morning of the Saturnalia, the Roman December festive season. The troops celebrated in style, since Cicero allowed them all the booty except the prisoners, whom he sold as slaves for the profit of the Treasury. For a self-confessed amateur at soldiering his achievements were remarkable, and his salutation as 'General' entitled him to a 'thanksgiving', perhaps even a triumph.

The Parthians disappeared, but Cicero still thought it wise to leave his troops in winter quarters in eastern Cilicia under his brother, while he himself went to administer justice in the western parts, which he referred to as 'Asia'. Here his arrival was keenly awaited, since it appeared that the communities could now hope for justice. The autumn was a season in which the governor usually lined his pockets by accepting bribes not to billet troops on those communities who paid him well enough: Cyprus, for example, had paid 200 talents regularly. The provincials were dumbfounded when they found a governor who made no demands and would take nothing.

Cicero announced the dates he would hold assizes at the different centres, and planned an itinerary for the rest of the year. This involved traversing the whole province, west to Laodicea in February for almost three months, back east into the Cilician plain in mid-May, spending June in Cilicia, and July on a westward tour so as to be ready to leave at the end of the month. He sent a deputy to Cyprus, since the Cypriots had the privilege of not having to leave the island in order to attend court, and

Cicero did not want the few Romans there to complain that they had had no access to the processes of law. He chose Q. Volusius – 'a reliable fellow, who sets a splendid example of integrity'.

For himself, he claimed that when he was on tour he made himself as approachable and humane as he had told Quintus a governor ought to be: 'I make myself available in a way most unusual in the provinces; I don't have a porter on the door, and stroll about at home before daybreak, just as I used to do when a candidate for office [with the result that people could come and talk to him]. This is very popular, and a great concession; I don't find it a bore because of my practice in it long ago.'

In Laodicea he was rejoined by the two young Ciceros, who seem to have had rather a wild time at the court of Deiotarus: 'I shall keep a tighter rein on Quintus your nephew when he gets here', he promised Atticus. The two young Ciceros were very different in temperament, he thought, Quintus headstrong and needing to be restrained, Marcus lazy and needing the spur. Their teacher was very good, though the boys complained of his temper. Cicero found Quintus quite a problem. At his brother's request he presented him with his man's toga, thus formally proclaiming him a citizen and no longer a mere boy; he could then begin to attend his uncle (or other relative) in public, and learn about public life by listening to councils or judgments or discussions of political and other matters.

There were family troubles too; Quintus had flown off the handle and threatened to divorce Pomponia, and had written to a freedman Statius to see about it. Atticus, who was the head of Pomponia's family, heard about it, and naturally wrote to Quintus. The younger Quintus opened the letter to his father and read all about what was in the air. He was naturally very upset; Cicero later informed Atticus that the boy was instrumental in bringing his father round to a reconciliation – aided and abetted by Cicero himself. This habit of opening one another's letters seems to have been accepted in Cicero's family, though it has much shocked most modern commentators. An explanation in the two cases we know of in Cilicia may be that Cicero's brother was in a remote part of the province, the posts were very irregular (non-existent for periods), and therefore what appeared to be merely a family letter was more or less common property, and for the consumption of all. If this was not accepted how did they

expect to explain the broken seals? The privacy of correspondence was clearly much less respected in ancient times. With no
public postal system letter-carriers of variable honesty had to be
employed; Cicero writes of their habit of 'lightening their load by
relieving it of the burden of their contents'. When he suspected
trouble in his own family he wrote to Atticus in code, and in
Greek, asking him to investigate. A freed slave of Terentia's
called Philotimus seemed to be cheating Cicero and his wife;
he had to ask Atticus to manage a legacy he received, and to
ask Terentia to leave it to Atticus. Philotimus' dishonesty and
Terentia's connivance, or wilful ignorance of it, played a large
part in the financial difficulties which led to Cicero's divorcing
her some three years later.

From Cilicia too he kept in touch with Rome; he had asked his
young friend Caelius to keep him posted with the news. Caelius
obliged by paying someone else to collect the materials, and
added comments himself (he was an engaging rascal). His first
letter enclosed a mass of materials: decrees of the Senate, edicts
(of the magistrates), gossip, rumours – 'no trivial gossip', Cicero
says in a reply, 'tell me what's going to happen in politics'.
Caelius was disarmingly frank:

Pompey always thinks one thing and says another, but he hasn't
enough character to keep what he really wants out of sight, ...
Hortensius got a terrible hissing in the theatre after getting Messalla
acquitted.... When you have a moment, what about writing an essay
dedicated to me? ... I wish you'd seen Lentulus' face when he was
defeated by Dolabella for a priesthood.... You know what'll happen
about Gaul: there'll be a decision, then someone to veto it, then another
who'll veto decisions on all the other provinces unless the Senate can
freely decide about all without exception. This prank will go on for
ages.... Now that Hirrus has been defeated at the polls he's all smiles,
plays the man of standing, speaks against Caesar, attacks delay in
allocating his provinces, and as for Curio – phew, how he goes for him!
He's really changed himself because of this defeat, ... but he never
works after noon.... Appius is an ape ... he got in a blazing temper at
me, kept shouting I was picking a quarrel so that I might attack him
under cover of it, just because he hadn't quite settled up with me....

He got his own back on Appius, who was now censor, by making
him look a fool as well as a knave.

Caelius also wrote about the main issues of the day, of Pompey and the termination of Caesar's command, and of Curio's tribunate – his initial blustering, and talk of a land-law, then his change of sides, and proposal for a roads-commission, and the immense political skill with which he prevented a decision about appointing a successor to Caesar's provinces until he had made it absolutely clear that there was only a tiny minority who were determined to fight Caesar. Other issues came in too, like the thanksgiving for Cicero's successes:

I can speak highly of Balbus' persistent efforts: he gave Curio a good talking to, told him if he didn't withdraw his objection he'd be incurring Caesar's deepest displeasure [this made Curio's disinterestedness seem a bit dubious] – some of those who spoke in favour were quite insincere about it, Domitius Ahenobarbus and Metellus Scipio were two of them ... You will find how everyone voted in my notes; you must pick out what is worth noting, just skip a lot of it, details about games and funerals and other things that don't matter.

When Cicero heard the results of the elections, he wrote to congratulate both the consuls elected for 50 B.C., also two of his young friends, Curio who had been elected tribune, and Caelius, aedile-elect; all were asked to see that his command was not prolonged. He wrote with this request to every senator but two, one of them Furius Crassipes, his ex-son-in-law. He also wrote to thank men like Caelius and Curio for supporting the motion to make a formal thanksgiving for his victories. Cato had opposed it; in a supercilious letter to Cicero he wrote:

I am glad that a formal thanksgiving was decreed, if you prefer us to thank the gods rather than give you credit for a success which owed nothing to chance, but has been secured for the Republic by your own prudent self-control – let me remind you that a triumph does not always follow a thanksgiving ... and for the Senate to declare a formal opinion that a province has been secured by the uprightness and mildness of the governor is a more brilliant honour than a triumph. .... On your journey home continue to secure to our allies and the Republic the advantages derived from your integrity and energy.

He also made a complimentary speech, which was sent to Cicero. Cicero, though pleased at the speech, was vexed at the vote and wrote a reply in which he virtually said he hoped that next time Cato would vote in favour of what he knew Cicero wanted.

In the administration of justice, Cicero had to deal mainly

with the problem of debt. In his edict he had laid down 12 per
cent per annum as the maximum rate of interest he would allow;
he now used this ruling to get the provincials to pay their debts
promptly:

I choose a day reasonably far in the future; I rule that if the
provincials pay up by the stated day, 12 per cent is the maximum
permissible rate, if they don't, they must pay the rate of interest in their
contract. So, the Greeks pay up at a reasonable rate of interest, the
contractors are happy to get the money, and especially if I'm polite to
them, compliment them, and give them plenty of invitations.

At his assizes in Laodicea: 'I achieved wonders', he said; 'many
communities are now clear of debt, many more have reduced
their obligations; all of them are looking up under a regime which
allows them local autonomy and the use of their own laws and
courts.' Cicero had laid it down as a principle that they could do
this.

The two ways I have provided for getting them out of debt are that I
make no demands – yes, literally no demands – on them for myself, the
other is that I have personally audited the accounts of all the
magistrates of the last ten years; their peculation was astonishing, but
they have made a clean breast of it. I therefore made them reimburse the
community they had defrauded, without making a public exhibition of
them. Thus, without a murmur the communities have paid the tax-
contractors what was due this quinquennium – not having paid a penny
yet – and the debts from the previous one as well. I'm the apple of the
tax-contractors' eye.

Though he could thus satisfy the tax-contractors and delight
the provincials, Cicero was unable to please a number of Roman
nobles. Their reactions to Cicero's government reveal much of
the Roman Republic, and also suggest reasons for its failure to
provide satisfactory government for an Empire.

Appius Claudius, Cicero's predecessor, resented the way
Cicero went round reversing his unjust decisions; he felt, quite
rightly, that they reflected on his own government, but also that
his reputation mattered more than the welfare of the provincials.
Similarly he was furious when Cicero encouraged the communities to reduce the cost of the embassies Appius had induced
them to send to Rome to praise his government. Cicero's letters to
him were masterpieces of tact, if not tissues of white lies, as when,

for example, he writes of Appius having been 'concerned to hand over the province to me in the best state, and free from troubles'. These expressions, and the reiterated assurances of friendship reflect Cicero's determination not to pick a quarrel with one who was now a central figure in Roman politics since his daughter had married Pompey's son. Cicero's patience with him snapped only when he accused Cicero of pride in refusing to come to meet him; he pointed out that the fault for that lay entirely with Appius, and that his attitude towards nobility had always been that what a man had done himself counted for far more than his ancestors' achievements. Appius accepted Cicero's assurances, and dedicated to him, as a new augur, a book on augural law, but no sooner had this occurred than Cicero's wife and daughter chose Dolabella as Cicero's new son-in-law – the very man who had prosecuted Appius for misgovernment in Cilicia. No wonder Cicero was acutely embarrassed, even though his explanation, that he knew nothing about it, was true.

Cicero's dealings with M. Brutus (who later murdered Caesar) illustrate the problems which had to be faced by a Roman provincial governor who wanted to rule justly. Before Cicero left Rome Atticus had pressed on him the interests of Brutus in Cilicia; and Brutus had asked him to look after 'two good friends of mine'. These two were creditors of the men of Salamis in Cyprus; Appius had made them prefects of the town with an escort of cavalry, which they had used to besiege the local council in their offices till five of them had died of starvation. They tried to get Cicero to intimidate the council, or to allow them to do so, then to falsify their accounts and allow them to charge four times the legal rate of interest Cicero had laid down. Cicero rejected all their demands, then was dumbfounded by the revelation that they were not Brutus' friends, but his agents. Even now, however, he would not change his ruling; all he would concede was not to allow the Salaminians' request to pay off the whole of their debt, and to adjourn the case. By doing this he made it possible for Brutus to resume his extortionate demands under his successor; he therefore thought that Brutus should accept the situation, and not insist that Cicero should aid and abet his extortionate demands. But he got no thanks from Brutus: 'He writes me nothing but haughty and arrogant letters', Cicero complained. Atticus pressed him, but he would not give way: 'You wrote that if I brought nothing else back from Cilicia but Brutus' goodwill I should be satisfied. All right, if that's what you wish, but I'm sure you'd add the proviso that it must not be at the price of misgovernment.... Brutus' uncle [Cato] will approve of my actions anyway.'

Cicero also wrote numerous letters to other governors asking them to look after the interests of friends, and he undoubtedly received them too. Cicero made no flagrant demands on others to behave the way Brutus had expected him to behave, but the recipients must have been expected to view the activities of the persons in question with a friendly rather than a disinterested eye. He also had a number of commissions; Atticus wanted a new horn for one of his musicians, and some dishes for the table, but Cicero had made it known through Atticus and Caelius that he would not make demands from the provincials for 'voluntary contributions' for political purposes, or for animals for shows in Rome – 'not a farthing is extracted from my province except in settlement of a debt' was his policy. He tried to keep his intellectual pursuits active too; he wrote to Atticus on various topics arising out of his *Republic*, defending his chronology, and asking Atticus to see that his slaves' copies all corrected his mistake in Greek grammar. The great abundance of Cicero's letters from Cilicia may reflect his increasing familiarity with Tiro his secretary. He had already given him his freedom in 53 B.C., but before Cilicia there is little sign of that intimate bond which appears in the letters to Tiro when he fell sick on the way home, and it was not till a later date that Tiro began to collect his ex-master's letters with a view to publication. It seems likely that their intimacy began in Cilicia, when they both had little other company, and where Tiro could have learned from experience to appreciate Cicero's humanity in dealing with his subjects. Certainly, when Tiro fell ill on the way home, and Cicero had to leave him at Patras in Greece, the letters he wrote to him show a deep concern for his welfare and recovery; so do his exhortations to the doctor he engaged and paid to do everything in his power to cure Tiro. Atticus commented on Cicero's concern for Tiro; Cicero replied that he was indeed concerned. Tiro was not just a valuable secretary, but a splendid person too. In fact, he was a friend to all the family, and the feelings of affection and respect between Cicero and Tiro were mutual.

In Cilicia, Cicero's final problem was handing over the province. He had been appointed for one year from the day he entered it. Hating his commission, he argued that this meant that, if his command was not explicitly extended, he was obliged to leave at the end of that period (although custom indicated that he could remain till he handed over to a successor). The Senate, however, did nothing except appoint new quaestors for the provinces, owing to the impasse over the question of when Caesar should be relieved of his Gallic command. To Cicero's relief there was no resolution of a general character instructing the proconsuls then in office to stay at their posts. He thus took the view that, provided there was not a major war on hand, such as might be provoked by a Parthian invasion, he would leave. There was a new quaestor to whom he could hand over, though he did not think much of him – nor did Atticus, who called him 'a boy, perhaps a silly one and not really responsible or capable of restraining himself'. But he was better than Cicero's own quaestor, Mescinius, who was described as 'irresponsible and licentious, and with sticky fingers', and there was no alternative in sight: Pomptinus had left long ago; he did not want to leave Quintus when there was no imminent threat (and, confidentially to Atticus, Quintus was not all that a governor should be: he was a bit quick-tempered and high-handed and careless). It would be an insult to his quaestor, who was a noble, to leave anyone of lower than praetor's rank in charge. Cicero eventually left the quaestor in charge, with the appropriate amount of money for a year's maintenance as quaestor (less, naturally, than a proconsul's allowance), and returned almost 2¼ million sesterces to the treasury (that is to the state's bankers, at Ephesus probably) despite the protests of his staff who wanted the profits split among them as was normal.

Cicero now wanted a triumph. To triumph would set the capstone on his return from exile, and he had in fact earned a claim to one when his troops saluted him as 'General'. Triumphs however involved patience and political influence, and Bibulus now claimed one too – probably in a desire to rival Caesar's glory. Cicero was furious; Bibulus' efforts against the tribes on the Syrian side of Mt Amanus, he said, had been a dismal failure; after that 'he had shut himself up behind the city walls of Antioch as he had shut himself up as consul in his house'. But Cato backed

Bibulus, his relative, not Cicero. Cicero was extremely angry with him.

He landed at Piraeus, the port of Athens, on 14 October. While in Cilicia he had thought of a benefaction to the city – and had proposed to present a portico for the Academy; Atticus had suggested that he think about it. In Athens, Cicero heard that the political situation in Rome was even worse than he had thought; he turned to Atticus for advice. Both Pompey and Caesar had told him that they were counting on his friendship; his sympathies were with Pompey, but he had spoken for the Law of the Ten Tribunes, and he had scruples about backing those who would regard it as null and void. He even wished he were back in Cilicia where nobody would ask him to give his opinion – still, he reflected, if he persisted in his request for a triumph he'd be able to stay out of the city, hence out of the Senate.

Cicero landed at Brundisium on 24 November 50 B.C., where he was met by Terentia. He had already been told about the mounting crisis by Caelius, whose analysis was deadly and shrewd:

> The point at issue, on which the bosses are going to fight, is that Pompey has decided not to allow Caesar to become consul on any conditions other than that he hands over his army and provinces, Caesar is convinced that he cannot be safe if he leaves his army, but is proposing that both should hand over their armies. I'm certain you have noticed that when there's a political tussle, one should take the path of honour as long as it's pursued without war; but when it's war, one ought to back the stronger, and think the more secure the better cause.... To sum up; what I think is going to happen is that unless one or the other goes to fight Parthia there is going to be a tremendous battle, which the edge of the sword will decide. Both have the will to fight, and the forces. Fortune's getting a magnificent spectacle ready for you to watch, if you can do so without risking your neck.

It is clear that Caelius could see no moral issues at stake in the struggle.

Nor could Atticus; though he warned Cicero that the roles of candidate for a triumph and independent statesman were incompatible, he approved of Cicero's remaining endowed with his military commission, and thus able to remain out of the Senate. He thought that neither side was genuinely republican, but that Cicero should not merely play the neutralist. Cicero agreed with this, and said he would urge Pompey to choose the path to peace. For the time being therefore he remained away from Rome: he saw Pompey twice, on 10 and 25 December; on the 10th Pompey could see nothing leading to any hope of an agreement, on the 25th he seemed not even to want one, and to be contemptuous of Caesar's power.

Cicero planned to reach Rome on his fifty-seventh birthday, 3 January 49, but postponed it till the 4th to avoid making work for Pompey's servants on a holiday (which shows him to be a considerate man). As he travelled round the country towns, he could not help noticing the strong opposition to the proposed showdown with Caesar. 'Peace is what we must have. A victory means a host of troubles, and an autocrat ... I have found scarcely anybody who does not think it would be better to grant Caesar's demands than to fight it out. . . .' But in the Senate he'd back Pompey up. Atticus wrote that everyone of any standing knew what Cicero would do – 'Who are these men of standing?' Cicero replied,

there aren't any – there are individuals of course, but no class as such – not the Senate, nor the tax-contractors, nor the bankers, nor the landowners; they're only interested in peace at home; they don't mind an autocrat so long as they have peace. . . . We ought to have stopped Caesar long ago, now it is too late. . . . Why fight? It will be autocracy, win or lose. . . . I'll follow the men of standing or those who pass for such, whatever they do, but I can see clearly enough the best way through the strait – that is, compromise.

But some would not compromise. These were the irreconcilable enemies of Caesar, who were determined not to allow him to be consul again, and his reckless, irresponsible supporters, like young Mark Antony, who made violent personal attacks on Pompey, and others. 'Day and night I am tortured', Cicero wrote to Atticus. He was destined to remain on the rack throughout the spring.

When he approached the city on 4 January he was received by a large demonstration which came out of the city in his honour. After this he did everything in his power to save peace, but he was too late: the die was cast, and irrevocable positions had been assumed; Pompey and the consuls would brook no compromise, Caesar insisted on his rights under the Law of the Ten Tribunes.

Both sides were certain that they would win if it came to fighting
– otherwise they would not have fought.

Caesar opened hostilities by crossing the Rubicon on 11
January, ostensibly in defence of the tribunes Q. Cassius and
Mark Antony, who, in Cicero's view, had lost their nerve,
and fled quite unnecessarily from the city. He grabbed the
Apennine passes, thus opening the way into Italy, and offered to
negotiate, but he was not heeded: he was told he must withdraw
from all occupied territories, then the Senate would negotiate;
it would not promise to concede what he asked, but it would
negotiate. No wonder Caesar refused, and began to move rapidly
down through Italy.

Rome was evacuated; Pompey asked Cicero to take charge of
Capua, but he declined. He wanted to be able to act as a go-
between and peacemaker, and took only the titular post of
supervisor of the Campanian coast round Formiae and Cumae
where he had houses. He moved there with his lictors, their *fasces*
still garlanded for a triumph, but he did so little that Pompey's
entourage criticized him – and he himself afterwards maintained
that he had done nothing to help Pompey's cause. He pleaded
whenever he could for peace: 'Even an unfair peace is more useful
than the fairest war.'

Quintus Cicero probably left Rome with Cicero and the two
boys. Their wives remained in the city. So did Tullia, whose
husband Dolabella soon joined Caesar; she was three months
pregnant in January. Cicero was very concerned that the women
should do the right thing: it would be better to stay in the city
unless Caesar was going to plunder it, he thought, but there
might be a food-shortage. They might also not be able to escape
when they wanted, for Dolabella's protection might not be
enough. Many women of rank had left; were there still honourable women there? If they were in the country they would be with
Cicero and among friends: they must make up their own minds,
he told them, and consult Atticus. Atticus advised them to stay;
Cicero instructed them to do so, but they left the city, and arrived
at Formiae on the coast on 2 February. He planned to send them
back but did not do so at once. They returned by the beginning of
April, but left again to be at Cumae with Cicero by 7 May.

Worry about Tullia was one of the things on Cicero's mind this
spring. The other, perhaps greater, worry was which side to join if

peace could not be saved. Cicero was important enough for both sides to want his support and he had many reasons for joining each of them. He felt a deep sense of gratitude to Pompey for his recall from exile, and most of those he respected were on his side, but he was repelled by their strategy of retreating through Italy to maintain contact with the eastern provinces, which were solidly behind Pompey. If Pompey could not raise enough support in Italy, Cicero thought he should come to terms: it was shameful to invade his native land with a train of eastern princes. He was even more repelled by Pompey's entourage who tried to frighten the hesitant into support for them: 'their talk is all of Sullas and proscriptions', he reported to Atticus.

On Caesar's side were his son-in-law, Dolabella, and his young friends, Curio, Caelius and Trebatius; Hortensius' son joined Caesar too, and Quintus Cicero's son nearly did so. Caesar himself tried hard to win Cicero over, writing to applaud his efforts for peace, and assuring him that he had no intention of imitating Sulla. Besides, his attempts to negotiate seemed to be sincere, and this appealed strongly to Cicero, but he was appalled at Caesar's entourage; Atticus had called them 'the Under-world', and Cicero thought the description apposite. Could Caesar provide good government with a following like that?

Some of Cicero's friends were determined to be neutral; Atticus was able to use a bad dose of fever as an excuse to remain in Rome through the spring, and thus sit on the fence; he told Cicero to join Pompey if he stood to fight in Italy, but not to follow him overseas. Servius Sulpicius, the jurist and an old friend, decided nervously for neutrality, so did other consulars like Volcatius Tullus and Manius Lepidus, Cicero's seniors, who were consuls in 66 B.C. A lot more would do so too, Cicero predicted, if Pompey abandoned Campania; he would do so himself, but for his lictors, since there was nothing to be ashamed of in such company.

The progress of the fighting made his decision ever more difficult. Little resistance was made to Caesar as he advanced through Italy, where the willingness of the Italian towns to accept him proved that Cicero's first impressions had been right – there was no will to fight. An attempt to hold Corfinium contrary to Pompey's orders resulted in a humiliation for the commander, Domitius Ahenobarbus, and an opportunity for Caesar to

demonstrate that his advertised policy of clemency and reconciliation was not a sham. A plan was made to concentrate at
Luceria; Pompey told Cicero to come there: 'it is the safest place
anywhere', he wrote. Cicero replied that he was not looking for
the safest place; he would come to Luceria in order to serve the
Republic, or Pompey himself if he wanted. He never went there
though; Pompey was too late and too slow, and Luceria was soon
abandoned.

As Pompey evacuated more and more of Italy, Caesar's
following grew. In mid-March, Cicero's wife, daughter, son and
nephew all urged him to join Caesar. Caesar wrote, urging him to
go to Rome that he might have the advantage of his counsel:
'What does that mean?' Cicero asked Matius, one of Caesar's
staunchest friends. Matius said he had no doubt that Caesar was
thinking of peacemaking. Much encouraged, Cicero wrote to
Caesar expressing his willingness to help with that. But he would
not go to Rome, which would symbolize his unequivocal support.

He remained in an agony of indecision. He wrote to Atticus
almost every day; seventy-seven letters have survived, many with
others enclosed, between 18 January when he left Rome, and 19
May when he ultimately acted on his decision to join Pompey in
Greece; a number more are lost. Most are gloomy, predictions of
doom, lamentations for the Republic, criticisms of Pompey's
strategy and attitudes: only a few, reacting to more cheerful news
from Atticus, are at all hopeful. He moved about, now overseeing
a little recruiting, but mostly listening to talk, rumours of the war,
speculations on what Caesar would do; and he reported to
Atticus what he had heard. To occupy his mind he wrote essays,
or declamations in the idiom of the Roman rhetorical schools, but
he was too distracted for serious work.

On 17 March Pompey followed the consuls to Greece. 'The
sun', as Atticus put it in one of his letters, 'has fallen out of the
heavens. It is said that there is hope for a sick man as long as there
is life, and so, while Pompey was in Italy, I never gave up hoping'
– that is, for a settlement. It was clear now that there must be a
war, and an attempted invasion of Italy from the east. Perhaps
the weapon of starvation would be used, with Pompey's powerful
fleet cutting off Rome's food supply from overseas. Cicero's first
instinct was to go and join him whatever the risk, but Atticus'
advice still was to wait and see. Certainly, it was now harder to

stay uncommitted, since those still in Italy had taken Caesar's part – or so Pompey's supporters understood it.

Unable to follow Pompey to Greece, Caesar decided to get the consular elections for 48 B.C. arranged, pay his troops, and consolidate the western provinces behind him. He summoned a meeting of the Senate for 1 April and asked Cicero to attend. This was the crunch; to attend would mean lending his authority to Caesar's proceedings. Caesar sent his friends to call; Matius came, so did Trebatius; Balbus and Caelius wrote to him. Cicero agreed to meet Caesar at Formiae on 28 March.

At the interview Cicero demanded the right to speak freely in the Senate, and to oppose sending armies to Greece and Spain. Caesar said he did not want that said; Cicero replied that that was what he must say if he attended the Senate. Caesar told him to think it over. He was far from accommodating, as Atticus and Cicero had hoped he would prove to be. 'I suppose I'm not in his good books', Cicero summed it up to Atticus, 'but I am in my own, anyway', he added.

This was one of Cicero's most dignified moments; to refuse to kowtow to the conqueror who had overrun the whole of Italy showed he could stick to his principles; he must have either freedom of speech or the right to stay away. Caesar's parting shot distressed him very much: 'If I cannot have you as a counsellor, I must use the advice of those I can, and I will stop at nothing.' Having seen his entourage, Cicero shuddered, and recalled Atticus' description of 'the Under-world'.

He now went to Arpinum to present young Marcus ceremonially with his white toga of manhood, probably on 1 April; his fellow-townsmen were pleased at the honour he thus did them. His next thoughts were of how and where to join Pompey in Greece; 'wait and see', said Atticus.

Cicero stayed on in Italy; the reports of Caesar's poor showing in the Senate on 1 April – losing his temper, doing violence to a tribune, defying the Senate's authority – all confirmed Cicero's view that Caesar was incapable of providing a truly republican government. Young Quintus Cicero caused trouble, going off to see Caesar's friends and perhaps Caesar himself; according to the gossip (perhaps true) he told Caesar that Cicero had no use for him and was going to join Pompey. Cicero thought Quintus had actually joined Caesar's army, but he came back and got a severe dressing down from Cicero: 'He's a bad character, a twister and insincere; my brother has spoiled him by being too lenient. He is estranged from all his family, quite without moral standards, and secretive', was Cicero's opinion of him. His parents also had a row about the boy; it distressed Cicero that he could do nothing about it.

When Caesar set off to overrun Spain, Atticus urged Cicero to await the result; Tullia and Terentia begged him to do so too, but he had resolved to go and join Pompey. Caesar tried to compel him to stay in Italy, and ordered Mark Antony to see to it. His tactlessness annoyed Cicero, and his progress round Italy flaunting his mistress, the lovely actress Cytheris, together with a bevy of disreputable followers, confirmed Cicero's low opinion of Caesar's party. Cicero refused to lead an insurrection, however; when he heard a cohort would mutiny at Pompeii and put themselves and the town under his care he was horrified, and quickly left the district.

Tullia's child was born two months prematurely on 19 May: 'I am thankful that she was safely delivered,' he wrote, 'but the baby is a poor weak thing.' It was Cicero's first grandchild, and did not live long.

He was then delayed by an illness affecting his stomach, but, as he wrote to Terentia, vomiting cured him miraculously one night. He set off from Formiae to sail to Greece on 7 June with his brother and their sons; 'I would exhort you to be brave', he wrote to Terentia, 'if I did not know that you and darling Tullia are braver than any man'; he also asked her to make a thank-offering to god for his recovery – 'as you always do'; her simple piety contrasts with his scepticism.

Cicero arrived safely in Pompey's camp. He had not been enthusiastic about going, and his reception dampened any enthusiasm there might have been. Cato, whom Cicero at least respected, took him to task severely for abandoning his role of peacemaker, but the talk in the camp was mostly about the vengeance the nobles would enjoy when they got back. They were all deeply in debt too, and stopped at no form of extortion. Moreover Pompey had no special use for Cicero: he was not thinking of peacemaking, he had no missions for him to fulfil, and collecting war supplies, especially money, required less scrupulous assistants than Cicero. Plutarch relates that Cicero did not disguise his regret that he had come, criticized the preparations and plans which Pompey made, and made biting witticisms about his comrades in arms. Worry even made him ill.

Nor did Caesar's successes relieve the gloom. A lightning campaign in Spain destroyed Pompey's supporters' forces there; Marseilles was compelled to surrender, and Caesar, as dictator, held the elections in which he was duly elected consul for 48 B.C. Early in 48 he crossed to Greece to confront his opponents' main forces. After a success at Dyrrhachium Pompey was compelled by his overconfident supporters to give battle on the plain outside Pharsalus in Thessaly. His forces were routed, and he fled by ship across the Aegean Sea, thence to Egypt. There he was murdered by the mercenaries of 'the Flautist's' son, who was at logger-heads with his sister and queen, Cleopatra. When Cicero heard of his murder, 'I cannot help grieving for his death', he wrote; 'as a man I knew him to be genuine, upright and dignified' – although of course in politics he was none of these things and had done Cicero many injuries.

Cicero was not on the fatal field at Pharsalus; he had stayed in the base camp in Epirus. He may have been ill again. Cato tried to get him, as the senior ex-consul, to assume command of the remnants of the Pompeian forces, but he refused: he had only come out of loyalty to Pompey; if Pompey was fled or dead he would return to Italy and make his peace with Caesar. Plutarch says he was nearly murdered by Pompey's sons for this, but in the late summer of 48 he returned to Brundisium in Italy to await Caesar's return. He had to wait over a year.

7
Under Caesar's Rule:
A New Ambition Dawns

In Brundisium Cicero's fortunes reached their lowest ebb. When he had been in exile ten years earlier he had been able to feel that it was not his fault, there were powerful forces working on his side, and the majority of those he respected were behind him. Now, however, he knew that his plight was his own fault, any future he had was entirely dependent on Caesar's goodwill, and the party with which Caesar had associated himself was the one Atticus had called 'the Under-world'.

Besides, in the winter of 48–47 B.C. Caesar's goodwill – even if Cicero could win it – seemed not to be worth much. After the rout at Pharsalus Pompey's supporters had rallied in Africa, where they now had a strong army and an even stronger navy, whereas Caesar had disappeared into Alexandria, from where he either could not, or, if scandalous rumours were correct, did not wish to extricate himself. All that had come from him was a peremptory order late in 48 expelling from Italy all Pompeians he had not himself pardoned; Cicero was bidden by Antony to leave, but allowed to stay when he replied that he had returned to Italy in response to a letter from Dolabella in Caesar's name. Antony then exempted him by name, thus further identifying him publicly with Caesar's cause.

When Cicero first returned to Italy, Caesar's deputies had welcomed him, but his relations with them deteriorated; evidently he criticized their government, and in August 47 B.C., Atticus warned him to mind what he said and did. Moreover, Caesar's resources seemed to be disintegrating: he had virtually lost control of Spain owing to the misgovernment of his commander there, his armies in Italy were mutinous, and the city of Rome was chaotic owing to the demagogic activities of Dolabella, Cicero's son-in-law, who had set himself up as a new Clodius.

Ten years earlier, in 58–57 B.C., Cicero's family had stood solidly behind him in his exile; his son-in-law, Piso, and Quintus his brother had worked loyally for him. Now, the Quintus Ciceros, father and son, had gone to Caesar's camp and blamed Cicero for their having joined Pompey's side; Cicero's nephew was particularly aggressive in his criticism. Cicero however was more honourable; he wrote to Caesar asking him not to allow his own conduct to be held against Quintus, his brother. Dolabella, Cicero's new son-in-law, was profligate, promiscuous and extravagant; but he had such an important position in Caesar's party that Cicero felt he could not seek a divorce for Tullia, and tried to scrape up enough money for the second instalment of her dowry, which was due in July 48. Cicero was also now completely estranged from Terentia, his wife, who had mismanaged, if she had not misappropriated, his funds, and in mid-47 cheated him blatantly over a small sum of money.

These monetary troubles were thought to have played a large part in Cicero's divorce, but they were more probably the reflection of a more long-standing estrangement which had deeper causes underlying it, such as Cicero's political failure, his wrong decision in joining Pompey, Terentia's disastrous choice of Dolabella as Tullia's husband and her lack of intellectual interests; perhaps she had quarrelled with Tullia too, since Cicero was convinced that Terentia intended to ignore her daughter in her will, and was unwilling to contribute to her support. Tullia remained devoted to her father, and she was uppermost in his thoughts: in July 47, he was asking Atticus to gather saleable articles so that she would not be destitute. In 47 too, he tried to provoke Dolabella into a divorce by withholding the third instalment of her dowry, which was due: 'My poor girl's forbearance affects me unendurably', he wrote to Atticus. She left her husband for a while, since she lived with her father in Brundisium from June 47 until at least August, but she must have gone back to Dolabella later, since she became pregnant during the spring of 46 after Caesar had put an end to Dolabella's antics on his return to Rome. Their resumed marriage did not last, however, and they were divorced later in 46, before the baby was born. In the late summer of 47, Caesar reappeared; Cicero received a friendly letter from him, and when he landed in Italy Cicero was among those who set out to meet him. When Caesar saw him, he not merely pardoned him but made a public demonstration of his respect, and of the warmth of his feelings towards him. Cicero thankfully left Brundisium and went to his favourite villa at Tusculum; his last, brusque, letter to Terentia asked her to see that everything, including the plumbing, was in order; he would stay there a long time; he would also renew acquaintance with his old friends, the books in his reading-room there, to which he assured the scholar Varro that he was returning.

In January 46, Cicero was sixty years old. He returned to the public life of Arpinum by procuring the election of his son Marcus and nephew Quintus as magistrates (the local name was 'aedile'), and writing to M. Brutus who was now governor of Cisalpine Gaul, asking him to assist the borough in collecting the rents which were due from the communities there, and which were the source of its public income. This association with Brutus was prompted by Atticus, perhaps for political reasons, but they never became close friends. Cicero however now dedicated to him a history of Roman oratory he called *Brutus*, or *On Famous Orators*.

Brutus was written in the winter and early spring of 47–46 B.C. and perhaps revised after Caesar's victory at Thapsus was announced. Brutus had adopted the 'Attic' style of oratory, which had been introduced by C. Licinius Calvus, who had died in 48 B.C. at the early age of thirty-four, and had advocated the use of a simple style and pure type of Latin, claiming the Greek orators as his models, especially Lysias. Cicero remarked of Calvus that, 'though well-trained in theory, he lacked vigour in his speeches through an over-exact concern with proper usage; thus, though scholars admired, the common people could not taste them at all. . . . And if a lack of flesh, a dry flavour, and a thin texture – polished of course and cultured and precise – is "Attic", that is all very well, but there is more to the genuinely Attic than that'; and among the Attic Orators Cicero thought that Demosthenes in his more fiery and highly-coloured style reached the apogee of achievement: this was proved by the way the Greeks had flocked to hear him; the Roman 'Atticists' could not

hold their audiences. The main argument of the *Brutus* thus seeks
to show that Cicero's own elaborate style was the true product
of the Roman oratorical tradition, and hence more genuinely
Roman than the 'Atticists'' style. Cicero approved however of
purity of language, and praised Caesar as a model of this, both in
the work he dedicated to Cicero on the principles of correct Latin
usage, and in his *Gallic Wars*, which Cicero compared to 'nude
figures, well proportioned and lovely, with every vestige of
rhetorical ornament stripped off' like clothes.

But *Brutus* is also a tribute to Atticus and Brutus, of whom the
former 'first revived Cicero's spirits with his letters', and perhaps
stimulated the historical interest which underlies this dialogue
(he himself published and dedicated to Cicero a book of *Annalistic
Notes*). Brutus had sent him from Asia 'a letter', perhaps to be
identified with his essay *On Moral Qualities*, in which the self-
sufficiency of the man of wisdom was set out. It was perhaps in
reply to this that Cicero also dedicated to Brutus his collection of
essays known as the *Stoic Paradoxes* which he wrote between *Brutus*
and *The Orator* in the late spring of 46. He took six of the Stoic
axioms and illustrated points in them from Roman history,
criticizing sharply two of the most conspicuous features of Rome
in his own day: the frantic desire for money and material
possessions, and the mad extravagance in spending them. The
heroes of Roman history, in seeking only praise and renown, had
proved the axiom that virtue is enough for happiness; the
destruction of the Republic under Clodius proved the axiom that
every foolish man is mad; to be wholly devoted to acquiring art
treasures is a form of slavery, because by axiom it is a form of folly.
The work is not serious philosophy, but an interesting illustration
of how the Romans used philosophy as a guide to living.

While Cicero wrote, Caesar resumed his war with the surviving Pompeians in Africa; the decisive battle was at Thapsus in
April 46 B.C., and was followed by Cato's suicide in Utica in order
to avoid having to submit. On Brutus' suggestion, Cicero wrote a
laudation of the dead Stoic, who was Brutus' uncle. It has not
survived, but its after-effects were important, since Cato became
a hero, and his example of suicide rather than submission an ideal
for those oppressed by the more tyrannous of Caesar's heirs. To
praise Cato without castigating Caesar and his allies, as Cato
had done, was a delicate task; so also was to do justice to his

seriousness of purpose and consistency, since Cato's wisdom was that he 'foresaw how the situation in Rome lay, and how it would develop (under Caesar), struggled to prevent it, and died to avoid seeing it'. Again Cicero provided one of his contemporaries with an unforgettable epitaph.

Perhaps *On the Best Sort of Orators* was also written now. This short work is designed as an introduction to never-completed translations from the Greek of Aeschines' speech *Against Ctesiphon* and Demosthenes' great reply *On the Crown*. Its date of composition is uncertain, but the context of the argument with the 'Attic' writers would certainly be appropriate.

Until the result of Caesar's African campaign was known, Cicero stayed either at his Tusculan villa, or in Rome and in the company of Atticus. He divorced Terentia, for which he was criticized – Antony later mocked him for 'having put out of his house the woman who had grown old and grey with him', and the repayment of her dowry left him still further in debt. Rome was an uncomfortable place; it is evident from a series of letters to Varro that neither that great scholar nor Cicero was popular with Caesar's partisans, and the dislike was mutual. When the news of Caesar's victory came many of them gloated openly over them and other pardoned Pompeians. Later in 46 B.C. Cicero wrote to his invalid friend Paetus:

This is my pattern of life now: I'm at home to callers first thing; I see a lot of men of my own political views, but they are glum; I see those exuberant victors too, though I must say they are extremely courteous and affable. When they've gone, I bury myself in my books, writing or reading. A few people call too, to listen to me as a scholar – well anyway a little more of one than they are. Then I just look after myself. I have mourned for my country more bitterly, and longer now, than any mother ever did for her only son.

Among those who came to listen was Hirtius, from whose pen we have the surviving Book VIII of Caesar's *Gallic War*; he was a particularly keen student. Cicero also dined out regularly, as a number of jesting letters reveal; this led on one occasion to an amusing contretemps when he found himself at dinner with Cytheris, the lovely actress (whose name means Venus, goddess of love) whose progress round Italy with Antony had caused so much offence in 48 B.C. 'But I'm not one for a mistress', he wrote, 'I wasn't even as a young man, let alone at my age. No, it's

dinners for me; there I talk on whatever comes my way, as they
say, and turn gloomy faces into hearty laughter.'

After Caesar came back from Africa, Cicero returned to public
life; he watched Caesar's quadruple triumph, and was upset at
the pictures of the capture of Marseilles and the leaders defeated
at Thapsus – triumphs were inappropriate in civil wars. He also
worked with Atticus on behalf of the people of Buthrotum in
Epirus where Atticus' estate was, and was concerned about the
lands in Italy chosen for allocation to veterans. But he was not in
the councils which made the decisions: 'Aren't you a joker', he
wrote to Paetus, 'Balbus was with you, and yet you ask me what I
think is going to be done about those communities and lands.
As if I should know anything he doesn't know – or as if I know
anything I don't get from him. Come on, be a good fellow, and
tell me what is going to happen to us; you have had the source of
information in your power, and could get it out of him, if not
when sober then when drunk for sure.' Later, he wrote in the
same vein:

Do you think there will be any fewer decrees of the Senate if I am in
Naples? Why, when I'm in Rome and pounding the Forum, decrees are
drafted in the house of our pal – you know who—; and whenever it
occurs to them my name is put down, and I hear that a decree passed on
my motion has reached the eastern frontiers before I've ever heard
about it, so I get a letter of thanks from the Kings of the Back of Beyond
thanking me for proposing that they be recognized – and I've never
heard of their existence let alone their recognition.

Cicero was also unsure whether Caesar was in fact in control,
and doubtful if he could govern his supporters:

Caesar has all the power; I see nothing to fear from him, but once you
have broken the law everything is thrown into doubt.... Suppose
Caesar wants us to have our Republic, he can't find a way to do it; he
has got himself tied up with so many people.... I tell you this, it is not
only I, who am not in his council, who do not know what is going to
happen, even the boss himself does not know. We are bound to his will;
he is bound to the times. So he cannot know what the times are going to
demand nor can we know what he has in mind.

Cicero's main part in public life was in working for the recall
and pardon of his friends still in exile. Letters to Plancius, for
example, assured him he was in no special danger, to Figulus he

wrote with great regret that he could promise nothing; Fadius Gallus, who had found fault with Cicero, and maintained that he was too scared to speak for him when he ought, received a very rude rebuff in a letter which has been described as the most unpleasant in the whole of Cicero's correspondence.

Cicero attended the Senate too, but he did not speak until late in the year, when Caesar suddenly announced that he would grant the appeals of C. Marcellus, consul of 50, for the recall of his cousin M. Marcellus, the consul of 51, who had contributed so much to the civil war. There was a dramatic scene worthy of Cicero's pen:

Caesar had himself criticized the 'acrimony' of Marcellus [Caesar's own word] ... when suddenly, contrary to all expectation, he said he would not refuse a request of the Senate, bad though the omen might be. The Senate had appealed to him, you see, when Caesar's father-in-law had spoken of Marcellus, and C. Marcellus had thrown himself at Caesar's feet, and the whole Senate had risen and approached Caesar as petitioners.... And so, though everyone who was called upon to speak before me had thanked Caesar (except Volcatius who said he would not have done it had he been in Caesar's shoes), when I was called, I changed my mind – you see I had decided to remain silent for ever, not from indolence I assure you, but in regret for my lost position of honour. Anyway, Caesar's magnanimity and the Senate's sense of loyalty to Marcellus broke my resolution, and I made quite a long speech of gratitude to Caesar. Now, when other questions come up, I'm afraid I may have deprived myself of the abstention with which alone I consoled myself. Of course, I have avoided offending Caesar – after all, if I never spoke at all he might think I questioned the freedom of the Republic – but I shall not speak much, only enough to please him and to do justice to my scholarship.

The speech *For Marcellus* was published, and survives; it cannot be exactly what Cicero said at the time since that was impromptu, whereas the speech we have has a high polish and a lofty spirit. Caesar is praised for his clemency in victory, which alone could bring reconciliation. Recalling Marcellus showed that he accepted that those who fought him were honourable men, and sincere, if mistaken, in their political convictions. Caesar must now complete the work of restoration; nobody else could do it: he must not take the view that he had lived long enough. He must now make posterity praise him for his civic achievements as they will marvel at his military feats.

This speech vividly illustrates the author's mercurial temperament; inspired by an act of magnanimity he threw aside his gloomy silence and proclaimed what is obviously a deeply-cherished aspiration that the Republic which he idealized would come to life again. He also stated frankly what Caesar himself later declared, that for the time being the stability of the state depended on Caesar alone.

Politics were tolerable to Cicero only when Caesar was present in person: 'I'll stay in politics as long as Caesar is here', he wrote to Paetus, 'but when he goes, it's the flesh-pots for me.' Until Caesar left for Spain, Cicero continued to work for his friends: he wrote that he was confident that Caecina would soon be recalled, though Caesar had been much angered by the bitter pamphlet he wrote: to Q. Ligarius, who had fought in Africa, Cicero felt sure that Caesar would not be very harsh, and shortly afterwards, when Ligarius was indicted for treason, Cicero undertook to defend him. Caesar decided to hear the case in his own private council, and Cicero was only with difficulty admitted to the hearing. When he arrived, Caesar had remarked, 'Why should we not hear Cicero speaking again after so long? There is no doubt that Ligarius has long been a villain and an enemy.' But as Cicero spoke Caesar was unable to control his emotions; he kept changing colour, and at the point where Cicero touched on the battle at Pharsalus his hand shook and he dropped some papers. Such was the effect of the speech *For Ligarius* on the most intrepid general and greatest administrator of the age. Cicero told Ligarius he believed that he would be acquitted, and he was.

In the middle of 46 B.C. Cicero wrote *The Orator*. This work is ostensibly a portrait of the ideal orator, but actually portrays Cicero himself, and gives an extended defence of his own style and diction against the 'Atticists'. It also includes an elaborate discussion of the place of rhythms in prose-writing. It is particularly interesting that Cicero uses his own published speeches for illustrating his points, thus assuming that they were familiar to his readers; he also announces that he is thinking of teaching oratory. He points out that in Rome there had long been a difference between men's attitude to knowledge of the law and their attitude to knowledge of the techniques of oratory. If it was thought honourable for men learned in the law to teach the civil law and to have their houses full of pupils, why should orators not do the same? After all, oratory is potentially the master of the civil law; it can defend and uphold it, and the civil law, if attacked by oratory, is often hard pressed to defend its own position; oratory has thus had a pre-eminent position in the affairs of the state in quiet times. If it is disgraceful to speak eloquently, let eloquence be banished, but if it is not disgraceful, why is it shameful to learn eloquence, and why is it not creditable to teach it? A scholar, says Cicero, must be judged by his scholarship, and scholarship is rooted in minutiae. Minutiae are like the roots and stem of a tree; what we admire is the tree, but it can only grow as well as its roots and stem allow. In his own case, since he knows the fundamentals of oratory, why should he not set them forth? Since his law-court practice and his contributions to public debate are at an end, literary studies are his alternative to sheer idleness or self-pity, and surely a better choice.

This self-defence, in the middle of the work, gives an important clue to Cicero's attitude to himself at the end of the year 46; teaching eloquence was to be the 'honourable life of leisure' that he had discussed with Varro. It is clear however that a scholar's life required an apology in Rome, for we find Sallust also writing elaborate apologies for taking to history instead of continuing in public life.

Perhaps as part of his educational programme for his son Marcus, Cicero wrote, sometime in 46, the *Classification* [or *Divisions*] *of Oratory*. This work, which takes the form of a discussion between himself and his son, might be described as an introduction to the whole subject of oratory. In the first part it covers the functions of an orator – to discover arguments, arrange them in an appropriate order, and present them in the appropriate style with the appropriate gestures; in the second part the divisions of a speech – introduction, statement of the case, proof of it by arguments, attack on the opponent's arguments and summing up; and in the third part the different sorts of speech – the exposition of a general or theoretical subject, or of a particular subject which raises moral issues, such as the praise or criticism of someone, or of some public policy, or a law-court speech, in which moral issues may come in under a number of headings. Of all Cicero's works on rhetoric this comes nearest to an attempt to unite oratory and ethical teaching, and thus make it a rival to philosophy as a suitable medium for instructing the young. By presenting these ideas in Latin, Cicero laid the foundations of one of the most important educational systems of the Roman Empire.

He also found that he had become something of a legend in his own life-time. In Cilicia he had complained to a friend of all the flat jokes that were attributed to him; now, collections of his witticisms were being made. Caesar was a connoisseur; he was said to have been able to pick out the spurious from the genuine at once, and at the end of 46 B.C., Trebonius, one of Caesar's long-standing supporters, published a volume of them, duly annotated, and each introduced with a preface.

In the autumn of 46, Caesar arranged the elections for 45 (Cicero had wondered whether even the pretence of an election would be made), and revised the calendar so that the months should have the numbers of days they now have, and 1 January 45 B.C. might coincide with the start of the solar New Year. He then left for Spain to fight Labienus and Pompey's sons, who had raised a last resistance among the discontented provincials. Cicero left public life again, and returned to his books. He was much concerned for his children; Tullia was pregnant again, but her divorce from Dolabella now went through. Young Marcus' career needed promoting; he might have been sent with Caesar to Spain, but Cicero was reluctant to have his own son actually fighting on Caesar's side. Besides, young Quintus had gone there, and Cicero had not yet forgiven his brother and his family, regarding as contemptible their acceptance of honours at Caesar's hand. Young Marcus was therefore to be sent to Athens to study; arrangements had to be made, and funds secured. In this, naturally, Atticus was to play a large part.

Cicero's studies now turned to philosophy, as the last part of the *Divisions of Oratory* had suggested they would, and as a letter to Servius Sulpicius in Greece had foreshadowed; perhaps he now started his important work, *De Finibus* (*On Different Views of the Ultimate in Good and Evil*). Much of the time he stayed in Rome with Atticus, whose magnificent library was at his disposal. Tullia was there too in an advancing state of pregnancy, and when Cicero went on a short tour of his country villas towards the end of the year, 'I wish,' he wrote to Atticus, 'I could run straight to her welcome, and to your little Attica's kisses.' But he had to meet Quintus.

Cicero now planned to marry again. In a society in which marriage was a business arrangement, a man might marry for prestige, political or financial reasons. Cicero was a good match for a family anxious to add to its distinction, though there was likely to be little political profit in it; he himself needed a wife with a dowry so that he could repay the dowry of the divorced Terentia. Discreet enquiries were made; Pompey's daughter, now a widow with two children by Sulla's son, was suggested, but Cicero did not approve of her; another suggestion, possibly Hirtius' sister, was 'the ugliest person ever'; various women had candidates. In the end he decided to marry Publilia, a very young woman to whom he was himself guardian; she was extremely wealthy and her mother was anxious for the match.

There was a great discrepancy in age between the two partners; Terentia and others said he was infatuated with her (to be in love was thought quite the wrong reason for getting married, and very reprehensible at Cicero's age, which was now almost sixty-two), but modern commentators generally agree that Cicero's motive in making the match was for money, her mother's for the distinction Cicero brought to the family. As her guardian, Cicero was responsible for her money, and benefiting from it himself while looking after it for her was something to be expected in the ancient world – and especially in the Greek world in which Cicero's intellectual sympathies lay. In fact, if he was her guardian because he was her next of kin, he would have been obliged to marry her under the laws of Athens. So, when her mother desired the match as well, it was quite natural for him to make it. Atticus also urged Cicero to make the match; it will have appealed to his business instincts, but it was a bad piece of advice – not the only one he gave Cicero.

Cicero seems to have suffered some measure of social ostracism at this period, since he wrote he had no callers at his house in Rome, and felt himself obliged to defend his divorce of Terentia: she and her relatives had let him down, he said; that was why he had decided to find new allies to take the place of the old dis-loyal ones. Nor was his new marriage a success. Publilia never came as close to her husband's heart as Tullia – it was perhaps impossible for her to do so, especially when Tullia died early in 45 B.C.

In Caesar's absence, political life came to a standstill; there was great nervousness about the outcome of the war in Spain, though everyone hoped Caesar would win. C. Cassius, later one of Caesar's assassins, found it prudent to leave Rome in case Pompey's sons were victorious and he had to flee to the East; to him Caesar was 'the old and gentle master', whose rule was much preferable to that of Pompey's brutal sons. To Cicero he wrote mostly about philosophy as a means of attaining peace of mind; Cicero believed that study and writing were the only way for him: 'My philosophy is my work now, for I am ashamed to be a slave in politics.'

Tullia gave birth to a son in January 45 B.C.; father and daughter moved to his favourite villa at Tusculum, but her health deteriorated, or failed to recover after her confinement, and she died about the middle of February. Cicero was desolate. He could not bear to stay at Tusculum, so he moved to Atticus' house in Rome and read every book about the lessening of grief he could find in the library there. Three weeks later he moved to Astura, a lonely house by the sea, where he could sit and watch the grey waves rolling in.

He wanted to be alone, except for Atticus – yet he was solicitous for his friend, the one person he desired to see: 'Are you sure it's not awkward for you to come? It's an awful long way – and I shall hate to let you go, as you may have to do soon', he wrote. At first, Cicero wrote to him every day, then almost every day, and this continued until the end of August. After the initial shock, Cicero burned up his energies in reading and writing, and in planning a memorial for Tullia. He planned a shrine rather than a tomb, and exhausted Atticus and himself in futile negotiations for a place which would serve both as a shrine to her and a retreat for his own old age, and which would be secluded and yet visited by many people, thus keeping Tullia's memory green; he thought at one time even of selling his splendid town house, but nothing came of it all, and the whole scheme faded from the front of his mind.

A number of people wrote to console him: Brutus' letter was sensible enough, but not really very helpful; Hirtius and Lucceius were very kind. Caesar wrote from Spain, but not till after his victory at Munda; the letter, written from Seville and dated 30 April, arrived early in July. But the truly memorable letter came from his old friend Servius Sulpicius, now governing Greece:

When I heard the news of Tullia's death, I was most deeply moved,
and terribly shocked, of course, and I thought what a blow it was to
both of us. Had I been with you, I should have called round to express
my sympathy to you in person.... But why does your personal tragedy
affect you so much? Just think how fortune has treated us up to now; we
have lost everything which men ought to regard with as much affection
as their families – our country, our integrity, our standing, all our
offices; what could be added to our distress by this single additional
tragedy? Or, what spirit that has had experience of these public
catastrophes should not now steel itself, and think that nothing is so
bitter a blow? You are grieving for her, of course; but you must very
often have come to the same conclusion as I have, that in this day and
age those people who have been allowed to pass from life to death
without suffering have not been harshly treated. What had Tullia now

got to inspire her with any great passion to live? What material things
            ⁣t her heart? Did she
            ⁣ie young man of good
            ⁣ildren, and to enjoy
            ⁣ld, maintaining the
            ⁣anding for the public
            ⁣om of action in public
            ⁣ls? Every one of these
            ⁣ell, it is hard to lose a
            ⁣ler still to put up with
            ⁣ts away from all that,

            ⁣a contemporary of the
            ⁣praetor, then consul,
            ⁣married young men of
            ⁣ll the blessings of life;
            ⁣complaint can you or
            ⁣do not forget that you
            ⁣dvise, and to discuss
            ⁣loctors, who profess a
            ⁣er people are ill, but
cannot look after themselves; treat yourself with what you are always
prescribing for other people, and take your own advice to heart.

No grief exists which time cannot reduce and cure. It is not worthy of
you to wait for this to happen rather than to meet its challenge with your
education. Besides, if the dead have any power to feel, Tullia's love for
you and devotion to all her family make it certain that she does not want
you to be prostrated. For her sake, for the sake of your friends and
relatives and other sympathizers, for your country's sake, continue your
public service whenever it is needed. I know, of course, that we have lost

our independence, but do not give men a chance to think that you are not grieving for your daughter so much as for the plight of our free Republic in the grasp of conquerors.... On a number of occasions before this we have admired your character in times of success and the credit you have earned for it; now show us that you can equally well endure adversity, and that you do not exaggerate your burden of grief unduly; we don't want this one defect to mar your character.

Cicero replied. After thanking Servius for his kind letter, and praising his son for his sympathy and devotion, he wrote:

It is not only what you say, and your companionship in troubles, but your leadership which consoles me. I think it is discreditable for me not to live up to the expectations of a man of your education, but sometimes I am overcome, and can hardly endure my grief, since I have not got the compensations which the other men had, whom I regard as having been fellow-sufferers.... They all lived in ages when the standing they had themselves attained in the free Republic compensated for their loss. My situation, though, is that I have lost the honours of which you speak, and which I obtained by strenuous exertion, and the one consolation left to me was what death has now torn from me. You see, my thoughts had nothing to engage them, there was no business to be seen to for my friends, no affairs of state were demanding my attention; I had no stomach for the Forum; I could not endure the sight of the Senate; I thought that I had lost all the fruits of the success that I had won by my hard work. Nevertheless, when I reflected that I was in the same plight as you and others, and when I was getting the better of my mood, and making myself put up with it all, I had someone to go to, someone to bring me relaxation, someone in whose delightful society I could get rid of all the anguish I felt. But now, this savage blow has opened even those scars which seemed to have healed. Now I cannot escape from the sorrow of my home into public affairs, and find anything in them to console me, whereas before I had always a place at home to cheer me up when I came home depressed from public life. So I'm not at home, and I'm not in public life; my home cannot console me for the sorrow I feel for the free Republic, nor can public life compensate for the grief I feel at home.

Few daughters have had a finer epitaph.

Atticus was asked to handle all his business affairs: Terentia's dowry must be repaid; let her be demanding if she must; Cicero would rather be overreached than give her grounds for criticism. Young Marcus' allowance must be settled, and arrangements made for him to be paid it in Athens; Cicero would make over the rents from some properties in Rome, which should be quite enough. Of course he had made provision for Tullia's child in his will – Terentia should mind her own business. To his new young wife, Publilia, who wrote asking to be allowed to visit him, he replied that he was in an even poorer way than when he had sent her away – but he must take evasive action to escape a visit from her mother and relatives.

Men criticized him for being unsociable. This was most unfair, he wrote; when he'd stayed with Atticus in Rome he had received all who called; when he'd been at Astura he'd worked like mad; then, when he had been with Atticus again at Ficulea, he had seen anyone who called. Early in May nobody was in Rome, and he did not want the gay crowds of the popular resorts; he had a good example to follow in preferring the solitude of Astura. When he came back to Rome, he declared, he would not give anyone grounds for criticism, but he would not resume the consolations of the previous year, the dinners and entertainments of which he had written to his friend Paetus. In the middle of May he moved to Tusculum despite its memories of Tullia. He stayed there until 21 June, whence he went to visit his birthplace at Arpinum, then round his country houses in turn.

He refused to attend to public affairs, even to witness a will, or do jury service – Atticus must please plead ill-health, chronic if necessary. Nor could he bear to live in Rome; his house was too near the Forum, and he could not endure the Forum without taking part in the courts or the Senate, where all he could do was criticize the loss of the free Republic. People who criticized him for being so grief-stricken did not know the facts; he was being true to himself, as a man of letters. Writing, and especially writing on difficult questions, was a sign of a clear mind, not of one prostrate with grief. Why, he said, he had written as much as some of his critics had ever read.

Of these works, the first, *On the Lessening of Grief*, or *Consolatio*, is almost entirely lost. It distracted him, but did not console him, and he kept asking Atticus to tell him if other noble Romans who had lost their children provided valid examples. In this work Cicero also seems to have felt what would now be called a growing faith in the existence of an eternal, imperishable soul, or non-material element in men, what the Greeks called a spark of the divine intellectual and cognitive power.

Cicero then wrote a series of dramatized dialogues – the *Academics*, the *De Finibus*, and the *Hortensius*. It is not certain what the order of production was. *De Finibus* was probably started first, before Tullia's death, but *Hortensius* was probably published first.

In it Cicero set out the arguments in favour of the life of the scholar as opposed to the traditional Roman activities of money-making, politics, war and the exploitation of empire. Its most important achievement was that more than 400 years after it was written its exhortation to pursue wisdom made such a deep impact on a dissolute youth in Carthage that it started him on the path that led him to become St Augustine.

Cicero wrote quickly all through the early summer. In the long days of May he was writing even at night, as he could not sleep. The first draft of the *Academics* was completed on 13 May, but it was expanded and almost completely rewritten in order to give a part to Varro, who was anxious to appear in some work of Cicero's. Varro had promised to dedicate to Cicero his work *On the Latin Language* on which he had worked for at least two years. Varro's work was one of greater pains, Cicero told Atticus; his own productions were mere transcripts, requiring much less work – all he did was to find words, of which he had plenty.

This humorous depreciation of his philosophical writings has been taken as a serious assessment of them, but Cicero in fact regarded the *Academics* as a work both worth-while in itself and an achievement to write; its subject is epistemology, and in it Cicero discusses the development of the Platonic theories of cognition and knowledge as altered by his successors in the Academy, Carneades, Antiochus, and Philo. Cicero told Atticus that he regarded it more highly than anything else of the kind, even in Greek; this being so, he was sure that Atticus would not mind the time that had been wasted by the copyists on the abortive first draft – publishers must smile at the unchanging character of authors! He was nervous, however, about Varro's reactions, even though the presentation copy was on the best paper, and Cicero's letter to go with it a masterpiece of careful composition. 'I did not dictate it – not even to Tiro who can take down whole paragraphs at a time; every syllable was given separately to Spintharus.' The letter survives, very careful and very dull, reminding Varro of his promised work, criticizing the political situation, and expressing the hope that the two men might enjoy in better times an intimate familiarity they had in fact never enjoyed at all. Of the whole work there survives an exposition of the positions of Antiochus and Philo as given in the second (revised) version, and the attack on the defence of Carneades' position as given in the original version, in which Lucullus was assigned the part later given to Varro.

At the end of May Cicero sent Atticus the first book of *De Finibus*, though it was not yet ready for publication. A number of historical points had to be cleared up; would Atticus help? As an expert in the history of the second century B.C. they were in his field. The work was completed by the end of June; it had apparently aroused great interest, and some people got a hold of parts of it before it was published. Cicero was annoyed with Atticus, as he had wanted Brutus, to whom it was dedicated, to be the first to see it.

De Finibus consists of three separate dialogues, in all of which Cicero himself acts as critic of various points of view on the ultimate aim of life as they are expounded by spokesmen for the principal philosophical schools. In the first, which is set in Cicero's villa at Cumae, the Epicurean view is given by Manlius Torquatus (Cicero's opponent in the speech *For Sulla*), who is represented as having made a social call in the company of a young friend. In his reply, from a Stoic viewpoint, Cicero argues that the Epicurean ultimate aim of pleasure is not enough: since the intellect is superior to the senses, it must be the instrument for determining the ultimate good, hence all theories that exclude virtue must be inadequate. Virtue, being based on reason, has its roots in human society. 'Man was not born for himself alone but for his country and his kinsmen; only a very small part of him is for himself alone.' The four cardinal virtues, Wisdom, Justice, Courage and Temperance, must be exercised in society. Morality is instinctive, not a mere convention; examples of disinterested fair dealing show that justice is not always prompted by self-interest. Moreover, since man is naturally a part of society, Epicureanism, which teaches men to reject political commitment, is contrary to human nature.

The scene of the second dialogue is a chance meeting in the fine library of Lucullus at Tusculum; M. Cato expounds the Stoic views, and Cicero criticizes them from the standpoint of the contemporary head of the Academy which, though Antiochus denied it, was very far from Plato's. The ultimate Stoic aim was to achieve Virtue, which was identified with Wisdom. Wisdom enabled a man to live 'in accordance with Nature', because the 'wise man' understands Nature's plan, and willingly co-operates with it by choosing an 'appropriate' course of action. An 'appropriate' act contains in its appropriateness the element of Wisdom, hence of Virtue. Man was endowed with the primary instinct of self-preservation, and for the things that ensure it, health and knowledge, so that the acquisition of Wisdom through knowledge is living 'in accordance with Nature', and the 'wise man', having done that, is the only one who is fully happy. Morality consists in aiming at this end, and the intention is more important than success in the aim. In reply, Cicero answers that the nature of man includes body as well as mind, so that happiness must include the well-being of the body if man is to live 'in accordance with Nature', and desiring things good for the body is part of man's nature. The Stoic syllogisms (concise proofs) fail to satisfy if they are illogical, and they can be proved so because they are incompatible with the four cardinal virtues, Wisdom, Courage, Justice and Termperance, all of which belong to Nature.

The scene for the third dialogue is a walk in the Academy in Athens; it opens with a discussion of the inspiration to be gained from places associated with great men such as the grove of Plato's Academy, or Sophocles' home at Colonus, or Epicurus' garden. This leads on to Antiochus, who claimed to 'go back to Plato, Aristotle and the "ancients" ' in his views on the ultimate good. The first principle is that it must be based on the natural instincts, so that it involves achieving knowledge of oneself and of human nature. It is natural to desire the four cardinal virtues which are instinctive and also developed by reason. The dialogue ends inconclusively in a discussion of how far there are fundamental differences between the various systems, and how far the differences are merely of terminology.

Little of this work is likely to be original, but the criticism of the Epicureans in Book II, with its abundance of Roman examples, probably contains more of Cicero's own thought. Originality, however, was not the aim of Cicero's philosophy; as he put it in *Tusculan Disputations*, his next work: philosophy is the study of all the subjects relevant to right conduct, and a training in them; it

was Cicero's duty to illuminate it by a study of the subject in
Latin. Though study of Greek works was always possible, the
Romans had always proved themselves superior to the Greeks in
every field to which they had applied themselves; they were
superior in morality and social usages, ran their families and
personal affairs better, and their ancestors at least managed
public life under better political institutions and laws. The
Romans were superior militarily and in their natural talents; the
Greeks' superiority in learning and literature was due only to a
lack of competition – poetry had never been highly thought of
in Rome and hence was neglected, as were painting, music and
mathematics; but in oratory, in which the Romans had always
had an interest, they were as good as the Greeks. Cicero now felt
it his duty to use his leisure to serve his countrymen by making
philosophy available to them in Latin in a readable form, 'for
writing books on philosophy without proper arrangement or
clear expression, and without giving the reader pleasure by the
attractiveness of the style, is unpardonably to misuse one's time
and one's ability to write'.

Cicero described his *Tusculan Disputations* as 'the declamations
of his old age'. The questions he dealt with were appropriate to
an elderly man; he defined them in a later work as being 'the
things requisite for happy living: the first dialogue defends
the view that death is not a great evil, the second deals with the
endurance of pain, the third with the control of grief, the fourth
with the other emotions which upset men, the fifth teaches the
self-sufficiency of virtue'.

The points of view cited are those of the Epicureans, Stoics,
Peripatetics and others, but the examples are often Cicero's own.
Pompey is a man who lived too long – he would have died much
happier had he succumbed to his serious illness in 50 B.C., before
the Civil War. Cato is compared to Socrates; both died content
because they had a reason to die; Metellus Macedonicus died
happy because he left all his four sons and many grandchildren
alive, and was thus much happier than Priam, who lost all his
much more numerous family. Marius gave an example of how to
endure pain when he had his varicose veins cut open; he gave an
example of endurance also when leading his men under a blazing
sun, and all Roman soldiers show great toughness as they carry
their arms and equipment, food, tools and palisade-stake

everywhere – indeed they are so used to their shield, sword and helmet that they do not really count them as a load at all – and as a result of their hard training veterans bear wounds much more easily than young soldiers do.

In dealing with the control of grief Cicero alludes to his own work on the subject; he seems to have been able to use his own experience to reflect on the validity of the various theories on the alleviation of grief for the dead, and comes to the perhaps surprising conclusion that what evil there is in grief is not caused by nature, but by an act of judgment based on a mistaken belief. The fourth discussion goes on to argue that this is generally true, that all feelings which upset men's equanimity arise out of error, whether the feelings be faults like fear, lust and anger, or more pleasant feelings like delight and love. The fifth book contains Cicero's sketch of the supremely happy man, who is the supremely wise one; he will be outstandingly intelligent, eagerly enthusiastic in the pursuit of truth, and capable of logical analysis, and thus be able to see correctly what follows from any premise and what does not, and be able to argue and judge truly.

There is less Roman colouring in the later dialogues, though each bears a preface which refers to the general introduction at the beginning and must therefore be an original composition. In his blending of Roman thought and personal experience with Greek models Cicero resembles contemporaries like Catullus (who translated Sappho and others), Gallus, and the poets of Augustan Rome, Horace and Virgil, who were now approaching manhood; their literary claims, like Cicero's, were to have made Greek literature available to Romans in Latin.

During the course of 45 B.C., Cicero gradually began to take more interest in public affairs. At the end of March he wrote to Lucceius the historian that he could see no hope anywhere – every faculty of the free Republic was shattered. When the news of Caesar's victory at Munda came, he was indifferent to the fates of Pompey's sons, whose victory he had feared, but he showed some interest in the war. He drafted an open letter of advice to Caesar, but it was never sent or published, since he deemed it prudent to submit it not merely to Atticus, but also to Caesar's closest counsellors, Balbus and Oppius, and to Hirtius, and the changes they advocated were too many for Cicero to feel it was still his work. At about this time Hirtius published an attack on

Cato in which he combined praise of Cicero with criticisms of
Cato; Cicero was happy enough to send it to Atticus' clerks to
have multiple copies produced for circulation; he thought it
foreshadowed the line that Caesar himself would take. Brutus'
eulogy of Cato now reached Caesar; Caesar remarked that he
learned from Cicero's *Cato* how to write, from Brutus' that he
himself knew how to write.

In May 45, Cicero received an appeal from an adventurer who
called himself C. Marius, son of the great Marius' son, to defend
him in court, but he refused to resume his career at the bar and
referred him to his all-powerful 'relative', Caesar.

As Caesar's officers returned from Spain, Cicero renewed his
contacts: he wrote to Dolabella and welcomed him (a diplomatic letter, surely, since Dolabella owed Cicero the money for
Tullia's dowry). Dolabella had embarrassed Cicero by asking for
a work to be dedicated to him; as Cicero said to Atticus, treatises
on morals would hardly do; public opinion must be considered.
In the middle of June, Brutus reached Tusculum, a week later
Trebatius came to stay; Curtius called, then Dolabella, paying
their respects. Torquatus called too, to thank Cicero for persist-
ing in trying to get him recalled. They all talked till late in the
day.

Cicero still avoided public commitments like serving on a jury-
panel, but in July he had to go to Rome to see to his will (his
grandson must have died by now; he did not live long). However,
he was glad of every chance to postpone his visit for as long as
possible. A hint from Brutus that an open letter to Caesar would
be welcome stimulated this activity again for a time, but the
procession at the games in honour of Caesar's victory at Munda
put him off.

This summer he received a very large legacy, from a banker at
Puteoli; his income was expected to rise by something like 80,000
to 100,000 sesterces per year. But, generous and open-handed as
ever, he planned to help his brother Quintus out of debt with
what he had to spare. It is probable that this legacy enabled
Cicero to go through with his divorce of Publilia, as we hear of
negotiations with a certain Publilius, conducted by Atticus:
Cicero could not stand being in Rome during the progress of this
business.

Tusculan Disputations was started by August, and so, perhaps, was *On the Nature of the Gods*, but Cicero's philosophical writings were interrupted by Caesar's return, which he had announced would be by 5 September. Cicero was uncertain of Caesar's attitude towards him, since his nephew Quintus was always attacking him and his own father in front of Caesar and his leading officers (though he had heard that Hirtius and Brutus defended them). Brutus now divorced Appius Claudius' daughter and married Cato's daughter; to please him Cicero wrote a eulogy of Porcia, Cato's sister and Brutus' aunt, commemorating her death. About now too, Cicero received a copy of Caesar's attack on Cato, and wrote to him in admiration of the work; he assured Atticus that his admiration was genuine, not feigned. He thought also of going to meet Caesar, but he showed no signs of moving from Tusculum and Astura until a letter from Lepidus came, asking Cicero in Caesar's name not to miss the Senate on 1 September.

Cicero went to Rome, telling Atticus that he would return at once to Tusculum. He probably remained in Rome, however, since there is a break in their correspondence till after the Ides of March 44 B.C. Caesar returned to Rome, and ceremonially deposited his will with the Vestal Virgins; nobody knew who his heir would be. Young Octavius his great-nephew was sent, like Marcus Cicero, to study in Greece; but politically the signs of favour pointed to Antony and Dolabella who were designated consuls for 44 B.C., while Caesar was appointed dictator for ten years, annually renewed.

Peace reigned in Rome, though Cicero felt that Caesar too must notice many objectionable features: 'The results of Civil War are not always just what the victor wants: he has to consider his lieutenants too.' Cicero became hardened to sights he thought he never could endure; he took some part in public life, spoke on behalf of the towns of Volaterrae and Atella to prevent their lands being earmarked for allocation to Caesar's veterans; he also spoke for some of his friends, and when King Deiotarus of Galatia was accused of plotting against Caesar Cicero defended him. He recalled the king's loyalty to Rome when he was in Cilicia, and urged the claims of clemency as he had urged them on behalf of Ligarius. Deiotarus had followed Pompey becase he was misled, and was in no position to hear Caesar's side of the case. Besides, everyone had heaped distinctions on Pompey, and even if Caesar had eclipsed all men, Pompey was not forgotten. Caesar must also remember how much insecurity must be created by revoking a pardon once given. This, the last of the speeches published under Caesar's rule, was delivered at a court held in Caesar's palace.

At the end of the year Cicero left Rome, as he usually did in periods of holiday; Caesar left too. Both moved to Puteoli. Caesar had an escort of 2,000 men, and many domestics and slaves; it was an army. On 19 December, he invited himself to dine with Cicero, and thoroughly enjoyed himself, eating and drinking freely – 'but you'd not say "do come again next time you are here" '. The talk was all literary: no state affairs. Cicero had been a generous host too; the higher echelons of attendants had been well entertained, the humbler ones and slaves got all they needed, each group in their own dining room. Caesar had spent the day in accounts – nobody was admitted at all; then he had walked on the beach, bathed, heard something about Mamurra with whom he was supposed to have had homosexual relations – he was quite unmoved. Next day he moved off, escort and all; it was all a bit much, but not disagreeable really. Such was the impression the dictator made on one of Rome's leading citizens.

Cicero went to Rome for the New Year; augurs had to be present at the dedication of a new temple to Fortune. While there he witnessed the farce of the six-hour consulate: Caesar was holding elections for quaestors when the death of the consul Fabius Maximus was announced just after noon. Caesar turned the elections into consular elections, and Caninius Rebilus was elected for the rest of the year: 'What a vigilant consul, he never slept; nobody had lunch in the whole of his consulship, nor was there any evil done.' So Cicero scoffed to a friend at what was a gross abuse of the most highly honoured office in the state.

Cicero was also present in the Senate for the New Year debate in 44 B.C. Though Dolabella had been promised the consulship, Caesar became consul himself with Antony as his colleague; Dolabella made a furious attack on Caesar to which Antony replied with an equally furious tirade. It was a violent row which Caesar tried to calm down by saying that Dolabella could take over his consulship when he himself went to fight the Parthians. Antony was not mollified: he swore he would prevent Dolabella's election by using his powers as an augur – it was a 'ridiculous,

ignorant assertion', Cicero said, and the whole affair reflected
still more discredit on the Republic under Caesar's rule.

We do not know how much Cicero was in Rome before the
Ides of March. It seems unlikely that Plutarch is right in saying
that Cicero took a leading part in promoting the absurd and
flattering decrees the Senate passed in Caesar's honour, or in
granting the perpetual dictatorship which Caesar received this
spring, or that he approved when Caesar punished the tribunes
who removed emblems of royalty from his statue. Cicero may
however have supported, if he did not promote, the oath of the
senators to guard Caesar themselves, since this oath prompted
the dismissal of the bodyguard which had visited him the
previous December. He wrote that he had nothing to do; public
affairs must be in the hands of one man now, the Republic was
defunct. After Caesar's death he claimed that he did not either
hide himself, or abandon everything, or torture himself into a
state of misery, nor on the other hand did he parade a con-
tumacious attitude to Caesar or his government, or fawn on
Caesar and flatter him as though in remorse for his own fortune;
we should probably believe Cicero rather than Plutarch, who
may have read some hostile propaganda, or fraudulent decrees.

Some incidents however prove that Cicero was in Rome: once
he went to call on Caesar to plead again for Atticus' neighbours
in Epirus; afterwards he heard that while he was waiting Caesar
had said: 'Can I doubt that I am an object of deep dislike when
M. Cicero has to sit and wait and cannot see me at his own
convenience? If anyone is easygoing it is he, but I have no doubt
that he hates me.' Cicero did not hate Caesar the man; whenever
he met him he came under the spell of his personal magnetism,
but he did hate what Caesar had done to the political life of the
free Republic which he loved. This does not mean that Cicero
wanted him killed; he probably agreed with Caesar himself that
his death would only provoke a new civil war.

Cicero was probably also in Rome on 15 February; his brilliant
account of Mark Antony's attempt to crown Caesar at the
Lupercalia appears to be that of an eyewitness. He also made the
acquaintance of Cleopatra, whom in his letters he always refers to
as 'the queen'. She came to Rome at this time bringing a child
which she alleged was Caesar's. So far as we know Caesar never
denied this, though he made not the slightest attempt to

recognize it in his will. Modern scholars have laboured much to prove it could not have been his for chronological reasons of which contemporaries could scarcely have been unaware, but Cicero refers to the child as 'that Caesar', and this suggests that he did not regard Caesar's paternity as impossible.

Cicero approached the queen with requests for some favours, possibly Greek manuscripts from Egypt; she seems to have later turned these into allegations of improper demands, to his immense indignation: 'I hate the queen; Hammonius, the fellow who said he'd see to her promises, knows perfectly well that I am in the clear; my requests were scholarly and perfectly in tune with my position; I would be ready to speak of them anywhere.'

Under Caesar's dictatorship Cicero wrote *On the Nature of the Gods* and began *On Divination*. In the former, he traces the Greeks' views on the gods from Thales and the Milesian physicists, and gives an account of Socrates' supposed views, and those of Plato, Aristotle, Antisthenes, founder of the Cynic school, and Chrysippus the Stoic. As Book I is written from the Epicurean standpoint, Cicero naturally condemns the popular myths of legend and saga which he calls 'the religion of the poets', and proceeds to elaborate the Epicurean view, though oddly enough without any reference to Lucretius' poem, and he ends the book with Euhemerus' view that the gods are men who have been deified by later generations.

Book II presents the Stoics' views; the basic thesis is that the material universe shows clear signs of design, hence of reason. This is God, who permeates all the universe, including man, the apex of creation, who alone is capable of conceiving God. God is one but evidences himself in physical forces to which the Greeks gave the names of the traditional anthropomorphic gods. This view is supported by some incredible etymology. Book III consists of a critique from Carneades, a successor of Plato in the Academy. It denies the indestructibility of the material, and the argument for God based on the apparent signs of design in nature: periodicity, as of the sun and stellar movements, no more proves them divine than it does the tides or recurrent bouts of fever (such as malaria). Moreover reason cannot be the divine in men, since men misuse reason, and the prosperity of the successful wicked is a denial of a beneficent divine will. The dialogue ends with these statements of position; it makes no attempt to make a personal statement of faith, though there is at the end a suggestion that Cicero himself found the positive Stoic view the most attractive.

Cicero then began *On Divination*, a work which naturally arose out of the work *On the Nature of the Gods*, since divination cannot possibly have any validity unless there are gods. In this work Cicero may have been influenced too by his own position as augur and the fact that divination played a very important part in Roman state religion. In this age of civil war too, which brought violent fluctuations in fortune, there was naturally a particular interest in any available means of foretelling the future, and an undoubted growth of superstitions likely to be useful in this respect. The work, however, was not completed when Caesar's assassins struck him down on the Ides of March 44 B.C.

8
After Caesar:
Cicero's Return to Politics

On the Ides of March, as Caesar fell mortally wounded, Brutus
raised aloft his dripping dagger and called on Cicero by name,
congratulating him on the recovery of liberty – that is, the
recovery of the free Republic. Antony later alleged this meant
that Cicero had been the mastermind behind the plot; Cicero
said that Brutus recognized him as the other man who had saved
Rome from a tyranny. Antony's version seems undoubtedly false:
none of the conspirators ever named Cicero, and Cicero most
emphatically denied complicity, though there were many who
falsely claimed it. Moreover, he did not retreat to the Capitol
with Brutus and the other assassins – nor flee as precipitately as
Antony, who would surely have thrown it in his teeth if he had.

In the evening he went with Atticus to visit the assassins on the
Capitol, and urged Brutus who was urban (hence the senior)
praetor to summon the Senate at once if the surviving consul
(Antony) was not willing to do so. Brutus however refused,
whether out of a regard for constitutional niceties, or the sort of
scruples which made him forbid the assassination of Antony
along with Caesar, or out of timidity – for Caesar's troops were
very angry, especially the veterans who were waiting to have
lands allocated to them; and Lepidus, Caesar's Master of the
Horse, had wanted to use them to strike down the assassins at
once.

After his precipitate flight home Antony negotiated with
Lepidus and other leading supporters of Caesar, and with
Dolabella – whom he now recognized as consul, conveniently
overlooking the omens alleged at his election. On the following
day, 16 March, negotiations took place between Decimus Brutus

on behalf of the assassins and Hirtius, who made it clear that Caesar's party believed that co-existence was not possible. Brutus thought that the assassins had better go into voluntary exile, and hope that Caesar's party would adopt a moderate tone; a bodyguard for M. Brutus and Cassius was also proposed, but it was doubtful if the soldiers would allow the people to vote for it.

In this atmosphere of threatening violence the Senate met in the guarded Temple of Tellus on 17 March. Cicero later said he had been unwilling to attend, but in the event he took a leading part in promoting the amnesty which was agreed upon. The historian Dio, writing in the third century A.D., reports a long speech by Cicero in this debate; if it is based on a genuine original, Cicero appealed for that harmony and sinking of personal differences for which he had long pleaded, and for the abandonment of feuds – the Senate was deliberating for the welfare of the nation, not sitting in judgment. Having been neither a partisan of Caesar's nor an assassin, he could be disinterested and have only the common welfare in view. The amnesty was modelled on the famous Athenian amnesty of 403/2 B.C.; it indemnified the assassins for their murder, confirmed all Caesar's acts, and indemnified his followers against accusations of having made war against the free Republic.

Though Atticus had vigorously urged Cicero to prevent it, it was also agreed to give Caesar a public funeral. When this took place, it demonstrated clearly the violence of the feeling against the assassins, for when the terms of Caesar's will were read, and it was known that he had vindicated his claim to the patronage of the whole common people of Rome by leaving every man a sum of money, and his gardens as a public domain, they joined the veterans in expressing their resentment at the murder, and some houses were set on fire in the riots that followed.

The murder of Caesar interrupted the flow of Cicero's philosophical work. Under Caesar's dictatorship he had in-tended his philosophy to be his contribution to the welfare of his country, and so a continuation of his previous services; educating the youth aright would be the best contribution he could make; besides, it would be a splendid thing if Romans did not have to learn Greek in order to study philosophy, but had a complete course available in Latin. At the time of Caesar's murder he had been pressing on with enthusiasm. In the days that followed, as he became involved in political consultations again, he felt his duty to the Republic outweighed his philosophical responsibilities. He therefore stopped work for a time on *On Divination* and *On Old Age*, or *Cato the Elder* as he sometimes called the latter, both of which he had started before the Ides of March.

In spite of his speech at Caesar's funeral, Antony at first convinced many of the Senate that he would obey the constitution; he secured the passage of a decree abolishing the office of dictator and other decrees which seemed to symbolize the restoration of the free Republic. We cannot now determine his motives or his sincerity; Cicero later asserted that he had never been convinced of it; certainly, in less than four weeks he told Atticus that there was no free Republic, by which he meant no restoration of the constitutional processes of debate and decision by the Senate. Antony, however, was probably not fully in control of affairs, and many of Caesar's partisans were most unwilling to accept the amnesty which had been decreed. Cicero discovered as much when he left the city on 7 April and stayed with Matius, who told him he did not think things could rest as they had been agreed at the amnesty. Cicero moved slowly round his country properties; in the country towns he found men delighted at Caesar's assassination, no doubt because they felt it meant that there would be no more land allocations to veterans. When he reached the popular Campanian coast in the last week of April, he found many important people there, including the two consuls-elect for 43 B.C., Hirtius and C. Pansa, both Caesarians but out of sympathy with Antony. Cicero was persuaded to help them with their oratory, somewhat against his will, but 'that's what comes of my being too easygoing', he said. Octavius, Caesar's heir, arrived from Greece, and moved into the house next to Cicero's on 21 April. Cicero regarded him with distrust: 'I do not see how he can be a good citizen. He has so many in his entourage who threaten death to the assassins and say that things are intolerable as they are.'

By the end of April, Cicero thought another civil war probable, and this time without the possibility of neutrality, since Caesar's more extreme partisans would consider as enemies anyone who had shown pleasure at Caesar's death; civil war was certain if Sextus Pompeius (Pompey's surviving son) remained defiant in Spain, or moved on Italy as Cicero was certain he would. Cicero's first instinct was to go abroad on a travelling embassy, and visit Athens to see how his son Marcus' studies were progressing; he feared however that he would be criticized for deserting, and when Atticus urged him to wait and see what happened, he shelved his plans for the time being in the hope that he might be able to serve the cause of the Republic more effectively in Italy. Atticus also kept encouraging him to write contemporary history, and he took this in hand, though he did not publish it.

Cicero was also concerned with family affairs: he tried to act as peacemaker in a row between his brother and his nephew over his brother's projected re-marriage (his divorce from Pomponia had evidently now taken place and there were financial complications). Antony wrote to him about the recall of Sextus Cloelius, one of Clodius' henchmen; Antony had now married Fulvia, Clodius' widow, and said he was anxious to teach his stepson (Clodius' son) that quarrels should not be hereditary; there was a thinly veiled threat of blackmail too in Antony's letter which Cicero ignored in acceding to his request. Cicero also wrote a fulsome letter of congratulation to Dolabella when he suppressed the cult of Caesar in Rome. Atticus agreed with the sentiments, but said Cicero had laid it on too thick; Cicero however was concerned to get Dolabella to repay Tullia's dowry, which he still showed no sign of doing. Atticus also asked Cicero to write a speech for Brutus, but Cicero refused: 'There never yet was any poet or orator who thought anyone better than himself; since that's true of bad performers, how much more true of Brutus who has both talent and training?' Brutus had in fact already preferred a draft of his own for an edict; he and Cicero had quite different views on style.

By 11 May, *On Old Age* had gone to Atticus; Cicero dedicated it to him in order to lighten the burden of old age for them both. He enjoyed writing it, he said, and it is a pleasant work, predominantly Roman, making much use of Latin sources; Ennius' *Annals* and Cato the Elder's historical work and speeches are quoted, and Atticus' own work on second-century chronology. It also reasserts the view that there is an after-life for those who have reached the necessary level of attainment in public life; its Greek inspiration was probably the concluding passages of Plato's *Phaedo* and Xenophon's *Education of Cyrus*, both favourite works of

Cicero's. Atticus praised it enthusiastically, and whetted Cicero's appetite to write more. *On Divination* was probably the next work to be published, followed by *On Fate*, which was designed as a sequel, and to complete Cicero's work on the gods. *On Fate* survives only in fragments: unfortunately these do not include the statement of the Stoic views on fate, which were based on the premise that fate is the rational principle in the world. What survives is only the criticism of the Stoic point of view from the standpoint of the Academy; the most interesting part is the discussion of the problem of free will and fate. Naturally, no conclusion is reached on this difficult question.

On Divination has come down to us, in two books, of which the first sets out the arguments for its validity, the second attacks them. The standpoint for asserting its validity is that of the Stoics, though there is much Roman colouring, as for example in the inclusion of auspices and augury among the 'external' means of foretelling the future (by phenomena), as opposed to the 'natural' means, by experiences which originate in men themselves, such as dreams and prophecies made in a state of frenzy or ecstasy. The book closes with a denunciation of charlatans like fortune-tellers, snake-charmers and astrologers. The attack on the validity of divination is based on the views of the contemporary Academy. Many examples are taken from Roman history: Pompey, Crassus and Caesar are all examples of men who had no idea what their ultimate fate would be, and would have been most unhappy had they known; this showed the disadvantage of knowing the future. There is also a gently humorous account of the Roman institutions which owed their origin to the primitive belief in divination. The dialogue ends by dismissing dreams as no more useful than the rest: 'the truth is that superstition has become widespread everywhere, and has played on men's weakness.' This remark suggests that it was probably one of the objects of the dialogue to counter superstition, for Cicero thought it would be a great public service if he could root out such beliefs altogether. Here we find Cicero of the same mind as his great contemporary, the poet Lucretius.

In Rome, an important debate was fixed for 1 June. Cicero at first intended to go, since evidently it would provide a test of Antony's intentions, but before the middle of May he had been advised not to do so; there would be troops there, and perhaps

violence against Caesar's assassins and those who had sympathized with them. Atticus kept his ear close to the ground: he
heard more than Cicero, and was present at many of the caucus
discussions; he too advised Cicero not to go.

Cicero decided that, if he could not attend the Senate, he would
go to Athens to visit Marcus. Evidently he held Antony largely
responsible for the present situation, since he agreed with Hirtius
and Pansa that he would return for their consulship at the start of
43 B.C. Hirtius was very critical of Antony, and Pansa seemed to
want the amnesty upheld. Hirtius was also very critical of the
assassins, criticizing M. Brutus and Cassius for their wish to go
abroad during their praetorship, since he thought they wanted to
raise an army, and to do so would give Antony's more violent
partisans a chance to use force in Italy. Antony was gathering
bands of veterans in Rome; there were rumours that a posse
would be organized to harass Cicero, and perhaps all the leading
men with houses at Tusculum. Cicero decided to write a letter to
ask for a commission which would allow him to leave for Athens.
Tiro took the letter to Rome; in case Tiro could not see Antony (it
was difficult to do so), Cicero also wrote to a friend, Eutrapelus,
patron of Cytheris, Antony's mistress, to ask him to see that
Antony got it – bedroom government had returned.

On 1 June, Antony's province was changed to Cisalpine Gaul,
with a long tenure: on 2 June, Dolabella's tenure of Syria was
extended to five years, and he named Cicero as one of his
lieutenants, which gave him the excuse he needed for going to
Athens. On 5 June, the Senate gave M. Brutus and Cassius a
commission to procure corn for Rome in Asia and Sicily. Such
commissions were humiliating for praetors, but Cicero thought it
better to take them than to go on skulking in Brutus' villa because
they dared not appear in Rome. The effect of these dispositions
was to give Antony a position from which he could threaten
Rome with an army, once Decimus Brutus had handed over the
province to him; the question now was whether Decimus would
agree to do so.

After this meeting Cicero was invited to attend M. Brutus'
party's council at Antium. He was very unwilling to go, but when
he arrived he urged M. Brutus to accept the corn-commission.
Cassius came in during the discussion, breathing fire and
asserting that he would not accept the job in Sicily, but would go,

illegally, to Greece. Brutus wanted to visit Rome, but Cicero urged him against it. General recriminations followed about what ought to have been done, which ended in Brutus' mother cutting Cicero short with the sarcastic comment that 'nobody I've heard has ever said that before'; he was repeating stale views. However, she promised to see that the 'corn procurement' bit should be removed from Cassius' commission, thus making it a regular governorship of Sicily. Cicero thought that Brutus would go to Asia, and he decided that it was time that he left Italy himself. He could not affect the main political issues, which were whether Caesar's heir could be trusted (his father-in-law thought that he couldn't), and whether he could be dissociated from Antony, thus weakening the Caesarian party by dividing it.

Cicero still procrastinated for some time over whether or not to leave for Athens; he had to straighten out his finances; Dolabella had not yet given him a specific job to do, and this looked bad; he wanted to avoid an open breach with Antony, so he must write to him; Atticus must advise him about the date for his return. Eventually, he left Tusculum on 30 June. Atticus wrote that he had wept when they parted: 'I'm sorry', Cicero wrote. 'Had you done that in my presence I might not have started.' This was uncharacteristic behaviour for Atticus; he was probably ill and was worrying about death; he had been deserting his brand of Epicurean principles and fortifying himself against the fear of death by reading Cicero's *Tusculan Disputations*, and counselling submission to the Caesarians; Cicero would not hear of it. Atticus had cause to worry too, for M. Brutus and he were deeply attached – 'doesn't Brutus' grave old face deter you from talking like that?' Cicero had asked him when he had advocated an Epicurean detachment from the affairs of the state in April. Atticus found himself in grave danger of being dragged by the heels off the pitch of neutrality which it was his habit to cultivate – indeed, one might wonder whether Atticus had anything to do with the continuing ineffectiveness of Brutus in this period, and his apparent lack of will to resist Antony.

All this time Cicero was writing. *On Friendship* followed *On Fate*, and then the two (now lost) books *On Glory*. *On Friendship* is sub-titled *Laelius*, after the great friend of Scipio Aemilianus. Contrary to what we might expect, the tone of this work is rather grim, and inclined to raise awkward questions, such as perhaps arose from Cicero's personal experience of political friendships. Compensation for one's own inadequacies is acknowledged (rather unhappily) as a motive for true friendship, but friendship must be subordinate to patriotism, since friendships which involve sacrifices of principles are necessarily limited. The Epicurean standpoint is criticized, along with friendships based on kinship, moral similarity, and the need to get on in the world. The whole discussion is carefully removed from the current social and political scene. *On Glory* was sent to Atticus just before Cicero left Tusculum for Greece; when it went, it had the wrong prologue attached – Cicero had inadvertently re-used one he had previously put into the *Academics*. The stock of prologues from which this one was drawn illustrates Cicero's facility for literary production, as does the writing of a new one on board ship – would Atticus please see that the old one was removed from the copies of the work he had already had produced? Also written on board ship to relieve the tedium of the voyage was *Topics*, addressed to Trebatius. Cicero says it was prompted by a request from Trebatius to explain Aristotle's *Topics*, but it completely fails to do this, omitting some of Aristotle's topics and including much other material. Evidently it was largely written from memory and was not a work of serious scholarship.

Cicero's memory was not failing, however; when he looked up a point of law about which he had argued with Trebatius at dinner, he found he was right, and the jurist wrong. He also promised to hammer out 'something after Heracleides' for Atticus to put away in his safe; was this some astronomical work, or was it historical? Heracleides of Pontus wrote both; the 'hammering out' suggests something intellectual, the secrecy something of more current importance than astronomy, perhaps the contemporary or secret history Atticus kept suggesting.

Cicero travelled slowly south through Italy, writing to Atticus at his daily stops, reacting to the news as he heard it. He was very shocked to hear that July was now so named, after Julius Caesar; there was also a good deal to report about the younger members of the family – of Marcus in Athens and Quintus, who had now quarrelled with Antony and left the Caesarian party; he was certainly much improved.

Cicero embarked at Pompeii, but even as he went on board he felt he was a fool to go; ships were uncomfortable for a man of his age; it was a ridiculous time of year to be sailing; he'd be much better off in one of his country houses: the feelings are familiar to all who have made long journeys by sea. He coasted southwards, paused at the villa of Trebatius at Velia, and reached Vibo in Bruttium where he stayed with his friend Sicca. He planned to go on to Rhegium, thence by merchant-ship to Patras or by a smaller, faster, rowing-boat to Leucopetra, thence to Corcyra (Corfu).

On the way to Corfu Cicero's ship met a strong headwind and turned back. At Leucopetra he met men from Rome who told him that there were hopes of a settlement. Brutus and Cassius had asked all ex-consuls and ex-praetors to attend the Senate on the first of the month; there was a good hope that Antony would give up his claim to Gaul, which was now the root of the trouble, and there had been conciliatory edicts from both sides. Cicero heard from Atticus too, reproaching him most bitterly for going away. It seems clear that letters had gone astray; the meeting had been scheduled for 1 August, but on that day, for some reason we do not know, all that happened was that L. Piso (Caesar's father-in-law) made a bitter, but unsupported, attack on Antony. Antony replied, and then issued a violent edict repudiating Brutus and Cassius, and wrote them a letter which they told him in a reply 'was like your edict, insulting, intimidating and quite improper for you to send to us'.

The close of their letter was no less threatening:

Just reflect how intolerable it is for praetors to be unable to resign some of their prerogatives in the interest of civil harmony and freedom without being threatened by the consul with military force. As we are sure of our ground, we are not to be intimidated by you. We do not think it right to submit to threats, nor do we agree to do so; nor do we think it is the business of Antony to issue orders to those whose actions have made him a free man. If other circumstances demanded that we should engage in a civil war, your letter would be useless; letters full of threats carry no weight with free men. You know perfectly well that we are not to be pushed around; we think that your threats are designed to make our sensible approach seem to be motivated by fear. We are anxious that you should have an important and honourable position in a free Republic; we shall not provoke you, but we value our own freedom more highly than your friendship. Please review very carefully what you are undertaking, and the means at your disposal; reflect on how long Caesar reigned, not on how long he lived. We pray to the gods

that whatever you plan may serve the interests of the state and yourself;
if they do not, we hope that the free Republic may be preserved, and
that you yourself may suffer as little as possible.

The usual explanation for Antony's extraordinary changes of
front at this time is that he became reconciled with Brutus and
Cassius in order to undermine Caesar's heir, but when the
veterans demanded that the two Caesarian leaders be reconciled,
Antony abruptly resumed, or intensified, his attitude of hostility
to the assassins. This is probably correct. So, when Cicero re-
established contact with politics at the end of August, the
prospect was not one of reconciliation, but of an immediate and
serious crisis. Moreover, he found that his departure had been
criticized, and that it would have been regarded as unforgivable
frivolity if he had gone to the Olympic games. He was glad to
be back too, since debts were being called in; the fear of war
was responsible, and money was tight. He reached Rome on 31
August; his arrival there was public, and he was warmly
welcomed. When he found that the subject of debate on 1
September was not public business generally but honours to
Caesar he decided to stay away, and sent Antony a note of
apology. Antony lost his temper, delivered a violent attack on
Cicero, and declared he'd go in person and demolish Cicero's
house. The next day, 2 September, Dolabella took the chair for a
debate on 'public business'; contrary to everyone's expectations,
Cicero arrived, and delivered what he subsequently called his
First Philippic Oration.

For a speech composed in one day this is a masterpiece. After
defending his own return and rebuking Antony for his temper,
he took his stand firmly on his old policy of compromise and
harmony. Caesar's acts must of course be upheld, he said; they
were the only foundation on which to build – but Antony had
passed new laws which cut across them. Antony's acts which
served the cause of harmony are praised; both consuls are warned
not to disregard the common people, who had showed their
feelings for Brutus at games in July. Cicero concludes by saying
that he will come to the Senate and speak again if he is not
subjected to threats; if he cannot come, he will still be ready to
serve the Republic. This dignified and temperate reply was all
that Cicero said in public, but he wrote to Munatius Plancus,
governor of the 'long-haired' Gauls (those still not Romanized,

whom Caesar had conquered), to Cassius, and to Cornificius in Africa. These are the first trickle of what was to become a mighty spate of letters which Cicero wrote in the interest of the Republic during the next six months. Over one hundred of them survive, and there were many more, probably suppressed later because of criticisms they contained of Caesar's heir and others.

After the *First Philippic* Cicero retired from the Senate; whether he also retired from Rome is uncertain. The absence of letters to Atticus till November may mean he was in the city, or it may mean that both men were at Tusculum. Antony certainly left Rome, to draft a reply. According to Cicero, it was written at Tibur, in the villa that once belonged to Metellus Scipio, Pompey's last father-in-law, amid scenes of drinking and violent debauchery. It was delivered on 19 September, and consisted of criticisms of Cicero for violating ties of friendship, an attack on his whole political career, and mockery of him as a man. This we can gather from Cicero's reply. Because of the soldiers, Cicero was afraid to appear in the Senate in person; the *Second Philippic Oration* was written over several weeks from late September, sent to Atticus for criticism on 25 October, but probably not put into public circulation till after Antony left Rome for Gaul on 29 November.

Though not spoken, the pamphlet is written as a speech delivered in the Senate in Antony's presence; it consists of two parts, an answer to Antony's attack of 19 September, and a review of Antony's career. The principal charges made against him are immorality, lack of principles, and inconsistency in political alliances: he had been now a friend, now an enemy of Clodius, now Caesar's favourite for his recklessness, now disgraced for his dishonesty; similarly with Dolabella, with his wife Fulvia, with the Senate, and with Cicero; with all of them he was at one time on terms of closest intimacy, at another at enmity. Cicero closes the pamphlet with a comparison between Caesar and Antony:

Caesar was a man of genius, intellect and memory, literate and careful, with the ability to plan and the industry to execute. His military achievements, though disastrous to the state, were immense. He planned a monarchy for many years and laboured through immense dangers to effect his plan. By his gifts, public works, distributions of food, and public hospitality he reconciled the uneducated masses to his rule. He attached his supporters to him by rewards, his enemies by an exhibition of mercy. In brief, partly by fear, partly by resignation to their lot, he imposed on a free Republic the habit of subservience.

Antony had neither Caesar's gifts nor his ability to apply them; the Roman people had now learned whom to trust and whom to fear; men had also learned the glory of tyrannicide. As for Cicero himself:

> I defended the Republic as a young man, I shall not desert it in my old age. I scorned the swords of Catiline, I shall not fear yours.... Twenty years ago in this very temple I said that a man of consul's rank could not die prematurely – how much more true that is for an elderly ex-consul now.... Two hopes I have: one is that when I die I shall leave the Roman people free; this is the greatest gift the gods could bestow; the other is that every man may meet the deserts he has earned in public life.

This work has every ingredient of great oratory: description, narrative, mockery, pathos, humour, the thunder of resounding rhetoric, and the cold calm of softly-spoken contempt. Modern taste recoils from the charges of sodomy and unchastity, but they were a regular part of the vocabulary of ancient abuse; on Antony's wild carousings and financial dishonesty the facts speak for themselves; examples of what Cicero cites are repeated in his later life. But this pamphlet made it clear that Cicero and Antony could hardly live together in the same free state. Atticus, despite his advice to wait and see, approved the pamphlet, and his clerks produced the text for publication.

While Cicero wrote this pamphlet, he was also completing his treatise *On Duties*, in three books, and dedicated to his son. On 25 October, he told Atticus he was getting on with it splendidly; two weeks later he requested the loan of a book to help him with Book III. Like his other philosophical works, this treatise is based on a Greek original but has its examples derived from Roman history, many from the orator's own experience of life. Cicero starts with a statement of his aim in philosophy: to use the orator's special talent of speaking appropriately, clearly and elegantly, for expressing philosophical ideas. Having spent his whole life in this, he intended to extend the range of expression in the Latin language; in his writings he had shown himself master of both trades, rhetorical and philosophical – something few Greeks had attempted and no Roman. He then explains his subject: duties are practical rules for daily life; philosophers generally neglect these rules in favour of theoretical speculations on the Supreme Good, but Cicero will neglect the Supreme Good, and stick to practical rules based on what is right and what can be shown for sufficient reason to have a claim to be performed. In any situation, therefore, a man has to decide whether an intended action is morally right or morally wrong and whether it is conducive to his good (whether this good is his comfort, happiness, wealth, influence, or power for himself or his friends); that is, to utility for him. If the morally right and the useful conflict, on what basis can a choice be made? What also should a man do when there are conflicting courses, both right or both useful? which should he prefer? Reason, family ties, feeling for truth, and his sense of morality differentiate man from the animals, so that man has four cardinal virtues: Wisdom, Justice, Courage and Temperance, on which all duties are based.

Under the heading of Justice, Cicero discusses the characteristic Roman virtue of good faith (*fides*), then passive injustice (failing to do right) compared with active injustice (doing wrong), and excessive ambition, of which Crassus and Caesar are offered as contemporary examples. On judicial punishment, Cicero comments that there is a proper limit for avenging (or punishing) an injury; this is that the offender should regret his act and think twice before repeating it, and that others should be warned against it. He shows a similar attitude to war; the only right motive for war is to be able to live in peace without suffering injuries, so, when victory is won, an enemy who has not committed atrocities should be spared; this was the Romans' way (and incidentally a principle for Empire). In dealing with slaves, justice must extend to the humblest; the standard should be that appropriate for employees – fair treatment for honest work. Generosity excludes giving away other people's property, lavish expenditure beyond one's means, and giving without discrimination; though he does not say so explicitly, Cicero's mind must be on the games and public extravagance at Rome.

Turning to bravery, Cicero asserts it can only be exercised in accordance with Justice, and supports the Roman view of the superiority of public service over a private career: 'Those whom Nature has given the talent for public life must not hesitate to enter it, hold office and direct public affairs . . . but let a man be careful not to think only of its honour, but also of his own capacity.' Victories won without bloodshed are greater than those of the sword, and Cicero's own successes pre-eminently so: 'Let arms give place to civil garb, laurels of victory to words of panegyric', Cicero's own line had put it well.

After dealing with physical courage, Cicero passes to the more important courage, that of doing justly in public life. Public administrators must put the public interest above their own, and the interests of the whole Republic above that of one section; failure to do this results in party strife, the worst condition for a state in Cicero's view. He also strongly criticizes malicious misrepresentation of opponents, excessive competition for office, vindictiveness, and punishment under the stimulus of anger, though forbearance must always have the state's interest in mind, and not be connivance at wrongdoing. The section finishes with a defence of the intellectual life, and that of business and commerce, provided that wealth is honestly acquired and used generously in a man's own family and among his friends.

Temperance forms the last of the cardinal virtues; it is summed up as the subjection of one's passions, seeking what is moderate in all things, and what is proper. Propriety is then defined; its essence is seen in conjunction with justice: justice makes a man refrain from injuring his fellow men, being considerate prevents him wounding their feelings. In choosing a career, one's father's profession should first be considered, but the eventual choice may be a matter of accident, or the result of a natural bias in some direction. Different ages have their own duties: youthful inexperience requires the practical wisdom of the older, the older should try to help the younger, and not relax into sloth and luxury:

Magistrates have the peculiar duty to bear in mind that they represent the state: they must uphold its dignity and honour, preserve the laws, guarantee each man his rights, and remember that all are entrusted to them. . . . In public life, a private citizen should labour for the peace and honour of the state. . . . A resident alien should mind his own business, leave that of others alone, and keep entirely out of the public affairs of a country not his own.

Cicero then goes on to deal with propriety in private life, decency in action and appearance, and self-control in speech and conversation: 'one should note how far a conversation gives pleasure, and stop it if it ceases to do so, for that was why it was started.' A man's house should be appropriate to his standing; a spacious house is needed by a public man with many callers, but is ridiculously empty without them. Competition in luxury of appointments is reprehensible too – what we call 'keeping up with the neighbours'.

A man should recognize his faults; he may then be able to correct them by studying other people, or by listening to criticisms by experts or people with practical experience. Like an artist, a sensible man welcomes knowledgeable criticism. One does not argue with the laws though, just because a few exceptional people like Socrates did: 'It is our duty to respect, defend, and uphold the laws, which are the common bonds which unite men as human beings.' Dealing with occupations, Cicero's views sound strangely old-fashioned in an industrial society, but they are fully in conformity with the views of the ancient world: agriculture is far and away the most honourable occupation, working for wages a sort of slavery.

The treatise then passes to questions arising out of the conflict of duties, and the duties which arise out of maintaining a standard of life and the means of acquiring what people use and enjoy – the standard known as the useful. This does not necessarily conflict with the morally right, though some think it does, as Cicero admits. One reason is that civilization itself depends on men acquiring property and some measure of prosperity. Co-operation is thus itself a virtue, and actions motivated by love are superior to those motivated by fear. Hence the miserable situation of a tyrant, and also the deterioration in the quality of Roman public life once the principle of mercy was abandoned, especially from Sulla's time. Here Cicero seems to be making an important contribution to that strong sense that they had been punished for their loss of moral standards which is a notable feature in the Roman writers of the next generation.

Discussing glory, Cicero says that it is based on the love, confidence, admiration and high regard of the people – in a word, on popularity. Cicero concludes that as justice is the best source of popularity, so justice is also the way to achieve glory, but it cannot be achieved by pretence and empty show, or by hypocrisy. True glory has wide-spreading roots and a wide span, and a good name must be based on actions which are just, whatever the field in which the good name is sought.

Generosity is more nobly shown by personal service, though more easily shown by giving money; Cicero contrasts the waste of money on games and shows in Rome with kind acts towards individuals, such as acting as a defence lawyer or giving advice – activities which may promote both the interests of the public and those of private individuals. Hence comes the honour of the bar, at which it is better to plead the case of a poor man than a rich man's, for he will know that kindness was the motive. The interests of justice must be served too, since without it no services are praiseworthy.

Cicero then passes to services to the state, and the duty of the public man to maintain property, avoid direct taxation, and ensure that there is an adequate supply of food.

> But a public man's principal duty is to avoid any suspicion of self-seeking; he must maintain absolute integrity – there is no failing more offensive than avarice, especially in leaders of the state and those who form the government.... To exploit the state for profit is not just disgraceful, it is criminal and immoral.

Cicero then violently attacks agrarian legislation as a means of gaining popularity or support in politics:

> it is a matter of the highest principle, and the height of wisdom of a good citizen not to divide the interests of the citizens, but to embrace all with the same impartial justice.

Those who administer the laws equitably win great popularity and glory for themselves, and serve the state as well; such services call for great men, who were common among the Romans of old.

The third book deals with situations in which there is a conflict between principles, or between different things conducive to utility; the general standard of discussion is lower and perhaps illustrates the fact that Cicero's mind was by then actively engaged in public affairs.

While Cicero was in retirement completing these two major works, Antony's violence grew more extreme: he intimidated a tribune Cannutius on 2 October, and published a demand for the trial of Caesar's assassins, and of Cicero as an accomplice. He also accused Caesar's heir of trying to murder him – Cicero believed it true, though whether he was merely blinded by his hatred of Antony is not certain. However, Antony's attempt to outdo Caesar's heir as an extremist Caesarian resulted in the latter turning into a Republican, a result Antony can hardly have foreseen, and when Antony tried to distribute largesse in his own name (having neglected to pay it under Caesar's will because he had embezzled the money), he found he had been outbid by Caesar's heir and had to face a series of mutinies.

He was able to suppress one at Brundisium by executing three hundred officers and men; he could not suppress the others, and these mutineers formed the first army of Caesar's heir. 'At the age of nineteen years I raised an army at my own initiative and at my own expense, and with it I freed the Roman people from the domination of a faction which held it in its grasp.' So the heir of Caesar wrote some forty years later when he had become known as Augustus Caesar, son of the deified Julius. At this period he called himself C. Julius Caesar; his friends called him 'Caesar', modern scholars prefer 'Octavian', to remove ambiguity and prevent confusion with the dead dictator. Octavian's illegal army made a new civil war all but certain.

Immediately, however, he needed support, and someone to put the stamp of legality on his acts. He turned to Cicero. Cicero's first reactions were very cautious; he could not believe that the young man could be trusted, nor that a man with his name and backing could prove a supporter of the sort of republic Cicero believed in. As was his way when in doubt, he wrote to Atticus; a stream of letters, the last, begins on 2 November. He refused to make a secret rendezvous with the young man at Capua – an 'infantile idea' – but advised him to go to Rome and test the feelings of the common people of the city. Octavian asked Cicero to come too, to support him in the Senate. Cicero thought that the Senate could not act before the new consuls entered office on 1 January 43 B.C.; few men would come and affront Antony so openly. But Octavian persisted; he wrote every day, and as he toured Italy, he told Cicero of his welcome in the country towns. In the end, he went to Rome and made a popular harangue, which was not a success; anti-Caesarians were offended at his obeisance to Caesar's statue, the veterans were offended at his not taking a more extreme line, the common people disliked his soldiers. He withdrew north into Etruria to watch the situation.

Antony returned to Rome from Brundisium in a furious rage. He issued insulting edicts about Octavian, his family and morals, attacked Cicero, and called a meeting of the Senate for 24 November, uttering ferocious threats against any who failed to attend. But he was unable to implement his threats since the 'Legion of Mars' mutinied and occupied Alba Fucens, forty miles from Rome. Antony tried to recover their allegiance, but in vain; he returned to Rome on the 28th, called another meeting of the Senate in the evening, warned hostile tribunes not to attend on pain of death, and prepared to have Octavian declared a public enemy. Again he was foiled, as the Fourth Legion's mutiny was announced; all he could do was to propose a vote of thanks to Lepidus for concluding a deal with Sextus Pompeius in Spain, and allot provinces to the praetors. He then left at night to deal with the open rebellion of Octavian, not to return again during his consulate. When he left the city, many senators, equites and other citizens swore to obey his orders, and he moved to take possession of Cisalpine Gaul, which was still in the control of Decimus Brutus. Brutus was besieged in the town of Mutina (Modena); Cicero wrote to him urging him to stand against Antony, and to other governors to urge them to obey the Senate.

While Antony moved round Italy, Cicero kept track of his movements and managed to keep out of his way. Atticus still advised a policy of wait and see; Cicero should stay in Arpinum until the results of Octavian's illegal act were seen. Cicero however had to come to Rome. His finances were in another tangle, and he was determined not to allow his credit to collapse. Dolabella had still failed to repay Tullia's dowry, and from what Dolabella owed him Cicero could have met all his obligations. Since Dolabella had now deserted the assassins' side for money there was no reason for Cicero to use kid gloves any longer; he resolved to announce their friendship was at an end.

This is the subject of the last surviving letter to Atticus. It ends with peculiar appropriateness: 'I am coming' (to Rome). He came indeed, to try for the third time to take Rome's destiny out of the hands of nobles who planned a coup d'état.

We do not know why there are no more letters to Atticus. Various reasons have been offered; perhaps the simplest is that Atticus and Cicero now went different ways. Atticus' keen nose for politics and his determination to remain neutral carried him safely through the next civil war, and, by his daughter's marriage to Agrippa, into the heart of Octavian's party; Cicero disregarded Atticus' advice to wait and see, led the Senate against Antony, and died. It is hard to believe that they ceased to be friends, but after Cicero came to Rome they lacked the essential basis for those intimate consultations which play so large a part in the surviving letters.

The next day, 10 December, new tribunes entered office. They were hostile to Antony, and summoned the Senate to meet on 20 December to debate the question how the new consuls could secure the Senate's liberty after 1 January 43 B.C. Cicero wrote to Decimus Brutus about this meeting: 'Although I had intended not to attend the Senate before 1 January ... I came to the meeting early. On my arrival being noticed, a full meeting quickly convened; I should prefer you to hear from others what I said about you in the Senate, and at a very large public meeting afterwards.'

What Cicero said comprised the *Third* and *Fourth Philippic Orations*, two of the mightiest fighting speeches of antiquity. With them he threw down the gauntlet to Antony, and seized the leadership of the Senate from Caesar's partisans:

That day [he later declared] the foundations of a free Republic were laid. ... Men remember that on 20 December I was the leader of the fight for the recovery of liberty. ... I embraced the whole political scene in my speech; I spoke very forcefully, and recalled the Senate to its ancient courageous ways, when it was already exhausted and drooping in spirit. This very day, and the exertions I made in my speech, rekindled the Roman people's hope of recovering their freedom. Since then, I have never let up in my planning for a free Republic and acting on my plans as well ... That was the day I first entered upon the hopes of freedom, and, though others hesitated, I laid the foundations of a real, free Republic.

He was nearly sixty-three years old, and the greatest fight of his life was on.

9
The End of the Republic: Cicero's Last Fight, and Death

Cicero concluded his *Third Philippic Oration* with a series of motions. The most important was to instruct the men then governing provinces not to quit them without further orders from the Senate; others were to commend Decimus Brutus and Octavian for their actions against Antony, and the Legion of Mars and the Fourth Legion for their mutinies. These motions were carried, and Octavian later based the propaganda designed to justify his actions on what Cicero had said.

Constitutionally the Senate did not have the right to reverse popular decrees (which Antony's measures were) but they could suspend their implementation until they could debate a question afresh and put it to the people for reconsideration. Immediately, therefore, the effect of the adoption of Cicero's proposals was to suspend the measures by which Antony had had the provinces reallocated, first in June then in November, and in particular the allocation of Cisalpine Gaul to himself. Decimus Brutus was, in effect, decreed to be still the legitimate ruler of Cisalpine Gaul until the Senate decided otherwise, and the people voted on the Senate's decision; Antony was therefore attempting to seize Cisalpine Gaul illegally and by force, an act that amounted to treason. Thus, in adopting Cicero's proposals, the Senate presented Antony with a challenge of the most direct sort. More remarkable still, the tribune who convened the Senate called on Cicero to speak first after himself, and thus put the clock back nearly twenty years, restoring to Cicero the leadership which he had had in 63 B.C. Who prompted the tribune to do this? Was it Octavian, or was it the sheer power of the orator's presence at what was once again a moment of crisis?

For Cicero, the great difference between 20 December 44 B.C. and 17 March of that year was that in March he had spoken for harmony, now he spoke for defying Antony. What had caused Cicero to change? Apologists for Antony – of whom there are a number in the annals of scholarship – explain it as Cicero's personal antagonism towards a man, now the husband of Clodius' widow. But this cannot explain why the people had elected ten tribunes not one of whom was willing to veto the proposal, nor the fact that the Senate, which consisted predominantly of Caesar's partisans, passed Cicero's motion in less than one day, nor the tumultuous applause which greeted the *Fourth Oration* which was given in the popular assembly.

It is much more consonant with the facts to accept that Antony was seen as an adventurer, liberal with the money of Caesar, the Roman treasury, and other people, who held his position by making promises to troops, encouraging them to take a hostile attitude to the Republic's organs of government, and telling them that they would be cheated of their rewards unless they enforced their will, and that he had alienated the civilian population of Rome. Cicero had the courage to take the lead in encouraging civilians to defy soldiers and use the opportunity offered by Octavian to free themselves from Antony's arbitrary rule, since Octavian appeared ready to collaborate with Cicero, and with Decimus Brutus, though he was one of Caesar's assassins.

On 1 January, the Senate met again under Hirtius and Pansa, the new consuls. Though both were nominees of Caesar they had showed their hostility to Antony by ostentatiously absenting themselves from the meetings of the Senate he had so peremptorily called. They opened the usual debate on public business, and then passed to questions arising out of the decrees of 20 December. Pansa, in the chair, asked his father-in-law Fufius Calenus to speak first. Once an officer of Caesar's, Fufius was an old enemy of Cicero, though he had been formally reconciled to him only six months before; Fufius spoke generally on public affairs, and moved that an embassy should go to negotiate with Antony. Faced with the dissolution of their party, Caesar's friends approved. Cicero opposed him; he was probably the first speaker to do so, though whether he spoke next after Fufius is uncertain. He delivered a point-by-point denunciation of

Antony, and proposed that the 'Senate's Last Decree' should be passed, and an amnesty offered to all Antony's soldiers who deserted within the next month. He also moved that Octavian be invested with the rank of propraetor, and appropriate rewards given to Antony's opponents, the legions who had deserted him, and any others who now did so. This was the *Fifth Philippic Oration*.

The debate was stormy and protracted, and though the proposals to honour Octavian and the legions were agreed on 3 January, the 'Last Decree' was not passed, nor were the proposals aimed at Antony, though an ultimatum was eventually drawn up on 4 January for an embassy to deliver to him. Cicero's *Sixth Philippic Oration* was delivered to the people in the Forum that evening. It explains his own part in securing that the envoys presented a strongly-worded ultimatum, in which the sting was that it gave Antony a time-limit within which he must comply. Foolishly, however, the Senate agreed at the same meeting to declare invalid, as passed by violence, Antony's law assigning lands to veterans and the commission to implement it, for though this satisfied the Senate and other landowners, it fatally weakened their position in regard to the veteran troops. Cicero was one of those unwise enough to support this decree.

In the *Sixth Philippic Oration* Cicero declared that the Roman people must now fight for their liberty; in the *Seventh Philippic*, a speech in the Senate two or three weeks later, he roundly declared:

I am one who has always been an advocate of peace. I have always been among those principally concerned for peace, especially civil peace. Peace has always been the aim of all my supporters; the whole course of my efforts, in the Forum, in the Senate House, in my defence of friends, has been directed to peace. Peace has been the source of my highest honours, of my reasonable prosperity, of the position I enjoy in men's estimation, such as it is ... yet I do not want peace with Antony, ... firstly because it would be disgraceful, secondly because it would be dangerous, thirdly because it would be impossible to come to terms with him.

This speech achieved no immediate result since the envoys still had not returned, but it made Cicero's position unequivocal.

Early in February two of the envoys came back; the third was dead. As might have been expected, they brought with them a series of counter-demands from Antony, of which the most irreconcilable with the Senate's were that Antony's troops should have the same rewards as Octavian's, that the acts of his consulate should be ratified, including of course his allocations of the provinces, and that he should govern Further Gaul so long as M. Brutus and Cassius were consuls or proconsuls, which would in the normal course of events be five years. There was a stormy and confused debate, at which Cicero again spoke against negotiations or compromise. A 'Senate's Last Decree' was passed, but this was milder than Cicero wanted, since it instructed the consuls and other magistrates to deal with a disturbance; Cicero had wanted it called a war.

Next day the Senate considered a dispatch from the consul Hirtius who was now in Northern Italy. In his *Eighth Philippic Oration* Cicero again attacked Fufius Calenus and the others of Caesar's old supporters who were speaking for peace, that is, almost all the men of consular rank but Cicero himself; he succeeded in getting the Senate to offer an amnesty to all Antony's soldiers who deserted him by 15 March next. A public funeral was then decreed for Servius Sulpicius, the envoy who had died on the mission to Antony. It was proposed that he should also have the statue 'awarded to those whose death was caused by an embassy', a motion which would imply that Rome was at war. Cicero's *Ninth Philippic Oration* is both eulogy of Servius and a call to pass the proposal. When the Senate did so, it had been driven one step nearer to war with Antony.

Antony's supporters now rallied more effectively; one tribune and two of the praetors spoke for him, and one of the latter followed Octavian's example by raising a private illegal army in Italy. Perhaps his action was prompted by M. Brutus and Cassius; on the way to his mission to collect grain in Asia Brutus had gone to Greece; there he raised a military force, obtained adherents and money, and challenged Antony's brother Gaius when he came to take over Macedonia under Antony's provincial allocations. Gaius was deserted by his troops and was blockaded in Apollonia, on the Adriatic coast. In his *Tenth Philippic Oration* Cicero secured the Senate's approval for Brutus and had him appointed governor of Greece and Macedonia and commander of the armies there. Cicero wrote to Cassius urging him to do what Brutus had done, and seize the Asiatic provinces.

Asia was without a governor, since Dolabella had captured and killed Caesar's nominee, C. Trebonius. There were rumours that the murder had been treacherous and accompanied by torture, and it roused the deepest horror. Dolabella was unanimously declared a public enemy, and the next day Cicero warned the Senate in the *Eleventh Philippic* that Antony would follow Dolabella's example by killing off his enemies if he could; he was a true prophet. His proposal that Cassius be commissioned to replace Trebonius failed to pass, since the consuls wanted Asia for themselves, but this had no practical importance since Cassius had already illegally assumed control of Syria from the junior officers there. Cassius soon got the better of Dolabella, who killed himself; but this was not until May.

At the end of February, Cicero's campaign began to lose its impetus. There were a number of reasons for this: the first is that it was not clear that the Senate's cause was prospering. Decimus Brutus and his army were starving in Mutina, Gaius Antonius was still holding out at Apollonia, Dolabella had easily overrun Asia and nothing was yet known of Cassius. Another is that Antony's agents were now active in Rome; even in January one was present in the Senate, taking note of what men said, and thus intimidating the nervous with the fear of Antony's vengeance. A third reason is that the commanders of the armies in Gaul, Plancus and Lepidus, were sitting on the fence, despite the stream of letters directed at them by Cicero. They were Caesar's partisans – Lepidus had been among the foremost advocates of violence against the assassins on the Ides of March – and they had strong armies, mainly of veterans. A fourth, still more pressing, reason for a general wish to negotiate was that the treasury was now almost empty, and this meant that the civil population had to face new taxes and levies: a 4 per cent capital levy, and a tax on houses calculated by the number of tiles, fell heaviest on the rich. 'Voluntary contributions' were also called for from the city and the country towns. No quicker way of dousing enthusiasm for war could have been found.

In consequence, Antony's friends succeeded in getting another embassy approved; Cicero was to serve on it, but before the envoys set out, Antony's friends were unable to substantiate their indications of concessions from Antony, and this made all his opponents among the envoys withdraw; Cicero delivered the *Twelfth Philippic Oration* to explain his own withdrawal. Opinion then moved against Antony's party again. In March, Pansa the consul, who had persistently opposed severe measures, left to help Hirtius and Octavian relieve the siege of Mutina. Before he left Rome he named Cicero 'leader of the Senate', a title conferred formally only by censors, but now perhaps granted informally in the way that the leaders of various factions had for some years called themselves 'leaders'.

After Pansa left letters came from Plancus and Lepidus in Gaul urging peace, and these were debated along with a letter from Antony to Hirtius and Octavian accusing Cicero and the Senate of reviving the party of Pompey. Cicero spoke second in this debate; his speech was the *Thirteenth Philippic Oration*, in which he again called for the rejection of any form of compromise. In the evening afterwards (it was now 20 March) he wrote harsh, blunt notes to Plancus and Lepidus. Early in April, Plancus assured Cicero that he would be at the disposal of the Senate, news came that Brutus had captured Gaius Antonius, and was in complete possession of the eastern Adriatic coast, and on 9 April the news of Cassius' initial successes arrived.

Cicero's policy seemed to be about to bear fruit; hopes rose still further when news came that Hirtius had turned a defeat of Pansa's new legions into an important victory over Antony's veteran troops. Cicero was escorted by a jubilant crowd to the Capitol where he gave thanks for the victory, thence home. It was to be almost his last moment of triumph. The following day the Senate debated the consuls' despatch, and Cicero delivered the *Fourteenth Philippic Oration*. In it he argued that the thanksgiving requested by the consuls in honour of their victory compelled the Senate to decide who were its enemies, because, if Antony was not, no thanksgiving could be decreed. He also proposed rewards for the victorious troops, honours for the dead, and payments to the families bereaved. This is Cicero's last published speech, 'the monument', it has been called, 'not only of the Republican dead at Mutina, but of the Cicero who might have made a Demosthenes'. It has all the vigour of his greatest work: the power in the abuse of Antony, the swift-moving narration of the plot against himself, the skilful argumentation, and the rounded periods of praise which characterize the master's hand. At the age of sixty-three, after four strenuous months of leadership, his powers were in no way impaired.

For a brief while longer, Cicero's leadership flourished. A

second battle liberated Decimus Brutus' troops from Mutina, and Antony was declared a public enemy. The tide then turned: Decimus Brutus could not and Octavian would not pursue Antony's withdrawing forces; Decimus wrote to Cicero on 5 May that he could not control Octavian, and Octavian could not control his men.

Cicero was one of the few in the Senate who realized that all was not over yet; Octavian must be encouraged, and the feelings of the veteran troops respected. Cicero had himself been unwise enough to make some remarks critical of the veterans in his *Tenth* and *Eleventh Philippic Orations*, and he had rashly praised Sextus Pompeius in the *Thirteenth Philippic*. All this lent colour to Antony's accusation that the party of Pompey was being revived, and that Brutus and Cassius in Greece and Asia were planning a new civil war against Caesar's friends. Cicero therefore proclaimed his complete faith in Octavian and proposed a triumphal ovation for him (an ovation was the appropriate honour in a conflict between citizens), but this was probably not passed. The senatorial majority seemed determined to snub Octavian, and, since Hirtius had fallen in battle and Pansa had died of wounds, they voted to hand over command in Cisalpine Gaul to Decimus Brutus, one of Caesar's assassins, who was also voted a full triumph. The debate on this proposal was probably the context of Cicero's famous comment that Octavian was 'a young man to be praised, honoured and promoted', but the Latin word 'to be promoted' can also mean 'to be disposed of', and Cicero's remark was thus ambiguous; he was really urging his fellow-senators to win Octavian's support now; they could (if need be) dispose of him later. Octavian heard of the remark, and was not amused.

Disregarding Cicero, the Senate persisted in an extremist policy. They recognized Sextus Pompeius as an admiral of the Republic, not a pirate, and thus further strengthened the impression of wanting to revive Pompey's old party. In consequence, Caesar's old generals in the West deserted with their armies of Caesar's veterans, first Lepidus in Southern Gaul, who was outlawed, then Pollio in Spain, then Plancus in Further Gaul. Octavian then changed sides too. In his memoirs he naturally did not explain why; at the time he gave the excuse that the Senate would not allow him one of the vacant consulships. This was true, but even in a time of civil war it was an outrageous demand; Octavian was less than half the age legally necessary. The truth is much more likely to be that he had now obtained what he wanted – a position in which Antony would have to listen to him, and bargain; he could therefore dispense with the Senate's help.

In August, Octavian crossed the Rubicon and marched on Rome. Panic rose. Negotiations were attempted. A plan to defend the city was drawn up, and preparations were begun. Octavian ignored the one and swept the other aside. Mutinies in the defence put the entire city into his hands. On 19 August he was declared consul with Q. Pedius, his cousin and one of Caesar's minor heirs. His first action was to procure a law to ratify his adoption, and thus make legal the name he had used for over a year. He then repealed the decree outlawing Dolabella, and set up a court to punish Caesar's assassins. Naturally, the defendants did not appear, and all were outlawed. When Pedius later carried another law revoking the outlawry of Antony and Lepidus, the field was free for the Caesarian party to re-unite. Many tales were told about the leaders' mutual suspicions, but the veterans of the battles at Mutina were unwilling to fight one another again, and virtually forced them into a conference near Bononia. There it was agreed to set up Octavian, Antony and Lepidus as a Triumvirate, a commission of three, to reorganize the state, with autocratic power for five years.

The triumvirs also agreed to proscribe their opponents and confiscate the lands of eighteen towns of Italy to reward their veterans. Two days, it was said, were spent in debating the list of the towns and citizens to be victimized, as each triumvir tried to save his own kinsmen and the towns of which he was patron. Later historians, who favoured Octavian, claimed that he had tried to save Cicero, but this is not easy to believe.

Rumours of the impending proscription spread before the details were known; Pedius received orders at night to kill the most prominent victims, and a panic spread through the city as his agents set to work. He tried to pacify the people by announcing that there would be lists, and by publishing the first of them which contained only seventeen names; the eventual total reached three hundred senators and two thousand equites, many of whom were proscribed simply for their property. The proscription edict has been preserved, in Greek. It violated almost every principle of Roman law; it was directed against named persons, condemned them without trial, and ordered the mutilation of their corpses by decapitation. Money was offered to each man's assassin, and freedom to slaves who gave their services. Assistance to the proscribed was punishable by proscription.

It is not known what Cicero did during the summer. Presumably he wrote up his *Philippic Orations* for publication; some letters, probably only a small proportion, are preserved, but none after July. The rest presumably were suppressed, perhaps on the orders of Octavian. According to one anecdote Cicero was in Rome when Octavian marched on the city, and he requested an interview. On gaining it he excused himself, and said he had proposed Octavian's consulship (or perhaps supported the proposal). He received the sarcastic reply that he seemed to be the last of Octavian's friends to call. Had Cicero not criticized Octavian in some lost (or suppressed) works it is hard to see why he needed to excuse himself, or be nervous about an interview. We must assume there had been some, perhaps strongly worded, criticism.

Cicero must have known that he was doomed, but he would not commit suicide, as Cato had done, and as some others now did. Whether suicide is braver than remaining to face the inevitable is a matter of opinion. Romans (whose unpleasant habits included crucifixion and other methods of torturing their victims) generally preferred suicide; Greeks had usually preferred to try to fight again another day if that were possible. Greeks were no less brave than Romans, and in this respect Cicero was a Greek. He left Rome and awaited events at his villa at Tusculum. Quintus was with him.

When the news of their proscription came, they moved south, towards the sea, but not in a determined flight, though their departure was hasty and both forgot to take much money. Quintus went back to fetch some, but was killed when his slaves betrayed him. Cicero moved on to his house at Astura, from where he put to sea to go to join M. Brutus in Greece. Whether through contrary winds, or because he decided to die in Italy, he came ashore again, fell a victim of his characteristic indecision, and was overtaken by assassins at his villa at Formiae on the Campanian coast. His slaves eventually induced him to fly, and told the assassins they did not know his whereabouts. He had, however, gone no further than the garden when he was overtaken by two officers, a centurion called Herennius and a military tribune called Popilius whom Cicero had once defended. Seeing his doom now certain he faced it stoically, looking steadily at his assassins till they struck off his head. They also cut off his hands and carried these grisly relics to Antony, who gloated over them himself and then gave them to his wife. She mutilated the head and tongue which had so bitterly castigated two of her husbands, Clodius and Antony. Antony had them displayed on the speaker's platform in Rome. It was Cicero's last appearance there.

It was 7 December 43 B.C. when Cicero was killed; he was within a month of his sixty-fourth birthday. He died at a moment and in a manner peculiarly appropriate to his whole career. Arms had not given place to civil garb, nor had laurels of victory to words of panegyric. Moreover, nothing could have been more contrary to his ideals of a free Republic than this massacre of free men unheard and uncondemned at the bidding of a military junta who sought only to secure power for themselves and the resources with which to bind their armies to their service.

10

Epilogue:
Cicero's Posthumous Achievement

Cicero was dead, but in death he proved more influential than he had ever been in life. Within ten years his death was being used by Octavian as part of his propaganda against Antony; before the end of the century his biography had been published by Tiro. His own published works spoke for themselves. In the Roman Empire, Cicero became the model for oratory, and for the study of literary theory that the Romans called 'rhetoric', and which became the normal educational course for public men. Quintilian, the first holder of a 'Chair of Latin Rhetoric' in Rome, was a devoted follower of Cicero; in his *Training of an Orator* he wrote a full educational curriculum based on Cicero's works; it was aimed at producing a model orator who was also a model of moral excellence, for to Quintilian the two went hand in hand, and Cicero was both the Roman Demosthenes and the Roman Plato.

As Christianity gained ground, Cicero continued to influence its intellectuals; Augustine (A.D. 354–430) and Jerome (*c.* A.D. 350–420) were both Ciceronians, and were largely responsible for the survival of classical philosophy by converting it to the service of Christianity. Thanks to them, the Roman church was able and willing to present itself as the heir to the heritage of Rome, as it appeared for example to Dante (1265–1321).

Virgil was Dante's guide, and he, Aristotle and Ovid are the most-quoted authors in *The Divine Comedy*, but Dante himself wrote that Cicero's *On Friendship* was the chief philosophical influence he felt, and he quoted Cicero some fifty times. *De Inventione* was part of the curriculum of the Carolingian teachers (ninth century, and on), and Sedulius Scottus, the ninth-century

Irish monk, included selections from Cicero's speeches and
Tusculan Disputations in his influential *Collectaneum*. After about
A.D. 1000 and the revival of the towns which marked the start of
the High Middle Ages, the search for an identity within the world
of feudal lord and church led the townspeople to the Roman
Republic, and to Cicero. His ideal of service to the community,
his praise of men of practical achievement and common sense
rather than noble birth, and his abhorrence of violence and
extremism, spoke to their needs. His proposals for practical
morality, and his respect for reason, education and culture
established a goal alternative to the monastic search for salvation
through celibacy and withdrawal from the world.

In England in the thirteenth century, the manuscript attributed to Alexander Neckham, Abbot of Cirencester, lists eight
of Cicero's works to be read in the second stage of the schools'
curriculum. The catalogues edited by M. Manitius show Cicero
the most-mentioned author in the libraries of all Europe, the
mentions of his rhetorical works alone outnumbering those of any
other author.

In the fourteenth century the period of Cicero's greatest
influence began, with Petrarch (1304–74) and Boccaccio
(1313–75) and the start of the Humanist movement. What Virgil
was to Dante, Cicero was to Petrarch. Born a political exile,
gaining early recognition as a poet, passionately anxious for
fame, and convinced that public recognition of real talent was
proof of its existence, Petrarch was a natural Ciceronian, and he
adopted Cicero as his model; the cadences of Ciceronian Latin
appealed to his poetic and musical ear, and Cicero's emphasis on
the music of words and the musical effects of stylish writing
captivated him. Cicero became the paragon of excellence, the
man of rounded attainment to which all Humanists should
aspire, the orator, statesman, poet, and practical moralist, who
knew alike how to lead in politics and how to write on friendship
and the right uses of leisure.

Petrarch believed that imitation is the most sincere form of
admiration, and in that belief urged the imitation of Cicero. But
his imitation of Cicero was of the ideal of eloquence which made
the orator the master of every type of prose-writing, with enough
ideas and vocabulary at his disposal to express his views in a
manner appropriate to any subject. Under his influence the

Humanists sought eloquence through the study of Cicero and Quintilian, and supported their assertion that virtue is attainable through eloquence, since a bad man cannot be a good orator, and vice versa.

Coluccio Salutati, the most devoted of Petrarch's admirers, quoted Cicero as often as he quoted the New Testament, and by the clarity and elegance of his style, which he modelled on Cicero, he set a standard in his diplomatic correspondence as Chancellor of Florence from 1375 to 1400 which made others try to imitate him if they could not emulate him. Coluccio was thus responsible for turning all aspiring diplomats to the study of Cicero, and in consequence for centuries the diplomacy of Europe was conducted not only in the language, but in the precise vocabulary, word-order and cadences of Ciceronian Latin. All Humanists tried to write like Cicero, and the imitation became even more exact after Cardinal Bembo (1470–1547) had started the practice of rejecting as un-Ciceronian any phrase that could not be paralleled verbatim in Cicero's works – a touchstone by which much of Petrarch's own work would have failed to pass as Ciceronian.

The Humanists were enthusiastic collectors and discoverers of manuscripts; thanks to Petrarch, Boccaccio, Coluccio, Poggio Bracciolini (1380–1459) and others the range of known Latin literature was vastly increased, and many new works of Cicero were discovered. Among these were his *Letters to Atticus* and *To Quintus his Brother* which Petrarch himself found, and the *Letters to his Friends*, which Coluccio was the first of the Humanists to own. These almost at once became the models for correspondence, and were made part of the school curriculum. Philip Melanchthon (1497–1560), friend of Martin Luther, produced an influential anthology in which a large part was taken by Cicero's *On Duties* and letters, and this is typical of the shift in interest from the style and language of Cicero to the content and thought of the classical writers that went with the Reformation. In Wittenberg, in 1546, Cicero was the principal prose author studied in the Latin course at the University; nine tenths of Melanchthon's own Latin courses were devoted to Cicero, and Cicero's ideals for public life were thus put before the youth of Protestant Germany as a standard and a guide.

In Catholic Europe the Jesuits also favoured Cicero; *Selections from Cicero's Letters* was the first literary work in their Grammar classes, and in the next year *On Friendship* or *On Old Age* was read, along with Ovid and either Terence or Sallust. The Humanities class read *Tusculan Disputations* along with Erasmus and Horace *On the Art of Poetry*, and after that, the Rhetoric class used Cicero as its model; the Jesuits produced a remarkable series of Humanists, many of them Ciceronians – Descartes, Tasso, Voltaire, Montesquieu, Corneille, Bossuet and others.

In England, which wavered between Protestantism and Catholicism, the spirit of the Humanists began to penetrate the schools at the start of the sixteenth century. The arrival of Erasmus in 1499 may have given an initial impulse, which was taken up by Colet when he organized St Paul's School, and by Wolsey at his school at Ipswich. Erasmus was an enthusiastic educationalist, and wrote manuals for his pupils, but he was also an enthusiastic Ciceronian, and the *Selections* produced by Johann Sturm at Strassburg following Melanchthon became the first prose work in his course.

The Universities of Oxford and Cambridge also studied Cicero enthusiastically; the Latin Lecturer for the University of Oxford installed by Richard Fox at Corpus Christi College was to lecture on Cicero's *On Duties*, and his rhetorical works were prescribed for more advanced pupils. In Cambridge, Cicero was the one Latin author in Thomas Cheke's list of works which 'an excellent man may dwell on' – the others were the Bible and Greek authors – and this choice was possibly fairly general in the age when the biblical languages were receiving most encouragement by the founding of Regius chairs.

The study of Cicero needed no special encouragement, however; the best writers of Latin were sure of employment in the diplomatic service, and professors were often called away for public service, or even to tutor the royal family, as Cheke tutored Edward VI, and Roger Ascham Elizabeth I. Ascham's tutoring was very modern in its slant, since he aimed not at making his pupil speak Latin, but at mastering Latin syntax and constructions by translating Cicero into English and retranslating back into Latin.

In Tudor England, both Protestant and Catholic parties favoured classics, and Cicero; Ascham was a Protestant, but More was a Catholic, so was Stephen Gardiner; Wolsey decided to endow professorships, then a College at Oxford, and at Trinity College, Cambridge, founded by Henry VIII, the Elizabethan statutes established a Latin lecturer who lectured principally on Cicero. However, it was in the Protestant party that Cicero flourished most, and Cicero's *On Duties* became a daily standby for men who were prepared to be burned for their belief in the individual's responsibility for his own morality. Lord Burghley, for example, is said to have often carried a copy in his breast pocket.

The Puritans attacked the classics as heathen, and tried to focus all study and learning on the Bible, but the Restoration brought fresh enthusiasm for Cicero in particular, and *On Duties* (under the familiar title of '*Tully's Offices*') returned to it position as a handbook for all who thought themselves civilized.

As the vernacular languages took over from Latin as the languages of diplomacy, Cicero's letters faded from their position in the schools, but his style became naturalized in the languages of Europe, as it had been in Italian ever since Boccaccio. In France, Balzac (1597–1632), Bossuet (1627–1704), and Fénelon (1651–1715) were all Ciceronians, and Voltaire decided to express his unorthodox religious views as *Letters from Memmius the Epicurean* to Cicero. In England, Addison (1672–1719), Swift (1667–1745) and Dr Johnson (1709–84) followed Cicero, and so did Edward Gibbon (1737–94), though Gibbon was not fully a Ciceronian in that he failed to provide the variety in tone and texture which is an essential ingredient in the master's own work. Burke (1729–97), perhaps the greatest English-speaking orator, spoke with the richness and sonority of Cicero's style, and the power and force of his thought; the imitation was deliberate, as is clear from his impeachment of Warren Hastings in 1788, which was modelled on Cicero's indictment of Verres.

Burke's contemporaries and rivals, William Pitt (the Younger) (1759–1806), Charles James Fox (1749–1806), and Richard Brinsley Sheridan (1751–1816), were no less devoted followers of Cicero. All used the Ciceronian rhetorical devices – pairs of synonyms and homophones and frequent anaphora (words resembling one another in sense or sound and repetition of the same word) – and searched for the balance and symmetry combined with variety in sentences and paragraphs which is obtained by creating now an antithesis, now a climax, and very often by the use of a tricolon, a group of three balancing or echoing phrases.

Cicero was also the model for the orators of the French Revolution; when Louvet attacked Robespierre in 1792, he called him Catiline, and Danton Crassus, and modelled his speech on Cicero's speeches against Catiline. Robespierre modelled his reply on Cicero's *For Sulla*, comparing his opponents to demagogic tribunes; the names of Clodius, Catiline and Cicero became regular descriptions of political enemies and friends in the Revolution. When Napoleon took power, he called himself 'consul'; 'Senate', 'tribunes', and 'Emperor' (or 'General') all appear in the vocabulary of the day. Likewise, the revolutionary architecture is Roman – the Arc de Triomphe, for example, the Panthéon, and the Madeleine. No less Roman were the founders of the United States; 'Senate' and 'Capitol' formed the council of state and the seat of government; Washington, like Cicero, became 'Father of his Country'. Thomas Jefferson was a Ciceronian, and, in a later age, there is no more Ciceronian speech than Lincoln's Gettysburg address (1863).

Nationalist Germany, by contrast, had little use for Cicero; Goethe (1749–1832) had been one of the true Humanists, but his influence appears more in his passion for Greek studies and in the other non-Roman elements in his work. In Bismarck's Germany the great Roman historian Mommsen's cult of Caesar reflected his countrymen's militaristic interests, and this is paralleled by their devotion to Tacitus and the myth of German invincibility and the 'Watch on the Rhine'.

In nineteenth-century Britain the use of the classical languages as a rigorous mental discipline for schools and the passion for 'composition' rather than for understanding the literatures of Greece and Rome turned many able minds – like Darwin's – away from classics. In the public schools too, Cicero's defence of property came to be stressed at the expense of his attacks on the claims of birth and secret faction-politics; his ideal of *optimates* became identified with the rich rather than with the opponents of military junta and coup d'état. Yet even in the twentieth century, when only a handful of school pupils study Latin at all, the resistance to tyranny has been led by orators who, whether they were aware of it or not, found themselves using Ciceronian echoes.

In the House of Commons on 3 August 1914, Edward Grey concluded his speech with the following truly Ciceronian passage: 'I wanted to bring out the underlying issues which would affect our own conduct, and our own policy, and to put them clearly. I have put the vital facts before the House, and if, as seems not improbable, we are forced, and rapidly forced, to take our stand upon these issues, then I believe, when the country realizes what is at stake, what the real issues are, the magnitude of the impending dangers in the West of Europe which I have endeavoured to describe to the House, we shall be supported throughout, not only by the House of Commons, but by the determination, the resolution, the courage, and the endurance of the whole country.' A generation later, against the shapeless German ravings of Adolf Hitler, Britain was inspired to resist when all seemed lost by the Ciceronian cadences of Winston Churchill, no great classical scholar, but a true orator, who turned, instinctively perhaps, to Ciceronian devices for his defence of the values of civilized Europe.

Bibliography

Since this book was written Elizabeth Rawson has published her *Cicero*
(Allen Lane, 1975); this is the best of recent biographies, combining as it
does an excellent analysis of Rome's political structures with a feeling
for Cicero's humanity. Cicero's identification with the *res publica* seems,
however, to be less than fully brought out, and his abiding importance is
underestimated. An earlier work is D. R. Shackleton Bailey's *Cicero*
(Duckworth, 1971). Dr Bailey has an unequalled mastery of Cicero's
Correspondence (especially with Atticus) and he excels as an accurate
and interpretative translator, but he has no use for the oratory of Rome's
greatest orator or the treatises of the man who tried to be the Roman
Plato, and he has the honesty to say so. Since, politically, Dr Bailey
admires Caesar, the destroyer of the *res publica*, his Cicero wins
sympathy only on the personal side, and this biography is essentially a
selection of Cicero's letters in translation, to be compared with L. P.
Wilkinson, *Letters of Cicero* (Geoffrey Bles, 1949), now available in
Hutchinson's University Library (paper covers), a finely sensitive
collection of extracts strung upon a thin historical framework, but
revealing much of Cicero the man.

Earlier in 1971 appeared *Cicero, a Political Biography*, by D. L.
Stockton (Oxford University Press). Mr Stockton is a 'Greats' don, and
he writes for Oxford students who already know the basic outlines of the
period, and introduces a number of the favourite controversies of the
Greats school. There is sound advice – such as warning students not to
endow ancient politicians with foresight, and a refusal to be dazzled by
prosopographical research, but there is an unwillingness to accept, until
the very end, that the prerequisite for maintaining the *res publica* was the
abandonment of military (and para-military) force as an instrument in
politics. Moreover, in a political biography, one whole dimension of
Cicero is side-stepped: his quest for fame in literary work when
frustrated in politics. Cicero's own views on politics are set out in *Res
Publica* (Oxford University Press, 1970) by the present writer and
B. W. J. G. Wilson, a selection, mostly from the published speeches, of
how Cicero interpreted in public the major problems of his lifetime. Other

recent translations of Cicero's works are Michael Grant, *Cicero, Selected Works* (1960), *Selected Political Speeches of Cicero* (1969), *Cicero on the Good Life* (1971) and *Cicero Murder Trials* (1975): all Penguin Classics. The first is a wide general selection with no special theme; the second illustrates the fundamental importance of oratory in Roman political life, hence its systematic study in education, and argues that Cicero's boastfulness is not mere vanity, but a political answer to the nobles' claims based on heredity; in the third, Grant selects widely from the treatises on ethics and literary theory to show Cicero as perhaps the first great popularizer, as he took the widely differing, speculative arguments of Greek philosophers to produce a code of practical morality whose influence is traceable through the centuries. The last is a less coherent selection, but the four speeches translated further highlight the differences between Roman and modern lawcourt procedures.

World War II stimulated two most interesting interpretations of Cicero: *This was Cicero*, written by J. J. Haskell in the U.S.A. in 1942 (Fawcett Publications Inc.), emphasized the place of Cicero in the tradition of western humanism; Hartvig Frisch, a Danish statesman who knew the meaning of being driven out of politics by a military junta (in his case the Nazi invaders), wrote *Cicero's Last Fight for the Republic* (Glydendal, Copenhagen, 1946). Frisch's summary of his predecessors is an admirably judicious one. Prominent among those praised is Matthias Gelzer, whose own *Cicero* (Franz Steiner, 1969) provides an excellent annotated account for those who read German.

Cicero appears prominently in all outline histories of this period. In English the best is *From the Gracchi to Nero* by H. H. Scullard (Methuen, 4th edn 1976); if heavy going at times, it is based on scholarly, sober judgment, is clearly expressed, and has an ample supply of notes and references to modern discussion. More easily readable, if less reliable, is F. B. Marsh, *A History of the Roman World, 146–30 B.C.* (Methuen, 3rd edn 1964). *The Last Generation of the Roman Republic* (E. S. Gruen, University of California Press, 1974) represents an attempt to break away from the political type of history, not altogether successfully. It contains a huge bibliography. *A History of Rome* (Macmillan, 2nd edn 1965) by M. Cary belongs firmly to the tradition of *Cambridge Ancient History, IX* (1932), to which Cary contributed. This older tradition is also represented by R. E. Smith, *Cicero the Statesman* (Cambridge University Press, 1966). As the title suggests, Smith is somewhat over-generous to Cicero, and his reaction against the prosopographical method is excessive; the abiding fact of nobility and its methods and claims demand recognition. P. A. Brunt, *Italian Manpower, 235 B.C.–A.D. 14* (Oxford University Press, 1971), sets out in impressive detail the social resources behind the struggles of the age of Cicero, the previous and subsequent generations.

F. R. Cowell, *Cicero and the Roman Republic* (Pitman, 1948, now Pelican), tells much of the Republic, but hardly takes Cicero seriously as a writer, though he points out well the contrast between Cicero's and Caesar's views on politics. Of the biographers of Caesar, J. P. V. D. Balsdon, *Caesar and Rome* (English Universities Press, 1967), is a model of compression and judgment where Caesar is concerned, though frequently less than fair to Cicero. Gelzer's *Caesar* (6th edn 1959; in English, Blackwell, 1966), though now somewhat old, is also an excellent account, stressing the fundamental importance of patron/client and family relationships. Visually more rewarding is M. Grant's *Julius Caesar* (Weidenfeld and Nicolson, 1969), though his Caesar is less convincing than Balsdon's.

For further reading, Lily Ross Taylor, *Party Politics in the Age of Caesar* (Berkeley, California, 1948), has stood the test of time well, and so have R. Syme, *The Roman Revolution* (Oxford University Press, 1939), a revolutionary book mostly about Caesar's heir, and Ch. Wirszubski, *Libertas as a Political Ideal* (Cambridge University Press, 1960). More recently, Donald Earl, *The Moral and Political Tradition of Rome* (Thames and Hudson, 1967, shows how far Cicero belonged to and moulded the Roman tradition of the good life, and John Crook, *Law and Life of Rome* (Thames and Hudson, 1967), shows the part of Cicero and his contemporaries in moulding Roman Law. R. Syme, *Sallust* (Berkeley, California, 1964), has many stimulating things to say on Rome in Cicero's day. An abundance of other studies exists as well; lists of titles are in most of the above books. There is also an excellent discussion by A. E. Douglas in *Cicero* (New Surveys in the Classics No. 2, *Greece and Rome*, Oxford University Press, 1968); Mr Douglas is himself the leading writer in English on Cicero's philosophy, as may be seen in the generally useful collection *Studies in Latin Literature and its Influence: Cicero*, ed. T. A. Dorey (Routledge and Kegan Paul, 1965).

M. L. Clarke's chapter in this collection would provide a good starting-point for studying Cicero's posthumous influence. More wide-ranging discussions are in R. R. Bolgar, *The Classical Heritage and its Beneficiaries* (Cambridge University Press, 1954), and Gilbert Highet, *The Classical Tradition* (Oxford University Press, 1949). The fundamental work is T. Zielinski, *Cicero im Wandel der Jahrhunderte* (St Petersburg, 1897), in German. A list of the dates of the re-discovery, publication and subsequent editions of Cicero's works is in J. E. Sandys, *History of Classical Scholarship* (Cambridge University Press, 3 vols, 1903–8); M. L. Clarke, *Classical Education in Britain* (Cambridge University Press, 1959) illustrates Cicero's importance in this field.

Index

General

Art collection, 19, 23, 118
Assemblies, 3–4, 6, 23, 35, 47

Bribery, 5, 21, 23–4, 27, 29, 35–6, 38, 47–9, 53, 56, 87, 99, 156, 157

Cappadocia, 98
Centuries, *see* Assemblies
Civil Wars, 26, 28, 107, 109–14, 118–19, 124, 134–5, 136–8, 143, 157, 162ff
Clients and patrons, 3, 18, 32, 43–4, 76, 142
Clubs (collegia), 4, 14, 29, 64, 69–71, 116
Concord, *see* Harmony
Corn, 18, 34, 42, 62, 64, 69–70, 76–7, 111, 146–7, 156

Debt, interest rates, 34, 36, 39, 42, 54, 63, 65, 89, 98, 103–4, 113
Demonstrations, 34, 43, 48, 57, 61–2, 65, 68, 101, 108, 142

Education, 6–8, 10–12, 16, 44, 79–80, 85, 94, 100, 123–4, 136, 142, 144, 170ff
Egypt, 57–8, 73, 86, 114
Elections, 3–4, 10, 26, 28–9, 36–7, 55–6, 62, 70, 82, 88, 112, 114, 124, 137, 141
Embassies, 38, 84
Equites, 3–4, 6, 11, 16, 17, 21–2, 24, 28, 33–4, 37, 44, 49–50, 57, 62–3, 65, 86, 158, 167
Extortion, 5, 25, 27, 58, 97–8, 113

Finances (Cicero's), 2, 17, 22–3, 26, 31, 44–5, 71–2, 96, 101, 106, 125, 128–9, 135, 147, 158

Games and shows, 5, 10, 20, 22, 28, 33–4, 54, 83, 85, 89, 102, 105, 135, 150, 153, 156

Harmony (concord, peace), 30, 33, 49, 54, 65, 74, 78, 82, 87, 91, 94, 108ff, 121, 142, 149, 150, 162–3
Historians and writers: Archimedes, 19; Catullus, 75, 134; Dio, 57, 64, 77, 142; Lucretius, 85, 145; Plutarch, 7, 8, 17, 23, 65, 113–14, 138; Quintilian, 15, 170; Sallust, 28, 41, 123; Suetonius, 41–2
History, 7, 12, 79–80, 118, 131
Houses, 44, 71, 72–3, 78, 85, 89, 126, 155

Interest rates, *see* Debt
Italy (towns and peoples of), 3, 11, 28, 40, 64, 68, 69, 108, 110, 117, 136, 143, 157, 164, 167

Land settlements, 11, 30–2, 53, 56–8, 69, 76–7, 120, 136, 141, 143, 156, 162
Law, 7, 22–3, 25, 41, 74, 79–80, 94–5, 122–3, 155, 168
Law-courts, 5–6, 11, 14, 18, 21–2, 31, 46–8, 62–3, 70–1, 81, 85, 86, 89–90, 153, 167
Lawyers, 4, 8, 156

Magistracies, 3–5, 42, 48, 154; aedileship, 20–8; censors, 21, 28, 73, 94; consulship, 5, 26, 58, 137, 166–7; dictatorships, 10, 14, 89, 114, 136, 138, 143; praetorship, 5; quaestorship, 4; tribunate, 58, *see also* Tribunes

Selected Persons
(cos. = consul, trib. = tribune: figures in brackets are dates B.C.)

Cicero's Speeches and Writings

Roman Money and Cost of Living

The Romans calculated in *sesterces* and talents. A *sestertius* (literally 2½ *asses*) was one quarter of a *denarius*, a silver coin. A talent was 6000 denarii. For sums below one *denarius*, a token copper coinage was mostly used.

The subsidized price of corn (i.e. wheat) was 6⅓ *asses* per measure (*modius*). At ½ kg of bread a day, a man would eat about 30 *modii* a year. Romans (except for the rich) ate little but bread, lard and vegetables. About 5 *modii* of corn per family per month may have been available at the subsidized price. Rents of apartments in the city were thought very high, but we have no figures.

Date Due

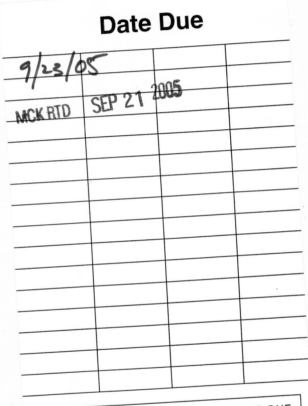

9/23/05

MCK RTD   SEP 21 2005

IF YOUR BOOK IS RECALLED YOUR DUE
DATE WILL BE SHORTENED. YOU WILL BE
NOTIFIED BY MAIL.